KB116457

TEPS

# 서울대 텝스 관리위원회 텝스 최신기출 1200제 1

## 문제집

**서울대 텝스 관리위원회 텝스 최신기출 1200제 문제집 VOL. 1**

문제제공 서울대학교 TEPS관리위원회
펴낸이 임상진
펴낸곳 (주)넥서스

초판 1쇄 발행 2015년 6월 25일
초판 33쇄 발행 2023년 10월 30일

출판신고 1992년 4월 3일 제311-2002-2호
10880 경기도 파주시 지목로 5
Tel (02)330-5500 Fax (02)330-5555

ISBN 979-11-5752-360-3 14740
979-11-5752-359-7 14740 (SET)



www.nexusbook.com

TEPS

# 서울대 텝스 관리위원회 텝스 최신기출 1200제

## 문제집

서울대학교 TEPS관리위원회 기출문제 제공

넥서스

# PREFACE

넥서스에서 정기 텝스 시험의 공식 출제 기관인 서울대 텝스 관리위원회가 제공하는 기출 문제를 독점 출간하게 되었다. 이미 최초로 TEPS 기출문제집 〈TEPS 기출 문제집〉, 〈유형별로 분석한 NEXUS 기출 800〉 등을 출간한 이후 〈서울대 텝스 관리위원회 최신기출 1000〉, 〈서울대 텝스 관리위원회 제공 최신기출 시크릿〉, 〈서울대 텝스 관리위원회 최신기출 1200 / SEASON 2, 3〉, 〈서울대 텝스 관리위원회 최신기출 Listening / Reading〉, 〈서울대 최신기출 TEPS VOCA〉, 〈서울대 텝스 관리위원회 공식 기출 1000 시리즈〉에 이르기까지 연이어 대표적인 TEPS 기출 교재로 자리매김할 수 있도록 많은 사랑과 관심을 보여준 TEPS 수험생들과 학교 및 학원에서 강의하시는 선생님들께 다시 한번 감사의 마음을 전한다. 다른 영어 능력 검정시험과 달리 많은 기출문제가 공식적으로 오픈된 TEPS 시험은 그만큼 과학적인 측정 도구와 신뢰할 수 있는 콘텐츠, 뛰어난 변별력 등 공인 영어 능력 시험으로서의 자격을 충분히 인정받았다.

TEPS 수험생들로부터 이 시험이 참으로 어렵다는 얘기를 많이 듣는다. 벼락치기가 가능할 만큼 단순한 실용 영어의 측정에 그치는 것이 아니라 그야말로 기초부터 고급까지 모든 수준의 영어를 심도 있게 측정하는 것이 바로 TEPS 시험의 목표이므로 TEPS 시험 준비에도 제대로 된 전략과 교재와 필요함은 두말할 나위가 없다. 따라서 지금까지의 출제 원리와 경향 분석을 위해서는 가장 확실한 기출 문제집을 하나 골라 반복해서 풀면서 정리하는 것이 무엇보다 중요할 것이다.

이번에 출간하는 서울대 텝스 관리위원회 최신기출 시리즈는 출제 기관이 지금까지 공개한 것 중 가장 최신의 공식 기출문제 6회분으로 구성했고, 학습자 편의를 위해 문제집과 해설집을 각각 별도로 제작했다. 또한 실제 TEPS 시험장에서 접했던 문제지와 동일한 페이지로 구성했고, 청해 방송에서 듣던 MP3 음원을 고스란히 그대로 실었다. 또한 별도의 해설집에는 마치 실제 해설 강의를 듣는 것 같이 정확하게 핵심을 짚어 주는 문제 해설로 수험생들의 만족을 높이고자 했다.

새로운 TEPS 기출문제집 출간을 위해 넥서스 TEPS연구소에서 참으로 많이도 성가시게 해 드렸는데도 그간 늘 한결같이 적극적으로 도움을 주신 서울대학교 TEPS관리위원회 관계자분들께 이 자리를 통해 감사의 마음을 전한다. 본 교재를 통해 수험생 각자의 목표가 제대로 실현되기를 진심으로 바란다.

목차

# CONTENTS

특징

# FEATURES

## 1 가장 최근에 공개된 공식 기출 1,200문항 독점 수록

서울대학교 TEPS관리위원회가 가장 최근에 공개한 현존 가장 최신 기출문제 1,200문항을 실제 TEPS 시험지와 동일한 페이지 구성으로 제공

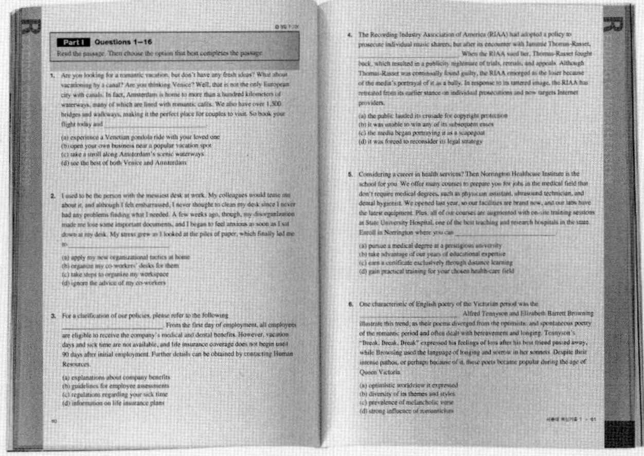

**Part I Questions 1–16**

Read the passage. Then choose the option that best completes the passage.

1. Are you looking for a romantic vacation, but don't have any fresh ideas? What about vacationing by a canal? Are you thinking Venice? Well, that is not the only European city with canals. In fact, Amsterdam is home to more than a hundred kilometers of waterways, many of which are lined with romantic cafés. We also have over 1,500 bridges and walkways, making it the perfect place for couples to visit. So book your flight today and ______________.
(a) experience a Venetian gondola ride with your loved one
(b) open your own business near a popular vacation spot
(c) take a stroll along Amsterdam's scenic waterways
(d) see the best of both Venice and Amsterdam

2. I used to be the person with the messiest desk at work. My colleagues would tease me about it, and although I felt embarrassed, I never thought to clean my desk since I never had any problems finding what I needed. A few weeks ago, though, my disorganization made me lose some important documents, and I began to feel anxious as soon as I sat down at my desk. My stress grew as I looked at the piles of paper, which finally led me to ______________.
(a) apply my new organizational tactics at home
(b) organize my co-workers' desks for them
(c) take steps to organize my workspace
(d) ignore the advice of my co-workers

3. For a clarification of our policies, please refer to the following ______________. From the first day of employment, all employees are eligible to receive the company's medical and dental benefits. However, vacation days and sick time are not available, and life insurance coverage does not begin until 90 days after initial employment. Further details can be obtained by contacting Human Resources.
(a) explanations about company benefits
(b) guidelines for employee assessments
(c) regulations regarding your sick time
(d) information on life insurance plans

4. The Recording Industry Association of America (RIAA) had adopted a policy to prosecute individual music sharers, but after its encounter with Jammie Thomas-Rasset, ______________. When the RIAA sued her, Thomas-Rasset fought back, which resulted in a publicity nightmare of trials, retrials, and appeals. Although Thomas-Rasset was continually found guilty, the RIAA emerged as the loser because of the media's portrayal of it as a bully. In response to its tattered image, the RIAA has retreated from its earlier stance on individual prosecutions and now targets Internet providers.
(a) the public lauded its crusade for copyright protection
(b) it was unable to win any of its subsequent cases
(c) the media began portraying it as a scapegoat
(d) it was forced to reconsider its legal strategy

5. Considering a career in health services? Then Norrington Healthcare Institute is the school for you. We offer many courses to prepare you for jobs in the medical field that don't require medical degrees, such as physician assistant, ultrasound technician, and dental hygienist. We opened last year, so our facilities are brand new, and our labs have the latest equipment. Plus, all of our courses are augmented with on-site training sessions at State University Hospital, one of the best teaching and research hospitals in the state. Enroll in Norrington where you can ______________.
(a) pursue a medical degree at a prestigious university
(b) take advantage of our years of educational expertise
(c) earn a certificate exclusively through distance learning
(d) gain practical training for your chosen health-care field

6. One characteristic of English poetry of the Victorian period was the ______________. Alfred Tennyson and Elizabeth Barrett Browning illustrate this trend, as their poems diverged from the optimistic and spontaneous poetry of the romantic period and often dealt with bereavement and longing. Tennyson's "Break, Break, Break" expressed his feelings of loss after his best friend passed away, while Browning used the language of longing and sorrow in her sonnets. Despite their intense pathos, or perhaps because of it, these poets became popular during the age of Queen Victoria.
(a) optimistic worldview it expressed
(b) diversity of its themes and styles
(c) prevalence of melancholic verse
(d) strong influence of romanticism

## 2 수험생들의 필살기 TEPS 만점 전략

청해–문법–어휘–독해 4영역 13개 파트에 대한 TEPS 출제 경향 및 고득점 대비 전략을 통합적으로 분석한 출제 비밀 노트 공개

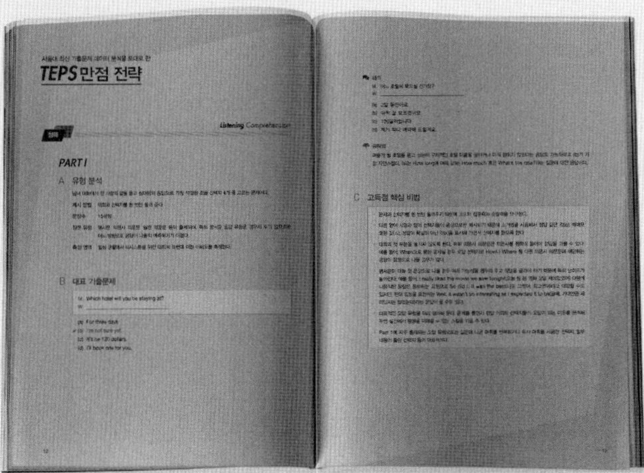

TEPS 만점 전략

Listening Comprehension

PART I

A 유형 분석

B 대표 기출문제

C 고득점 핵심 비법

## 실제 강의를 듣는 것 같은 완전 해설

넥서스 TEPS연구소의 오랜 노하우가 녹아 있는 콤팩트한 알짜배기 해설로 오답에 대한 속시원한 해결책 제시

## 문제집과 해설집 별도 제작

학습자 편의를 위해 방대한 분량을 문제집과 해설집으로 별도 제작, 휴대하기 편할 뿐 아니라 학습 목적에 맞게 구매 가능

## 실제 고사장에서 듣던 청해 음성

정기 TEPS 고사장에서 청해 시험 시간에 그대로 사용했던 MP3 음원을 수록, 생생한 실제 청해 시험 체험

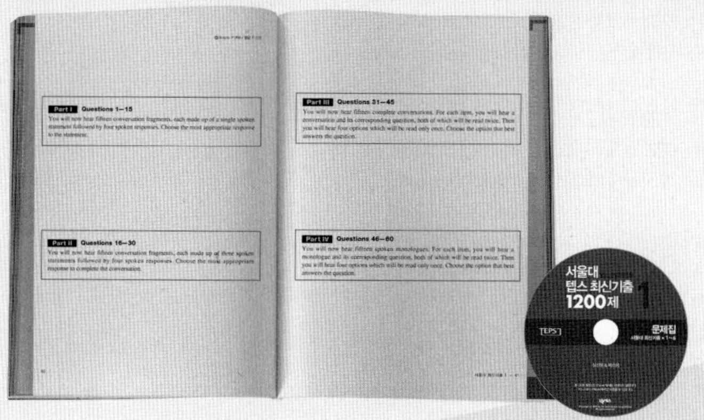

# 1 TEPS란?

❶ Test of English Proficiency developed by Seoul National University의 약자로 서울대학교 언어교육원에서 개발하고, TEPS관리위원회에서 주관하는 국가공인 영어시험
❷ 1999년 1월 처음 시행 이후 연 12~16회 실시
❸ 정부기관 및 기업의 직원 채용, 인사고과, 해외 파견 근무자 선발과 더불어 대학과 특목고 입학 및 졸업 자격 요건, 국가고시 및 자격 시험의 영어 대체 시험으로 활용
❹ 100여 명의 국내외 유수 대학의 최고 수준 영어 전문가들이 출제하고, 언어 테스팅 분야의 세계적인 권위자인 Bachman 교수(미국 UCLA)와 Oller 교수(미국 뉴멕시코대)로부터 타당성을 검증받음
❺ 말하기 – 쓰기 시험인 TEPS Speaking & Writing도 별도 실시 중이며, 2009년 10월부터 이를 통합한 *i*-TEPS 실시

# 2 TEPS 시험 구성

| 영역 | Part별 내용 | 문항수 | 시간/배점 |
|---|---|---|---|
| 청해<br>Listening Comprehension | Part I: 문장 하나를 듣고 이어질 대화 고르기<br>Part II: 3문장의 대화를 듣고 이어질 대화 고르기<br>Part III: 6~8 문장의 대화를 듣고 질문에 해당하는 답 고르기<br>Part IV: 담화문의 내용을 듣고 질문에 해당하는 답 고르기 | 15<br>15<br>15<br>15 | 55분<br>400점 |
| 문법<br>Grammar | Part I: 대화문의 빈칸에 적절한 표현 고르기<br>Part II: 문장의 빈칸에 적절한 표현 고르기<br>Part III: 대화에서 어법상 틀리거나 어색한 부분 고르기<br>Part IV: 단문에서 문법상 틀리거나 어색한 부분 고르기 | 20<br>20<br>5<br>5 | 25분<br>100점 |
| 어휘<br>Vocabulary | Part I: 대화문의 빈칸에 적절한 단어 고르기<br>Part II: 단문의 빈칸에 적절한 단어 고르기 | 25<br>25 | 15분<br>100점 |
| 독해<br>Reading Comprehension | Part I: 지문을 읽고 빈칸에 들어갈 내용 고르기<br>Part II: 지문을 읽고 질문에 가장 적절한 내용 고르기<br>Part III: 지문을 읽고 문맥상 어색한 내용 고르기 | 16<br>21<br>3 | 45분<br>400점 |
| 총계 | 13개 Parts | 200 | 140분<br>990점 |

☆ **IRT** (Item Response Theory)에 의하여 최고점이 990점, 최저점이 10점으로 조정됨.

3

## TEPS 시험 응시 정보

**현장 접수**

❶ www.teps.or.kr에서 인근 접수처 확인
❷ 준비물: 응시료 39,000원(현금만 가능), 증명사진 1매(3×4 cm)
❸ 접수처 방문: 해당 접수기간 평일 12시~5시

**인터넷 접수**

❶ 서울대학교 TEPS관리위원회 홈페이지 접속 www.teps.or.kr
❷ 준비물: 스캔한 사진 파일, 응시료 결제를 위한 신용 카드 및 은행 계좌
❸ 응시료: 39,000원(일반) / 19,500원(군인) / 42,000원(추가 접수)

4

## TEPS 시험 당일 정보

❶ 고사장 입실 완료: 9시 30분(일요일) / 2시 30분(토요일)
❷ 준비물: 신분증, 컴퓨터용 사인펜, 수정테이프, 수험표, 시계
❸ 유효한 신분증
성인: 주민등록증, 운전면허증, 여권, 공무원증, 현역간부 신분증, 군무원증, 주민등록증 발급 신청 확인서, 외국인 등록증
초·중고생: 학생증, 여권, 청소년증, 주민등록증(발급 신청 확인서), TEPS 신분확인 증명서
❹ 시험 시간: 2시간 20분 (중간에 쉬는 시간 없음, 각 영역별 제한시간 엄수)
❺ 성적 확인: 약 2주 후 인터넷에서 조회 가능

청해 **Listening** Comprehension

# PART I

## A 유형 분석

남녀 대화에서 한 사람의 말을 듣고 상대방의 응답으로 가장 적절한 것을 선택지 4개 중 고르는 문제이다.

**제시 방법** 대화와 선택지를 한 번만 들려준다.

**문항수** 15문항

**질문 유형** 평서문, 의문사 의문문, 일반 의문문 등이 출제되며, 특히 평서문 응답 유형은 경우의 수가 많으므로 어느 방향으로 응답이 나올지 예측하기가 어렵다.

**측정 영역** 일상 생활에서 의사소통을 위한 대화체 표현에 대한 이해도를 측정한다.

## B 대표 기출문제

M Which hotel will you be staying at?
W ________________________________

(a) For three days
✔ (b) I'm not sure yet.
(c) It'll be 120 dollars.
(d) I'll book one for you.

해석

**M** 어느 호텔에 묵으실 건가요?

**W** ______________________

(a) 3일 동안이요.

(b) 아직 잘 모르겠어요.

(c) 120달러입니다.

(d) 제가 하나 예약해 드릴게요.

공략법

머물게 될 호텔을 묻고 있는데 구체적인 호텔 이름을 말하거나 아직 정하지 않았다는 응답도 가능하므로 (b)가 가장 자연스럽다. (a)는 How long에 대해, (c)는 How much 혹은 What's the rate?라는 질문에 대한 응답이다.

## C 고득점 핵심 비법

- 예전보다 Part 1도 많이 까다로워졌으며 문제와 선택지를 한 번만 들려주기 때문에 고도의 집중력과 순발력이 요구된다.
- 다른 영어 시험과 달리 선택지들이 음성으로만 제시되기 때문에 소거법을 사용해서 정답 같은 것(o), 애매모호한 것(△), 정답이 확실히 아닌 것(x)을 표시해 가면서 선택지를 듣도록 한다.
- 대화의 첫 부분을 놓치지 않도록 한다. 특히 의문사 의문문은 의문사를 정확히 들어야 정답을 고를 수 있다. 예를 들어, When으로 묻는 문제일 경우 오답 선택지로 How나 Where 등 다른 의문사 의문문에 해당하는 응답이 함정으로 나올 경우가 많다.
- 평서문이 대화 첫 문장으로 나올 경우 여러 가능성을 염두에 두고 정답을 골라야 하기 때문에 특히 난도가 높아진다. 예를 들어, I really liked the movie we saw tonight(오늘 밤 본 영화 정말 재미있었어) 다음에 동의하는 표현으로 So did I. It was the best(나도 그랬어. 최고였어)라고 대답할 수도 있지만, 반대 입장을 표현하는 Well, it wasn't so interesting as I expected it to be(글쎄, 기대만큼 재미있지는 않았는데)라는 응답이 올 수도 있다.
- 대표적인 오답 유형을 미리 정리해 둔다. 문제를 풀면서 정답 이외의 선택지들이 오답이 되는 이유를 분석해 두면 실전에서 함정을 피해갈 수 있는 스킬을 키울 수 있다.
- Part 1에 자주 출제되는 오답 유형으로는 질문에 나온 어휘를 반복하거나 유사 어휘를 사용한 선택지, 일부 내용이 틀린 선택지 등이 대표적이다.

# PART II

## A 유형 분석

남녀 대화에서 세 번째 대화까지 듣고 그 다음 이어질 응답으로 가장 자연스러운 것을 4개의 선택지 중에서 고르는 문제이다.

**제시 방법** 대화와 선택지를 한 번만 들려준다.

**문항수** 15문항

**질문 유형** 평서문, 의문사 의문문, 일반 의문문 등이 출제되며, 이 중 특히 평서문인 경우 어느 방향으로 응답이 나올지 예측하기 어렵다.

**측정 영역** 일상 대화 속 표현에 대한 이해도 측정이라는 점에서 Part 1과 동일한데, 이와 더불어 전반적인 대화 흐름의 이해도를 측정하기도 한다.

## B 대표 기출문제

M Nice car, Mia. It looks pretty new.
W Really? It's actually a 2008 model.
M It's certainly in good condition.
W ____________________

(a) In that case, I'll buy it.
(b) I appreciate your advice.
✔ (c) Well, I take good care of it.
(d) True, but yours is no better.

해석

**M** 미아, 차 좋다. 꽤 새 차 같은데.
**W** 정말? 실은 2008년 식이야.
**M** 상태가 아주 좋구나.
**W** ____________________

(a) 그렇다면 내가 살게.
(b) 네 충고 고마워.
(c) 음, 내가 관리를 많이 하거든.
(d) 맞아, 하지만 네 차라고 더 나을 것도 없어.

공략법

여자가 연식에 비해서 차의 상태가 좋다고 칭찬을 했으므로 그만큼 많은 관리를 한다는 (c)가 남자의 응답으로 가장 적절하다. 충고가 아니라 칭찬이므로 (b)는 advice가 아닌 compliment가 되면 자연스러운 응답이 될 수 있다.

## C 고득점 핵심 비법

- 한 번만 들려주는 세 줄의 대화를 정확하게 잘 듣도록 한다. 첫 문장을 잘 들어야 그 다음에 이어지는 두 줄의 대화를 잘 이해할 수 있기 때문에 Part 2 역시 고도의 집중력을 요한다.
- 만일 첫 줄을 놓쳤다면 당황하지 말고 그 다음 이어지는 두 줄의 대화를 잘 듣도록 한다. 가장 이상적인 청취는 세 줄을 다 알아듣는 것이지만, 혹시 그렇지 못하더라도 선택지가 나오기 직전의 말을 잘 들으면 자연스럽게 이어지는 응답을 고르는 데 도움이 된다.
- 소거법을 활용해서 정답을 고르는 것도 들려주기만 하는 선택지에 대처할 수 있는 한 방법이다.
- 남녀 각각 어떤 말을 했는지 구분해서 들어야 오답을 피해갈 수 있다.
- 풀어본 문제의 오답을 매번 분석해서 실전에서 신속하고 정확하게 오답을 피하도록 한다.
- Part 2의 대표적인 오답 유형으로는 대화의 앞부분을 일부 놓치고 착각해서 선택할 만한 선택지, 대화에 언급된 어휘로 만든 선택지, 대화에 등장한 어휘의 또 다른 의미를 가지고 만든 선택지, 질문한 사람이 이어서 할 만한 말로 만든 선택지 등이 있다.

# PART III

## A 유형 분석

남녀가 세 번씩 주고받는 대화를 듣고 4개의 선택지 중 질문에 가장 적절한 답을 고르는 문제이다.

**제시 방법** 대화 → 질문 → 대화 → 질문 → 선택지 순으로 들려준다.

**문항수** 15문항

**질문 유형** 대의 파악(7문항) → 세부 내용 파악(6문항) → 추론(3문항) 순으로 나온다.

**측정 영역** 일상 대화에 등장하는 다양한 표현에 대한 이해도를 바탕으로 전체 대의 파악, 세부 내용 파악, 추론 능력을 측정한다.

## B 대표 기출문제

M Any special plans for your two-week vacation?
W I think I'll visit my family and relax somewhere.
M Where do you plan on relaxing?
W Oh, I don't know, maybe go somewhere warm.
M What about Jeju island?
W Actually, that sounds good. I'll put it on my list.

Q What is the main topic of the conversation?
(a) The best way to spend a vacation
✔ (b) The woman's vacation plans
(c) Popular holiday destinations
(d) Setting aside time to visit family

해석

M 2주 휴가 동안 특별한 계획이 있나요?
W 집에 들렀다가 어디 가서 좀 쉴 생각이에요.
M 어디서 쉬려고 하는데요?
W 글쎄요. 모르겠어요. 아마 따뜻한 곳으로 가겠죠.
M 제주도는 어때요?
W 좋은 생각이네요. 그곳도 고려해 봐야겠어요.

Q 대화의 중심 소재는?
(a) 휴가를 보낼 가장 좋은 방법
(b) 여자의 휴가 계획
(c) 인기 있는 휴양지
(d) 가족을 방문하기 위한 시간을 남겨 놓기

공략법

대화의 중심 소재는 여자가 휴가 동안 무엇을 하는지이다. 가족을 방문하고 나서 어디로 가서 좀 쉴 거라는 말에 제주도를 권하고 있으므로 (b)가 가장 적절한 답이다. 따뜻한 곳이나 제주도라는 특정 지명을 언급하긴 했지만 인기 있는 휴양지 자체가 대화의 소재는 아니므로 (c)는 오답이다.

## C 고득점 핵심 비법

- 처음 대화를 들을 때 전체 대화 내용을 파악한 뒤, 질문에 따라 집중할 부분에 더 집중하는 두 번째 듣기를 한다. 대화의 흐름을 파악해야 대의 파악 문제뿐 아니라 세부 내용 파악이나 추론 문제도 더 쉽게 풀 수 있다.
- 질문에 따라서 메모를 해야 하는 경우도 있다. 특히 세부 내용 파악 문제의 경우 숫자, 연도, 물건의 종류 등을 명확하게 기억하는 것이 유리하고, 남녀 각각 어떤 말을 했는지 구분해서 알아 두는 것이 오답을 피하는 데 많은 도움이 된다. 추론 능력은 대의 또는 세부 내용을 바탕으로 하기 때문에 세부 내용도 간과할 수 없다.
- 선택지를 한 번밖에 들려주지 않기 때문에 대화 내용을 다 이해하고도 선택지를 놓쳐서 정답을 고르지 못하는 경우가 있다. 이를 방지하기 위해 소거법을 적용해서 선택지를 차례대로 표시하면서 최종 정답을 고르도록 한다.
- 질문 종류별로 오답 확률이 높은 유형을 알아 두는 것도 도움이 된다.
  - 대의 파악 오답 유형: 대화 중 일부 세부 사항만 포함한 선택지, 너무 일반적인 내용의 선택지, 대화 중 특정 키워드를 조합한 전혀 엉뚱한 내용의 선택지 등이다.
  - 세부 내용 파악 오답 유형: 대화에서 언급된 어휘를 반복한 선택지, 대화와 전혀 무관한 선택지, 일부 내용만 사실인 선택지, 남녀의 역할이 뒤바뀐 선택지, 시제가 대화 내용과 일치하지 않는 선택지 등이 있다.
  - 추론 오답 유형: 상식적으로는 맞는 진술이지만 대화 내용과는 무관한 선택지, 대화에서 언급된 어휘로 만들었지만 대화 내용과 무관한 선택지, 추론 가능한 내용과 정반대인 선택지 등이 있다.
- 대의 파악이나 세부 내용 파악 유형에 대비해 패러프레이징(paraphrasing) 연습을 하는 것이 좋다. 대화에서 언급된 어휘가 그대로 사용된 경우는 오답일 확률이 높은 반면, 언급된 어휘를 비슷한 말로 바꾸어 만든 선택지는 정답일 확률이 높으므로 paraphrasing 연습이 많은 도움이 된다.

# PART IV

## A 유형 분석

담화문을 듣고 4개의 선택지 중 질문에 가장 적절한 정답을 고르는 문제이다.

**제시 방법** 담화문 → 질문 → 담화문 → 질문 → 선택지 순으로 들려준다.

**문항수** 15문항

**질문 유형** 대의 파악(7문항) → 세부 내용 파악(5문항) → 추론(3문항) 순으로 나온다.

**측정 영역** 연설, 강의, 라디오 방송 등에 나오는 다양한 표현에 대한 이해도 측정을 바탕으로 전체 대의 파악, 세부 내용 파악, 추론 능력을 측정한다.

## B 대표 기출문제

Wildlife officials announced today that a tiny snail that could harm American river trout populations is spreading throughout the country. The New Zealand mud snail was first discovered in Idaho's Snake River in 1987. Since then, it has shown up in eight more rivers. The snails reproduce rapidly and destroy the habitat of trout and other aquatic life. Fishermen are being asked to clean their boots, fishing equipment and boats to prevent the snails from spreading from one river to another.

Q Which is correct according to the news report?

(a) American river trout are damaging waterways.

(b) Snails from the U.S. have been found in New Zealand.

✔ (c) It was in Snake River that the mud snail was first found.

(d) Fishermen have been asked to collect the snails they find.

해석

야생 생물 관계자는 오늘 미국 민물송어 개체군에 해를 끼칠 수 있는 작은 달팽이가 전국적으로 확산되고 있다고 발표했습니다. 뉴질랜드 진흙 달팽이는 1987년 아이다호 주 스네이크 강에서 처음으로 발견됐습니다. 그 이후 이 달팽이는 8개 강에 추가로 나타났습니다. 이 달팽이는 번식이 빠르고 송어 및 다른 수생 생물의 서식처를 파괴합니다. 이들 달팽이가 하나의 강에서 다른 강으로 확산되는 것을 막기 위해 어부에게 장화와 낚시 장비, 배를 청소하도록 요청하는 바입니다.

Q 뉴스 보도에 따르면 옳은 것은?

(a) 미국 민물송어는 수로를 손상시킨다.

(b) 미국산 달팽이가 뉴질랜드에서 발견되었다.

(c) 진흙 달팽이가 최초로 발견된 곳은 스네이크 강이었다.

(d) 발견한 진흙 달팽이를 어부들에게 채집하도록 요청했다.

공략법

외래종의 확산으로 발생하는 문제에 대한 내용이다. 두 번째 문장에서 진흙 달팽이가 스네이크 강에서 처음 발견되었다고 했으므로 (c)가 정답임을 쉽게 알 수 있다. (a)는 언급되지 않은 내용이며, (b)는 정반대 진술이다. 또한 어부들에게 달팽이의 확산을 막기 위해 노력해 달라고 했으므로 (d) 역시 오답이다.

## C 고득점 핵심 비법

- 먼저 담화문의 전체 흐름을 파악한 뒤, 두 번째 듣기에서 질문과 연계된 부분에 집중하여 정확하게 듣는다.
- 질문 유형에 따라 맞춤식 메모를 한다. 특히 세부 사항 파악 유형 문제에 대비해서는 숫자, 연도, 물품 종류 등을 세세하게 메모해야 하고, 추론 능력은 대의 또는 세부 내용을 바탕으로 하기 때문에 세부 내용도 간과할 수 없다는 것을 기억한다.
- 질문 종류별로 오답일 확률이 높은 경우를 알아 두면 도움이 된다.
  - 대의 파악 오답 유형: 담화문 내용의 일부에 해당하는 세부 사항으로 만든 선택지, 주제와 관련은 있으나 너무 범위가 넓은 일반적인 내용의 선택지, 언급된 어휘로 구성된 점 외에는 내용과 전혀 관련이 없는 선택지 등이 오답일 확률이 높다.
  - 세부 내용 파악 오답 유형: 담화문에 언급된 어휘로 만들어진 선택지나 내용과 전혀 무관한 선택지, 일부만 사실인 선택지 등이 오답으로 제시될 가능성이 크다.
  - 추론 오답 유형: 상식적으로는 맞지만 내용과는 무관한 선택지, 담화문에서 언급된 어휘로 만들었지만 내용과는 무관한 선택지, 추론 가능한 내용과 정반대의 선택지 등이 종종 사용되는 오답 유형이다.
- 대의 파악이나 세부 내용 파악 유형의 문제를 대비하려면 paraphrasing 연습을 하는 것이 좋다. 언급된 어휘를 그대로 사용하면 오답일 확률이 높은 반면, 정답의 경우 언급된 어휘를 paraphrasing해서 만드는 경우가 많다.

# PART I

## A 유형 분석

두 줄의 대화문을 읽고 빈칸에 문법적으로 적절한 표현을 4개의 선택지 중에서 고르는 문제이다.

**제시 방법** 두 줄의 대화문이 주어진다.

**문항수** 20문항

**측정 영역** 실시간과 비슷한 시간 제약 속에서 문법적으로 정확한 영어를 대화 속에서 구사할 수 있는지 측정한다.

**빈출 토픽** 일상 생활 대화 중에 흔히 접할 수 있는 주제가 많이 사용되므로 청해나 어휘 영역의 대화 부분과 비슷한 내용이 나온다.

## B 대표 기출문제

A Don't take that last cookie. It's for Dan.
B But he ____________________ all the cookies last time.

✔ (a) ate
(b) eats
(c) has eaten
(d) had been eating

해석

**A** 마지막 쿠키 먹지 마. 댄 줄 거니까.
**B** 하지만 댄은 지난번에 쿠키를 다 먹었잖아요.

공략법

시제 문제는 함께 쓰이는 시간의 부사에서 힌트를 찾아야 한다. 이 문장에서는 last time이 시간의 부사 역할을 하고 있다. last는 지난 일을 나타내므로 항상 과거 시제와 함께 쓰인다. 따라서 (a)가 정답이다.

## C 고득점 핵심 비법

- 정확한 영어를 적재적소에 사용하는 능력이 중요하므로 눈으로만 익히는 문법 지식을 배제한다. 대화체를 소리 내어 읽는 연습을 해서 문법이 내재화되어 상황에 맞게 즉각적으로 사용할 수 있는 수준까지 끌어올리도록 한다.
- 문법 네 가지 Part 중 비교적 평이한 수준이기 때문에 시간 안배 차원에서 신속하게 풀고 다음 Part로 넘어가도록 한다. 단, 첫 줄은 빈칸에 올 적절한 답을 찾는 데 단서가 되므로 생략하고 넘어가면 함정에 빠지는 경우가 종종 있다. 신속하게 문제를 읽어나가되 읽지 않고 건너뛰는 일은 없어야 한다.
- 문법 문제의 빈칸은 주로 두 번째 줄에 오지만 일부 문제는 첫 번째 줄에 빈칸이 오기도 한다. 이런 유형에서는 두 번째 줄을 제대로 읽어야 출제자의 함정에 걸려들지 않는다. 즉, 빈칸 위치에 상관없이 문제에 나오는 대화는 모두 다 읽고 정확한 내용을 파악해야 오답 함정을 피해 정답을 찾을 수 있다.
- 문법 문제라고 해서 대화의 문법적인 요소만 신경 쓰면 안 된다. 상황에 적절한 어법을 고른다는 자세로 문제를 풀도록 한다. 예를 들어 대화 내용에 현재 시제가 여러 개 나온다고 무조건 현재 시제를 답으로 고르면 오히려 오답일 경우가 많다.
- 일상 대화 구문의 어법을 묻는 Part이므로 대화체의 정확한 표현을 익히는 것이 도움이 된다. 즉, 문법책의 모든 문법 요소를 처음부터 공부하는 것보다는 일상 대화 구문 표현 위주로 외울 수 있는 수준까지 익혀 두면 짧은 시간 내에 정확하게 구사할 수 있는 표현들이 많아지고 이렇게 되면 문법 Part 1도 쉽게 정복할 수 있다.

# PART II

## A 유형 분석

하나의 문장을 읽고 빈칸에 문법적으로 가장 적절한 표현을 4개의 선택지 중에서 고른다.

**제시 방법** 하나의 문어체 문장이 주어진다.

**문항수** 20문항

**측정 영역** 문어체 영어의 정확한 어법 구사력을 측정한다.

**빈출 토픽** 학술문과 실용문 등 일상에서 접하는 문어체 문장에 언급되는 주제가 주로 사용된다.

## B 대표 기출문제

__________________ the movie twice, Bob did not want to see it again.

(a) He had seen
(b) Had he seen
✔ (c) Having seen
(d) To have seen

해석

그 영화를 두 번 봤기 때문에 밥은 그것을 또 보고 싶지 않았다.

공략법

접속사가 없으므로 (a)와 같은 완전한 절은 올 수 없다. (d)와 같은 to부정사는 문두에 오면 보통 목적의 의미를 가지므로 문맥상 어울리지 않는다. 따라서 빈칸에는 분사구문이 나와야 하는데 주절의 주어 Bob이 영화를 직접 본 것이므로 능동의 현재분사 (c)가 정답이다. 영화를 본 것이 먼저 일어난 일이므로 완료분사 Having seen을 썼다.

## C 고득점 핵심 비법

- 구어체 문장보다 문어체 문장의 의미 파악이 까다로울 수 있으므로 평상시 문어체 문장의 직독직해 연습을 충분히 한다. 특히 관계사들로 연결된 문장, 절 안에 또 다른 절이 있는 문장 등 복잡한 문장을 평상시에 많이 접해 보도록 하자. 난해한 문장을 만났을 때 바로 의미를 파악할 수 있어야 문법 Part 2 문제를 신속하게 해결할 수 있다.
- 주어와 동사가 여러 개 나오는 긴 문장은 주절의 주어와 동사를 파악한 후, 다른 문법 사항들을 따져 보도록 한다. 특히 대표 빈출 유형이자 기본이 되는 주어-동사 수 일치 문제는 주절의 주어와 동사를 파악해야만 풀 수 있는 문제이다.
- TEPS 시험에서는 한국인이 특히 취약한 관사와 문장 구조 등에 대해 묻는 문제가 다수 출제된다. 이를 대비하기 위해서는 문장 내 쓰임새를 익혀 두는 것이 낱낱의 문법 지식을 알고 있는 것보다 신속하고 정확하게 문제를 푸는 데 많은 도움을 줄 것이다. 영어 활용 능력 수준 측정을 위해 TEPS가 고안된 점을 염두에 두고, 평소에 정확한 영어 구사 능력 함양에 집중하도록 한다.
- 문법 Part 1과 마찬가지로 정확한 어법을 익히려면 청해 Part 4 긴 담화문 속에 나오는 문장이나 어휘 Part 2 문장을 익혀 두는 것도 좋다. 각 분야별 어휘와 구문에 익숙해질수록 읽고 이해하는 속도가 자연히 빨라지게 되고, 아울러 문장 안에서 정확한 쓰임새도 익힐 수 있기 때문이다.

# PART III

## A 유형 분석

네 줄의 대화문을 읽고 문법적으로 이상한 부분이 있는 문장을 고르는 유형의 문제이다.

**제시 방법** 네 줄의 대화문이 주어진다.

**문항수** 5문항

**측정 영역** 길어진 대화에서 비문법적 요소를 가려내는 능력을 측정한다.

**빈출 토픽** 일상 생활에서 접하는 대화에 나오는 주제가 주로 사용된다.

## B 대표 기출문제

(a) A Let's go to an amusement park this weekend.
✔ (b) B Well, that's not what I had planned during the weekend.
(c) A Oh, are you going to do anything special?
(d) B Actually, I just want to stay home and relax.

해석

(a) **A** 이번 주말에 놀이공원에 가자.
(b) **B** 음, 그건 내가 주말에 계획한 게 아닌데.
(c) **A** 아, 뭐 특별한 거라도 하게?
(d) **B** 실은 그냥 집에서 쉬고 싶어서.

공략법

과거완료 had p.p.는 과거보다 더 앞선 시제를 나타낼 때 쓰므로 (b)에서처럼 현재 시제와 함께 쓸 수 없다. 다른 계획을 세운 것은 과거의 일이므로 had planned가 아니라 단순과거인 planned가 되어야 한다.

## C 고득점 핵심 비법

- 주어진 선택지가 따로 없어서 어떤 문법에 관한 문제인지 전혀 알 수 없고 주어진 대화 내용을 읽으면서 틀린 부분을 골라야 하기 때문에 보다 적극적인 태도로 문제에 임해야 한다. 즉, 각 대화에서 어느 문법 요소가 틀렸는지 모르는 상태에서 틀린 부분을 찾아야 하기 때문에 대화 내용을 파악함과 동시에 모든 품사와 구문 요소가 정확한지도 일일이 확인하는 습관을 평소에 들여야 당황하지 않고 실전에서 실력 발휘를 할 수 있다.
- 주어진 시간 내에 틀린 문법 사항을 골라야 하기 때문에 즉각적으로 비문법적인 부분을 찾아내는 훈련이 평상시에 필요하다. 이렇게 하기 위해서는 다른 문법 Part의 문제 대비와 마찬가지로 일상 대화 및 학술문과 실용문을 많이 접해서 다양한 문장에 익숙해져야 한다.
- 모든 문법 학습 요소들이 다 출제되는 것이 아니라 단골로 출제되는 문법 사항이 있음을 알자. 문장 구조, 시제, 수 일치, 관사 등에 해당하는 문법 요소들을 집중해서 훈련하는 것도 단기간에 Part 3을 정복할 수 있는 길이다. 물론, Part 3 역시 제한된 문법 사항에만 국한해 다른 문법 요소를 무시했다가 낭패를 볼 수 있다는 것을 유의하자.
- Part 4에 비해 짧은 대화체라 약간 수월하게 보일 수 있겠지만 선택지가 주어진 Part 1과 2보다는 고난도인 경우가 많다. 특히 재빨리 읽으면서 틀린 문법 사항도 찾아내야 하므로 평상시 대화문의 정확도를 분석하는 것도 실전에서 틀린 부분을 파악하는 데 도움이 될 것이다. 즉, 정답을 찾는 데에만 급급하지 말고 한 문제를 풀더라도 문법적으로 옳고 그른 부분들에 대한 분석을 자세히 하다 보면 실전에서 당황하지 않고 틀린 부분을 찾아낼 수 있다는 것이다.

# PART IV

## A 유형 분석

4개의 문어체 문장을 읽고 문법적으로 어색한 부분이 있는 문장을 고르는 유형의 문제이다.

**제시 방법** 4개의 문어체 문장이 하나의 지문으로 주어진다.

**문항수** 5문항

**측정 영역** 문어체 문장으로 구성된 지문에서 비문법적인 요소를 가려내는 능력을 측정한다.

**빈출 토픽** 신문, 잡지, 교재 등 일상 생활에서 문어체로 접하게 되는 주제가 등장한다.

## B 대표 기출문제

✔ (a) In a study, separate groups of men was asked to run as hard and as long as possible on a treadmill. (b) Each group was cheered and encouraged, but at different intervals—either every 20, 60 or 180 seconds. (c) Researchers perceived no gains among those who were given verbal cues every 180 seconds. (d) It was found, however, that performance did improve for men cheered every 20 or 60 seconds.

해석

(a) 한 연구에서 서로 다른 남성 집단에게 러닝머신 위에서 최대한 빨리 그리고 최대한 오래 달리도록 요구했다. (b) 각 집단은 각각 20초, 60초, 180초 간격으로 응원과 격려를 받았다. (c) 연구자들은 180초마다 응원을 받은 사람들에게는 이득이 없다는 것을 발견했다. (d) 그러나 20초, 혹은 60초마다 응원을 받은 남성들의 경우는 성과가 실제로 향상되었음이 밝혀졌다.

공략법

A of B 형태에서 동사는 A와 일치시킨다. (a)에서 주어 separate groups of men의 동사는 groups와 일치시켜 복수 동사를 취해야 하므로 was를 were로 고친다.

## C 고득점 핵심 비법

- Part 3 대화체에 비해 Part 4는 지문 길이도 더 길고 문어체라서 내용 파악이 훨씬 더 어렵고 시간도 가장 많이 걸린다. 그렇기 때문에 비문법적인 요소를 찾기가 특히 더 어려울 수 있으므로 신속하게 문어체 문장들을 읽고 직독직해를 통해 내용을 즉시 파악할 수 있는 능력을 평상시에 훈련하도록 한다.

- 지문 내용은 물론 문제에서 요구하는 문법 사항 예측이 어렵기 때문에 더욱 적극적인 문제 풀이 전략이 필요하다. 4개의 문장을 읽으면서 내용 파악을 하는 동시에 모든 가능성을 열어 두고 비문법적으로 보이는 부분을 찾아 나가야 하는데 이때 가능성이 있는 부분을 일단 밑줄 그어 놓은 뒤 신속하게 다시 그 부분들을 재확인하는 것도 정확도를 높이는 한 방법이 될 수 있다.

- 주어진 시간 내에 틀린 문법 사항을 골라야 하기 때문에 즉각적으로 비문법적인 부분을 찾아내는 훈련이 필요하다. 이를 위해서는 정확한 표현을 즉각적으로 사용할 수 있을 정도로 알고 있어야 한다. 즉, Part 3 대비를 위해서 대화체를 많이 익혀 둠으로써 신속하게 비문법적인 대화 부분을 알아차리는 훈련을 하듯이, Part 4 대비책으로 학술문과 실용문을 접하면서 거의 암기할 정도로 정독하는 것도 문법 내재화를 도울 것이며, 이런 훈련 과정을 거치고 나면 자연스럽게 틀린 부분이 눈에 잘 띌 것이다.

- Part 2에 나오는 문장 네 개가 한꺼번에 출제된다고 생각하면 좀 부담이 덜어질 것이고 Part 2 문장들에서 문법적 오류를 찾는다고 생각하면 이제 마음도 편해질 것이다.

  – 시제 문제: 각 문장마다 여러 시제가 혼합되어 있는 경우가 대부분이기 때문에 시제의 형태만 참고해서 틀린 시제를 찾는 것은 거의 불가능하다고 봐야 한다. 내용 파악이 선행되어야만 시제가 잘못 쓰인 곳을 찾을 수 있다.

  – 관사 문제: a와 the의 쓰임 여부는 4개 문장에서 어떤 명사가 이미 앞서 언급된 것이고 아닌지를 이해한 후에 결정되므로 내용 파악이 우선되어야 한다.

# PART I

## A 유형 분석

두 줄의 대화문을 읽고 빈칸에 가장 잘 어울리는 어휘를 고르는 문제이다.

**제시 방법** 두 줄의 대화문이 주어진다.

**문항수** 25문항

**측정 영역** 대화에서 사용하는 구어체 표현을 적절하게 활용할 수 있는지 측정한다.

**빈출 토픽** 일상 생활과 관련 있는 주제가 많이 출제된다.

## B 대표 기출문제

A What took you so long to get here?
B Sorry, I was __________________ a meeting.

✔ (a) attending
(b) including
(c) reducing
(d) skipping

**해석**

**A** 여기 오는 데 왜 이렇게 오래 걸렸니?
**B** 미안, 회의에 참석했었어.

(a) 참석하다
(b) 포함하다
(c) 줄이다
(d) 건너뛰다

**공략법**

시간이 오래 걸린 이유를 묻고 있으므로 회의에 '참석했다'는 문장이 되어야 한다. '참석하다'는 의미의 동사 (a) attend는 다음에 전치사를 쓰지 않는 타동사이므로 attend a meeting이 된다.

## C 고득점 핵심 비법

- 짧은 시간 내에 문맥에 어울리는 어휘를 골라야 하기 때문에 많은 어휘를 알고 있는 것뿐만 아니라 문맥(context)에 적절한 어휘를 사용할 수 있는 능력을 키우는 것도 중요하다. 따라서 어휘를 처음 접할 때엔 참고 자료를 동원해서 문장 내에서 쓰이는 다양한 예문을 동시에 익혀 두어야 한다. 시간 내에 모든 어휘 문제를 잘 풀기 위해서는 특히 문맥 속에서 각 어휘의 쓰임을 거의 외우다시피 알고 있어야 시간 낭비 없이 즉각적으로 빈칸에 올 정답을 고를 수 있을 것이다.
- 해당 어휘의 우리말을 단순하게 암기하는 것은 별 도움이 안 된다. 우리말로는 그럴듯해도 쓰임이 어색한 어휘의 뉘앙스 차이를 구분할 줄 알아야 하므로 문장 전체로 어휘를 이해하는 것이 장기적으로 유리하다.
- 청해의 대화 파트뿐만 아니라 문법 Part 1과 3에 언급된 대화들도 어휘 실력 향상을 위해 활용될 수 있음을 기억하고 어휘 영역 이외의 빈출 표현도 문맥 속에서 익혀 두도록 한다.
- 대화를 신속히 읽고 즉각적으로 빈칸을 채워 넣어야 하기 때문에 실제 대화를 하면서 적절한 어휘를 사용할 수 있을 정도의 실력이 되도록 많은 표현을 통째로 익혀 두어야 한다.
- 일상적인 대화 속에서 자주 등장하는 어휘뿐만 아니라 이어동사, 이디엄 등도 출제되므로 숙지해 두도록 한다.
- 형태상 · 의미상 혼동되는 어휘, 의미 덩어리로 사용되는 연어 등의 정확한 활용법도 아울러 알아 둔다.

# PART II

## A 유형 분석

한 개의 문어체 문장을 읽고 빈칸에 가장 잘 어울리는 어휘를 고르는 문제이다.

**제시 방법** 한 개의 문어체 문장이 주어진다.

**문항수** 25문항

**측정 영역** 일상 생활에서 접할 수 있는 문어체 표현을 문맥에 맞게 사용할 수 있는지 측정한다.

**빈출 토픽** 학술문뿐만 아니라 실용문에 이르기까지 매우 다양한 주제를 다룬다.

## B 대표 기출문제

To ___________________ military messages over radio, a secret code based on a Native American language was used by the US in World War II.

(a) infuse
(b) conflict
✔ (c) transmit
(d) intercept

**해석**

무선으로 군사 메시지를 전송하기 위해, 제2차 세계대전 당시 미국은 인디언 언어를 기반으로 한 비밀 코드를 사용했다.

(a) 불어넣다
(b) 상충하다
(c) 전송하다
(d) 가로막다

**공략법**

목적어가 메시지이기 때문에 '보내다, 전송하다'는 의미의 동사가 필요하다. 따라서 답은 (c)이다. 접두어 trans-에는 이동의 의미가 있다.

## C 고득점 핵심 비법

- 학술문과 실용문의 주제별 빈출 어휘를 익혀 둔다. 빈출 어휘는 정답 선택지뿐만 아니라 오답 선택지에 나오는 어휘도 포함한다. 주제별로 자주 출제되는 어휘는 한정되어 있기 때문에 기출 어휘가 다시 출제될 확률이 높다.
- Part1과 마찬가지로 각 어휘의 쓰임새를 알아야 하기 때문에 전체 문장을 익히도록 한다. 그래야만 문법적으로도 정확한 어휘 활용 능력을 키울 수 있기 때문이다.
- 미묘한 뉘앙스 차이가 있는 쉬운 어휘의 용례 예문을 적극적으로 활용해야 한다. 의미가 비슷해 보이는 어휘들끼리 묶어서 따로 정리하면 도움이 될 것이다.
- 신문 기사, 잡지, 광고, 학술지, 비평 등의 실용문과 전문적인 학술문에서 다양하게 출제되므로 평상시 이런 종류의 글을 많이 접하는 것이 도움이 된다. 15분이라는 짧은 시간 내에 50문항이나 되는 문제를 무리 없이 풀기 위한 대비법 중 하나가 주제별로 다양한 문장을 평소에 자주 읽는 것이다. 이렇게 함으로써 필수 어휘를 자주 접할 수 있을 뿐만 아니라 문장 이해 속도도 향상될 수 있다.
- 대화체 문제와 마찬가지로 주제별 어휘뿐만 아니라 연어 및 형태상 · 의미상 혼동되는 어휘도 잘 알아 두도록 한다.

# PART I

## A 유형 분석

100단어 내외의 단일 지문을 읽고 빈칸에 들어갈 적절한 선택지를 고르는 문제이다. 14문항은 구나 절을 고르는 문제이고, 나머지 2문항은 문장과 문장 사이를 이어주는 연결어를 찾는 문제이다.

**제시 방법** 지문의 처음 문장이나 마지막 문장, 드물게 중간 문장에 빈칸이 있는 한 개의 글이 주어진다.

**문항수** 16문항

**측정 영역** 글의 전반적인 이해 능력 및 논리적인 흐름 파악 능력을 평가한다.

**빈출 토픽** 학술문과 실용문에서 골고루 출제된다.

## B 대표 기출문제

Deerbar's annual sale is now on! To make way for next year's new models, Deerbar is selling off its entire remaining inventory at wholesale prices! This week only, get heavily discounted refrigerators, washer-dryer combos, freezers and microwaves. We will even include free delivery anywhere within the city limits! Don't delay. If you want __________________, come to Deerbar!

(a) this year's latest kitchen gear
(b) fashionable home furnishings
✔ (c) deals on major home appliances
(d) affordable equipment for the office

해석

디어바 연례 세일 중입니다! 내년도 신형 모델 입고를 위해 디어바에서는 남아 있는 전 재고 물량을 도매가에 처분하고 있습니다. 이번 주 단 한 주, 폭탄 세일가로 냉장고, 세탁기-건조기 콤보, 냉동고와 전자레인지를 들여가십시오. 시 경계 내라면 어디든 무료 배달까지 해 드립니다! 미루지 마십시오. 저렴한 가격의 주요 가전제품을 원하시면 디어바로 오십시오!

(a) 올해의 최신 부엌용품을
(b) 유행하는 가구를
(c) 저렴한 가격의 주요 가전제품을
(d) 적정한 가격의 사무용 장비를

공략법

디어바의 연례 세일 광고이다. 이 가게에서 취급하는 물건은 냉장고, 세탁기, 전자레인지 등이므로 가전제품을 구매하려고 하는 사람을 대상으로 하는 광고임을 알 수 있다. 가전제품은 home appliances라고 하며 정답은 (c)이다.

## C 고득점 핵심 비법

- 모든 지문을 자세히 읽겠다는 생각을 접는다. 1분에 한 문제씩 풀어야 하기 때문에 정독을 하기에는 절대적으로 시간이 부족하므로 주요 어휘 위주로 대의 파악 및 흐름 파악에 주력해야 시간 내에 문제를 다 풀 수 있다.
- 주제별 어휘를 평소 많이 알아 둔다. 청해, 문법, 어휘 등 TEPS의 다른 영역과 마찬가지로 방대한 어휘 지식을 갖추고 있어야 독해 속도도 빨라지고 정확한 이해가 가능하다.
- 빈칸의 위치에 따라 독해의 목적이 달라져야 한다. 빈칸이 첫 문장에 있는 경우 대의 파악만 해도 되지만 마지막 문장에 올 때에는 대의 파악뿐만 아니라 논리적 흐름도 염두에 두면서 독해를 해야 한다.
- 오답 함정 선택지 유형을 연습해 둔다.
  - 지문에 나오는 어휘로 만들었지만 문맥과 전혀 상관없는 선택지
  - 너무 일반적인 내용으로 만든 선택지
  - 상식적으로는 괜찮아 보이지만 내용과는 무관한 선택지
  - 지문 내용의 일부처럼 보이기는 하지만 논리적인 흐름 면에서는 어울리지 않는 선택지

# PART II

## A 유형 분석

100단어 내외의 단일 지문을 읽고 주어진 질문에 적절한 답을 4개의 선택지에서 고르는 유형이다.

**제시 방법** 한 개의 지문에 한 개의 질문이 주어진다.

**문항수** 21문항

**측정 영역** 단일 지문에 대한 전체 및 세부 내용 이해 및 추론 능력을 측정한다.
대의 파악(6문항) → 세부 내용 파악(10문항) → 추론(5문항) 순으로 나온다.

**빈출 토픽** 학술문과 실용문에서 모두 골고루 출제된다.

## B 대표 기출문제

Sam Cantwell and Jack Hansen are two of America's best-loved motivational speakers. They have each delighted thousands of listeners with their wit and wisdom, and now—in a never-before-held event—they have teamed up to create a unique, doubly rewarding experience. Join them as they tell their favorite tales of inspiration at Chancellor Hall this Friday and Saturday only, from 8:00 pm. Tickets are available at the door, or you may purchase tickets in advance through www.ticketsite.com.

Q What can be inferred about Cantwell and Hansen from the passage?

(a) They will stay together for a national tour.
(b) They are not likely to attract high ticket sales.
✔ (c) They are appearing together for the first time.
(d) They will give talks advocating a religious doctrine.

해석

샘 캔트웰과 잭 핸슨은 미국 내에서 가장 사랑받는 두 명의 동기부여 연사입니다. 이들은 각각 재치와 지혜로 수천 명의 청중들에게 기쁨을 주었으며, 이제 과거에 유례없던 한 행사를 통해 이들이 의기투합하여 독특하며 두 배로 보람 있는 경험을 만들고자 합니다. 이번 주 금요일과 토요일 단 이틀, 오후 8시부터 챈슬러 홀에서 이들이 가장 좋아하는 감동의 이야기를 들려주는 자리에 함께하십시오. 입장권은 행사장에서 구매 가능하며, www.ticketsite.com을 통해 예매를 하실 수도 있습니다.

Q 캔트웰과 핸슨에 대해 유추할 수 있는 것은?

(a) 전국 투어를 함께 다닐 것이다.
(b) 높은 입장권 판매를 유치할 것 같지 않다.
(c) 처음으로 함께 출연한다.
(d) 종교적 교의를 옹호하는 이야기를 할 것이다.

공략법

두 번째 문장에서 언급한 과거에 유례없는 행사(a never-before-held event)라는 표현으로 보아 두 사람의 연사가 함께 출연하는 것이 처음임을 추론할 수 있다. 따라서 정답은 (c)이다. (a)와 (b)는 지문의 내용만으로는 알 수 없으며, 사람들에게 영감을 주고 동기를 부여해 주는 내용의 연설을 할 것으로 예상되므로 (d)도 오답이다.

## C 고득점 핵심 비법

- 직독직해하는 습관을 들인다. 우리말로 해석부터 하려고 덤벼들지 말고 신속하게 영어 지문을 읽으면서 내용을 이해하는 습관을 들여야 한다.
- 지문을 다 읽겠다는 생각을 버려라. 대의 파악 문제의 경우 주요 내용어 중심으로 읽고, 세부 내용 파악 문제는 질문에 따라 선택지의 진위 여부를 한 개씩 확인해 가며 읽거나 육하원칙 문제는 질문 내용을 제대로 파악하고 해당 부분을 신속히 찾아서 그 부분을 자세히 읽는다. 추론 문제는 대의 파악 및 세부 내용 파악이 선행되어야 하기 때문에 좀 더 시간을 할애해야 할 것이다.
- 오답 함정을 각 문제 유형마다 미리 알아 두고 잘 피하도록 한다.
  - 대의 파악 오답 유형 : 세부 사실을 대의로 혼동하게 하는 오답이 자주 출제된다.
  - 세부 내용 파악 오답 유형 : 일부 내용만 사실인 경우, 지문에서 언급된 어휘로 만들었지만 내용과는 상관없는 선택지를 주의하자.
  - 추론 오답 유형 : 그럴듯해 보이지만 지문 내용과는 상관없는 오답, 정답과 정반대 진술이 선택지로 제시되기도 한다.

# PART III

## A 유형 분석

5개의 문장으로 구성된 100단어 내외의 단일 지문을 읽고 글의 흐름상 어색한 문장을 찾는 유형의 문제이다.

**제시 방법** 주제문에 이어 4개의 문장이 제시된다.

**문항수** 3문항

**측정 영역** 지문의 응집력 파악 능력을 측정한다.

**빈출 지문 토픽** 학술문과 실용문 모두 골고루 출제된다.

## B 대표 기출문제

See the memorable sights of London with Black Taxi Tours! (a) Our tour is the only one where you can enjoy seeing the sites of London in genuine London taxi cabs. (b) A detailed commentary from a trained London cabbie is included in your comprehensive two-hour tour. ✔ (c) To become a cabbie in London, you must have an extensive knowledge of the city's roads. (d) You won't find a better guide than our cabbies, so call our office now to book your tour.

### 해석

블랙 택시 관광으로 기억에 남을 런던 명승지를 돌아보세요! (a) 저희 관광은 진짜 런던 택시를 타고 런던의 관광지를 즐길 수 있는 유일한 관광 상품입니다. (b) 숙련된 런던 택시 기사의 자세한 해설이 전체 2시간 관광에 포함되어 있습니다. (c) 런던에서 택시 기사가 되려면 런던의 도로에 대한 해박한 지식이 있어야 합니다. (d) 저희 기사들보다 더 나은 가이드는 찾을 수 없을 것입니다. 그러니 지금 저희 사무실로 전화하셔서 블랙 택시 관광을 예약하십시오.

### 공략법

런던 택시를 이용한 관광을 홍보하는 광고문으로, 택시 관광에 대한 간단한 안내와 함께 빨리 예약을 하라는 광고 문구가 나와 있는 글이다. 그러나 (c)에는 관광과는 관련없는, 택시 기사가 되기 위해 필요한 조건이 나와 있으므로 전체 문맥과 어울리지 않는다.

## C 고득점 핵심 비법

- 처음 제시되는 주제문에서 벗어난 문장을 찾는 것이므로 4개의 선택지 문장을 읽을 때에 항상 주제문과의 연관성을 염두에 두고 읽도록 한다. 문법 Part 4의 경우 각 문장 간의 연관성까지 염두에 두고 내용을 파악할 필요는 없으나 독해 Part 3에서는 주제문과의 연관성이 문제 풀이의 핵심이다.
- 주제문과 연관성은 있으나 문장의 위치가 잘못되어 흐름을 깨는 유형도 있으니 흐름상 잘 어울리는지도 살피도록 한다.
- 글의 어조가 갑자기 바뀌는 경우도 어색한 문장에 해당하므로 어조의 변화도 주의하도록 한다.
- 주어진 주제문에 대한 문장이 3개 나온 뒤 새로운 주제문이 4번째 문장으로 나오게 되면 어색한 문장이 된다는 것도 기억한다.

# 서울대 최신기출

# 1

***Listening*** *Comprehension*

***Grammar***

***Vocabulary***

***Reading*** *Comprehension*

# LISTENING COMPREHENSION

## DIRECTIONS

1. In the Listening Comprehension section, all content will be presented orally rather than in written form.
2. This section contains four parts, each with fifteen individual items. For each part, you will receive separate instructions. Listen to the instructions carefully, and choose the best answer from the options for each item.

Scripts P 268 / 정답 P 328

**Part I** **Questions 1—15**

You will now hear fifteen individual spoken questions or statements, each followed by four spoken responses. Choose the most appropriate response for each item.

**Part II** **Questions 16—30**

You will now hear fifteen short conversation fragments, followed by four spoken responses. Choose the most appropriate response to complete each conversation.

**Part III** **Questions 31–45**

You will now hear fifteen complete conversations. For each conversation, you will be asked to answer a question. Each conversation and its corresponding question will be read twice. Then you will hear four options which will be read only once. Based on the given information, choose the option that best answers the question.

**Part IV** **Questions 46–60**

You will now hear fifteen short talks. After each talk, you will be asked to answer a question. Each talk and its corresponding question will be read twice. Then you will hear four options which will be read only once. Based on the given information, choose the option that best answers the question.

TEPS

# GRAMMAR

## DIRECTIONS

This section tests your grammar skills. You will have 25 minutes to complete the 50 questions. Be sure to follow the directions given by the proctor.

정답 P 328

## Part I Questions 1—20

Choose the option that best completes each gap.

1. A: Can we study together tonight?
   B: Sure. My classes end at 6 pm, ____________ is later than usual, but I'm free afterward.
   (a) that
   (b) what
   (c) when
   (d) which

2. A: How long have you known Elizabeth?
   B: We grew up together, so as far back ____________.
   (a) as remembering I can
   (b) remembering as I can
   (c) as I can remember
   (d) I can remember as

3. A: Didn't Joel come with you?
   B: No. He said he'd be late, so he should arrive after the show ____________.
   (a) began
   (b) begins
   (c) will begin
   (d) had begun

4. A: I'm afraid to tell my boss about losing that client.
   B: ____________ the way he overreacts, I don't blame you.
   (a) Considering
   (b) To consider
   (c) Considered
   (d) Consider

5. A: I heard the guest lecture was brilliant.
   B: Yeah. If I had known about it, I definitely ____________.
   (a) would have gone
   (b) would be going
   (c) had been going
   (d) had gone

6. A: How is your grandfather enjoying his retirement?
   B: He appreciates ____________ up early in the morning.
   (a) having not himself to wake
   (b) him having not to wake
   (c) having not to wake him
   (d) not having to wake

7. A: Was Zack dressed up for the party last night?
   B: Yeah, he was dressed in ____________ looked like a borrowed suit.
   (a) that
   (b) what
   (c) which
   (d) whose

8. A: It's really starting to rain hard.
   B: I regret not ____________ an umbrella.
   (a) to bring
   (b) bringing
   (c) have brought
   (d) to have brought

**9.** A: You're picking me up at 10, right?

B: Yes. Give me a call ___________ anything change.

(a) could
(b) might
(c) would
(d) should

**10.** A: I thought Cathy was staying late.

B: No. She ___________ even before I got back from lunch.

(a) has left
(b) had left
(c) was leaving
(d) had been leaving

**11.** A: Do you need to see my driver's license or passport?

B: ___________ is fine. I just need some form of identification.

(a) Either
(b) Other
(c) None
(d) Some

**12.** A: We really need to go shopping!

B: I know. We barely have ___________ food in the house.

(a) no
(b) few
(c) any
(d) little

**13.** A: Were you an early riser when you were young, Sarah?

B: Yes, and the first person ___________ to bed, too.

(a) went
(b) to go
(c) is going
(d) had gone

**14.** A: The park sure was crowded.

B: Yeah. I didn't expect ___________ many people to be there.

(a) that
(b) such
(c) even
(d) much

**15.** A: I can't put together this new bookcase. Can you take a look?

B: OK. Let me see how ___________.

(a) it is going about to you
(b) you are going about it
(c) about going to do it
(d) to be going about

**16.** A: How did your job interview go?

B: Not too well. ___________ a second chance, I'd do much better.

(a) Granted
(b) Granting
(c) Had granted
(d) Having granted

**17.** A: I heard you got a promotion.
B: No, and I don't know __________ like that.

(a) about where you heard
(b) how you would be hearing
(c) anything about how you hearing
(d) where you would hear something

**18.** A: Can I take this subway to City Hall?
B: No, you have to change __________ at Singil station.

(a) train
(b) trains
(c) the train
(d) the trains

**19.** A: These low-fat muffins taste just as good as regular muffins!
B: I'd even say they're superior __________ the full-fat versions.

(a) to
(b) than
(c) with
(d) above

**20.** A: Bruce won't accept my apology. I've tried four times already.
B: I know. Still, __________, you should keep trying.

(a) it may though be difficult
(b) though difficult may it be
(c) may it be difficult though
(d) difficult though it may be

**Part II** **Questions 21–40**

Choose the option that best completes each gap.

**21.** Brian plays the clarinet now, but years ago he __________ the horn.

(a) plays
(b) played
(c) has played
(d) has been playing

**22.** One of the topics that were addressed in the article __________ how solar power is becoming more practical.

(a) was
(b) were
(c) has been
(d) have been

**23.** Even healthy people __________ suffer from altitude sickness if they do not get enough oxygen at high elevations.

(a) may
(b) need
(c) may not
(d) need not

**24.** Next Friday will mark one year __________ the five-day workweek became law for all state-run companies.

(a) as
(b) until
(c) since
(d) when

**25.** According to the resort's rules, children cannot enter the pool area after 9 pm ___________ accompanied by an adult.

(a) if only
(b) even if
(c) as far as
(d) as long as

**26.** The computer virus ___________ rapidly through email for the past week.

(a) spreads
(b) is spreading
(c) was spreading
(d) has been spreading

**27.** New species of fish ___________ at such an astonishing rate that biologists are barely able to keep pace.

(a) have been identifying
(b) had been identified
(c) are being identified
(d) have identified

**28.** Many of the ailments ___________ with old age result from years of poor posture.

(a) associated
(b) associating
(c) to associate
(d) are associated

**29.** After years of living abroad, Marie bought a house close to her family, ___________ she felt the most comfortable.

(a) who
(b) what
(c) which
(d) where

**30.** By the time Regina was 13, she ___________ three operations on her feet.

(a) has already had
(b) had already had
(c) was already having
(d) will have already had

**31.** Most of the sports-related injuries treated by a doctor last year ___________ nothing more than twisted ankles.

(a) was
(b) were
(c) was being
(d) were being

**32.** SaleWorld is known for ___________ employees.

(a) its generous offering benefits for
(b) offering with generous benefits to
(c) generosity offering with benefit for
(d) its generosity in offering benefits to

**33.** With it ___________ for weeks, few people were surprised when Bill announced his resignation last Friday.

(a) rumoring
(b) having rumored
(c) having been rumored
(d) to have been rumored

**34.** If Jessica's grades ___________ have been, the university might take away her scholarship.

(a) fall continuously as to
(b) continue to fall as they
(c) are continued to fall as they
(d) fall as they are continued to

**35.** The lights ___________ in the park all night allowed residents to take walks whenever they wanted.

(a) shine
(b) shone
(c) shining
(d) were shining

**36.** The airline required that Leonard ___________ a fee for his overweight baggage.

(a) pay
(b) pays
(c) has paid
(d) would pay

**37.** April was forced to finish her plate of vegetables even though she did not ___________.

(a) want
(b) want to
(c) want it to
(d) want to do

**38.** Sheryl was disappointed to see that her hard work at the gym did not make ___________ difference on the scale.

(a) much of
(b) much the
(c) much of a
(d) much of the

**39.** Carl was exhausted, but since the party was in his honor, he did not think ___________.

(a) it appropriately to leave
(b) leaving was appropriately
(c) his leaving would be appropriate
(d) he was appropriate to leave

**40.** Out of ___________ job applicants, only two were chosen to be the final candidates.

(a) few hundred of
(b) one hundred
(c) any hundred
(d) hundred of

## Part III Questions 41—45

Read each sentence carefully and identify the option that contains a grammatical error.

**41.** (a) A: I'm so glad that all of my holiday shopping are finally done!
(b) B: Already? You must have gotten an early start this year.
(c) A: I did. Plus, I bought most of my presents at just two stores.
(d) B: What a great idea! Maybe I'll try doing that as well.

**42.** (a) A: The printer is out of paper again, and I need this report today.
(b) B: Have you asked to someone in administration to order more?
(c) A: Yes, but according to them, it won't arrive until next week.
(d) B: Then I guess we'll have to get some ourselves from the store.

**43.** (a) A: Have you purchased your plane ticket home yet?
(b) B: No, I've still got a month to go, so it hasn't been my top priority.
(c) A: Well, don't wait too long, or the flight will fully book.
(d) B: True. I guess I'd better call my travel agent to see about it soon.

**44.** (a) A: What issues do you plan on raising at the meeting today?
(b) B: I think we need to sort out which ventures are worth exploring.
(c) A: A few that seemed to show promise were discussed at the last meeting.
(d) B: Yes, but I feel the topic hasn't been thorough discussed yet.

**45.** (a) A: What's the weather going to be like today, Peter?
(b) B: It supposed to be windy, and the temperature will drop sharply.
(c) A: Then shouldn't we postpone our weekend camping trip?
(d) B: Let's look at the forecast before we make any decisions.

**Part IV** **Questions 46–50**

Read each sentence carefully and identify the option that contains a grammatical error.

**46.** (a) Arguably the most widespread sleep disorder, insomnia, involves falling asleep difficulty. (b) Many people have trouble sleeping, but insomniacs can suffer from sleeplessness for years. (c) As a result, they can experience chronic fatigue, irritability, and various health problems. (d) The good news is that most cases of insomnia can be treated without the use of medication.

**47.** (a) In 2011, Bangkok, the capital of Thailand, was struck by the worst flooding in its recorded history. (b) Torrential rains resulted in the Chao Phraya River flooding over into heavily populated areas. (c) Hundreds of factories were forced to shut down by the incessantly and muddy torrent. (d) However, walls and pumping stations around the business district saved that area.

**48.** (a) The most common of the three basic rock types is igneous rock. (b) Well-known types of igneous rock include granite and basalt. (c) This type of rock makes about 95% of the earth's crust up. (d) It is formed when hot magma cools on or under the earth's surface.

**49.** (a) Scientists are exploring ways of using dogs' keen sense of smell to detect health problems. (b) A recent study has already shown that the canine nose can sniff out cancer with surprising accuracy. (c) These results indicate that cancer may produce chemicals that can be picked it up using breath samples. (d) In the future, scientists can use this information to develop noninvasive cancer tests based on scent.

**50.** (a) The only wooden whaleship still in existence from nineteenth-century America is the *Charles W. Morgan*. (b) Launched in 1841, this 35-meter vessel sailed the South Atlantic, Pacific, and Indian Oceans. (c) In its 80 years of service, it made 37 voyages and hauled tens of thousands of barrels of whale oil. (d) Today it is undergoing restoration and is in display at the Mystic Seaport Museum in Connecticut.

This is the end of the Grammar section. Do NOT move on to the next section until instructed to do so. You are NOT allowed to turn to any other section of the test.

# VOCABULARY

## DIRECTIONS

This section tests your vocabulary skills. You will have 15 minutes to complete the 50 questions. Be sure to follow the directions given by the proctor.

정답 P 328

## Part I Questions 1–25

Choose the option that best completes each gap.

**1.** A: How about a scoop of this chocolate ice cream?

B: Thanks. That's my favorite ___________.

(a) style
(b) scent
(c) flavor
(d) appetite

**2.** A: I'd like to reserve a room at the special grand opening price.

B: To get that ___________, you need to use our website.

(a) fee
(b) rate
(c) fund
(d) charge

**3.** A: Is this the right way to the zoo?

B: Yes, just keep going in the same ___________.

(a) route
(b) avenue
(c) method
(d) direction

**4.** A: How about we save this food and eat it for dinner?

B: Good idea. I'd hate to ___________ all these leftovers.

(a) settle
(b) waste
(c) spend
(d) empty

**5.** A: Can we ___________ a different price for this car?

B: Sure, I'm willing to discuss a price we both can agree on.

(a) convey
(b) scheme
(c) discount
(d) negotiate

**6.** A: You're proficient in German, right?

B: Yes, I've studied it for a while and now I'm ___________.

(a) fluent
(b) affected
(c) adorned
(d) punctual

**7.** A: Do you think this 1975 article is too old to use as a source?

B: Yeah, its information is probably ___________.

(a) outdated
(b) drafty
(c) extinct
(d) elderly

**8.** A: The director came up with such a brilliant way to end that film!

B: I agree. It was a(n) ___________ conclusion.

(a) rectified
(b) rampant
(c) observed
(d) ingenious

9. A: Is there any particular color you prefer for your new cell phone?
B: Any color is fine with me. I'm ___________.

(a) tolerable
(b) satisfying
(c) acceptable
(d) indifferent

10. A: When can we meet?
B: I'll check my ___________ and let you know.

(a) index
(b) agenda
(c) register
(d) account

11. A: The food is so tasteless. I doubt I'll come back to this restaurant.
B: Same here. I had no idea their food would be so ___________.

(a) bland
(b) morose
(c) tranquil
(d) embittered

12. A: I can't believe Ann was so rude to Tim this morning.
B: I guess she wants to ___________ him for mocking her hair style.

(a) get back at
(b) come up to
(c) stick up for
(d) cut down on

13. A: Why don't you drive to work these days?
B: My driver's license has been ___________ for three months, so I can't drive.

(a) expelled
(b) diverted
(c) suspended
(d) intervened

14. A: Cooper is late for the meeting.
B: I'm not surprised. He's almost always ___________.

(a) tardy
(b) belated
(c) cursory
(d) overdue

15. A: How should I decorate this cake?
B: Try ___________ it with fruit and whipped cream.

(a) boarding
(b) garnishing
(c) illustrating
(d) elaborating

16. A: Why aren't you ___________ with our guests?
B: Oh, I've already talked to most of them.

(a) merging
(b) mingling
(c) coalescing
(d) combining

17. A: Do you think these tulip bulbs will be confiscated at customs?
B: Yeah, customs officials will probably ___________ them.

(a) partake
(b) arrest
(c) grasp
(d) seize

**18.** A: How could you forget my birthday?
B: I'm sorry. I had a ___________ in memory.

(a) lapse
(b) wane
(c) faction
(d) pretense

**19.** A: Something came up at the office, and I have to cut my vacation short.
B: Oh, it's too bad you have to ___________ your visit.

(a) postpone
(b) subside
(c) recede
(d) curtail

**20.** A: My terrible math grades prove that I don't have a knack for it.
B: Yeah, math isn't my ___________, either.

(a) forte
(b) ethos
(c) quirk
(d) caliber

**21.** A: Simon Caughlin's plays have such ___________ story lines, don't they?
B: Yes, he really knows how to hold the audience's interest.

(a) plebeian
(b) intriguing
(c) foreseeable
(d) anticipated

**22.** A: Did the judge find your sister guilty of the traffic violation?
B: No, she was ___________ of all responsibility.

(a) impeded
(b) absolved
(c) vindicated
(d) discharged

**23.** A: Do we want to continue to support this failing venture?
B: No. Let's ___________ now before it goes bankrupt.

(a) pull the plug
(b) turn a blind eye
(c) cry over spilt milk
(d) let sleeping dogs lie

**24.** A: Did Jean ever say why she quit her last job?
B: I asked, but her reply was so ___________ that I couldn't figure it out.

(a) cryptic
(b) motley
(c) distinct
(d) mundane

**25.** A: Could you please summarize the novel?
B: Well, the plot ___________ the struggle between right and wrong.

(a) gets rid of
(b) runs out of
(c) stands up to
(d) boils down to

**Part II** **Questions 26—50**

Choose the option that best completes each gap.

**26.** In democratic societies, citizens are granted the right to participate in __________ to choose their leaders.

(a) courts
(b) elections
(c) advisories
(d) applications

**27.** *Globe Monthly* reminds its readers to renew their subscriptions early to avoid missing a single __________.

(a) issue
(b) affair
(c) option
(d) broadcast

**28.** Physical therapy can facilitate __________ after surgery by helping restore mobility and strength.

(a) guidance
(b) recovery
(c) duration
(d) support

**29.** Neil's thesis was rejected because he relied on assumptions that could not __________ careful analysis.

(a) contend
(b) survive
(c) hinder
(d) advise

**30.** Edward __________ the noise of his wife's party and continued to read his newspaper.

(a) cohered
(b) persisted
(c) disregarded
(d) transgressed

**31.** Union members want a peaceful resolution to the __________ with the administration over fair wages.

(a) debris
(b) pledge
(c) dispute
(d) recourse

**32.** Due to the food shortage, world health experts predict a __________ in malnutrition in the next decade.

(a) surge
(b) flutter
(c) quiver
(d) crevice

**33.** Queen Victoria __________ the throne at the age of 18 and reigned over the United Kingdom for 63 years.

(a) subdued
(b) divulged
(c) ascended
(d) condoned

**34.** Cantor Motor Oil is guaranteed to ___________ the life of your engine, so you can enjoy driving your car for years to come.

(a) unfold
(b) reprise
(c) overlap
(d) lengthen

**35.** ___________ by nature, Vanessa never lived in one city for a long time.

(a) Transient
(b) Credulous
(c) Meticulous
(d) Evanescent

**36.** Sharing a membership card is prohibited and may result in the gym ___________ your membership.

(a) avoiding
(b) silencing
(c) revoking
(d) extracting

**37.** The judge ordered the vandals to pay $1,000 as ___________ for the damage done to the shop owner's property.

(a) suffrage
(b) impunity
(c) restitution
(d) attainment

**38.** Gina complained that Martin was ___________ for not wanting to spend more than five dollars a day on food.

(a) stingy
(b) blatant
(c) nominal
(d) redundant

**39.** The recent decline in Lucky Motor's share price is ___________ to weak demand for its new line of luxury sedans.

(a) variable
(b) verifiable
(c) attributable
(d) accountable

**40.** Hugh Latimer, a Protestant preacher in the sixteenth century, became a ___________ when he died for his convictions.

(a) novice
(b) martyr
(c) vagrant
(d) neophyte

**41.** In a rush and unable to find a spot for her car, Jamie parked in a space ___________ for disabled people.

(a) designated
(b) sanctioned
(c) summoned
(d) deliberated

**42.** Hummingbirds are known for their ___________ size as they are usually no more than 8.5 cm long.

(a) tantamount
(b) diminutive
(c) embryonic
(d) immature

**43.** Alexander the Great defeated the Persians and ___________ their lands, which greatly expanded his empire.

(a) lauded
(b) annexed
(c) enshrined
(d) patronized

**44.** All boats in the area gathered to help rescue the thousands of passengers ___________ on a stranded cruise ship.

(a) ejected
(b) abdicated
(c) marooned
(d) relinquished

**45.** The building was flooded not because of one storm but because of the ___________ effect of several weeks of heavy rainfall.

(a) cumulative
(b) compulsive
(c) incorrigible
(d) irretrievable

**46.** Although most people do not believe in ___________ practices, the attraction to the supernatural, such as psychic powers or astrology, remains strong.

(a) occult
(b) opaque
(c) equivocal
(d) epicurean

**47.** Many social critics claim that ___________ celebrities perpetuates a culture in which stars feel they deserve such iconic status.

(a) lionizing
(b) extricating
(c) gentrifying
(d) substantiating

**48.** The government should commit to one course of action and stop ___________ among other possible resolutions.

(a) splurging
(b) deflecting
(c) eschewing
(d) vacillating

**49.** Confronted by conflicting testimonies, the judge felt that at least one witness must be guilty of ___________.

(a) imposition
(b) epiphany
(c) perdition
(d) perjury

**50.** The social ___________ that novelists create in their novels are oftentimes directly related to the sociocultural contexts they experience firsthand.

(a) milieus
(b) auspices
(c) homilies
(d) accolades

This is the end of the Vocabulary section. Do NOT move on to the Reading Comprehension section until instructed to do so. You are NOT allowed to turn to any other section of the test.

# READING COMPREHENSION

## DIRECTIONS

This section tests your ability to comprehend reading passages. You will have 45 minutes to complete the 40 questions. Be sure to follow the directions given by the proctor.

정답 P 328

**Part I** **Questions 1–16**

Read the passage and choose the option that best completes the passage.

**1.** Are you looking for a romantic vacation, but don't have any fresh ideas? What about vacationing by a canal? Are you thinking Venice? Well, that is not the only European city with canals. In fact, Amsterdam is home to more than a hundred kilometers of waterways, many of which are lined with romantic cafés. We also have over 1,500 bridges and walkways, making it the perfect place for couples to visit. So book your flight today and ______________________________.

(a) experience a Venetian gondola ride with your loved one
(b) open your own business near a popular vacation spot
(c) take a stroll along Amsterdam's scenic waterways
(d) see the best of both Venice and Amsterdam

**2.** I used to be the person with the messiest desk at work. My colleagues would tease me about it, and although I felt embarrassed, I never thought to clean my desk since I never had any problems finding what I needed. A few weeks ago, though, my disorganization made me lose some important documents, and I began to feel anxious as soon as I sat down at my desk. My stress grew as I looked at the piles of paper, which finally led me to ______________________________.

(a) apply my new organizational tactics at home
(b) organize my co-workers' desks for them
(c) take steps to organize my workspace
(d) ignore the advice of my co-workers

**3.** For a clarification of our policies, please refer to the following ______________________________. From the first day of employment, all employees are eligible to receive the company's medical and dental benefits. However, vacation days and sick time are not available, and life insurance coverage does not begin until 90 days after initial employment. Further details can be obtained by contacting Human Resources.

(a) explanations about company benefits
(b) guidelines for employee assessments
(c) regulations regarding your sick time
(d) information on life insurance plans

**4.** The Recording Industry Association of America (RIAA) had adopted a policy to prosecute individual music sharers, but after its encounter with Jammie Thomas-Rasset, ______________________________. When the RIAA sued her, Thomas-Rasset fought back, which resulted in a publicity nightmare of trials, retrials, and appeals. Although Thomas-Rasset was continually found guilty, the RIAA emerged as the loser because of the media's portrayal of it as a bully. In response to its tattered image, the RIAA has retreated from its earlier stance on individual prosecutions and now targets Internet providers.

(a) the public lauded its crusade for copyright protection
(b) it was unable to win any of its subsequent cases
(c) the media began portraying it as a scapegoat
(d) it was forced to reconsider its legal strategy

**5.** Considering a career in health services? Then Norrington Healthcare Institute is the school for you. We offer many courses to prepare you for jobs in the medical field that don't require medical degrees, such as physician assistant, ultrasound technician, and dental hygienist. We opened last year, so our facilities are brand new, and our labs have the latest equipment. Plus, all of our courses are augmented with on-site training sessions at State University Hospital, one of the best teaching and research hospitals in the state. Enroll in Norrington where you can ______________________________.

(a) pursue a medical degree at a prestigious university
(b) take advantage of our years of educational expertise
(c) earn a certificate exclusively through distance learning
(d) gain practical training for your chosen health-care field

**6.** One characteristic of English poetry of the Victorian period was the ______________________________. Alfred Tennyson and Elizabeth Barrett Browning illustrate this trend, as their poems diverged from the optimistic and spontaneous poetry of the romantic period and often dealt with bereavement and longing. Tennyson's "Break, Break, Break" expressed his feelings of loss after his best friend passed away, while Browning used the language of longing and sorrow in her sonnets. Despite their intense pathos, or perhaps because of it, these poets became popular during the age of Queen Victoria.

(a) optimistic worldview it expressed
(b) diversity of its themes and styles
(c) prevalence of melancholic verse
(d) strong influence of romanticism

**7.** A recent survey shows, unsurprisingly, that the majority of adults are concerned about children being exposed to inappropriate material in the media. Among those surveyed, 79% indicated that they believed that violent and sexual content on television negatively affects youths. However, when asked about furthering governmental control of the media, 61% opposed, expressing their concern that such control could constitute an infringement on freedom of speech. The study shows that while many adults are concerned about media content, they ______________________.

(a) believe that censorship could have more negative effects
(b) argue that the government needs to step in and regulate it
(c) do not think that it actually has a detrimental effect on youths
(d) do not use parental control to effectively monitor their children

**8.**

Dear MensWear Customer Service,

Recently I purchased a shirt for my husband, only to find out that it didn't fit. When I took it back to your store, I was told that not only was it the largest size you carry, but that for returns you only offer store credit. Since none of your clothing will fit my husband, store credit will do us no good. In light of the situation, a refund would be more appropriate. Therefore, I would appreciate it if you would consider

______________________.

Sincerely,
Loretta Jameson

(a) stocking a wider variety of clothing styles
(b) making an exception to your return policy
(c) simplifying the procedure for returning gifts
(d) offering cash refunds for credit card purchases

**9.** When Jonathan Franzen expressed reluctance to accept Oprah Winfrey's invitation to have his novel *The Corrections* be one of her official book club selections, the public branded Franzen a snob. In his defense, Franzen pointed out that even though being one of "Oprah's Picks" would garner him huge sales, just as many people avoided Oprah's book club picks—men, in particular—as flocked to buy them. So what others took to be a haughty attitude, Franzen asserted, was a justifiable desire to ______________________.

(a) try to control critics' reaction to his work
(b) use a public forum to promote his novel
(c) write a novel aimed specifically at men
(d) not limit his book's potential audience

**10.** Although today's American newspapers cover a wide variety of topics, they ______________________. Today newspapers contain articles on everything from current events to stocks to celebrity culture. Earlier versions, on the other hand, were relatively short and limited in content. Most were either of a partisan nature, designed to support a political party's aims, or of a commercial nature, used only by traders and merchants. Nevertheless, these early publications established important reporting traditions that still continue today.

(a) were initially published for niche markets
(b) are being accused of pandering to their readers
(c) should strive more to maintain political objectivity
(d) could lose their status as the main providers of news

**11.** Advancements in technology often lead to unemployment, which can have dire effects on rural areas. For example, harvesting, usually a process requiring a lot of manpower, produces the same yield with fewer people when it is automated. Those who lose their jobs as a result of this migrate to urban areas to seek work. This is followed by a domino effect as services in rural areas that rely on residents, such as stores and schools, are also impacted. As this process continues, ______________________.

(a) agricultural areas witness a spike in employment opportunities
(b) the encroaching effects of urbanization are effectively reversed
(c) rural governments anticipate a significant increase in revenues
(d) more rural inhabitants are forced to relocate to urban cores

**12.** Jean-Paul Sartre's philosophical theories garnered considerable respect in academia, yet their format was not digestible for the masses. Thus, he presented his ideas via short stories and plays, which became commercially successful and extended his thoughts beyond the academic community. In fact, the popular exposure got his works noticed by friends and foes alike, and his books even landed a place on the Roman Catholic Church's index of prohibited books. This, however, did not affect their reception, and it was his works in narrative forms rather than his academic papers that ______________________.

(a) generated a large body of literary criticism
(b) allowed his ideas to infiltrate a wider audience
(c) were considered too abstruse for the average reader
(d) were criticized for having little philosophical substance

**13.** Entries in the Chinese version of the online encyclopedia Wikipedia ______________________. Although many articles are written, translated, and edited outside of mainland China, and thus are not subject to government censorship, contributors seem to be treading warily when dealing with topics that could potentially incur the displeasure of the authorities. Some entries differ substantially from the original English version, having erroneous facts or leaving out touchy issues. When questioned, contributors insist that they are not self-censoring; however, these entries appear to be highly edited and subjective.

(a) appear unaffected by potential political repercussions
(b) show the difficulty of producing accurate translations
(c) are mostly exempt from government retribution
(d) tend to distort politically sensitive information

**14.** In 2006, a controversial "Clean City" law banning advertising in all open-air public spaces was passed in São Paulo, Brazil, which resulted in ________________________________. When the law was implemented, businesses had no choice but to adapt to it. Advertisers started reevaluating their strategies, which led them to employ unconventional means of promotion. Televised and electronic ads proliferated in indoor public spaces, and social media campaigns offered new ways for businesses to interact with consumers. The law eventually benefited not only citizens but also advertisers and businesses as it forced advertisers to be more creative.

(a) the virtual demise of São Paulo's advertising industry
(b) innovative and creative methods of outdoor advertising
(c) businesses being driven out of the city for lack of exposure
(d) the development of alternative ways of product promotion

**15.** Renting a car in Europe can be expensive and complicated. But when the cost is split among several people, each person's share is no more than the cost of a rail pass. It can also allow you more, and often cheaper, options for accommodations, as you can look for hotels away from train stations. Besides, cars offer much more freedom than traveling by train, allowing you to explore the countryside. ________________________________, renting a car is more convenient than traveling by train and well worth the expense.

(a) Likewise
(b) Ultimately
(c) Regardless
(d) Specifically

**16.** Some researchers suggest that our daily efforts to keep germs away actually hurt our ability to fend off infections. These scientists say that contact with germs exercises our immune systems and actually decreases the likelihood that we will get sick. ________________________________, our immune system is like a muscle that becomes weaker when we do not use it. According to this theory, when our immune systems lack the opportunities to do their jobs, they become less effective and we become more vulnerable to diseases.

(a) Next
(b) Granted
(c) By contrast
(d) In other words

**Part II** **Questions 17—37**

Read the passage, question, and options. Then, based on the given information, choose the option that best answers the question.

**17.** The Academy Awards, given out every year by the Academy of Motion Picture Arts and Sciences, are also known as the Oscars. No one, including the Academy, knows how this nickname was acquired, although some popular theories exist that attempt to explain it. Some trace the name back to an employee of the Academy who thought the trophy resembled a relative of hers named Oscar. Another possible explanation is that the Academy Award-winning actress Bette Davis called her award Oscar after her husband, and other people followed suit.

Q: What is the best title for the passage?
(a) Davis's Husband Confirmed to Be the Oscars' Namesake
(b) Newly Uncovered Facts about the Name "Oscar"
(c) The Unknown Origin of the Name "Oscar"
(d) The Recipient of the First Oscar Trophy

**18.** Today, the most famous depiction of a sphinx, a mythical creature with the head of a human and the body of a lion, is the Great Sphinx in Egypt. Because of this iconic image, most references to sphinxes are associated with Egypt. However, likenesses of half-lion, half-human creatures can be found in many cultures across the globe. Sphinxes were carved by the ancient Greeks, and the image continues to be part of the art and traditions in India and Southeast Asia.

Q: What is the writer's main point about the image of the sphinx?
(a) It is not unique to Egyptian culture.
(b) It spread from Egypt and Greece to India.
(c) It is no longer integral to Egyptian mythology.
(d) It has its ideal expression in Egypt's Great Sphinx.

**19.** Scientists speculate that past ice ages were the result of the combination of variations in ocean currents, fluctuations in the composition of the atmosphere, and changes to Earth's orbit. The oceans play a huge role in climate regulation by carrying warm water from tropical regions to the poles. If this flow is blocked, ice in polar regions increases. Meanwhile, changes in atmospheric concentrations of carbon dioxide and methane, as well as Earth's variations in distance from the sun, can cause an overall decrease in Earth's temperature.

Q: What is the writer's main point about past ice ages?
(a) They caused tropical currents to be rerouted to the poles.
(b) They have usually been modeled on one ecological variable.
(c) They resulted from the interplay of various global phenomena.
(d) They were succeeded by climate conditions similar to those seen now.

**20.**

Dear Ms. Heighton,

I'm writing to the Foundation for Literacy on behalf of Garfield Elementary School regarding the Reading Success project we discussed earlier. As we have not heard back from you yet, I would like to reiterate my hope that you consider our request for the much needed funding. The program, which is designed to help our at-risk students by providing free after-school lessons to improve their reading skills, cannot be launched without the generous support of organizations like yours. Thank you.

Sincerely,
Shirley West

Q: What is the main purpose of the letter?
(a) To show gratitude for sharing information on a successful reading program
(b) To request support for a recently launched extracurricular activity
(c) To follow up on a prior funding request for a literacy project
(d) To seek advice on creating an after-school program

**21.** Eastern Orthodoxy and Roman Catholicism, two of the largest Christian denominations, were once part of the same religious body. Their distinct attitudes toward the power of the Pope eventually separated them, as Eastern Orthodox churches balked at the Pope's claim to universal jurisdiction. Disagreement over the supremacy of the Pope in all social, educational, and economic matters finally came to a head in the eleventh century, when the branches officially split.

Q: What is the main purpose of the passage?
(a) To compare the religious doctrines of Catholicism and Orthodoxy
(b) To show how conflicting views of authority divided the Church
(c) To provide examples of various sects within Eastern Orthodoxy
(d) To contrast the way Catholicism and Orthodoxy were formed

**22.** Traditionally, the disadvantaged in rural India have been burdened by high interest rate loans doled out by private lenders. To lessen the suffering of borrowers, government financial institutions recently intervened and regulated the practice, but the intended effects have not been achieved. Public bank loans are still inaccessible to many, and private lenders remain a strong presence in rural areas. In fact, studies have shown that the cost of private loans has actually risen with increasing institutional finance.

Q: What is mainly being said about borrowers in rural India?
(a) Traditional types of financial transactions are their best option.
(b) They have no recourse after taking loans from corrupt lenders.
(c) They did not benefit from government intervention in loan markets.
(d) Longer loan terms and lower interest rates should be offered to them.

**23.** The deltar is a new type of stringed instrument, based on mathematical principles and years of acoustic research. Its shape is similar to a three-sided pyramid, and it is played with the instrument hanging from the shoulders with a standard guitar strap. The music comes out of a large opening on the side, which allows a deltar to be quite loud. As the deltar is still a new invention, each one created today is handcrafted. It can also be made to the musician's specifications, using different types of wood or strings.

Q: Which of the following is correct about the deltar according to the passage?
(a) It was reconstructed after being lost for years.
(b) It is played placed on the shoulder like a violin.
(c) It is currently manufactured exclusively by hand.
(d) It must be built with a particular type of wood.

**24.**

Dear Mr. Kelvin,

It is with mixed feelings that I tender my resignation to you, effective July 21. As we discussed on July 7, I have been considering an offer to work in Milan, and I have finally decided to take the offer. It has long been a dream of mine to move to Italy, and the opportunity is too good to pass up. My three years here at Kelvin Design have been wonderful, and I will miss you and all the friends I have made here.

Yours truly,
Adam Benford

Q: Which of the following is correct about the writer according to the letter?
(a) He will be leaving Kelvin Design in early July.
(b) He has discussed his job offer with Mr. Kelvin.
(c) He had not considered living abroad before.
(d) He began working at Kelvin Design last year.

**25.** Acceptance of papers submitted to *Today's Scholar* is determined by the journal's editor in consultation with the editorial board. Rejected papers will not be returned, although the writer will be sent the reasons for rejection. Writers may appeal a rejection by writing to the editorial board directly, which will result in a meeting between the editor and the board. Writers may not submit previously published papers, and by submitting a paper to *Today's Scholar*, writers agree to not submit it to any other publication until a decision is made.

Q: Which of the following is correct according to the passage?
(a) All rejected submissions are returned to the writer.
(b) Writers are not notified of the reason for rejection.
(c) Appeals are discussed by the editor and the board.
(d) Papers can be submitted to multiple journals at once.

**26.** Get the Pritchard Cashback Card and start building up credit! The Pritchard Cashback Card is a credit card designed exclusively for currently enrolled Pritchard University students. We offer low introductory rates, and there is no annual fee. Earn up to 5% cash back when shopping on campus and up to 1% everywhere else. No co-signer is required to sign up, even for those who have no credit history, so apply today!

Q: Which of the following is correct about the Pritchard Cashback Card according to the advertisement?
(a) Any student enrolled in any university is eligible for one.
(b) It offers a low introductory annual fee to new cardholders.
(c) A uniform cash-back rate applies to all purchases made with it.
(d) Students without established credit do not need a co-signer.

**27.** The Mayan civilization of Mesoamerica went through three distinctive periods, called pre-classic, classic, and post-classic. The last period ended with the first coming of Spanish conquistadors in 1502. Though the arrival of the Spanish meant the destruction of Mayan civilization, it did not mean the end of the Mayan people. Today, some six million Mayas still live in Guatemala, Belize, and Mexico, where they continue to maintain their traditions and native language.

Q: Which of the following is correct about the Maya according to the passage?
(a) Their civilization is broken into four main periods.
(b) The Spanish arrived during their pre-classical period.
(c) Sixteen million of them are now living in South America.
(d) The Mayan language survived after their defeat by the Spanish.

**28.** As identical twins, my sister and I grew up very close to each other. Until second grade, we were inseparable: we were in the same classes and always dressed the same, and we relished the attention that was bestowed upon us. However, when we started third grade, my mother stopped dressing us in the same clothes and asked that we be placed in different classrooms. We resented the separation at first, but we made new friends and learned to enjoy school life as distinct individuals. Looking back, I think being raised as independent individuals strengthened our relationship and helped us mature.

Q: Which of the following is correct about the writer according to the passage?
(a) She resented the attention she received as an identical twin.
(b) She stopped wearing the same clothes as her sister in second grade.
(c) She was initially upset about being put in a different class from her sister.
(d) She believes her mother's decision to separate the twins estranged them.

**29.** The Chadwick Seminar is a monthly forum dedicated to exploring law-related topics such as free speech, justice, and equal rights. Every seminar features a keynote speaker who shares his or her insights before opening discussion to the entire floor. Those interested in delivering a keynote address should send a synopsis of their topic to the Chadwick committee at least two months prior to their intended presentation date. Topics are approved one month before each seminar and announced on our website two weeks prior to the event, usually in the first week of every month.

Q: Which of the following is correct about the Chadwick Seminar according to the passage?

(a) It does not include topics with legal implications.
(b) Time is allotted for discussions with the audience.
(c) Presentations must be submitted in full for consideration.
(d) Topics that are accepted are advertised a month in advance.

**30.** The Industrial Revolution spurred a significant increase in wealth throughout Europe, and the nobility were not the only ones to reap its benefits. New technology led to the establishment of factories, which were a boon for those who owned and operated them: middle-class businessmen. Indeed, the middle class eventually overtook the nobility in influence and status. Meanwhile, the working class who labored in these factories experienced the opposite: the same factories that provided such riches to their owners were also known for exploiting employees.

Q: Which of the following is correct about the Industrial Revolution according to the passage?

(a) The nobility alone profited from the growth it initiated.
(b) Factories were owned exclusively by members of the nobility.
(c) It was marked by a partial reversal in power in the class system.
(d) It saw the working class advance through lucrative factory jobs.

**31.** Mayumba National Park is one of 13 national parks that were established in 2002 to preserve the natural beauty of Gabon. Combined, the network of parks protects 11% of the country's diverse geography. Consisting of a narrow strip of coastal land and a large ocean area, Mayumba National Park is Gabon's only park dedicated to supporting marine life, and its beaches host one of the largest populations of nesting leatherback turtles in the world. The park has yet to build infrastructure to attract many tourists, and currently the park is visited mainly by scientists on research missions.

Q: Which of the following is correct about Mayumba National Park according to the passage?

(a) It currently occupies 11% of Gabon's land.
(b) It is one of Gabon's 13 national marine parks.
(c) Its beaches rarely see nesting leatherback turtles.
(d) Its tourists are outnumbered by research scientists.

**32.** Martin Luther King Jr. came under federal surveillance in 1957, when government authorities suspected that civil rights leaders might have been influenced by communism. Six years later, Robert Kennedy authorized investigators to use a wire tap to record King's phone conversations, despite King publicly disavowing support for communism. The wire tap turned up no proof of communist sympathies, but it did turn up evidence of marital infidelity. Investigators used this information to shame the typically outspoken King into silence. The records of the government's activities still exist, though access to them has been blocked until 2027.

Q: Which of the following is correct about Martin Luther King Jr. according to the passage?

(a) The recording of his telephone conversations was approved in 1957.
(b) His public embracing of communism spurred the government's scrutiny.
(c) The wire tap yielded no information that could be used to silence him.
(d) Records of the government's surveillance of him have yet to be made public.

**33.** Welcome to your new apartment in the wonderful community of Prestige Village! For all new tenants, we would like to stress the importance of reporting problems in your apartment. Issues with plumbing, gas service, and electricity should be reported to management as soon as they arise, so that they can be addressed promptly and further damage can be prevented. Damage resulting from late reporting of maintenance issues may be charged to tenants.

Q: What can be inferred from the passage?
(a) Prestige Village is a fully furnished rental apartment.
(b) Tenants should personally repair all damages they cause.
(c) All malfunctioning appliances will be replaced with new ones.
(d) Damages due to wear and tear are not usually charged to tenants.

**34.** Federal officials and wildlife advocates are meeting today over Congress's recent decision regarding gray wolves. Congress has removed gray wolves from endangered species protection in Montana and Idaho and lifted hunting bans on them, deeming the wolf population sufficient in these states. Advocates of wolf protection oppose the decision, saying that discontinuing the decades-long protection of the wolves could put the animals at risk again. But federal officials stand by their decision and insist that effective population checks are in place to keep the wolves secure.

Q: What can be inferred from the article?
(a) The gray wolf population has been decreasing.
(b) Congress is considering reimposing the hunting ban.
(c) Montana and Idaho are the only US states with gray wolves.
(d) Wolf advocates believe that protection has benefited the wolves.

**35.** In 1959, physicist Richard Feynman issued an open challenge to the world to build a working motor no bigger than 1/64th of an inch long. The competition was an attempt by Feynman to spur development in nanotechnology as he believed the solution necessitated its use. In 1960, Feynman conceded that William McLellan had succeeded in constructing a minuscule motor that fit the specifications of the challenge. However, McLellan had built the motor without using nanotechnology, using a microscope and some simple tools instead.

Q: What can be inferred from the passage?
(a) McLellan became an innovator of nanotechnology.
(b) Feynman refused to pay out the competition prize money.
(c) Feynman's original intent was subverted by McLellan's motor.
(d) McLellan's motor was considerably smaller than the specified size.

**36.** The French New Wave tradition, although not formally organized, produced films that shared common themes. These filmmakers rejected classical cinematic forms, and their films reflected the social and political unrest of their era—the late 1950s and early 1960s. Filmmakers experimented with radical visual and narrative styles as well as unconventional editing, pioneering a simple documentary-like style of film. Many of the editing and filming decisions were not only artistic but also practical, as the majority of New Wave films were produced on small budgets.

Q: What can be inferred about New Wave filmmakers from the passage?
(a) They shared conservative views about filmmaking.
(b) Their financial limitations affected their filming style.
(c) They pioneered innovative methods to create traditional films.
(d) Their films eschewed contemporary events in favor of past ones.

**37.** In today's increasingly globalized market, many international companies staff their home base of operations with foreign workers, as well as send domestic employees abroad. This strategy has the advantage of allowing companies to bring global perspectives to their firms. While this may have its merits, the extra costs involved could far exceed initial calculations. Transferring employees, helping them adapt to new environments, and facilitating relocation of temporary employees can be significantly expensive, so decisions about making these investments should be made with caution.

Q: Which statement would the writer most likely agree with?
(a) Investments made to globalize companies usually prove profitable.
(b) Rash decisions to globalize companies are likely to result in financial losses.
(c) Transferring domestic workers abroad is better than importing foreign workers.
(d) Large-scale international operations are more profitable than smaller-scale ones.

**Part III** **Questions 38–40**

Read the passage and identify the option that does NOT belong.

**38.** Feldman Organics specializes in organic and fair trade groceries from around the world. (a) Our fruits and vegetables are harvested from farms completely free of pesticides and chemicals. (b) Our bags of coffee beans are also organic and come from rural communities in South America. (c) South American coffee is the most flavorful on the planet, especially when grown in the shade. (d) Even our beef is organic and comes from Australian free-range cows that have been grass fed.

**39.** When ballet stars Natalia Osipova and Ivan Vasiliev announced their intention to leave the Bolshoi Ballet, the dance world was shocked. (a) The Bolshoi had experienced several difficulties lately, losing its artistic director, who resigned in the midst of a scandal. (b) They had left one of the world's premier dance institutions to join an upstart company in St. Petersburg called the Mikhailovsky Theater. (c) Despite the Bolshoi's intimations of financial motivations, the pair claimed their resignation was due to creative reasons. (d) Both dancers said that the Bolshoi was based on a limited repertoire and that they wanted to explore more dynamic roles.

**40.** The socially and environmentally conscious attitude that Bradestar brings to its business extends well beyond the boardroom. (a) While we have always prided ourselves on dealing with ecologically friendly companies, we also donate to various causes. (b) In fact, the recyclable products that we produce are now showing higher market values than they did a decade ago. (c) Over the last 12 years, we have made substantial contributions to over 150 charities throughout the world. (d) On the local level, we host food and clothing drives and fund several education programs for those in need.

This is the end of the Reading Comprehension section. Please remain seated until the proctor has instructed otherwise. You are NOT allowed to turn to any other section of the test.

# 서울대 최신기출 2

**Listening** *Comprehension*

**Grammar**

**Vocabulary**

**Reading** *Comprehension*

# LISTENING COMPREHENSION

## DIRECTIONS

1. In the Listening Comprehension section, all content will be presented orally rather than in written form.
2. This section contains four parts, each with fifteen individual items. For each part, you will receive separate instructions. Listen to the instructions carefully, and choose the best answer from the options for each item.

Scripts P 278 / 정답 P 329

**Part I** **Questions 1–15**

You will now hear fifteen individual spoken questions or statements, each followed by four spoken responses. Choose the most appropriate response for each item.

**Part II** **Questions 16–30**

You will now hear fifteen short conversation fragments, followed by four spoken responses. Choose the most appropriate response to complete each conversation.

**Part III** **Questions 31–45**

You will now hear fifteen complete conversations. For each conversation, you will be asked to answer a question. Each conversation and its corresponding question will be read twice. Then you will hear four options which will be read only once. Based on the given information, choose the option that best answers the question.

**Part IV** **Questions 46–60**

You will now hear fifteen short talks. After each talk, you will be asked to answer a question. Each talk and its corresponding question will be read twice. Then you will hear four options which will be read only once. Based on the given information, choose the option that best answers the question.

TEPS

# GRAMMAR

## DIRECTIONS

This section tests your grammar skills. You will have 25 minutes to complete the 50 questions. Be sure to follow the directions given by the proctor.

정답 P 329

## Part I Questions 1–20

Choose the option that best completes each gap.

**1.** A: I can't believe our paper almost went out with a typo in it.
B: I know. I'm so glad the typo ___________ before publication.

(a) caught
(b) catches
(c) is caught
(d) was caught

**2.** A: Have you been to Japan?
B: Yes. In fact, I ___________ there for six months in 2007.

(a) live
(b) lived
(c) have lived
(d) have been living

**3.** A: How was the company outing?
B: Oh, I had so much fun last year, but this year, it was even ___________.

(a) enjoyable
(b) more enjoyable
(c) much enjoyable
(d) the most enjoyable

**4.** A: Why didn't you wait for me after class yesterday?
B: I had to babysit my sister. Otherwise, I ___________.

(a) waited
(b) would wait
(c) was waiting
(d) would have waited

**5.** A: Have you turned in your essay yet?
B: No, a few changes still ___________ to be made.

(a) need
(b) needs
(c) is needed
(d) are needed

**6.** A: Are you going to the conference?
B: Yes, I'm sure it will be ___________ event.

(a) beneficial
(b) a beneficial
(c) the beneficial
(d) every beneficial

**7.** A: How long will this jam be good to eat?
B: ___________ properly, it will be fine for a couple of months.

(a) Preserves
(b) Preserved
(c) Preserving
(d) To preserve

**8.** A: You have to renew your passport before we travel.
B: Don't worry. It ___________ done in time for the trip.

(a) is
(b) was
(c) will be
(d) was being

**9.** A: Did you like the movie?

B: Not really. It was __________.

(a) needless crude with scenes packed
(b) packed with scenes needless crude
(c) packed with needlessly crude scenes
(d) with scenes packed needlessly crude

**10.** A: Should we take the highway?

B: No, all the commuters make that route __________. Let's take side streets.

(a) congest
(b) congested
(c) to congest
(d) congesting

**11.** A: Where did Kathleen get the idea for her latest novel?

B: Actually, __________ related to her aunt.

(a) her story was based on events were
(b) she based her story on events were
(c) her story she was based on events
(d) she based her story on events

**12.** A: Did you buy a birthday gift for Sean?

B: Yeah. I got him __________ I thought he really needed, a new wallet.

(a) that
(b) who
(c) what
(d) which

**13.** A: Why is Jean acting so strangely?

B: __________, I'm afraid I can't offer any insights.

(a) To have recently met only her
(b) Having only met her recently
(c) Recently having only met her
(d) To meet her only recently

**14.** A: I'm sorry that our party is so loud, Mr. Tomkins.

B: I don't mind __________ it doesn't run past midnight.

(a) until
(b) unless
(c) or else
(d) as long as

**15.** A: I heard you asked the boss for a raise.

B: Yes, and __________ for an answer all week. I hope to find out by tomorrow.

(a) I wait
(b) I am waiting
(c) I'd been waiting
(d) I've been waiting

**16.** A: How is your psychology class going?

B: It's so tough that __________ times I feel like quitting.

(a) for
(b) on
(c) in
(d) at

**17.** A: I'm shocked at how messy Lionel's desk is!
B: I agree. ___________ such a cluttered office space.

(a) I have seen never
(b) Have I never seen
(c) Never have I seen
(d) Never I have seen

**18.** A: Are you satisfied with your new job?
B: I enjoy the work, but I'm not getting all the benefits ___________.

(a) I was promised
(b) that promised to me
(c) that I was promising
(d) were promising to me

**19.** A: Is it true that Jon is dating three women?
B: No, I think that's probably just ___________.

(a) gossip
(b) gossips
(c) a gossip
(d) the gossips

**20.** A: Have you and your roommate decided how to split living costs?
B: Yeah, she'll take care of the utilities ___________ I pay for the groceries.

(a) wherein
(b) whether
(c) as though
(d) provided that

## Part II Questions 21–40

Choose the option that best completes each gap.

**21.** The father told his children that they had to leave the beach because ___________.

(a) was the storm coming
(b) of the coming storm
(c) the coming storm was
(d) of the storm was coming

**22.** After returning home from the store, Joan realized that she ___________ to buy milk.

(a) is forgetting
(b) has forgotten
(c) had forgotten
(d) was forgetting

**23.** Clinical studies indicate that women experience depression ___________ men do.

(a) as twice as much
(b) twice as much as
(c) as much as twice
(d) much as twice as

**24.** Seeing her parents for the first time since her wedding, Grace noticed how much they had aged ___________ the years.

(a) between
(b) among
(c) over
(d) past

**25.** Bryce felt guilty for lying to Mrs. Hilbert because he knew he ___________ always tell the truth.

(a) should
(b) would
(c) might
(d) can

**26.** Gourmet chefs put ___________ thought and care into preparing appetizing dishes.

(a) much
(b) many
(c) much of
(d) many of

**27.** It is a common misconception that people ___________ faces are red from rosacea are merely blushing.

(a) who
(b) when
(c) which
(d) whose

**28.** Due to recent security concerns, anyone ___________ the office building is required to wear an identity badge.

(a) enter
(b) enters
(c) entered
(d) entering

**29.** Darryl's mother suggested ___________ a writer since he had always enjoyed writing.

(a) him to become
(b) that he become
(c) it becomes him being
(d) that he becomes being

**30.** The store's entire stock of delicate silk handbags ___________ destroyed twice due to floods on two separate occasions at its warehouses.

(a) is
(b) are
(c) was
(d) were

**31.** ___________ books remaining after the liquidation sale will be donated to charity.

(a) Any
(b) Each
(c) Every
(d) Almost

**32.** Inflation rates across Europe have reached levels similar to ___________ in many developing countries.

(a) that
(b) them
(c) those
(d) theirs

**33.** Because the factory inspection took less time than expected, production could continue without ___________ for a week.

(a) the factory to need being shut down
(b) needing to be shut down the factory
(c) the factory needing to be shut down
(d) need to shutting down the factory

**34.** Winner of the 2010 Giller Prize for literature, *The Sentimentalists* is a book ___________ worth reading.

(a) such
(b) well
(c) that
(d) far

**35.** Michael Steele's upcoming TV series on global warming issues ___________ serious concerns about the future.

(a) raise
(b) raises
(c) was raising
(d) were raising

**36.** If you have a disability and need a trained service animal ___________ you, you can receive the animal license at no cost.

(a) assisted
(b) to assist
(c) has assisted
(d) to be assisting

**37.** Come the end of the year, Mr. Sorenson ___________ in Bloomington for ten years.

(a) will have lived
(b) will be living
(c) has lived
(d) is living

**38.** Younger people usually forgo mailing thank-you notes, as they consider writing them time-consuming, ___________.

(a) not to mention outdated
(b) and outdated to mention
(c) not to mention as outdated
(d) and outdated as mentioned

**39.** Rosalie forgot to bring her briefcase again, although everyone at the office was always ___________.

(a) reminding
(b) reminding to
(c) reminding her to
(d) reminding her to do

**40.** It was cold when Brad started his daily trek through the woods, the temperature below zero and the snow ___________ under his boots.

(a) crunched
(b) crunching
(c) was crunched
(d) was crunching

GRAMMAR

**Part III** **Questions 41–45**

Read each sentence carefully and identify the option that contains a grammatical error.

**41.** (a) A: Oh, no! I think the copier is jammed again!
(b) B: Well, we had better send for the repair man.
(c) A: He was just here to fix it a few days ago.
(d) B: Then he should not have fixed it properly.

**42.** (a) A: Are you all ready for your business trip to Brazil?
(b) B: I'm just about set. I do need to finish packing, though.
(c) A: Have you double-checked the time of your flight?
(d) B: Yes, I called the airline this morning and it confirmed.

**43.** (a) A: Would you keep an eye on my stuff for a few minutes?
(b) B: Do you think you're going to be gone for a long time?
(c) A: Probably not. I'm just going to ask someone how I can access to the Internet.
(d) B: I'm only going to be here for another 15 minutes, so please don't be too long.

**44.** (a) A: I can't wait for exams to wrap up and summer vacation to start.
(b) B: You can say that again. Have you got any special plans?
(c) A: I was thinking of taking the Trans-Siberian Express to Beijing.
(d) B: Wow! If I could take just one journey by train, that would have been it.

**45.** (a) A: Joe Clarkson starts today as head of marketing.
(b) B: I know. We're lucky to have him, to consider his track record.
(c) A: I just hope he's a good match with the rest of the staff.
(d) B: No need to worry. I'm confident we made the right decision hiring him.

**Part IV** **Questions 46–50**

Read each sentence carefully and identify the option that contains a grammatical error.

**46.** (a) To dry fresh herbs, start by rinsing them under cold water to remove any dirt. (b) Then shake off any excess water and place the herbs in a clean paper bag. (c) Gather the bag around the stems and tie up it to prevent moisture from getting in. (d) Poke a few holes in the bag for ventilation and store it in a dry area for two weeks.

**47.** (a) Though the number of individual sales had dropped, Burton Company was still earning the same profit. (b) Perplexed by the numbers, the store's owners hired independent analysts to investigate the situation. (c) The analysts determined that the more expensive merchandise was outselling the less expensive. (d) The finding explained how the company was as profitable as ever even though individual sales were indeed declined.

**48.** (a) Words such as "mankind" are perhaps not deliberate sexist but are problematic nonetheless. (b) Such words subtly position men as the norm and women as being outside of, or secondary to, that norm. (c) Having a gender hierarchy built into language in this way can reinforce gender stereotypes. (d) Because of this, it is recommended that writers strive to use gender-neutral language.

**49.** (a) In their haste to flee Vienna after their defeat in 1683, Turkish soldiers left a large amount of coffee behind. (b) After claiming the forgotten coffee beans, Jerzy Franciszek Kulczycki opened the city's first cafe. (c) In doing so, Kulczycki pioneered the coffee culture Vienna subsequently became famous for. (d) He introduced the idea of filtered coffee as well as to soften the beverage with sugar and milk.

**50.** (a) Violin making demands more than mere construction skills—mastery of many areas of expertise is required. (b) First, the materials and design must be carefully chosen as they determine the potential of the violin. (c) The craftsperson must use his or her tools properly and take good care of them because they are of the utmost importance as well. (d) If constructed well, what results is a magnificent instrument of which is totally responsive to the player.

This is the end of the Grammar section. Do NOT move on to the next section until instructed to do so. You are NOT allowed to turn to any other section of the test.

# VOCABULARY

## DIRECTIONS

This section tests your vocabulary skills. You will have 15 minutes to complete the 50 questions. Be sure to follow the directions given by the proctor.

정답 P 329

## Part I Questions 1—25

Choose the option that best completes each gap.

**1.** A: When should we meet for coffee?
B: You can ___________ the day. I'm free all week.

(a) refer
(b) pick
(c) pull
(d) hit

**2.** A: Is Alex really graduating ahead of schedule?
B: Yes. He finished his thesis one semester ___________ than he expected.

(a) fuller
(b) easier
(c) earlier
(d) lighter

**3.** A: Yesterday's festivities were very well organized.
B: Yes, the events were ___________ well.

(a) assumed
(b) measured
(c) prescribed
(d) coordinated

**4.** A: Can I borrow your stopwatch? I want to see how fast I can run a mile.
B: Sure, but you can use your cell phone to ___________ yourself, you know.

(a) time
(b) total
(c) score
(d) oppose

**5.** A: Excuse me, concierge. I'm not happy with my suite.
B: I'm sorry it's not to your ___________. I'll see what else is available.

(a) liking
(b) catering
(c) emotion
(d) suitability

**6.** A: Has the meeting started?
B: No, it is scheduled to ___________ at 10 am.

(a) impart
(b) stimulate
(c) engender
(d) commence

**7.** A: If Dave doesn't pay his rent this month, he's going to be thrown out.
B: I had no idea he was in danger of being ___________.

(a) stifled
(b) evicted
(c) trampled
(d) excavated

**8.** A: What have you heard about that big accident on the highway?
B: Nothing. The police are ___________ the details for the time being.

(a) undermining
(b) withholding
(c) illustrating
(d) expressing

**9.** A: These inline skates are still usable, but I don't need them.

B: Do you want my old bike? I'm willing to ___________ it for your skates.

(a) trade
(b) mark
(c) change
(d) purchase

**10.** A: How about taking a trip to the coast?

B: I'd love to, but there's no ___________ in my budget for it.

(a) area
(b) void
(c) room
(d) range

**11.** A: Promise me you won't get angry if I tell you something.

B: Don't worry. You have my ___________ that I won't get upset.

(a) faith
(b) truth
(c) word
(d) credit

**12.** A: I've been asked to settle a dispute between my brothers.

B: I advise you to be ___________ and avoid any favoritism.

(a) forsaken
(b) censured
(c) impartial
(d) untenable

**13.** A: I can't tolerate Diana constantly being late.

B: I'm ___________ her tardiness, too.

(a) fed up with
(b) done for
(c) toned down
(d) strung along

**14.** A: Have you been won over by Wendy's argument?

B: Yes, she has ___________ me.

(a) implicated
(b) persuaded
(c) proposed
(d) involved

**15.** A: Can I take the expressway to the theater?

B: Yes, but that's a rather ___________ route. Highway 41 is more direct.

(a) aberrant
(b) maligned
(c) circuitous
(d) scrambled

**16.** A: Hi, I'm calling to see if you are still hiring security guards.

B: Yes, we still have several ___________ to fill.

(a) situations
(b) intervals
(c) careers
(d) posts

**17.** A: I'm surprised Ralph was fooled by that old email scam.

B: I never thought of him as the ___________ type, either.

(a) decrepit
(b) posturing
(c) credulous
(d) impervious

**18.** A: The novel *Flinty's Nightmare* sure has become popular with critics recently.

B: That's odd, since the first reviews of it were rather ___________.

(a) tepid
(b) intact
(c) streaming
(d) meandering

**19.** A: Is your new assistant learning the job?

B: Yes. She's ___________ really fast.

(a) giving in
(b) turning in
(c) passing on
(d) catching on

**20.** A: Coach Higgins, what's your response to the violent protests by the fans?

B: It's terrible. I don't ___________ that kind of violence.

(a) avert
(b) lament
(c) condone
(d) fabricate

**21.** A: How was Rupert able to afford such an expensive car?

B: Apparently, he had to ___________ for years to save enough money.

(a) wince
(b) writhe
(c) scrimp
(d) splurge

**22.** A: Sarah was somewhat presumptuous in calling your parents by their first names.

B: Yeah. They'd just met, so it did seem a bit ___________.

(a) forward
(b) engaged
(c) insidious
(d) scrupulous

**23.** A: I think I accidentally threw away the report I was writing!

B: If it really is gone, then that's a lot of hard work ___________.

(a) off the record
(b) down the drain
(c) behind the times
(d) out of this world

**24.** A: Do I need a strong grasp of biology to join the Introduction to Anatomy course?

B: No, you only need a ___________ knowledge of biology for the course.

(a) permeable
(b) punctilious
(c) rudimentary
(d) reprehensible

**25.** A: I can't stand the sappy plots of TV dramas.

B: I know. The writing on those shows is a bit ___________.

(a) ebullient
(b) mawkish
(c) boisterous
(d) vociferous

## Part II Questions 26–50

Choose the option that best completes each gap.

**26.** The airline's policy ___________ carry-on baggage to one item not exceeding ten kilograms per person.

(a) limits
(b) retains
(c) imports
(d) describes

**27.** The manufacturing company ___________ more than one hundred full-time workers at its Hamilton factory.

(a) invites
(b) spends
(c) employs
(d) computes

**28.** Clariview tablets relieve common allergy ___________ such as itchy, watery eyes and runny noses.

(a) qualities
(b) emblems
(c) symptoms
(d) predictions

**29.** Although the possibility of another tsunami is low, officials are evacuating people from coastal areas as a ___________.

(a) forecast
(b) recession
(c) suspicion
(d) precaution

**30.** The accident put a huge ___________ in the side of the man's car, leaving a large depression above the left rear wheel.

(a) shot
(b) dent
(c) crash
(d) spark

**31.** The ancient document was so old and worn that the letters were barely ___________.

(a) legible
(b) feasible
(c) coherent
(d) transparent

**32.** Every year, Monarch butterflies ___________ across a huge distance to hibernate in Mexico during the winter.

(a) pursue
(b) radiate
(c) migrate
(d) exchange

**33.** Mr. Northwood sent the managers a letter of thanks to show his heartfelt ___________ for their hard work.

(a) integrity
(b) gratitude
(c) impression
(d) competency

**34.** The bread recipe can be modified for a low-fat diet by __________ the optional cup of butter.

(a) abating
(b) omitting
(c) canceling
(d) departing

**35.** During an emergency, there is no time for doctors to __________, as they must act quickly and decisively to save patients' lives.

(a) vibrate
(b) hesitate
(c) enervate
(d) conciliate

**36.** Library patrons will be required to __________ any unpaid fees before checking out new books.

(a) place
(b) settle
(c) grant
(d) compose

**37.** Anyone who neglects to install anti-virus software will be held accountable for any problems caused by their __________.

(a) variant
(b) liability
(c) oversight
(d) hindrance

**38.** Hardly a blessing, natural resources such as oil can be a __________ to countries without the necessary infrastructure to handle them.

(a) taboo
(b) tirade
(c) burden
(d) slander

**39.** Inequality harms social __________ and leads to a divided society, as the rich and poor retreat into separate spheres.

(a) rupture
(b) cohesion
(c) discharge
(d) vindication

**40.** Political candidates manipulate their public image so that voters will have a favorable __________ of them.

(a) attention
(b) affluence
(c) perception
(d) conscience

**41.** After the experiment, the students had to open the windows because the school laboratory __________ of ammonia.

(a) pined
(b) reeked
(c) coaxed
(d) fathomed

**42.** A personal identification number is required for all __________ on Goldsmith's bank machines, including withdrawals and transfers.

(a) stipulations
(b) occupations
(c) perforations
(d) transactions

**43.** The data Harrison stored in the document file had been __________ and was rendered unreadable.

(a) dilated
(b) corrupted
(c) predicated
(d) conscripted

**44.** Jin-ho was never one to ___________, but his parents happily bragged about how their son had graduated from Oxford.

(a) bawl
(b) flash
(c) boast
(d) flatter

**45.** Activists abhor the common ___________ of using animals for medical experiments and advocate other methods.

(a) motion
(b) practice
(c) exertion
(d) disposition

**46.** In his hurry to get home, Martin ___________ left his keys at the office and was locked out of his apartment.

(a) incorrigibly
(b) unreservedly
(c) unrelentingly
(d) inadvertently

**47.** Although Tom had meant his comment to be ___________, Maria failed to see its humor and took offense.

(a) volatile
(b) redolent
(c) facetious
(d) corpulent

**48.** The current ___________ of information related to populations in Africa is due to the scarcity of records.

(a) spate
(b) dearth
(c) sludge
(d) demise

**49.** When left ___________ by regulations, large corporations tend to act in their own interests, to the detriment of the environment.

(a) abridged
(b) distended
(c) unfettered
(d) depreciated

**50.** Silver, which ___________ when exposed to oxygen, can be cleaned using baking soda and hot water.

(a) stipples
(b) deposits
(c) tarnishes
(d) burnishes



This is the end of the Vocabulary section. Do NOT move on to the Reading Comprehension section until instructed to do so. You are NOT allowed to turn to any other section of the test.

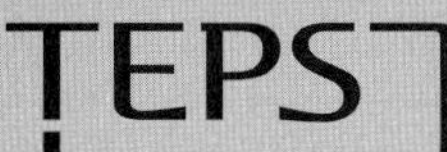

# READING COMPREHENSION

## DIRECTIONS

This section tests your ability to comprehend reading passages. You will have 45 minutes to complete the 40 questions. Be sure to follow the directions given by the proctor.

정답 P 329

**Part I** **Questions 1–16**

Read the passage and choose the option that best completes the passage.

**1.** Erma Stone's *The Healthy Kitchen* is a cookbook with a difference: the book ______________________________. Many of us want to cook healthy food but need more help than a recipe. That's why Stone created an online component to her cookbook. Have a question? Log in to *The Healthy Kitchen*'s website using the ID number printed inside your book's front cover to access a members-only portion of the website. When you type your question, you'll get a personalized answer within 24 hours.

(a) can be downloaded for free
(b) customizes your favorite foods
(c) lets you post recipes on the web
(d) comes with personalized online help

**2.** The Emancipation Proclamation of 1863 ______________________________. Lacking their own farmland, most slaves who were freed remained too poor to start new lives. They had no choice but to continue working on plantations, where their wages and social status remained low. "Emancipated" men were largely confined to unskilled labor and service jobs, while women remained private cooks and maids. It would take decades for abolition to have a positive effect on the lives of these victims of an inhumane institution.

(a) did not immediately alter the lives of former slaves
(b) improved working conditions for liberated slaves
(c) prompted the freed slaves to flee plantations
(d) helped to end racial prejudice in America

**3.** Please check your application form carefully before submitting a request for a replacement birth certificate. All fields on the form must be filled in completely and accurately. Incomplete application forms will be returned to the sender. As your birth certificate is one of the most important forms of identification, the government must verify your personal information before issuing a replacement. So please ensure your application form is complete; otherwise ______________________.

(a) it cannot be processed by the government
(b) your birth certificate will no longer be valid
(c) additional forms of identification will be required
(d) the government will be unable to return your forms

**4.** When studying the religions of ancient peoples, a useful clue in uncovering the nature of their gods is to know ______________________. For example, if the celebration falls on the new moon, it is logical to connect the deity to the worship of the moon. If the festival falls during the winter or summer solstice, it is likely that the god is linked with sun worship. Moreover, if worship occurs during the harvest, it is probable that the god is an embodiment of the earth.

(a) the culture's understanding of astronomy
(b) how the religious hierarchy was organized
(c) the time when their festivals were celebrated
(d) whether the society was primarily agricultural

**5.**

Dear Mr. Richards,

Football season is almost over, and we hope that you will ______________________. As you may already know, the cost of stadium development has strained the club's finances. As a result, the price of season tickets for next season will increase from $590 to $650. However, since you are a current season ticket holder, we are offering you a 5% discount to show that we appreciate your business. If you're interested, you can go online or call 221-887-6234.

Sincerely,
Andy Bayville

(a) take advantage of our new lower ticket prices
(b) support our athletes by considering a donation
(c) renew your status as a valued season ticket holder
(d) enter our upcoming contest for season ticket holders

**6.** Shakespeare lover Eugene Schieffelin changed New York City's ecology in a lasting way. Wanting to recreate the avian imagery in Shakespeare's poems, Schieffelin imported all the birds mentioned in Shakespeare's works to North America. In 1890, he released 60 European starlings in Central Park, and over the years, their numbers exploded. With their shrill cries and voracious appetites, these birds are now a major nuisance to New Yorkers. So though Schieffelin's intention to honor Shakespeare was pure, ______________________________.

(a) he failed to save the European starling from extinction
(b) many wish he had understood Shakespeare more thoroughly
(c) few people appreciate his introduction of a bothersome species
(d) he is most remembered for bringing a blessing in disguise to New York

**7.** The evaluation committee reviewed Haliford School's updated testing methods and found that problems remain. Following complaints of scoring irregularities, Haliford School agreed to implement grader training to improve inter-grader consistency and stabilize scores. The committee notes that the necessary training has occurred, but that the graders have not been able to bring their subjective grading criteria in line with each other. Basically, scoring irregularities remain, and it appears that ______________________________.

(a) the training has failed to deliver the desired outcomes
(b) test takers have demonstrated insufficient achievement
(c) the proposed solutions have been ignored by the school
(d) school officials were unaware of the scoring irregularities

**8.** Though the poet and novelist Jack Kerouac was deeply influenced by the writer Thomas Wolfe, Kerouac was ______________________________. Kerouac famously idolized Wolfe. In fact, Wolfe is often cited as the writer who inspired him to write and whom he sought to model himself after. With regard to Wolfe's language, though, Kerouac believed that it lacked focus and clarity. These conflicting attitudes Kerouac had towards his literary idol exemplify what literary critic Harold Bloom called "the anxiety of influence."

(a) blinded to Wolfe's faults by his adoration
(b) at once admiring and critical of the author
(c) reluctant to credit the author as an influence
(d) the first to admit he never fully grasped Wolfe

**9.** To make better use of its personnel, the army might consider ______________________. Currently, the personnel management of the army is somewhat inefficient. Soldiers are recruited, trained, and then promoted simply on the basis of seniority. This results in soldiers serving in positions that may not match their abilities. It would be much more beneficial if the army modeled itself after private businesses and evaluated candidates through interview processes and offered promotions on the basis of skill, not simply time served.

(a) redesigning its training to be more efficient
(b) promoting more officers to command positions
(c) offering better benefits to attract more new recruits
(d) replacing its seniority-driven system with a merit-based one

**10.** The twentieth century saw the rise of the planned community, where land development is carefully arranged from its inception. Such centralized planning has various advantages: it allows builders to lower costs by streamlining construction and reduces the chance of conflict over land use. In many cities, the development of attractive suburban subdivisions has created picturesque communities and increased property values. It is true that some such communities have been criticized for their homogeneity, but ______________________.

(a) the basis of such complaints is likely the drop in home prices
(b) their practical benefits have ultimately made them successful
(c) the real problem is the land-use conflicts they have provoked
(d) city planners have responded by giving free reign to developers

**11.** In the early days of mass-market perfumery, there were no major distinctions between men's and women's fragrances. Perfumes were no more considered to be "masculine" or "feminine" than foods were. Today, however, that has changed. Women's fragrances are often soft, fruity, and floral. Men's scents, which are commonly citrusy or aquatic, are distinguished by what they do not contain—notes of flowers, sweet fruits, or anything that might be construed as feminine. In essence, the commercial perfumers of today have ______________________.

(a) expanded their palette for crafting male fragrances
(b) stopped catering exclusively to female consumers
(c) reintroduced the former androgyny of perfumes
(d) designated scents for one gender or the other

**12.** Looking back on my 40-year career as a diplomat, I often ponder how my life would have been if I had chosen a more stationary profession. I realized that my professional mobility would put a strain on my family life and so refrained from committing to personal relationships. Though the work was mostly fulfilling, there was always a nagging voice in my mind asking, "What if?" I didn't listen, though, and over the years, the rewards of my job waned and the misgivings I had about forgoing family life morphed into outright regrets. I realize now I should have ________________________.

(a) known that I preferred adventure to family life
(b) heeded my own doubts about the choices I was making
(c) integrated overseas travel into my work on a regular basis
(d) consulted my spouse before devoting so much time to my career

**13.** Insectivorous plants such as flypaper traps capture their prey ________________________. Flypaper traps of the genus *Drosophyllum* release a sweet aroma that attracts insects, which get trapped when they land on the plant's sticky surface. Struggling to free themselves, the insects eventually die of exhaustion. In contrast, flypaper traps of the genus *Drosera* do not just wait for their prey to become stuck but actually manipulate sticky tentacles to ensnare insects and hold them in place until they are killed.

(a) with their sticky tentacles and squeeze them to death
(b) using smaller insect species as bait to lure bigger ones
(c) by actively ensnaring or passively luring them to their death
(d) after releasing sweet smells that actually contain a lethal poison

**14.** As the United States has stepped up its criticism of whaling in other countries, countries that practice the tradition have turned the tables on their accuser. Noting that the US lobbies against whaling in Japan and Sweden, supporters of whaling from these countries ask why the US allows its own aboriginal communities to harvest highly threatened bowhead whales. They also note that their own hunts target abundant species, while the US decimated the global blue whale population at the start of the last century. These countries use these arguments to claim that the US has ________________.

(a) remained too silent about whale hunting issues
(b) shown a double standard when it comes to whaling
(c) proven why whaling should be outlawed worldwide
(d) been unfairly banning aboriginals from hunting whales

**15.** With reports of chimpanzees learning sign language and dogs that are trained to recognize hundreds of words, some people believe that animals can use language. And it can be argued that these animals' behavior resembles the linguistic abilities of, for example, young children. ________________, it is not accurate to say these animals possess real language skills. They are really using a simplified animal communication system, which does not share all the features of human language.

(a) Even so
(b) As a result
(c) In particular
(d) In the same sense

**16.** Going undercover into a major garment factory, reporters found evidence substantiating complaints of worker exploitation. In addition to late paychecks and long working hours, the factory's management imposed harsh restrictions on workers' freedoms, including charging them to use the bathroom. ________________, the factory's owners were taking advantage of workers in any way they could. They have been getting away with it because workers were impoverished and desperate to support their families.

(a) In effect
(b) Otherwise
(c) For instance
(d) Nevertheless

**Part II** **Questions 17–37**

Read the passage, question, and options. Then, based on the given information, choose the option that best answers the question.

**17.** Lightning can seem magical and awe-inspiring, but the physical causes of lightning are actually fairly simple. Within a storm, a negatively charged electrical field develops. And while the ground normally has a negative electrical charge, the negative charge in storm clouds induces a positive charge on the ground for several kilometers around the storm. Lightning occurs when the two opposite charges build up enough to overcome resistance in the air and an electrical current flows between them.

Q: What is the main topic of the passage?
(a) How storms produce lightning
(b) Why air resists electrical currents
(c) The size of electrical fields from storms
(d) The cause of lightning's negative charge

**18.** Beautiful new holiday homes await buyers on the Mediterranean coast, but with recent trends in the real estate market, Spanish property is not a risk-free investment. A clear understanding of Spain's real estate market is essential to investing wisely. That's why we have created *Spanish Property Secrets*, an e-book and software package that will help you find your dream vacation home and ensure that your investment is secure.

Q: What is mainly being advertised?
(a) Software for first-time property owners
(b) Homes currently on the real estate market
(c) A resource for potential property investors
(d) Realtors that can maximize home sale profits

**19.** Winston's Bar and Grill will be hosting the Mishima Corporation's annual staff dinner party on Saturday, February 18. We regret to inform customers that the second floor dining area is reserved for their exclusive use on that evening and that only limited menus will be available for patrons at the first floor bar. We appreciate your understanding, and we will be fully open again for a roast dinner on Sunday.

Q: What is the main purpose of the announcement about Winston's Bar and Grill?
(a) To advertise a special roast dinner on Sunday
(b) To announce a partial closure for a private event
(c) To notify patrons that the bar is fully booked on Saturday
(d) To welcome guests to the Mishima Corporation's staff party

**20.**

To the Editor:

Wednesday's article "Post-War Vision of Growth" examines several reasons why the economy grew after World War II. But there was really only one reason. The federal government kick-started things by removing growth restrictions and tax threats. After that, commerce and industry sped ahead, manufacturing goods and creating jobs. In other words, economic progress came about with the government's withdrawal of business costs, which gave the private sector the confidence to expand and encouraged consumers to start spending.

George Andrews

Q: What is the writer's main point about the post-war economy?
(a) Increased manufacturing abruptly drove up business costs.
(b) Job creation occurred despite the government's interference.
(c) Eliminating hurdles to business led to rapid economic growth.
(d) Consumer spending initiated a revival in commerce and industry.

**21.** In certain individuals, intense feelings of social rejection can have serious consequences. Those who feel isolated and excluded by society are more likely to interpret others' actions as hostile, and they begin to behave in hurtful ways themselves. The important thing to note is that others' actions are not necessarily hostile and that they are only being interpreted that way. The exclusion causes the injured parties' outlook to change, leading them to see hostility in neutral actions and react in kind.

Q: What is the writer's main point?
(a) Excluded people are the typical victims of aggression.
(b) Some people seek to isolate themselves to avoid rejection.
(c) Society excludes certain people to prevent acts of aggression.
(d) Feelings of social rejection can distort how a person views others' actions.

**22.** As a staff member of the online division of Mina's Boutique, you are responsible for ensuring our customers' satisfaction. When placing their orders online, customers expect to receive the right products. The last thing they want is the disappointment of receiving the wrong products and the hassle of waiting for us to correct the mistake. Anyone who has gone through such an ordeal is unlikely to become a repeat customer, which is why it is vital to avoid errors when processing orders.

Q: What is the passage mainly about?
(a) The best way to correct problems with online orders
(b) The importance of filling online orders without errors
(c) Why customers must confirm their order before paying
(d) How online feedback helps gauge customer satisfaction

**23.** Aspirin can cause problems to the digestive organs. Coated aspirin, which does not dissolve until after it passes through the stomach into the small intestine, is often believed to be less damaging. However, no matter where it dissolves, aspirin still blocks substances that protect the stomach lining. Furthermore, such coating also delays aspirin's pain relieving effects. To mitigate its damaging potential, doctors recommend taking it with food and not mixing it with other painkillers with which it can interact dangerously.

Q: Which of the following is correct according to the passage?
(a) Coated aspirin tablets dissolve before entering the stomach.
(b) Coating aspirin does not eliminate its damaging effects.
(c) Non-coated aspirin takes longer to act than the coated version.
(d) Doctors suggest avoiding taking aspirin with food.

24. Individuals with dyslexia read at significantly lower levels than their peers. This has created an erroneous belief that dyslexic people have lower intelligence. At its root, dyslexia is a problem in linking written words with their sounds, which can interrupt silent "mental" reading as well as the speaking out loud of printed words. Although there is no medical cure for the disorder, there are a number of teaching methods that can help dyslexics successfully overcome their reading difficulties.

Q: Which of the following is correct about dyslexia according to the passage?
(a) It is accompanied by lower levels of intelligence.
(b) It is an inability to separate words from sounds.
(c) Its sufferers can read well silently but not out loud.
(d) It can be helped through certain teaching methods.

25. Always having earned a modest living, Margaret Jones was astonished to learn last week that the local government was going to give her approximately $100,000. Clerks in the office of records discovered that in 1899, Jones's great-grandfather bought investment bonds in the newly established town of Stockville. He had stored the bonds in the records office after a fire had nearly destroyed his personal papers. As Margaret was her great-grandfather's only surviving descendant, she is the rightful—and thrilled—heir of the bonds.

Q: Which of the following is correct about Margaret Jones according to the article?
(a) She had a sizable income before learning of her new wealth.
(b) She discovered hidden money while looking through old records.
(c) Her new wealth comes from an ancestor's investment in bonds.
(d) Her great-grandfather's personal papers were destroyed in a fire.

26. This Christmas, give Silverman Bank Gift Cards. These convenient cards come in denominations ranging from $50 to $500 and can be used anywhere that accepts credit cards, including bank machines. Simply fill out the online order form, and your card will be placed in an attractive envelope and sent to you or directly to the recipient by priority shipping. Safer than cash and easily replaced if lost, these gift cards are perfect for the holidays!

Q: Which of the following is correct about Silverman Bank Gift Cards according to the advertisement?
(a) The minimum value they carry is $50.
(b) They cannot be used at bank machines.
(c) They come as a downloadable online coupon.
(d) The bank will not reissue any lost cards.

**27.** Though some flowers are pollinated by the wind, most rely on insects for pollination. For this reason, many flowers have adapted to either nocturnal insects—insects that sleep during the day and are active at night—or diurnal insects, who are on the opposite schedule. Flowers that rely on nocturnal insects for pollination often bloom at night. Such flowers are typically white and heavily scented so that insects can find them in the dark. Day-blooming flowers are vividly colored and have lighter scents since insects can find them in the sunshine.

Q: Which of the following is correct according to the passage?
(a) All flowers rely on diurnal or nocturnal insects for pollination.
(b) Insects are only able to pollinate flowers during daylight hours.
(c) Night-blooming flowers do not typically give off strong scents.
(d) Flowers that bloom during the day tend to have bold colors.

**28.** The University of Nevada's email service will be down from 6 am to 6 pm on June 10 while the staff updates the system's software. Account information including saved correspondence will be unaffected; however, please be aware that messages received during the update interval will be automatically rejected. Senders will receive a reply to advise them that their message was not delivered and that they should resend their message after 6 pm on Sunday.

Q: Which of the following is correct according to the announcement?
(a) The email update will take place over two days.
(b) Saved correspondence may be lost as a result of the update.
(c) Incoming messages will be stored during the maintenance.
(d) Correspondents will be notified about undelivered messages.

**29.** Dubbed the "boomerang generation," North American young adults who left home to go to college are increasingly moving back in with their parents. This generational change in living arrangements has been attributed to the decade-long upheaval in the global economy and the ensuing lack of jobs available to young adults trying to enter the workforce. The trend is occurring across the developed world, and other countries have fashioned their own terms for it, including the Italian "big babies" and Japanese "parasite singles."

Q: Which of the following is correct about the boomerang generation according to the passage?
(a) The term applies to the parents of adult children living at home.
(b) It is caused by increased unemployment among young people.
(c) It has not yet impacted young people in the developed world.
(d) The term has been mistranslated in Japan as "parasite singles."

**30.** Containing the earliest signs of human life in India, the Rock Shelters of Bhimbetka feature detailed depictions of prehistoric life. The images were created over time, with the earliest ones featuring life-sized animal figures and later ones featuring more ornate depictions of communal dances and slaughtered animals. Artists painted over the work of previous artists, and archaeologists have used carbon dating to establish seven distinct periods of composition. Despite this wealth of information, however, the societies responsible for the paintings remain mysterious.

Q: Which of the following is correct about the images at the Rock Shelters of Bhimbetka according to the passage?
(a) They gradually became more spare and minimalist over time.
(b) They contain overlapping works completed by different artists.
(c) Carbon dating shows they were made in three different periods.
(d) Archaeologists have identified the civilizations that created them.

**31.** In early 2011, a proposal was made to build a "dry canal" in Colombia. The project, which involves 250 miles of rail connecting Colombia's Pacific coast to its Atlantic port of Cartagena, received significant support from the Chinese, who would benefit greatly from the more efficient transport of Colombian coal exports. However, political considerations may affect how the project goes forward. As a longtime ally of the US, Colombia risks damaging its relationship with Washington by partnering with China, particularly on a transit corridor that would compete with the American-built Panama Canal.

Q: Which of the following is correct about the dry canal according to the passage?
(a) It will bypass Colombia's port of Cartagena.
(b) It intends to link Colombia's ports to Panama.
(c) It has incited retaliation from China and the US.
(d) It would be a competitor to American interests.

**32.** Willa Cather is now counted among America's finest writers, but her popularity fluctuated while she was alive. Her career flourished in the 1910s and 1920s, with critics lauding her stories about common people told in spare prose. The 1930s brought the Great Depression and with it a shift in how Cather's work was viewed. Her style, which was once deemed deft and "deeply felt," was condemned as nostalgic and out of step with the current social atmosphere by critics. Demoralized, Cather became a recluse, going so far as to burn all her correspondence.

Q: Which of the following is correct about Willa Cather according to the passage?
(a) Reaction to her work grew steadily more positive over her career.
(b) Her flowery and emotional prose drew criticism for being overly wordy.
(c) Critics felt her work took on greater meaning during the Great Depression.
(d) She was driven to seclusion by the unfavorable reception of her work.

**33.** The so-called personal luxury car made by American automakers dominated the American mass market in the 1960s. Large, highly stylized cars like the Cadillac Eldorado and Ford Thunderbird had their heyday then, when gasoline prices were low and consumers were highly conscious of design. But when the oil shocks of the 1970s sent gas prices soaring, Americans suddenly became concerned with fuel efficiency and turned to more compact European and Asian cars, which could go farther on a tank of gas.

Q: What can be inferred from the passage?
(a) Large luxury cars declined in popularity in 1970s America.
(b) European cars were seen as flashy but inefficient in the 1970s.
(c) The Eldorado and Thunderbird were designed to conserve gas.
(d) Imported cars were prized in America for having bigger gas tanks.

**34.** Jim Henson, the American puppeteer famous for the Muppets and his characters on the children's show *Sesame Street*, revolutionized the art form. Prior to his creations, puppets were manipulated by strings, which made their movements somewhat jerky. But Henson moved his puppets using rods, which gave them smoother movements. He also made puppets' faces out of foam rubber instead of fabric, so that their facial expressions could convey a greater range of emotions, and he matched their mouth movements more closely with their speech.

Q: What can be inferred about Jim Henson from the passage?
(a) His innovations made puppets more lifelike.
(b) His puppets' popularity came as a surprise to him.
(c) He felt overly realistic puppets would scare children.
(d) He modeled his puppets after *Sesame Street* characters.

**35.**

Dear Ms. King,

I am writing to you to see if you are coming to the Winger Hall Association meeting this weekend. As time is short, it is important for us to resolve our differences and come to a decision regarding the allocation of the funds we have raised for next year. Your views carry substantial weight with all of the organization's members. Thus, I believe your participation could help facilitate a compromise among some of our more inflexible members. Please RSVP at your earliest convenience.

Warm regards,
Janet Warren

Q: What can be inferred about the Winger Hall Association from the letter?
(a) It is seeking advice on how to raise funds for next year.
(b) It has lost key members of its leadership group recently.
(c) It has had trouble raising enough funds over the last year.
(d) It is locked in a disagreement about its spending priorities.

**36.** I go to a university renowned for its basketball team, though it was the school's academic reputation that attracted me. Knowing almost nothing about sports had never been a handicap before, and I was surprised to feel distinctly left out of a lot of small talk. Our team's activities seemed like the main topic classmates used to grease the wheels of social interaction. I've recently started to peruse the sports section of the school paper each day, and although I am still not a huge basketball fan, at least I find myself fitting into conversations much better now.

Q: What can be inferred about the writer from the passage?
(a) He has a social motive for following college basketball.
(b) He feigns ignorance of sporting events as a conversation starter.
(c) His preference of other sports over basketball has alienated him.
(d) His strategy for making friends has been playing on sports teams.

**37.** The recent Supreme Court ruling that allows companies to block consumers from mounting lawsuits has set a dangerous precedent. From now on, companies can include a clause in service contracts that forces customers with a complaint into individual arbitration. In essence, a company can use contractual arbitration clauses to specify and limit how consumers can complain and seek restitution. The danger now is that when consumers sign a contract for a cell phone, for example, they may be giving up their rights to have their day in court if they feel they were wronged by the company.

Q: What can be inferred from the passage?
(a) Companies fear the ruling will encourage frivolous lawsuits.
(b) The ruling is more of a boon to companies than to consumers.
(c) Arbitration has usually been how consumers resolve complaints.
(d) Consumers will now have greater say over service contract terms.

**Part III** **Questions 38 — 40**

Read the passage and identify the option that does NOT belong.

**38.** More and more book lovers are discovering the advantages of owning an electronic reader. (a) Since the devices are very light, they are easy to carry and hold while reading. (b) They can also save money in the long term since e-books are cheaper than paper ones. (c) Paper books also have the element of nostalgia and become cherished objects that we love to hold. (d) And there is the added convenience of being able to download new books anywhere, at any time.

**39.** Few materials have had such a profound impact on modern engineering as steel. (a) Aircraft carriers, oil tankers, and cranes are just a few of the inventions it has made possible. (b) Steel manufacturing has generated great wealth in a variety of developing economies. (c) Invisible but equally important are items such as the girders that hold up our skyscrapers. (d) It is almost impossible to go anywhere without encountering some kind of steel structure.

**40.** Richmond officials have hit yet another roadblock in their efforts to modernize the city's historic waterfront. (a) The waterfront area has needed a makeover for decades, but something has always come up to halt the project. (b) In 1995, the funding for the renovations suddenly fell through, just weeks before the work was set to start. (c) Because of this, the radical changes made by the renovations drove up rent prices, causing the area to lose residents. (d) Now, the latest obstacle is coming from Richmond's historical society, which claims that the area's buildings are historical sites and must be preserved.

This is the end of the Reading Comprehension section. Please remain seated until the proctor has instructed otherwise. You are NOT allowed to turn to any other section of the test.

# 서울대 최신기출 3

***Listening*** *Comprehension*

***Grammar***

***Vocabulary***

***Reading*** *Comprehension*

# Listening Comprehension

## Directions

1. In the Listening Comprehension section, all content will be presented orally rather than in written form.
2. This section contains four parts, each with fifteen individual items. For each part, you will receive separate instructions. Listen to the instructions carefully, and choose the best answer from the options for each item.

Scripts P 288 / 정답 P 330

**Part I** **Questions 1–15**

You will now hear fifteen individual spoken questions or statements, each followed by four spoken responses. Choose the most appropriate response for each item.

**Part II** **Questions 16–30**

You will now hear fifteen short conversation fragments, followed by four spoken responses. Choose the most appropriate response to complete each conversation.

**Part III** **Questions 31–45**

You will now hear fifteen complete conversations. For each conversation, you will be asked to answer a question. Each conversation and its corresponding question will be read twice. Then you will hear four options which will be read only once. Based on the given information, choose the option that best answers the question.

**Part IV** **Questions 46–60**

You will now hear fifteen short talks. After each talk, you will be asked to answer a question. Each talk and its corresponding question will be read twice. Then you will hear four options which will be read only once. Based on the given information, choose the option that best answers the question.

# GRAMMAR

## DIRECTIONS

This section tests your grammar skills. You will have 25 minutes to complete the 50 questions. Be sure to follow the directions given by the proctor.

정답 P 330

**Part I** **Questions 1–20**

Choose the option that best completes each gap.

**1.** A: I think I'm coming down with a cold.

B: You ___________ to me when I told you not to go jogging in the rain yesterday.

(a) would listen
(b) should listen
(c) would have listened
(d) should have listened

**2.** A: Want to see that new vampire movie?

B: No, I've never found ___________ horror films enjoyable.

(a) watch
(b) watching
(c) having watched
(d) to have watched

**3.** A: You really got a lot of mail today.

B: ___________ my roommate, actually.

(a) It most is for
(b) Mostly for it is
(c) For it mostly is
(d) Most of it is for

**4.** A: Should I get these black shoes or those brown ones?

B: Just buy the ones ___________ best match your work uniform.

(a) that
(b) what
(c) to what
(d) to which

**5.** A: I can offer $10 off the price of this desk.

B: Thirty five dollars ___________ still too much.

(a) is
(b) are
(c) was
(d) were

**6.** A: Max, how about getting some coffee?

B: Sorry, I've got ___________ that I need to finish up.

(a) work
(b) works
(c) a work
(d) the works

**7.** A: When will Dr. Lim start interviewing assistants?

B: He'll begin ___________ all the applications are in.

(a) once
(b) while
(c) unless
(d) though

**8.** A: Is everyone able to attend today's meeting?

B: Yes, I planned it ___________ account of staff availability.

(a) took
(b) taken
(c) taking
(d) being taken

**9.** A: Is Greg still single?

B: No, he ___________ married for five years.

(a) is
(b) was
(c) has been
(d) was being

**10.** A: Are you getting a ride to the conference with Jeff?

B: I'm not sure. I'll be going with ___________ has space in their car.

(a) that
(b) who
(c) whoever
(d) whichever

**11.** A: What's the weather like?

B: Fine, but take an umbrella ___________ it rains later.

(a) as if
(b) in case
(c) even if
(d) in order that

**12.** A: Do you think this campfire will get us through the night?

B: Sure. When ___________ properly, a good fire can last all night.

(a) built
(b) building
(c) to be built
(d) having built

**13.** A: I think I left my cell phone on the bus!

B: Not again! You ___________ your cell phone.

(a) always lost
(b) had always lost
(c) are always losing
(d) had always been losing

**14.** A: You must be excited about being selected for the quiz show.

B: Yes! The cash prizes ___________ to participants total one million dollars!

(a) awarded
(b) awarding
(c) are awarded
(d) will be awarded

**15.** A: Are you going to finish that project before the deadline?

B: I'm not sure. I'll email you if I don't think I ___________.

(a) can
(b) can't
(c) can be
(d) can't be

**16.** A: Who's getting that promotion?

B: ___________ Alice is being considered.

(a) It's that rumor
(b) Rumor that it is
(c) Rumor is it that
(d) It's rumored that

**17.** A: Can we afford such a pricey TV?
B: Of course. I'm sure ___________.

(a) it's within our budget well
(b) it's well within our budget
(c) our budget is well within it
(d) our budget is within it well

**18.** A: It was nice of David to help you get that job.
B: Yeah, if it weren't ___________ his help, I would still be looking.

(a) without
(b) from
(c) after
(d) for

**19.** A: Did you like the escargot that Marianne served at her party?
B: No. But I ___________ just have weird taste, since everyone else loved it.

(a) can
(b) must
(c) would
(d) should

**20.** A: Did Mr. Enson attend the marketing proposal alone?
B: No. ___________ three members of his staff.

(a) He accompanied with
(b) Accompanying him were
(c) He was being accompanied
(d) Accompanying with him were

## Part II Questions 21–40

Choose the option that best completes each gap.

**21.** Irene felt sad ___________ because it had been a gift from her grandmother.

(a) for her clock breaking it
(b) when broke it her clock
(c) her clock for breaking
(d) when her clock broke

**22.** The case for Lionel's cello was heavy, but when he held it by ___________ it was much easier to carry.

(a) handle
(b) the handle
(c) some handle
(d) neither handle

**23.** Highly combustible materials ignite at relatively low temperatures and therefore ___________ fire easily.

(a) catch
(b) are caught
(c) are catching
(d) were caught

**24.** Since she wanted to stay home, Marilyn tried to get her husband ___________ his mind about traveling during Christmas.

(a) to change
(b) changed
(c) changes
(d) change

**25.** Leaders must communicate their vision ___________ clearly that no doubt remains among followers about how to execute it.

(a) so
(b) far
(c) such
(d) much

**26.** ___________ her mother call her name, Peggy ran down the stairs into the kitchen.

(a) Hear
(b) Heard
(c) Hearing
(d) To be heard

**27.** *Reach for the Stars* is a televised singing competition that ___________ next June in downtown Los Angeles.

(a) will hold
(b) was held
(c) is holding
(d) is being held

**28.** Although his roommate could study ___________ the TV blaring in the background, Albert found that the noise made it hard to concentrate.

(a) in
(b) as
(c) with
(d) about

**29.** Kendra's humanitarian efforts were all the more ___________ to others because she did not boast about them.

(a) inspired
(b) inspiring
(c) to inspire
(d) to be inspired

**30.** Famous for ___________ to national news magazines, Hank Buckley has also authored three books on democracy.

(a) regularly being to contribute
(b) being contributing regularly
(c) regularly contributing to be
(d) being a regular contributor

**31.** Leonard could not imagine buying a new car while still in debt and ___________.

(a) neither could his wife
(b) his wife could neither
(c) his wife neither could
(d) could neither his wife

**32.** Hardly had the festival's opening ceremony gotten underway when it ___________ to pour.

(a) started
(b) has started
(c) has been starting
(d) had been starting

**33.** The Friday after Thanksgiving is important for the US economy because it is ___________.

(a) a huge popular day shopping
(b) huge popular a day for shopping
(c) a hugely popular day for shopping
(d) shopping for a day hugely popular

**34.** On his third trip to the zoo, the boy's expression of wonder made him look as though he ___________ wild animals before.

(a) has never seen
(b) had never seen
(c) was never seeing
(d) were never seeing

**35.** Since he already has ___________, Tim will not renew his contract with the company unless he gets a considerable raise.

(a) job offer
(b) any job offer
(c) other job offer
(d) another job offer

**36.** Some of today's most important research on cognitive processes ___________ on the connections between neurons.

(a) focus
(b) focuses
(c) was focusing
(d) were focusing

**37.** ___________ amount of cramming can help students who have not properly prepared for exams.

(a) None
(b) Few
(c) All
(d) No

**38.** This language immersion class will be multicultural, so it is essential that each student ___________ his or her classmates.

(a) respect
(b) respected
(c) has respected
(d) would respect

**39.** Tonight's meeting will give ___________ have not yet been heard the opportunity to share their opinions.

(a) voices to those who
(b) those voices to who
(c) whose voices those
(d) those whose voices

**40.** Dr. Cho told students that assignments need ___________ on paper and that she would accept them via email.

(a) no longer be submitted
(b) not to be submitted any longer
(c) being not submitted any longer
(d) to be no longer being submitted

GRAMMAR

## Part III Questions 41—45

Read each sentence carefully and identify the option that contains a grammatical error.

**41.** (a) A: Hey, Gary. What are you doing after class this afternoon?
(b) B: I'm supposed to meet Margaret at the library. How come you're asking?
(c) A: I was going to see if you wanted to go to the mall with me.
(d) B: Maybe some other time. I've really needed to study after class today.

**42.** (a) A: How would you like to go sailing with me next Saturday?
(b) B: I'd love to! Is your boat moored around somewhere here?
(c) A: Yeah, it's at the marina located at the foot of Lakeview Drive.
(d) B: Great. I'll just check my schedule to make sure I'm free.

**43.** (a) A: Do I look all right? I have a fellowship interview this afternoon.
(b) B: Maybe you should change your pants. Wearing jeans might make you look too casual.
(c) A: OK, then I'll wear the new slacks I bought yesterday. It's in the closet.
(d) B: Good idea. And you might consider wearing a tie with that shirt, too.

**44.** (a) A: It's already dark out and we haven't done a single thing all day.
(b) B: Sometimes people just need to spend a day to relax it, though.
(c) A: Why don't we at least go outside and get some fresh air for a while?
(d) B: OK. I suppose I could be persuaded to take a short walk.

**45.** (a) A: Don't you feel that Carol is a little rude to you sometimes?
(b) B: Yeah, I guess she is kind of condescending when I ask for help.
(c) A: Exactly. She treats people as if they were children.
(d) B: I know what you're meaning. But I don't think she realizes she's doing it.

## Part IV Questions 46–50

Read each sentence carefully and identify the option that contains a grammatical error.

**46.** (a) Storybooks can play an instrumental role in developing a child's literacy. (b) Reading stories to young children helps them connect sounds to printed letters. (c) However, it is important that the stories be engaging and exciting for the child. (d) Children whose view reading as a pleasant experience become better readers.

**47.** (a) Youth courts are special judicial venues where teenage offenders can be tried for delinquent acts. (b) The goal of these courts is to handle cases involving young offenders who are not old enough to be tried as adults. (c) Such courts are not part of the official judicial system, but their judgments and sentences are legal valid. (d) Many youth courts operate in conjunction with youth centers and schools, and are staffed by volunteers.

**48.** (a) Since olives are naturally hard and bitter, they are rarely eaten right off the tree. (b) In preparation for consumption, they are usually fermented or cured with lye. (c) This process allows olives to be preserved and significantly alters their flavor. (d) Most olives are canned after curing, though some varieties, like the throubes olive, is eaten raw.

**49.** (a) Many people believe that layoffs have the greatest effect on the person who has been let go. (b) But research shows that those who remain behind suffer a much strong psychological impact. (c) This is due to "layoff survivors," as they are known, feeling an overwhelming sense of loss. (d) The sense of loss can develop into feelings of resentment, which can lead to a decreased sense of loyalty.

**50.** (a) Everywhere you look on Jupiter, and you are able to see clouds. (b) They form multicolored bands that run parallel to the equator. (c) The lighter bands, called zones, are composed mainly of ammonia. (d) However, the chemical composition of the darker sections, called belts, is unknown.

This is the end of the Grammar section. Do NOT move on to the next section until instructed to do so. You are NOT allowed to turn to any other section of the test.

# Vocabulary

## Directions

This section tests your vocabulary skills. You will have 15 minutes to complete the 50 questions. Be sure to follow the directions given by the proctor.

정답 P 330

## Part I Questions 1–25

Choose the option that best completes each gap.

**1.** A: Did the resort have a gym and swimming pools?
B: Yes, their sports ___________ were excellent.

(a) facilities
(b) addresses
(c) installments
(d) conveniences

**2.** A: I just finished painting the deck.
B: Thanks for helping me fix the place up. I really ___________ it.

(a) admit
(b) capture
(c) appreciate
(d) compliment

**3.** A: I don't feel like cooking tonight.
B: Then let's ___________ at that new sushi place.

(a) let up
(b) eat out
(c) pan out
(d) work off

**4.** A: Hello, I'm new at the company. My name is Andy White.
B: Hi, I'm Tim Ramsay. It's great to meet a new ___________.

(a) accessory
(b) colleague
(c) accomplice
(d) component

**5.** A: If you're free, let's go get lunch.
B: I can't. I'm still ___________ with projects, and my deadlines are approaching.

(a) devoured
(b) plundered
(c) overloaded
(d) understated

**6.** A: Do you have much time for hobbies or going out with friends?
B: No, I'm so busy at work that I rarely have any ___________ time.

(a) leisure
(b) privacy
(c) novelty
(d) solitude

**7.** A: It's getting late. I'd better ___________.
B: Drive carefully—it's dark.

(a) hit the road
(b) rise and shine
(c) hold your horses
(d) go the extra mile

**8.** A: Are we still going to the beach tomorrow?
B: Our plans are ___________ on the weather. We'll see a movie if it rains.

(a) provident
(b) redundant
(c) dependent
(d) convenient

**9.** A: I heard you bought a new keyboard for half price.

B: Yeah, it was on clearance, so I got a good ___________.

(a) pledge
(b) token
(c) deal
(d) fare

**10.** A: I bet you had a tough time teaching that kindergarten class.

B: Yeah, it didn't go ___________.

(a) willingly
(b) smoothly
(c) reluctantly
(d) subsequently

**11.** A: I love this pub. It's just like being hosted by a friend.

B: You're right—the atmosphere really is ___________.

(a) internal
(b) robust
(c) vapid
(d) cozy

**12.** A: I tried to calm Jonas down but he was too furious to listen.

B: It's impossible to ___________ him when he's like that.

(a) instill
(b) verify
(c) pacify
(d) alleviate

**13.** A: I wish Eric would learn to drive. He's old enough, and it's about time.

B: Don't be so ___________. He'll do it when he's ready.

(a) vivid
(b) rapid
(c) impatient
(d) imperative

**14.** A: Look at all this food my mom sent us.

B: Wow, that's enough to ___________ us for a month!

(a) last
(b) bear
(c) spare
(d) endure

**15.** A: How many frequent flyer miles do I have saved up?

B: You've ___________ 5,000 miles.

(a) accrued
(b) engrossed
(c) consigned
(d) summoned

**16.** A: How is Norman? Is he regaining his strength?

B: He's still quite ___________, but his recovery is progressing.

(a) barren
(b) spoiled
(c) defunct
(d) fatigued

VOCABULARY

**17.** A: How did your salary negotiations go?

B: Terribly. I tried to get a raise, but management wouldn't ___________.

(a) ply
(b) alter
(c) push
(d) budge

**18.** A: Is this shirt too wrinkled?

B: Yeah, you should iron out the ___________ before you wear it.

(a) flakes
(b) creases
(c) swivels
(d) ruptures

**19.** A: Did you try explaining that statistics problem to Roy again?

B: Yeah, but he didn't get it. He doesn't quite ___________ the underlying idea.

(a) muster
(b) collide
(c) grasp
(d) rally

**20.** A: Is the soccer game going ahead today?

B: No, they ___________ because of the stormy weather.

(a) left it out
(b) called it off
(c) played it up
(d) backed it up

**21.** A: Have you ever tried durian fruit, Logan?

B: No, but I've heard the smell is ___________ to rotting garbage.

(a) akin
(b) joint
(c) overt
(d) docile

**22.** A: What were those inspectors in here for last week?

B: They were checking our ___________ with fire safety regulations.

(a) abdication
(b) compliance
(c) subscription
(d) concurrence

**23.** A: How did Lisa do on her final exam?

B: She didn't say directly, but she ___________ that she might have to take the course again.

(a) subsumed
(b) insinuated
(c) ingratiated
(d) supplanted

**24.** A: I don't think we can get that bed frame through this door.

B: You're right. We'll need to ___________ it to get it in here.

(a) dislodge
(b) perforate
(c) segregate
(d) dismantle

**25.** A: It was really bold of Alexis to dye her hair pink.

B: Yeah, it certainly takes a lot of ___________ to pull off a hairstyle like that.

(a) audacity
(b) extremity
(c) propensity
(d) perspicacity

VOCABULARY

## Part II Questions 26—50

Choose the option that best completes each gap.

**26.** The plane ___________ Seoul and arrived in Hong Kong a few hours later.

(a) lifted
(b) began
(c) removed
(d) departed

**27.** In coherent writing, every sentence is clearly ___________ to the previous sentence, thus creating a smooth flow.

(a) linked
(b) crossed
(c) bunched
(d) regulated

**28.** Drinking coffee helps people remain ___________ even if they have not had enough sleep.

(a) curt
(b) alert
(c) facile
(d) drowsy

**29.** After twenty years with the company, the manager ___________ in order to start his own business.

(a) waived
(b) negated
(c) resigned
(d) reversed

**30.** ___________ among the top ten places to stay in Cebu by Traveler Magazine, the Beacon Hotel guarantees you the perfect getaway.

(a) Tilted
(b) Ranked
(c) Surveyed
(d) Calculated

**31.** The commanders of the two rebel groups agreed to ___________ their troops to form a unified fighting force.

(a) combine
(b) perform
(c) remark
(d) obey

**32.** With Sandy's amazing lap times, her swimming coach thought she could ___________ to participate in Olympic trials.

(a) allow
(b) prove
(c) qualify
(d) conflict

**33.** An exciting, risky, and visually spectacular sport, snowboarding has now ___________ worldwide popularity.

(a) perceived
(b) conveyed
(c) imposed
(d) attained

**34.** Filing tax returns electronically significantly ___________ the number of errors, since software can check for and repair mistakes in real time.

(a) lessens
(b) neglects
(c) converts
(d) computes

**35.** With her highly original and unique literary works, Virginia Woolf was regarded as one of the most ___________ writers of the nineteenth century.

(a) plausible
(b) symbiotic
(c) innovative
(d) engendered

**36.** In hot weather, a fan cools your skin by speeding the ___________ of sweat from its surface.

(a) exposition
(b) evaporation
(c) precipitation
(d) condensation

**37.** The League of Nations, the intergovernmental organization that was formed after World War I and lasted until 1946, was the ___________ to the modern United Nations.

(a) precursor
(b) aftermath
(c) frontrunner
(d) intermediary

**38.** As a great ___________ of the arts, Pope Julius II supported many Renaissance artists, including Michelangelo and Raphael.

(a) suitor
(b) envoy
(c) patron
(d) disciple

**39.** After his injury, Ben could not walk, so he was temporarily ___________ to a wheelchair.

(a) ascribed
(b) confined
(c) delegated
(d) attributed

**40.** After appealing for more public parks for years, Meadville citizens have finally had their ___________ granted.

(a) motive
(b) petition
(c) argument
(d) insistence

**41.** Researchers questioned the ___________ of the new cholesterol medication, as it failed to reduce cholesterol levels in most participants.

(a) vehemence
(b) exertion
(c) efficacy
(d) verve

**42.** Before the hikers set out on their trek, the park ranger ___________ them of the possible dangers lurking in the woods.

(a) sanctioned
(b) forewarned
(c) reprimanded
(d) remonstrated

43. Marie Antoinette became an archetype for ___________ nobility after disdainfully declaring that starving peasants should eat cake if they had no bread.

(a) precocious
(b) factitious
(c) reserved
(d) haughty

44. Whether this is your first ___________ or you have had a home loan before, Delaware Union offers you the best lending terms.

(a) warranty
(b) mortgage
(c) allowance
(d) stipulation

45. After scanning the computer's hard drive, the technician ___________ it with a disk fragmentation problem.

(a) proposed
(b) diagnosed
(c) scrutinized
(d) commended

46. After countless bribery scandals involving politicians, the public came to believe that corruption was ___________ in their country's politics.

(a) accustomed
(b) prescient
(c) inclusive
(d) rampant

47. New legislation ___________ deceptive advertising by making it illegal for companies to provide misleading or confusing information.

(a) discharges
(b) vindicates
(c) outlaws
(d) deports

48. Linda could play memorized music well, but she found it difficult to ___________ on the spot.

(a) oscillate
(b) emanate
(c) improvise
(d) aggrandize

49. Chairman Wright had expected to retain his title, so being ___________ by an unknown candidate this year surprised him.

(a) dethroned
(b) disowned
(c) devolved
(d) disposed

50. Lexington Systems offers attractive ___________ packages for managers, including housing assistance and performance bonuses.

(a) restitution
(b) requisition
(c) repatriation
(d) remuneration

This is the end of the Vocabulary section. Do NOT move on to the Reading Comprehension section until instructed to do so. You are NOT allowed to turn to any other section of the test.

# READING COMPREHENSION

## DIRECTIONS

This section tests your ability to comprehend reading passages. You will have 45 minutes to complete the 40 questions. Be sure to follow the directions given by the proctor.

정답 P 330

## Part I Questions 1—16

Read the passage and choose the option that best completes the passage.

**1.** The Slater College Central Library would like to remind students that ______________________. Whether you are interested in the basics of a statistical analysis software package or need help with the latest developments in web design, these courses are an opportunity to keep your IT skills up to date. Classes begin in the second week of each term and are completely free. Schedules and registration information are available on the library's website.

(a) free one-on-one research assistance is available
(b) we provide a variety of courses for computer training
(c) online writing clinics are offered throughout the semester
(d) we are now accepting applications for peer tutor positions

**2.** Used by many gardeners to lighten up spring flower beds, daffodils ______________________. Even when incorporated into a garden already arranged in orderly rows, daffodils should be placed randomly. In the fall, plant daffodil bulbs in clusters with a few scattered outside the main group. When they bloom in the spring, these hardy plants add a lovely touch of spontaneity to any garden.

(a) seem out of place in formal gardens
(b) require careful tending after planting
(c) must be planted at the beginning of spring
(d) look best when planted in an irregular pattern

**3.** I have always regarded teaching as my true calling, but after thirty years in public schools, the emotional and physical stress became too much, and two years ago, I retired. However, I missed working with children, and to fill this void, I took up tutoring. My current life as a tutor is very satisfying, as I can choose whom to work with and set my own schedule while continuing to teach. Ultimately, tutoring allowed me to ______________________.

(a) consider going into education as a career
(b) realize how much I wanted my old job back
(c) work with students in a less demanding way
(d) refine my lessons for my public school students

4. If you need an exterminator to get rid of unwanted guests in your house, call Exterminator Plus. No need to look elsewhere because we ________________________________. With our years of expertise, we pinpoint the reason for infestation instantly and start treating it immediately. While one round of extermination is sufficient for some infestations, more serious cases require multiple steps, so we tailor our service to meet your needs. Don't be fooled by cheap extermination services that only provide temporary solutions. Exterminator Plus will take the time to make sure your pests don't return, or your money back.

(a) can solve any pest infestation with one simple procedure
(b) exterminate pests twice as fast as other exterminators
(c) guarantee to solve your pest problems permanently
(d) will match the advertised price of any competitor

5. Here at Merit Construction and Design, we are dedicated to building eco-friendly commercial high rises. Sustainable development is the driving force behind our high-end buildings, from using low-wattage lighting to installing efficient air conditioning systems in our skyscrapers. Our commitment to reducing our buildings' carbon footprint has earned us the endorsement of the Environmental Protection Foundation. We are proud to say that our mission is to ________________________________.

(a) provide housing for residents of all income levels
(b) lead the industry in preserving historic construction
(c) make a better future for the planet with our buildings
(d) build a city with lower skylines and more green spaces

6. The Columbia River dam system, with 14 dams on the river's main branch and hundreds more on its tributaries, has caused considerable controversy. Environmentalists protest that some dams should be torn down because they are damaging salmon populations by impeding their migration up and down the river. On the other hand, the system's advocates argue that the dams should be maintained because they provide much needed hydropower to the entire region. The debate between the two groups centers mostly on whether ________________________________.

(a) repairs to the tributary dams would be economical
(b) nature's needs should be put ahead of human needs
(c) the dams are hurting the region's population density
(d) it is ethical to fish for salmon in the Pacific Northwest

7. *Hamlet* has elicited more critical responses than any of Shakespeare's other tragedies, and critics have recently commented that ______________________________. For instance, compared with the protagonists in Shakespeare's other tragedies, *Hamlet* has many more opportunities to display his wit and humor to the audience. And perhaps in proportion to the immensity of its tragedy, the play contains more subtle moments of comic relief than either *King Lear* or *Macbeth*. The stark contrast between the play's comic elements and its woeful conclusion contributes to its enduring appeal.

(a) it is flawed because of its over-reliance on comedic elements
(b) it deserves to be eclipsed by other tragedies such as *Macbeth*
(c) its use of humor is well-intentioned but ultimately misplaced
(d) its greatness stems partly from the effective use of comic relief

8. Authors Per Wahlöö and Maj Sjöwall have long been known in their native Sweden for the masterful crime novels they wrote together in the 1960s, some of which have been adapted for the screen. After the recent phenomenal global success of fellow Swedish author Stieg Larsson's *Millennium* trilogy, ______________________________. The spotlight on Swedish crime novels has encouraged English-speaking readers unfamiliar with Sweden's tradition of excellent crime fiction to seek out other Scandinavian crime fiction, and they have discovered Wahlöö and Sjöwall. Publishers have issued new English editions of the couple's ten-novel series about the detective Martin Beck.

(a) the pair's crime novels have started to gain a wider audience
(b) the suspicious similarity between the authors has been pointed out
(c) there are calls to adapt more English novels into Swedish crime films
(d) the pressure is on to find the next popular fiction genre in Scandinavia

9. Traditionally, newspaper editors have been careful in handling political scandals of a personal nature. For instance, during President Clinton's extramarital affair, writers followed guidelines that directed them to publish stories appropriate for readers of all ages. However, in the era of Internet news, ______________________________.Websites often have looser restrictions on what they will publish and can disseminate graphic images and salacious details, which tend to attract readers. This has presented traditional news editors with a difficult choice between lowering standards to satisfy readers' curiosity on one hand and maintaining their commitment to decorum in news coverage on the other.

(a) politicians cannot count on constituent support during scandals
(b) government officials are using websites to spread their message
(c) subscribers are demanding more discretion on the part of editors
(d) newspapers face a dilemma competing with online media's candor

**10.** Throughout his reign, King James I of England ______________________. James espoused the view that a king's rule was a manifestation of the apostolic succession of the Christian Church. He believed in the divine right of kings and saw himself as a superordinate ruler with no obligation to submit to any authority. His Parliament took a different view, however. They claimed that the king was bound by Parliamentary decisions and that the subsidies Parliament granted the Crown should ensure royal cooperation. These opposing views led to tremendous strife during James's reign, and he twice dissolved the Parliament over financial and diplomatic disputes.

(a) criticized Parliament for demanding large grants from the Crown
(b) disagreed with Parliament over the extent of royal prerogative
(c) struggled with the Church over claims to apostolic succession
(d) challenged those who questioned the authority of Parliament

**11.**

Dear Editor:

I am writing to complain about ______________________. Last week your newspaper published an editorial by Jerry Grey in favor of the proposed Delanco County landfill. Grey wrote persuasively about the project's benefits for the community but neglected to mention that he's not just expressing the interests of a concerned citizen: he owns a business which is bidding for the contract to manage the landfill and stands to profit greatly from the project. I ask that The Delanco Times be more honest about writers' motivations.

Sincerely,
John Manus

(a) Delanco County's inefficient waste management
(b) the huge profits being made from landfills in our town
(c) the lack of coverage of Delanco's new landfill proposal
(d) your newspaper's failure to disclose a writer's affiliation

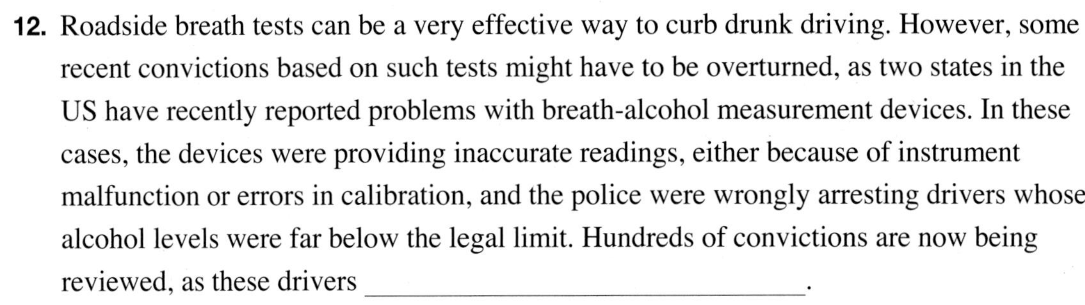

**12.** Roadside breath tests can be a very effective way to curb drunk driving. However, some recent convictions based on such tests might have to be overturned, as two states in the US have recently reported problems with breath-alcohol measurement devices. In these cases, the devices were providing inaccurate readings, either because of instrument malfunction or errors in calibration, and the police were wrongly arresting drivers whose alcohol levels were far below the legal limit. Hundreds of convictions are now being reviewed, as these drivers ______________________________.

(a) have successfully completed driver alcohol education programs
(b) would have tested below the new legal blood alcohol limit
(c) were found to have been offering bribes to police officers
(d) may have merely been victims of faulty equipment

**13.** Recent trends in the video game market have defied game creators' expectations about women's preferences. Historically, the gaming world has been dominated by men, but now 42% of serious gamers in the US are women, and many of them are playing the same games that have typically appealed to men. The long-held belief that women are turned off by games' violent storylines and male protagonists appears to be untrue, and game creators are pleased that ______________________________.

(a) their forecasts about market trends turned out to be accurate
(b) their attempts to make games more female-friendly have worked
(c) they have attracted a new audience without altering games' content
(d) women's increased participation will moderate the violence of gamers

**14.** Cultural critic and media commentator Marshall McLuhan distinguished between "hot" and "cool" media based on ______________________________. According to him, hot media like photographs or lectures usually engage one sense predominantly and allow the audience to be passive. On the other hand, cool media like television or seminars ask for more effort on the part of consumers, who must be more actively involved in the perception of meaning. Some critics have objected to the obscurity of the distinction between hot and cool media, but the idea still holds its place as a pioneering theory in media studies.

(a) the emotional impact they have on consumers
(b) how popular they are with modern audiences
(c) the degree of user participation they require
(d) how susceptible they are to critical reviews

**15.** Applicants to Bremer University are required to submit a statement of purpose along with the general application form. This should include information about the applicant's background and abilities, as well as long-term career plans. This essay is an opportunity for applicants to express their goals more thoroughly than the fill-in-the-blank application allows for. ______________________________, it gives admission officers a chance to gauge the applicant's ability to write a well-organized and coherent essay.

(a) Again
(b) Even so
(c) In addition
(d) Admittedly

**16.** Traditionally, linguists were limited to academic jobs, and many people believed that theoretical linguistics was an esoteric, ivory-tower pastime. However, this image has changed, as technology firms have realized the importance of linguistics for their industry. It is theoretical linguists who have modeled the syntactic and phonetic processes of natural language and made them accessible to computer science. ______________________________, many of the modern developments in automatic translation and voice recognition technology would not have been possible without the contributions of linguists.

(a) Indeed
(b) Eventually
(c) Regardless
(d) Meanwhile

**Part II** **Questions 17–37**

Read the passage, question, and options. Then, based on the given information, choose the option that best answers the question.

**17.** Although the Solar System is commonly thought of as the sun and its orbiting planets, it actually extends much farther. Beyond Neptune lies the Kuiper belt, a region similar to an asteroid belt except that it is much larger. The Kuiper belt itself is roughly one-thousandth the size of the Oort cloud, which is a spherical cloud of comets that extends one light year out from the sun. The edge of the Oort cloud is commonly accepted as the outer limit of the Solar System.

Q: What is the main purpose of the passage?
(a) To classify different types of planets
(b) To explain the Kuiper belt's location
(c) To propose the existence of the Oort Cloud
(d) To describe what the Solar System encompasses

**18.** Worried about looking your best this summer? Then visit Dr. Kline at the Nirvana Medical Center today! Dr. Kline is a leading specialist in all areas of medical aesthetics including hair removal, liposuction, botox, and skin rejuvenation. With over twenty years of experience and hundreds of satisfied patients, Nirvana Medical Center can get you the results you want. We're conveniently located in the heart of downtown, right across from Nirvana Fitness and Swimming. Come in for your free consultation today!

Q: What is mainly being advertised?
(a) A cosmetic medical clinic
(b) A newly opened medical center
(c) A summer skin-care package special
(d) A diet clinic and fitness membership deal

19. Sleep deprivation has tremendous observable effects on brain function. Namely, unrelated areas of the brain activate to compensate for lost functioning in the target areas. For instance, when sleep-deprived subjects are presented with a verbal test, instead of showing activity in the brain's temporal lobe, which is responsible for language, they show increased activity in the parietal lobe, which is mainly responsible for quantitative reasoning. In tests of movement, sleep-deprived subjects also exhibit activity in areas of the brain where motor functions are not normally processed.

Q: What is the writer's main point about sleep deprivation?
(a) It increases neural activity in the temporal lobe.
(b) It causes brain functions to be re-distributed.
(c) It can permanently damage the brain's circuitry.
(d) It impairs cognitive tasks more than locomotive ones.

20.

Dear Clark City Resident:

This winter, the city will implement temporary on-street parking bans on major side roads in order to facilitate street snow plowing. Affected roads will have "No Parking" snow removal signs posted in November. When 3 inches or more of snow is forecasted or when a snow emergency is declared, residents are not allowed to park on these streets. Any cars left on the street will be towed at the owner's expense.

Sincerely,
Clark City Public Works

Q: What is the letter mainly about?
(a) A temporary parking ban on all city streets
(b) New harsher penalties for parking violations
(c) The city's street parking policy in snowy weather
(d) How snow emergencies will be declared to citizens

**21.** Technology has made bullying a more complicated phenomenon than ever, and while many parents are rightly worried about schoolyard bullying, text messaging through cell phones may actually be of greater concern. Bullying via text messaging is on the rise: according to one recent study, the incidence of harassment via texting was up 10% from the previous year, while outright physical bullying at schools was up only 2%. The fact that text messaging is difficult to monitor and control makes this form of bullying particularly pernicious.

Q: What is the main idea of the article?
(a) Cell phone usage should be banned during school hours.
(b) Texting has spurred an increase in physical bullying.
(c) Texting has become a serious means of harassment.
(d) Acts of bullying have diminished in recent years.

**22.** The Great Alaskan Earthquake of 1964, with a record-breaking magnitude of 9.2 on the Richter scale, was crucial in establishing the West Coast and Alaska Tsunami Warning Center. The earthquake itself caused considerable property damage, but it was the subsequent tsunamis that caused the majority of the 143 fatalities. Government officials were awakened to the importance of proper monitoring systems, and they collaborated with seismologists to set up the center in the hope that similar disasters could be predicted in the future.

Q: What is the writer's main point about the Great Alaskan Earthquake of 1964?
(a) Seismologists working in Alaska predicted it.
(b) It caused a record amount of property damage.
(c) It highlighted the need for effective alert systems.
(d) Officials disregarded seismologists' warnings about it.

**23.** The university offers special transportation services during the last week of each semester. A free airport shuttle bus, which runs once at 7 am and then again at 1 pm, departs from the main campus gate. Students must sign up for this shuttle bus at the Student Union as space is limited. Also, students can purchase reduced-rate intercity bus tickets at the Union for several major cities in the state. Tickets are non-refundable, but dates may be changed at no extra charge based on availability.

Q: Which of the following is correct according to the announcement?
(a) Airport shuttle services operate throughout the semester.
(b) The airport shuttle runs once an hour from 7 am to 1 pm.
(c) The Student Union offers reduced-rate bus tickets for cities nationwide.
(d) The date of an intercity bus ticket can be altered without additional costs.

**24.** Excavations of the ancient city of Guzana have shown that it thrived in trade even though contemporary civilizations nearby were in decline at the time. Taking advantage of its fortunate location along a tributary of the Euphrates river, the city amassed a fortune trading ivory carved from Mesopotamian elephant tusks. It used its profits to build a massive citadel-palace surrounded by walls 12 meters high. The opulent fortress housed mysterious, human-sized statues of griffins, sphinxes, and other mythical creatures.

Q: Which of the following is correct about Guzana according to the passage?
(a) It was surrounded by similarly flourishing civilizations.
(b) It benefited from its prime location near a waterway.
(c) It traded its massive fortune for elephant tusks.
(d) It used its wealth to build 12-meter statues of sphinxes.

**25.** Most urban areas are noticeably warmer than the surrounding rural areas, a phenomenon known as the urban heat island (UHI) effect. Compared with trees, grass, and bodies of water, the materials used in urban development, such as bricks and cement, retain the warmth of sunlight for longer. As cities grow, they employ more heat-absorbing materials and use more sources of artificial heat, such as interior climate control, so a proportional increase in temperature can be observed. The UHI effect is most clearly observed during the night, when natural terrain quickly cools but the built environment remains warm by comparison.

Q: Which of the following is correct according to the passage?
(a) Building materials lose heat faster than natural terrain.
(b) Interior climate control does not contribute to UHI effects.
(c) An increase in UHI effects is proportional to a city's growth.
(d) UHI effects are most noticeable when the sun is out.

**26.**

> To the director:
>
> Due to a medical problem, I could not attend the scheduled level test for Summer Spanish School on May 24 nor make the full payment by the May 25 due date. I wrote an email on May 17 explaining the situation and requested a make-up test and a payment deadline extension. I received no reply and found that my name had been removed from the registration list. I still wish to take the course and will make the payment as soon as I take the placement test. Please contact me to discuss this further.
>
> Sincerely,
> Katie Price

Q: Which of the following is correct about Katie Price according to the letter?
(a) She is writing to request a refund for a Spanish course.
(b) She had notified the school that she would miss the test.
(c) She was removed from the class at her own request.
(d) She made the full payment after the due date passed.

**27.** Looking for a fun-filled weekend getaway? Take a trip to Atlantic City! Weekend express trains from New York City cost only $60 round-trip, and trains from Philadelphia are just $20 there and back. Home to eleven casinos and America's first oceanfront boardwalk, Atlantic City has activities to suit every taste. Not interested in gambling? Check out one of the city's six malls, or visit the Atlantic City Convention Center for an interactive display about the city's history as the former home of the Miss America beauty pageant.

Q: Which of the following is correct about Atlantic City according to the advertisement?
(a) It is cheaper to get there from New York City than from Philadelphia.
(b) It is home to more shopping malls than gambling establishments.
(c) It boasts the oldest oceanfront boardwalk built in the nation.
(d) It is currently the host of the Miss America competitions.

**28.** In Bali, *ngerorod*, or elopement, is the most common form of marriage because it is much cheaper than a traditional, more formal ceremony, *mapadik*. In the former practice, the honeymoon actually precedes the wedding ceremony. *Ngerorod* also reflects the playful and theatrical tendencies of the Balinese people in that it involves a staged kidnapping of the bride by her future husband. Even the bride's parents, who are often knowing participants in the whole scheme, make a great show of pretending to be opposed to the event.

Q: Which of the following is correct about *ngerorod* according to the passage?
(a) It is considered more formal than *mapadik*.
(b) It features the wedding after the honeymoon.
(c) It tends to be subdued and carried out in secret.
(d) It is always performed without the parents' consent.

**29.** ProSearch provides quality human resource solutions for the financial sector internationally. Whether you need to fill temporary or permanent positions, our recruiters will find you the best candidates in accounting, asset management, commercial banking, and other financial services roles. Since opening our headquarters in Canada more than a decade ago, we at ProSearch have built up a network of more than 200 employment agencies, serving clients in the US, Canada, and Europe.

Q: Which of the following is correct about ProSearch according to the advertisement?
(a) It only offers short-term job placement services.
(b) It specializes in finance-related job recruitment.
(c) It has its headquarters in the United States.
(d) It has been in operation for almost ten years.

**30.** Using tree growth rings, archaeologists have found a connection between climate and the rise and fall of civilizations. When the climate is conducive to plant growth, trees form broad rings, but when the climate discourages growth, such as during a drought, the rings are much closer together. Researchers examined nearly one thousand cross-sectional slices of trees, dating from 2000 BC to the present, and found that favorable climate conditions, as evidenced by broad growth rings, corresponded with periods of prosperity, while periods of difficult weather coincided with turmoil and hardship.

Q: Which of the following is correct according to the passage?
(a) Trees form narrowly spaced rings in favorable climates.
(b) The study looked at about two thousand tree samples.
(c) Researchers did not examine modern trees in the study.
(d) Broad growth rings corresponded with periods of affluence.

**31.** "Pediatric Allergies in America" is the largest and most comprehensive quantitative study on the extent to which allergies affect children. The study surveyed 500 children with allergies, an equal number of those without, and 500 physicians who had treated children with allergies. It found that allergies often interfered with children's sleep and daily activities: 40% of children with allergies suffered from sleep deprivation, and 28% of them reported having to avoid certain daily activities to prevent a flare-up of their symptoms. The majority of allergy sufferers took both over-the-counter and prescription medicines to cope with the condition.

Q: Which of the following is correct according to the passage?
(a) The research examined allergies in both children and adults.
(b) The study included 500 children who did not suffer from allergies.
(c) Allergies forced 40% of child sufferers to refrain from daily activities.
(d) Children used over-the-counter medications but not prescriptions.

**32.** Many people know that French artist Edgar Degas was a talented painter, but few are aware that he was also a prolific sculptor. This is likely because Degas only exhibited a single sculpture during his lifetime. His bronze statue *Little Dancer Aged Fourteen*, sculpted first as a wax figure, was shown in Paris at the Sixth Impressionist Exhibition of 1881. After his death in 1917, over 150 of his wax sculptures were discovered, most of which had already begun to deteriorate. Seventy-three of these were in sufficiently good condition to be cast in bronze and were eventually presented at posthumous exhibitions.

Q: Which of the following is correct about Degas according to the passage?
(a) He was very well known for his various sculpture exhibitions.
(b) He cast *Little Dancer Aged Fourteen* in bronze after sculpting it in wax.
(c) The only sculpture he ever made was shown at an 1881 exhibition in Paris.
(d) All wax sculptures found posthumously were sufficiently intact to be cast in bronze.

**33.** My wife and I usually spend our holidays at home doing activities we enjoy, such as gardening. Although we had originally planned to spend last Memorial Day weekend at home, we abruptly decided to travel to the mountains. However, the highway was jam packed, and it took us twice the normal travel time to get there. Also, all the nice hotels were all booked up, and we ended up staying at a shabby motel. In the end, our attempt at spontaneity did not work out.

Q: Which statement would the writer most likely agree with?
(a) Vacations are too stressful to plan in advance.
(b) Staying home during holidays wastes vacation time.
(c) Spontaneous vacations are the best way to increase satisfaction.
(d) Advance planning increases the likelihood of an enjoyable vacation.

**34.** The American Library of Congress hosts a collection of endangered music, aimed at preserving traditional musical forms. The Endangered Music Project, as the collection is called, includes recordings of traditional music from the indigenous cultures of Brazil, Indonesia, and West Africa, among others. Globalization and modernization have caused the loss of countless traditional musical cultures. Yet these same forces have made it easier than ever to preserve and disseminate humanity's musical heritage. The Endangered Music Project is dedicated to ensuring the survival of traditional music.

Q: What can be inferred about the Endangered Music Project from the passage?
(a) Its main purpose is to help indigenous cultures develop new musical techniques.
(b) It enables Americans to experience music that is difficult to access otherwise.
(c) Its mission is to educate indigenous cultures about modern instruments.
(d) It houses its recordings in diverse countries around the world.

**35.** Standard English is held in higher regard than other dialects of English, but it is important to remember that this is only due to social motivations. While standard English may be the most socially accepted dialect of English, it is simply one set of grammatical and pronunciation rules. Like standard English, ethnic dialects or regional variants of English feature regular, observable patterns in pronunciation, vocabulary, and grammar, and they are no less valid from a structural perspective.

Q: Which statement would the writer most likely agree with?
(a) Regional dialects are less controversial than ethnic ones.
(b) Standard grammar usage reflects a speaker's intelligence.
(c) No dialect of English is linguistically superior to any other.
(d) Most regional dialects tend to share the same grammar patterns.

**36.** Used books in good condition are accepted for donation at Antioch Public Library. Donations can be made at any time during library hours. Please note that if you wish to donate books, you must first bring them to the collections manager for inspection. Books must be deemed current, relevant, and in demand in order to be accepted. Some books in good condition that do not meet these criteria may still be accepted and put aside for our monthly book sales.

Q: What can be inferred about the library from the passage?
(a) It only welcomes donations shortly before book sales.
(b) It will accept donated books in place of overdue fees.
(c) It passes unneeded donations on to other charities.
(d) It reserves the right to reject unwanted donations.

**37.** With an aging population straining the country's health services, it is clear that health care spending needs to be reined in to avoid incurring severe deficits. Surely politicians are well aware of this, but both parties have produced very similar plans that include health care spending increases of 6% per year over the next five years. With an election looming, it seems that neither conservatives nor liberals are willing to risk the electorate's wrath by administering a healthy dose of reality about health care.

Q: Which statement would the writer most likely agree with?
(a) Politicians in both major parties are pandering to the electorate.
(b) Major spending increases should be made to maintain health care.
(c) Raising taxes is the only solution to the government's budget deficit.
(d) Collaboration between parties is addressing health care budget problems.

## Part III Questions 38–40

Read the passage and identify the option that does NOT belong.

**38.** Fruit juice is often criticized for having poor nutritional value, but it can be a good source of vitamins and minerals. (a) Nutritionists recommend that people consume five portions of fruit per day, and fruit juice fulfills this requirement. (b) In fact, pure fruit juice that does not contain additives or extra sugar is just as nutritious as fresh fruit. (c) Many juice companies advertise "superfruits," such as the acai berry, the health benefits of which may have been overstated. (d) Ultimately, fruit juice is an easy and convenient way to reach the recommended daily servings of fruit.

**39.** While some people take up bicycling for health reasons, many choose to do it on ecological grounds. (a) They claim that it is irresponsible to add to carbon emissions by using a car, when bicycling is an alternative. (b) And evidence supports their claim: researchers estimate that about 40% of hazardous air pollutants come from cars. (c) The National Highway Transportation Administration reports that cycling's new-found popularity has caused an increase in accidents. (d) Biking advocates note that, in addition to its ecological benefits, cycling cuts down on traffic congestion as well.

**40.** In 2011, the hole in the ozone layer above the Arctic was larger than it had ever been before. (a) The hole, which has been observed every year since 1980, appears most clearly in winter and early spring. (b) It occurs when the stratosphere is cold enough to enable the formation of ozone-destroying chlorine compounds. (c) The ultraviolet light absorbed by the ozone layer can harm plants and animals if they are overexposed to it. (d) And since global warming actually cools the upper stratosphere, where ozone is located, the hole is predicted to grow.

This is the end of the Reading Comprehension section. Please remain seated until the proctor has instructed otherwise. You are NOT allowed to turn to any other section of the test.

# 서울대 최신기출 4

***Listening*** *Comprehension*

***Grammar***

***Vocabulary***

***Reading*** *Comprehension*

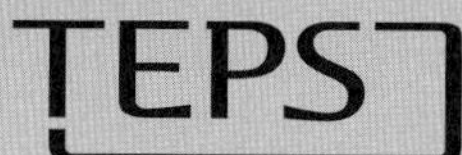

# LISTENING COMPREHENSION

## DIRECTIONS

1. In the Listening Comprehension section, all content will be presented orally rather than in written form.
2. This section contains four parts, each with fifteen individual items. For each part, you will receive separate instructions. Listen to the instructions carefully, and choose the best answer from the options for each item.

Scripts P 298 / 정답 P 331

**Part I** **Questions 1–15**

You will now hear fifteen individual spoken questions or statements, each followed by four spoken responses. Choose the most appropriate response for each item.

**Part II** **Questions 16–30**

You will now hear fifteen short conversation fragments, followed by four spoken responses. Choose the most appropriate response to complete each conversation.

**Part III** **Questions 31—45**

You will now hear fifteen complete conversations. For each conversation, you will be asked to answer a question. Each conversation and its corresponding question will be read twice. Then you will hear four options which will be read only once. Based on the given information, choose the option that best answers the question.

**Part IV** **Questions 46—60**

You will now hear fifteen short talks. After each talk, you will be asked to answer a question. Each talk and its corresponding question will be read twice. Then you will hear four options which will be read only once. Based on the given information, choose the option that best answers the question.

TEPS

# GRAMMAR

## DIRECTIONS

This section tests your grammar skills. You will have 25 minutes to complete the 50 questions. Be sure to follow the directions given by the proctor.

정답 P 331

## Part I Questions 1—20

Choose the option that best completes each gap.

**1.** A: Are you familiar with Jane Ingle's books?

B: Yes, ___________ of her recent novels was part of my summer reading.

(a) such
(b) this
(c) any
(d) one

**2.** A: May I have another slice of cake?

B: Sure, help yourself to ___________ piece.

(a) last
(b) the last
(c) any last
(d) some last

**3.** A: Did Jen come to the meeting on time?

B: No, she was late again, ___________ is why I'm so annoyed with her.

(a) that
(b) what
(c) when
(d) which

**4.** A: Are the steaks done? Remember, I like mine rare.

B: That's dangerous. You ___________ let me cook it to be at least medium.

(a) can
(b) may
(c) would
(d) should

**5.** A: Is everyone eligible to register for the marathon?

B: Only those who have qualified in a previous run ___________.

(a) is allowed
(b) is allowing
(c) are allowed
(d) are allowing

**6.** A: Did you happen ___________ the telephone bill, by any chance?

B: I think it's on the kitchen table.

(a) to see
(b) seeing
(c) to be seeing
(d) having seen

**7.** A: Do you work out every single day?

B: Yep, I ___________ regularly since high school.

(a) have been exercising
(b) am exercising
(c) had exercised
(d) exercise

**8.** A: Eric, you look worried.

B: Oh, I ___________ about tomorrow's math exam.

(a) think
(b) was thinking
(c) have thought
(d) will be thinking

**9.** A: Have you bought your textbooks for this semester?

B: Not yet, but ___________ to the bookstore later.

(a) I've been going
(b) I'll have gone
(c) I'm going
(d) I've gone

**10.** A: I haven't seen David around for a while.

B: I heard he changed schools, ___________ I don't know why he did.

(a) once
(b) although
(c) as though
(d) provided that

**11.** A: I'm moving to New York next year.

B: I used to live there, so just ask if you want ___________.

(a) advices
(b) an advice
(c) any advice
(d) any advices

**12.** A: Thanks so much for picking up my mail while I was gone.

B: You live right next door so it was ___________.

(a) at all no bother
(b) no bother at all
(c) not at all bother
(d) bother not at all

**13.** A: Andrew's really interested in cars.

B: I know. He's dedicated to ___________ everything he can about them.

(a) learn
(b) learning
(c) be learning
(d) have learned

**14.** A: Dr. Peters, can Ted leave the hospital today?

B: I suggest he ___________ the night, just to be safe.

(a) spend
(b) spends
(c) will spend
(d) is spending

**15.** A: My children ___________.

B: Mine are too busy with their own lives, as well.

(a) barely ever call
(b) never barely call me
(c) barely ever call to me
(d) never call to me barely

**16.** A: Would you rather have dinner at home or go out?

B: I'm fine with ___________ option is easiest for you.

(a) every
(b) either
(c) another
(d) whichever

**17.** A: How's Emily doing with the baby?
B: Just great. She's __________ I've ever seen.

(a) a mother as loving anyone as
(b) as loving a mother as anyone
(c) a mother loving as anyone as
(d) as loving anyone as a mother

**18.** A: Did you pick up our dry cleaning?
B: No, __________ swamped at work, I couldn't.

(a) been
(b) to be
(c) being
(d) to have been

**19.** A: Did you hear that a movie ticket is $10 __________ person now?
B: Yes. Going to the movies is unaffordable these days.

(a) with
(b) per
(c) for
(d) to

**20.** A: How can we increase the competitiveness of our company?
B: I think we should __________ the quality of our products.

(a) set our sights on improving
(b) improve setting on our sights
(c) improve on setting our sights
(d) set on our sights on improving

## Part II Questions 21–40

Choose the option that best completes each gap.

**21.** Tom always promises that he __________ the dog for a walk but then ends up just watching TV instead.

(a) took
(b) takes
(c) will take
(d) has taken

**22.** __________ more support to win the election, the gubernatorial candidate made more public appearances.

(a) Needed
(b) Needing
(c) To be needing
(d) To have needed

**23.** When she picked up her son from the babysitter's, Rosemary was upset to hear he __________ since she left.

(a) has cried
(b) will have cried
(c) has been crying
(d) had been crying

**24.** The dilapidated houses, or at least __________, illustrated just how deserted the neighborhood had become.

(a) what they remained of
(b) they remained of what
(c) of what remained them
(d) what remained of them

**25.** The judge said that the claims presented by the advertising company ___________ nothing more than lies.

(a) was
(b) were
(c) is being
(d) are being

**26.** The financial planner advised Paula and Gary that their assets, ___________, should be thoroughly reviewed.

(a) be they liquid or otherwise
(b) they are liquid or otherwise
(c) to be liquid or otherwise not
(d) otherwise they are liquid or not

**27.** Lawrence canceled his trip since he is busy with work and will have ___________ time for a vacation.

(a) a few
(b) few
(c) any
(d) no

**28.** At $21,000, the car was ___________ over the couple's budget of $20,000.

(a) so
(b) just
(c) that
(d) quite

**29.** ___________ in the context of other industrialized nations, the speed of South Korea's development was unprecedented.

(a) Viewed
(b) Viewing
(c) To be viewed
(d) Having viewed

**30.** The teacher laughed at Mary's tale about why her homework was late because ___________ such an absurd story.

(a) had a student before never told
(b) never had before a student told
(c) had never a student told before
(d) never before had a student told

**31.** If Carl had not put on a helmet when he went for a bike ride, he ___________ much more seriously hurt when he fell.

(a) was
(b) could be
(c) had been
(d) could have been

**32.** The outcome of the experiment was the opposite of ___________ scientists had expected to happen.

(a) that
(b) what
(c) which
(d) whom

**33.** Marion ___________ that she already had an invitation to next week's ball.

(a) has flattered
(b) was flattered
(c) had been flattered
(d) had been flattering

**34.** Sheila wore her red dress to her job interview even though her sister ___________.

(a) urged not
(b) urged to not
(c) urged her not
(d) urged her not to

GRAMMAR

**35.** After being stopped unfairly by a police officer, Robert went to appeals court, and the ticket ___________ for speeding was dismissed.

(a) issued
(b) issuing
(c) to issue
(d) was issued

**36.** Gina felt an instant kinship with Robin and considered her a good friend despite ___________.

(a) her just being introduced to
(b) she had just been introduced
(c) she had just introduced to her
(d) having just been introduced to her

**37.** A recent study ___________ that emotional and physical pain are similar may explain the brain's response to unpleasant events.

(a) to have demonstrated
(b) demonstrating
(c) demonstrated
(d) demonstrates

**38.** The newest hybrid car from the automaker Venus gets up to 400 miles ___________ a single tank of gas.

(a) by
(b) on
(c) at
(d) in

**39.** Music programs are one area ___________ many school districts often make cuts during periods of budgetary difficulty.

(a) that
(b) which
(c) in that
(d) in which

**40.** Meteorologists failed to ___________ and were surprised when the hurricane missed Florida's coast.

(a) account the winds for changing
(b) account for changing the winds
(c) take changing winds into account
(d) take account into changing winds

GRAMMAR

## Part III Questions 41–45

Read each sentence carefully and identify the option that contains a grammatical error.

**41.** (a) A: When was the last time you paid a visit to the dentist?
(b) B: It's been quite some time, but I haven't had any problems.
(c) A: Well, it's important to get your teeth checked regular.
(d) B: I know, but as far as I can tell, my teeth seem just fine.

**42.** (a) A: Do you have a copy of my schedule for this afternoon?
(b) B: Yes. You have two meetings, including one with the boss.
(c) A: What's on the agenda for that meeting? Is there anything major?
(d) B: No, it's just about advertising, and it will hold at 5 pm.

**43.** (a) A: I'm usually a fan of horror movies, but that one was a letdown.
(b) B: Still, I thought it was better than the original version from the 1970s.
(c) A: I haven't seen that one I can't compare them, but the acting in this one was horrid.
(d) B: I'd agree it was a little exaggerated, especially toward the end.

**44.** (a) A: What did you think about the countryside bike tour last week?
(b) B: It was fun, but I need to have done without the visit to the winery.
(c) A: But the vineyards are what make the region famous with tourists.
(d) B: I know, but the markup on the wine struck me as ridiculous.

**45.** (a) A: I wonder what's on the cafeteria's menu for today.
(b) B: It doesn't matter to me. Everything there tastes the same.
(c) A: Really? I have been rather pleased with the variety of meals offered there.
(d) B: Trust me, you'll find yourself getting tired of soon.

## Part IV Questions 46–50

Read each sentence carefully and identify the option that contains a grammatical error.

**46.** (a) Known for their incredibly bright colors, poison dart frogs are fascinating animals. (b) Although typically small, the more larger species grow up to six centimeters. (c) They are poisonous, secreting toxins through their skin for defense. (d) The brighter their color, the more toxic they are to predators.

**47.** (a) Even though both are classified as arthropods, spiders and insects are considerably different. (b) For one, insects have three body parts, six legs, two compound eyes, and two antennae. (c) Spiders, on the other hand, have a different anatomy, including two body parts, eight legs, and four eyes. (d) In addition to their physical differences, spiders are always predators, so insects are not.

**48.** (a) With the Great Depression of 1929 came significant changes to people's dietary habits. (b) Most families were too poor to be able to afford luxuries such as meat and produce. (c) And even if they could afford them, people still had to ration with their food, making it stretch. (d) Many people turned to bread and soup to fill themselves up throughout the economic downturn.

**49.** (a) Followers of the Paleolithic lifestyle attempt to live as ancient humans did. (b) They pursue a natural lifestyle similar to that of hunter-gatherers. (c) A Paleolithic diet including meat, fish, and produce are a major part of the movement. (d) Followers also replicate Paleolithic habits such as going barefoot and staying outdoors.

**50.** (a) The effects of obesity on the human lifespan have been the subject of scientific debate. (b) Some researchers point to a strong correlation between obesity and a shortened lifespan. (c) But others point out that the precise causal mechanism of this relationship to be unclear. (d) They insist on the need for evidence showing the biochemical effects of fat on a cellular level.

This is the end of the Grammar section. Do NOT move on to the next section until instructed to do so. You are NOT allowed to turn to any other section of the test.

TEPS

# VOCABULARY

## DIRECTIONS

This section tests your vocabulary skills. You will have 15 minutes to complete the 50 questions. Be sure to follow the directions given by the proctor.

정답 P 331

**Part I** **Questions 1—25**

Choose the option that best completes each gap.

**1.** A: So what are you going to call your newborn?

B: I think I'll ___________ her after her great-aunt.

(a) pick
(b) refer
(c) name
(d) assign

**2.** A: Did you buy a new kind of coffee? It's very weak.

B: Yeah, I should have just gone with our usual ___________.

(a) model
(b) badge
(c) brand
(d) mark

**3.** A: Would you please make me some tea?

B: Sure, let me ___________ some water.

(a) bubble
(b) steam
(c) steep
(d) boil

**4.** A: Did you get your soda for free?

B: Yes. I wasn't ___________ for it because I brought in a coupon.

(a) serviced
(b) charged
(c) spared
(d) paid

**5.** A: Bill and Janie are sure getting along well.

B: Yes, with all their shared interests, they do seem to be very ___________.

(a) inclusive
(b) equivalent
(c) compatible
(d) appropriate

**6.** A: Do you ever see deer at your cottage?

B: All the time. They're ___________ in the area.

(a) intimate
(b) common
(c) knowing
(d) particular

**7.** A: Front desk? We're out of towels.

B: I'll send someone up to ___________ your supply.

(a) generate
(b) restock
(c) exhibit
(d) hoard

**8.** A: Let's be sure to bring bug spray on our hike.

B: Right, we'll need something to ___________ the mosquitoes.

(a) repel
(b) violate
(c) neglect
(d) drizzle

**9.** A: Why do immigration officials have to scan our passports?

B: They do it to ___________ that the passports are genuine.

(a) ensure
(b) sustain
(c) accredit
(d) condone

**10.** A: Did my golf ball land on the green?

B: No, you've ___________ the green—the ball's in the bunker past it.

(a) outdone
(b) overshot
(c) overhauled
(d) outmatched

**11.** A: Do you keep in touch with Kyle?

B: Yes. We mainly ___________ by email.

(a) recall
(b) indicate
(c) announce
(d) correspond

**12.** A: I need some tips on making my accent less ___________.

B: Don't worry—it'll gradually disappear as your fluency improves.

(a) discreet
(b) genuine
(c) convincing
(d) pronounced

**13.** A: Was Kelly amazed by the new 3D movie?

B: Of course, she ___________ at the animation.

(a) scoffed
(b) exhaled
(c) marveled
(d) shuddered

**14.** A: Dad is furious because I dented his new car.

B: Just wait for his anger to ___________ and talk to him when he's calmer.

(a) hanker
(b) swerve
(c) subside
(d) devolve

**15.** A: Your watch looks quite old—is it a(n) ___________?

B: Yes, I inherited it from my great-grandmother.

(a) investment
(b) entailment
(c) heirloom
(d) heritage

**16.** A: How did your presentation turn out?

B: My hard work paid off, and the ___________ was great.

(a) stimulus
(b) outcome
(c) aftermath
(d) remainder

**17.** A: Participants on my tours seem bored by long explanations.

B: Then you'd better make your comments as ___________ as possible.

(a) docile
(b) concise
(c) taciturn
(d) brusque

**18.** A: Have you chosen a holiday destination yet?

B: No. I want to __________ for a few more days before deciding.

(a) see it through
(b) mull it over
(c) hash it up
(d) pass it off

**19.** A: Aren't roller coasters terrifying?

B: On the contrary, I feel __________ whenever I ride them.

(a) frugal
(b) ravenous
(c) exhilarated
(d) disheartened

**20.** A: The bribery scandal has really damaged the senator's public image.

B: Yes, the whole ordeal has __________ his reputation.

(a) etched
(b) tainted
(c) decayed
(d) disarmed

**21.** A: Do you think my speech will make the protesters less angry?

B: No, I don't think it's going to __________ the crowd.

(a) mediate
(b) muster
(c) mollify
(d) malign

**22.** A: Your abrupt outburst this morning really frightened Heather.

B: I know. I'll apologize for __________ at her later.

(a) razing
(b) clipping
(c) breezing
(d) snapping

**23.** A: Is there any way I can see a model of the new website?

B: Sure, I'll __________ a test page so you can check it out.

(a) pry into
(b) write off
(c) mock up
(d) leaf through

**24.** A: Maybe reinstalling the software will fix your computer.

B: That sounds like a(n) __________ solution. I'll give it a try.

(a) viable
(b) pristine
(c) animate
(d) inveterate

**25.** A: Kathy's really worked hard to make this party a success.

B: Yeah, she really __________ to make it happen.

(a) took a dive
(b) went belly up
(c) broke her back
(d) passed the buck

**Part II** **Questions 26—50**

Choose the option that best completes each gap.

**26.** Though they can hardly afford to buy them, many shoppers ___________ expensive handbags as status symbols.

(a) assume
(b) purchase
(c) commute
(d) distinguish

**27.** It is normal for youths to ___________ against their parents by breaking the rules during their teenage years.

(a) rebel
(b) recoil
(c) repeal
(d) retreat

**28.** Undercover journalists ___________ shocking company secrets to the public in their recent exposé.

(a) convinced
(b) purported
(c) revealed
(d) audited

**29.** A fire broke out on the ship, ___________ it so much that it needed to be towed to shore.

(a) disabling
(b) unfolding
(c) detracting
(d) undertaking

**30.** The basketball players were full of confidence going into the season, but their ___________ dropped after losing the first three games.

(a) morale
(b) affinity
(c) aptitude
(d) penchant

**31.** Readers can leave ___________ on any of our news stories by typing them in the feedback box on our website.

(a) remarks
(b) enclosures
(c) expositions
(d) publications

**32.** Management has decided to ___________ the project deadline, granting staff two more days to finish their work.

(a) vary
(b) extend
(c) overdo
(d) enlarge

**33.** The judge kept details of the trial from public knowledge by ___________ newspapers from publishing them.

(a) barring
(b) arresting
(c) excluding
(d) displacing

**34.** Because of its ___________ nature, mild depression usually disappears with time, leaving no long-term consequences.

(a) elusive
(b) addictive
(c) transitory
(d) contagious

**35.** Thick fog has created ___________ driving conditions tonight, so police are advising people not to take the risk of driving.

(a) abusive
(b) hazardous
(c) demeaning
(d) contaminated

**36.** Before the use of ___________ evidence, criminal cases relied on witness testimony rather than science.

(a) legal
(b) judicial
(c) forensic
(d) punitive

**37.** The belief that dogs have especially keen vision is a ___________, as their eyesight is actually inferior to that of humans.

(a) bluff
(b) fallacy
(c) forgery
(d) impostor

**38.** An ___________ collector of old coins, Sally travels around the globe in search of ancient currency.

(a) avid
(b) archaic
(c) exempt
(d) exorbitant

**39.** Jane's parents ___________ her from going out after she broke curfew, so she had to go straight home after school.

(a) quelled
(b) forsook
(c) forbade
(d) annulled

**40.** Although Trofim Lysenko's theories were once officially ___________ by the Soviet government, they were eventually dismissed as pseudoscience.

(a) endorsed
(b) tantalized
(c) exasperated
(d) beleaguered

**41.** The prime minister promised to unite the country by embracing its regional differences rather than trying to ___________ them.

(a) traverse
(b) eliminate
(c) adjudicate
(d) requisition

**42.** *Romeo and Juliet* centers on a ___________ between two families, with the members of each household fighting throughout the play.

(a) gale
(b) feud
(c) peril
(d) lapse

**43.** *Attracted to War* delves into the often deadly ___________ of combat, showing why it is so enticing to some young men.

(a) allure
(b) breech
(c) allusion
(d) reticence

**44.** The professor had a good ___________ with his students, and so his seminars often resulted in fun and lively discussions.

(a) rapport
(b) junction
(c) partiality
(d) confluence

**45.** The Bee Hummingbird has ___________ feathers, so their bright colors emerge in certain lights and at certain angles.

(a) wavering
(b) saturated
(c) iridescent
(d) oscillating

**46.** Historically, dictators have censored writers in order to ___________ any criticism of the regime that could lead to revolution.

(a) forfeit
(b) protract
(c) forestall
(d) languish

**47.** When the Carthaginians surrounded their Roman enemies, things quickly began looking ___________ for the Romans, who soon fell in defeat.

(a) ominous
(b) desultory
(c) precipitous
(d) exculpatory

**48.** Jamie's tires were nearly ___________, as they had been worn down by years of driving.

(a) glib
(b) bald
(c) blank
(d) shorn

**49.** When exercising, polyester clothing should be avoided as it traps perspiration and thus does not ___________ well.

(a) puff
(b) whiff
(c) distill
(d) breathe

**50.** Because of Gertrude Stein's ___________ for Cubism, she employed literary techniques that mimicked the style.

(a) prevarication
(b) ambivalence
(c) antecedence
(d) predilection

This is the end of the Vocabulary section. Do NOT move on to the Reading Comprehension section until instructed to do so. You are NOT allowed to turn to any other section of the test.

# READING COMPREHENSION

## DIRECTIONS

This section tests your ability to comprehend reading passages. You will have 45 minutes to complete the 40 questions. Be sure to follow the directions given by the proctor.

정답 P 331

## Part I Questions 1–16

Read the passage and choose the option that best completes the passage.

**1.** Call CityRentals today for an appointment to check out downtown Bellevue's ______________________________. Boasting large windows overlooking the city, units in Bellevue Court are fully furnished with wood desks, chairs, and movable partitions. Phone systems come pre-installed, and parking spaces for up to ten employees are available at no extra cost. So if you're looking to rent in downtown Bellevue, don't hesitate to call us for a tour of the luxury units in Bellevue Court.

(a) wide array of furniture rentals
(b) luxury apartments that await you
(c) newest office-equipment rental outlet
(d) premier offices waiting for you to move in

**2.** The latest Lake County census reports reveal ______________________________. The census shows that the county's overall population has continued its twenty-year falloff. However, the population of residents from minority cultures has significantly increased since the previous census five years ago. Also, this is the first time that the percentage of minority residents, mainly from African American and Hispanic backgrounds, is slightly more than the percentage of Caucasian residents.

(a) a shift in the makeup of Lake County residents
(b) Caucasian residents holding on to the majority
(c) the effects of a boom in the overall population
(d) Lake County's current lack of racial diversity

3. A chain is only as strong as its weakest link, and so it is with your company's security. That is why you need the Global Security Training program, a course specially designed to ______________________________. It introduces employees to basic security measures and shows them how to handle potential security threats. Topics covered include email security, identity theft, and password and access control. Digital security should not be left to a few specialists; everyone in your company should know how to keep confidential files confidential. Try our training program today!

(a) keep intruders off of the company's premises
(b) seek out hackers before they breach your system
(c) train experts to develop security software for businesses
(d) equip employees to safeguard sensitive digital information

4. Various factors must be taken into consideration when deciding on a water intake plan. Many people recommend eight eight-ounce glasses a day, a practice known as the "8 x 8" rule. While this may be suitable for healthy adults leading largely sedentary lifestyles, active individuals or those with water deficiencies need more. For others, the "8 x 8" rule may be excessive and induce water intoxication, a state of reduced solutes in the body, which can be fatal. Thus, when it comes to water consumption, ______________________________.

(a) there is no single universal formula
(b) it is safer to consume more than less
(c) bottled water is no better than tap water
(d) eight glasses per day is ideal for everyone

5. The idea of the unconscious mind, so strongly associated with Freud and psychoanalysis, ______________________________. The writings of philosopher Karl Eduard von Hartmann, who in turn drew from Arthur Schopenhauer's earlier philosophical works, greatly influenced Freud's theories. In fact, Schopenhauer is seen as the originator of the concept of the unconscious, and his ideas on human motivation closely parallel some of Freud's theories. Until Freud, however, these concepts had not received scientific recognition in the field of psychology or been applied in psychiatry.

(a) did not originate with Freud at all
(b) was initially dismissed in other fields
(c) had a strong influence on Schopenhauer
(d) had been utilized to treat psychiatric patients

**6.** Developers are working on creating new software that ______________________. This has special significance in the fashion and advertising industries, which depend on digital enhancement to create highly idealized images. The software will rate retouched digital photos on a five-point scale, from minimally altered to substantially changed, exposing the extent of retouching done on advertising images. Developers hope the software will discourage digital retouching and bring more natural, real-life representations back to advertising.

(a) can automatically correct flaws in photographs
(b) has long been awaited by the advertising industry
(c) is intended to advance digital retouching technology
(d) will make it possible to detect digital photo alterations

**7.** Diamond rings were not considered necessary accompaniments to marriage proposals until the twentieth century. No doubt jewelers' advertising campaigns played a big part in popularizing the diamond engagement ring, but there is a social factor behind the custom. Until the 1930s, a law gave brides-to-be the right to sue men who failed to follow through on marriage proposals. After this legislation was repealed, an expensive engagement ring replaced it as a de facto guarantee of a suitor's loyalty. In other words, the custom gained widespread appeal because it ______________________.

(a) emphasized romance over financial obligations
(b) allowed the groom to flaunt his wealth in public
(c) enabled the couple to announce their commitment
(d) offered women insurance against broken engagements

**8.** Social reaction theory, developed in the 1960s, posits that society's labeling of individuals as aberrant tends to perpetuate the cycle of deviant behavior. However, although the theory is useful in accounting for the increase in the likelihood that the behavior will recur, it ______________________. This is because the theory is only applicable after an individual has committed his or her first deviant act. The label does not exist prior to an individual's break from socially accepted behavior, and thus the first aberrant act could not have been driven by the label.

(a) alters the individual's sense of self
(b) offers no strategies for criminal reform
(c) provides no insights into its initial cause
(d) allows deviant behavior to pass as acceptable

**9.** Written at the turn of the twentieth century, Joseph Conrad and Rudyard Kipling's colonial novels ______________________________. Kipling's *Kim*, which chronicles the adventures of an Irish orphan in India during the height of the British Empire, shows the author as a patronizing imperialist who believes in the "white man's burden" to carry out the noble enterprise of imperialism for the benefit of other races. Conrad's *Heart of Darkness*, set in the dark wilderness of Congo, exposes the hypocrisy behind such ideologies by demonstrating the evil that results when European powers force their cultural values on other people.

(a) take widely disparate stances on imperialism
(b) provide multi-leveled criticisms of the British Empire
(c) were curiously indifferent to the political turmoil of the age
(d) failed to resonate with readers because of their criticisms of colonialism

**10.** A firm believer in the virtue of the free market, Austrian economist Friedrich Hayek was strongly opposed to government intervention in the market. He even argued that monopolistic industries, such as railways and utilities, should be privatized. However, he overlooked the ______________________________. Since governments would not let such important public services collapse, private companies would have free rein to act recklessly. They could take imprudent risks or misappropriate funds, knowing that the government would eventually bail them out.

(a) social inequality that a free market engenders
(b) dangers of arbitrarily restraining capitalist tendencies
(c) potential abuses that such a system would be vulnerable to
(d) extent of corruption within publicly owned essential services

**11.** In accordance with a recently implemented change to our visa policy, applicants for spousal visas ______________________________. To take advantage of this new regulation, supplementary materials must accompany the application. These can include a receipt for a reserved wedding hall showing the intended wedding date or a notarized statement from a family member attesting to the plan to marry. Also, a valid marriage certificate must be submitted within a year of having been granted a spousal visa.

(a) no longer need to be married at the time of application
(b) can now have dual citizenship with their native country
(c) need to provide photos of their wedding with the application
(d) must submit a copy of their marriage license when they apply

**12.** A recent study in Florida focused on Burmese Pythons, snakes native to Southeast Asia but imported as pets to Florida. In the last couple of decades, thousands of these snakes, having either escaped from their backyard enclosures or been freed by their owners, have been spotted in the coastal wetlands of the Everglades. During the same period, native populations such as raccoons and deer have declined drastically, some as much as 99%. Scientists have definitively linked the two phenomena, concluding that ______________________________.

(a) the imported species is near extinction
(b) pythons cannot thrive in Florida's ecology
(c) the newcomers are preying on other species
(d) domestication has made the snakes vulnerable

**13.**

> To the Editor:
>
> Upon learning that Roger Cranston's work will be exhibited at the renowned City Museum, I was ______________________________. Cranston's pieces have languished in undeserved obscurity, displayed in out-of-the-way, nameless venues, and his talent has gone unrecognized. Critics still snub his art, dismissing him for his dedication to primitive forms. I hope this exhibit will provide them with a chance to reconsider his work. At any rate, I believe Cranston is now somewhat vindicated to be represented at a prestigious institution such as the City Museum.
>
> Beth Harper

(a) elated to finally see his work get its day in the sun
(b) convinced of what my fellow critics have been saying
(c) glad to see that most critics have come around to my view
(d) impressed that the museum attracted such a prominent artist

**14.** Upon seeing a predator, ground squirrels emit a high-pitched shriek so that nearby squirrels can escape. This behavior is not in their immediate best interest, as the alarm could betray the squirrels' location and endanger their lives. Ultimately, though, their actions actually ensure the survival of their DNA by helping fellow squirrels, including their own offspring and other kin, get to safety. Thus, it turns out that ________________________________.

(a) their shriek does little to actually deter predators
(b) they only shriek in non-life-threatening situations
(c) the alarms were solely to protect their own offspring
(d) their altruism promotes the continuation of their species

**15.** Many child psychologists have suggested that birth order influences personality, and some use such theories when diagnosing psychological disorders in patients. But there is a lack of consensus on this issue, partly because these claims are hard to prove scientifically due to the difficulty of controlling external variables. ________________________________, published studies on birth order vary widely in their findings. Until there is conclusive evidence, basing diagnoses on birth order has no place in the psychiatric community.

(a) Indeed
(b) Granted
(c) However
(d) Otherwise

**16.** Scientists believe that they have found the Achilles' heel of the HIV virus, which may be an important breakthrough in the fight against AIDS. When viruses are under attack, their internal structures usually mutate to withstand that attack; however, researchers have found parts of the HIV virus that do not mutate, even when the virus is under attack. ________________________________, researchers are now attempting to design drugs that target those specific parts of the virus, in hopes of finding a cure for AIDS.

(a) In sum
(b) In contrast
(c) Accordingly
(d) Nevertheless

## Part II Questions 17—37

Read the passage, question, and options. Then, based on the given information, choose the option that best answers the question.

**17.** Throughout her career, four-time Olympic medalist Joan Evrett has held 5 world records, won 3 Olympic gold medals, and earned 11 Canadian Championship titles in speed skating. Now more than six years after her last competitive event, the 32-year-old is back. This September, she will be trying out for the 1,000-meter track, one of her signature events, in a bid to represent Canada at the 2013 World Skating Championships. She says her ultimate goal is to qualify for the 2014 Sochi Olympics.

Q: What is the best title for the passage?
(a) Evrett Wins Her Signature Event
(b) Evrett Returns to Competitive Skating
(c) Evrett to Retire after 2014 Sochi Olympics
(d) Evrett Qualifies for 2013 World Championships

**18.**

Dear Ms. Potter,

Because of competition from two new nearby restaurants, our sales have dropped 30% over the last six months. For this reason, we have been forced to get rid of several server positions, including yours. I'm sorry to say that this is effective immediately. Your final paycheck will be mailed to you shortly. We thank you for your service during your year with us and wish you the best of luck.

Sincerely,
Thomas Morelli
Chickeria

Q: What is the main purpose of the letter?
(a) To announce the closing of a restaurant
(b) To inform Ms. Potter that she is being laid off
(c) To update Ms. Potter on changes in the work shift
(d) To explain why the restaurant's profits are dropping

19. In the past, Antarctica's forbidding climate and terrain prevented scientists from conducting the necessary surveys to establish reliable estimates of the Emperor Penguin population. Researchers working on a three-year project, however, have utilized modern technology to overcome these problems. The team used satellite photography to identify the black-plumed birds against the white snow. This method has yielded an estimated population of 595,000 Emperor Penguins, almost twice the previous estimate.

Q: What is the passage mainly saying about Emperor Penguins?
(a) Their population in Antarctica is declining.
(b) Using satellites to count them brings many challenges.
(c) Weather patterns caused a change in their population.
(d) Technology facilitated an estimate of their population.

20. Are you fed up with telemarketers calling you even though you've repeatedly asked to be taken off their lists? Then try the TeleRepellent! It is the only gadget on the market that can detect and block telemarketing calls. Just connect it to your phone, and whenever it detects a call from a known telemarketing service, it will prevent your phone from even ringing. With our comprehensive, continuously updated database of telemarketers, you'll never have to worry about unwanted sales calls again.

Q: What is mainly being advertised?
(a) A device to reject phone solicitations
(b) A service that hides a caller's identity
(c) An innovative telemarketing technology
(d) A new way to report unwanted sales calls

21. Nonverbal communication, such as body language, is essential to human communication. However, the extent to which such nonverbal cues impact human interaction varies greatly by culture. High context cultures, which have little racial diversity and an established tradition of shared values, rely heavily on nonverbal communication, as individuals know that they can often leave things unsaid and still be understood perfectly by their peers. In contrast, low context cultures, which have more racial diversity and fewer shared values, lack such strong nonverbal cues and often require verbal confirmation of what is being said.

Q: What is the passage mainly about?
(a) Word connotations as they are used in various cultures
(b) The effect of a society's class structure on various speaking styles
(c) The varying extent to which different cultures rely on nonverbal cues
(d) Nonverbal cues shared by both high context and low context cultures

**22.** Thank you all for your patience during the construction of Altbiz's annex building. With the completion of the new building, we have been able to relocate the marketing and accounting departments, which has freed up a lot of space in the main building. Our retail department is currently setting up where marketing used to be, and the IT department is to take over the third floor. The bridge connecting the annex to the main building will be accessible Monday.

Q: What is mainly being announced?
(a) The opening of Altbiz's new branch offices
(b) Details of Altbiz's expansion to two buildings
(c) Altbiz's plans to relocate to a new neighborhood
(d) The impending completion of Altbiz's annex building

**23.** Are you looking for a faster Internet connection? For a limited time, existing Ditycom customers will be able to upgrade to Premium Plus, our fastest high-speed Internet, and pay their current subscription fee for three months, with a fixed monthly price of just $21.95 thereafter. With our unmatched speeds, you can experience faster surfing and downloading. Also, you keep your current Ditycom account, so there is no need to pay activation fees. Sign up today for a new level of Internet service!

Q: Which of the following is correct according to the advertisement?
(a) The advertisement is aimed at customers without Ditycom accounts.
(b) Upgrading customers pay no subscription fees for the first three months.
(c) Upgrading to Premium Plus will add $21.95 to the current monthly bill.
(d) Customers upgrading to Premium Plus are not charged any activation fees.

**24.** I used to dread going to work every day. It wasn't the lack of a raise during my two-year tenure or the twenty-minute lunch breaks that I loathed. Nor did I mind being the only 23 year old, one of two males, surrounded by twenty middle-aged women. I just grew sick of addressing customer complaint calls every day. Eventually, I couldn't take it and quit. It was difficult at first, being out of work, but eventually I found another job and I have been much happier ever since.

Q: Which of the following is correct about the writer according to the passage?
(a) His salary stayed the same for two years.
(b) He quit because of his short lunch breaks.
(c) His office had two other male employees.
(d) He had another job lined up before he quit.

**25.** In honor of the one hundredth anniversary of the birth of the composer John Ulrich, the Center of Arts will host two nights of rare performances and never-before-seen collaborations this Friday and Saturday. Pianist Robert Tierney will open both nights with solo performances of Ulrich's most beloved sonatas, followed by the Century Orchestra in a modern rendering of Ulrich's Symphony No. 2. Saturday's performances include group pieces by violinist Clara Chiu and the Center of Arts' students.

Q: Which of the following is correct about the concert according to the advertisement?
(a) It commemorates the centennial of Ulrich's passing.
(b) It will take place over three consecutive nights.
(c) Robert Tierney will perform on Friday and Saturday.
(d) Pianist Clara Chiu will collaborate with students.

**26.** Although German-American anthropologist Franz Boas had been deeply interested in the history of culture, his PhD degree, which he received from the University of Kiel in Germany, was in physics. After graduation, he pursued another of his interests, geography, by going to Baffin Island for work. There he came to know the Inuit people, which cemented his interest in human cultures and led him to pursue anthropology. Boas believed that anthropologists needed to employ personal rather than detached methods for studying human subjects. He also believed that anthropologists had an obligation to be socially active by speaking out against social inequality.

Q: Which of the following is correct about Franz Boas according to the passage?
(a) He received a PhD degree in anthropology from a German university.
(b) He conducted fieldwork in Baffin Island after receiving his PhD degree.
(c) He argued for a detached approach to the study of human subjects.
(d) He believed anthropologists should not become involved in social issues.

**27.**

> Dear Sally,
>
> My neighbors often play music after 9 pm, and it keeps me awake. I know that isn't the middle of the night, but my job requires me to wake up at 6 am and I need to go to bed early. I've never met them before, so it seems awkward to just confront them suddenly about it. I've been to the landlord to request his help, but he has refused to intervene. How can I get them to turn off the music without offending them?
>
> Yours truly,
> Suffering in Silence

Q: Which of the following is correct about the writer according to the letter?
(a) She complains that her neighbors play music in the middle of the night.
(b) She goes to bed early because she is required to be at work at 6 am.
(c) She prefers not to confront her neighbors because they are friends.
(d) She has already asked her landlord for his assistance in the matter.

**28.** Now that we have completely transitioned away from our previous paper-based applications, all applicants for admission to Brookings University must use our website to apply. In addition to completing the Applicant Information section, applicants must upload a statement of purpose, résumé, and three recommendation letters. All applications must be accompanied by a nonrefundable $50 application fee. Applicants may apply for more than one program and must submit a separate application and fee for each program.

Q: Which of the following is correct according to the passage?
(a) Traditional paper-based applications are no longer allowed.
(b) Recommendation letters must be mailed directly to the school.
(c) Rejected applicants will get a partial refund on the $50 application fee.
(d) Applicants need only pay one fee when applying to multiple programs.

29. The Maasai are a group semi-nomadic people who began migrating south from Northwest Kenya in the fifteenth century and now inhabit modern-day Kenya and Tanzania. Their territory reached its largest size in the mid-nineteenth century, but it has been reduced by half, as a large portion of it was confiscated in the twentieth century to make way for agricultural areas and game reserves. Governments of both countries have tried to pressure the Maasai to adopt an agricultural lifestyle, but many are averse to such changes and proudly maintain the traditions of their ancestors.

Q: Which of the following is correct about the Maasai according to the passage?
(a) They migrated south to Northwest Kenya from modern-day Tanzania.
(b) Some parts of their former land have been converted into game reserves.
(c) Governments are encouraging them to retain their traditional lifestyle.
(d) They unanimously regard the move towards agriculture as positive.

30. Born in 1907, the Mexican painter Frida Kahlo struggled with ill health and pain for most of her life. At age six, Kahlo contracted polio, which left one leg permanently disfigured. Her experience influenced her to aspire to be a doctor. However, in 1925, the bus she was on collided with a streetcar, which rendered her temporarily immobilized. During her long recovery, Kahlo began painting and discovered her true passion. Before passing away in 1954, she created around 200 artworks, 143 of which were paintings, but her work gained widespread recognition only posthumously in the 1980s.

Q: Which of the following is correct about Frida Kahlo according to the passage?
(a) She was afflicted with a severe case of polio from birth.
(b) She realized her love of painting after a traffic accident.
(c) She produced approximately 200 paintings in her lifetime.
(d) She garnered widespread acclaim for her work while alive.

31. Prostate-specific antigen (PSA) is a protein that is produced by the prostate gland. Men with healthy prostates normally have low levels of PSA. The PSA level often rises when men develop prostate cancer, but it can be high for other reasons, making the test not a completely reliable indicator of the disease. Meanwhile, men with normal PSA levels can also have prostate cancer, so normal numbers are no guarantee, either. Thus, many doctors recommend that most men opt out of routine PSA tests.

Q: Which of the following is correct according to the passage?
(a) PSA levels are usually low for men who have healthy prostates.
(b) A high PSA level is a conclusive indicator of prostate cancer.
(c) Prostate cancer does not afflict those with normal PSA levels.
(d) Experts unanimously recommend routine PSA screening

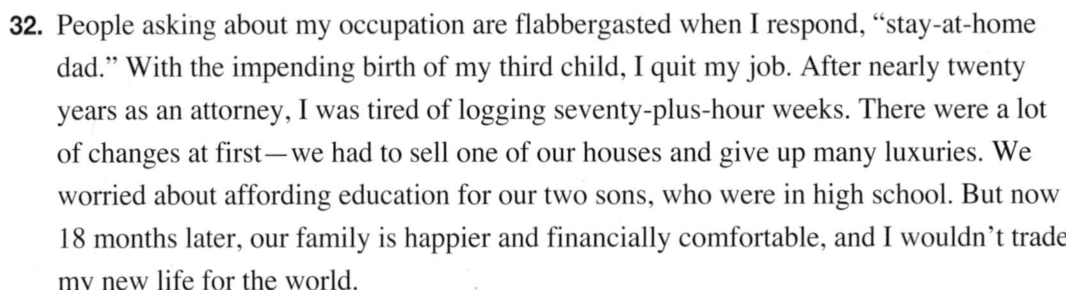

**32.** People asking about my occupation are flabbergasted when I respond, "stay-at-home dad." With the impending birth of my third child, I quit my job. After nearly twenty years as an attorney, I was tired of logging seventy-plus-hour weeks. There were a lot of changes at first—we had to sell one of our houses and give up many luxuries. We worried about affording education for our two sons, who were in high school. But now 18 months later, our family is happier and financially comfortable, and I wouldn't trade my new life for the world.

Q: Which of the following is correct about the writer according to the passage?
(a) He quit his job 18 months after his child's birth.
(b) He worked as an attorney for over twenty years.
(c) His family previously owned more than one house.
(d) His two sons were college aged when he quit his job.

**33.** Since 1950, *Good Buy* magazine has been testing products and publishing its findings in the interests of consumers. The magazine accepts no compensation, financial or otherwise, from the manufacturers under review, and all merchandise and services are purchased at retail prices. Threats of lawsuits have not deterred *Good Buy* in its attempts to provide consumers with objective reviews. The magazine's findings have brought about many improvements, even compelling several manufacturers to conduct their own retesting, occasionally leading to item recalls and improved releases.

Q: What can be inferred about *Good Buy* from the passage?
(a) It is distributed to readers free of charge.
(b) Its findings are mostly dismissed by consumers.
(c) It refuses compensation in order to maintain objectivity.
(d) Its lawsuits are usually settled in favor of the companies.

**34.** When *Mistaken Affair* was reissued on DVD recently, it drew attention to the controversy surrounding its first screening in the 1960s. Back then it experienced an undeserved death-by-critic like few others, with such a unanimous savaging from critics that box office failure was guaranteed. *Mistaken Affair* was no dud—it was simply before its time, which is evidenced by the apology of one of its fiercest critics, who later declared the film a masterpiece. These days it is rare for critics to label what deserves praise as a flop. If anything, the converse happens too frequently.

Q: Which statement would the reviewer most likely agree with?
(a) Today's critics too readily extol undeserving movies.
(b) Masterpieces are harder to produce by today's movie standards.
(c) Movies that are denounced by critics are usually enjoyed by the public.
(d) Film critics are far more sophisticated now than they were in the 1960s.

**35.** With profits plummeting, some airlines are taking extreme measures to cut costs. Last Sunday, Northeastern Airways incurred the wrath of passengers, who are vowing never to fly with the airline again. Passengers on Flight 086 were given no advance notice of increased baggage fees, and when the weather delayed the flight a staggering seven hours, requests for complimentary beverages were denied. Additionally, a substantial fee for those wanting a flight change was strictly enforced. The airline might believe it is saving costs now, but it should be rethinking its policy after the passenger backlash over the incident.

Q: Which statement would the writer most likely agree with?
(a) Choosing a low-budget carrier is well worth the savings.
(b) Passengers should be more understanding of inevitable delays.
(c) Northeastern Airways would do well to further curb its spending.
(d) Northeastern Airways' attempts at increasing revenue are short-sighted.

**36.** Although often referred to as the "father of American education," Horace Mann grew up poor and received little schooling before entering university. As secretary of the Massachusetts Board of Education, he played a crucial role in establishing tax-funded public schools in America. An advocate of equal access to education for all, he believed that students from various social backgrounds should be educated together. Mann also believed that schools should share parents' responsibilities of instilling values in children and preparing them to become judicious citizens.

Q: What can be inferred about Horace Mann from the passage?
(a) His view of education marginalized parents' role in education.
(b) He saw a need to tailor education to fit each student's social background.
(c) His privileged background weakened his credibility as an education reformer.
(d) He thought exposure to others from different backgrounds would benefit children.

**37.** Director Duncan Kanu's film *Genovia's Quest*, based on the immensely popular novel *Crusade of the Genovians*, caused a stir among fans of the book. The original novel was a sprawling epic, rich in both character and plot development, but many of its scenes and characters were cut to fit in the movie's allotted 120 minutes. The scriptwriters' attempts to adapt the novel into a fast-paced film have fallen short of their intentions, and the audience is left wondering if the task of condensing this epic into a feature-length film was feasible in the first place.

Q: Which statement about *Genovia's Quest* would the writer most likely agree with?
(a) It suffers from the same flaws that the novel had.
(b) It merits the negative response of the novel's fans.
(c) Its source material translates well to a feature film.
(d) Its only strong point is its well-developed characters.

**Part III** **Questions 38 – 40**

Read the passage and identify the option that does NOT belong.

**38.** Napoli's Café and Grill in Ridgeford Heights has been serving the area's finest Italian food and wine since 1952. (a) Italian food was first made popular in America due to the abundance of Italian immigrants. (b) Our appetizers include Italian favorites such as garlic bread, sumptuous olives, and homemade antipasti. (c) For your main course, choose from a variety of dishes, large enough to share and sure to please any palate. (d) To top it all off, spoil yourself with a traditional Italian dessert like our homemade cannoli and tiramisu.

**39.** The newest concept in zoos aims to help children connect with nature by incorporating interactive activities. (a) Many facilities run programs that offer children the chance to touch live animals, hunt for insects, or slosh in mud between their encounters with animals. (b) The Cantrece Zoo, outside Glenville, for example, offers children a chance to help prepare treats for the animals and feed them. (c) Also, a hands-on facility in New Jersey encourages kids to get their feet wet as they identify aquatic invertebrates. (d) Moreover, parents should take care that their children do not bother the animals or spook them by getting too close.

**40.** Offering financial donations is not the only way to spur human progress and help fellow human beings. (a) Making charitable donations to promote a noble cause or help the less fortunate is no doubt laudable. (b) Even the most skeptical among us cannot fail to notice that our nature resembles that of the social animals. (c) However, the people who are really remembered for their services to mankind are selfless leaders such as Gandhi or Mother Teresa. (d) The examples set by these historical figures prove that we can contribute in non-financial ways to making the world better.

This is the end of the Reading Comprehension section. Please remain seated until the proctor has instructed otherwise. You are NOT allowed to turn to any other section of the test.

# 서울대 최신기출 5

***Listening*** *Comprehension*

***Grammar***

***Vocabulary***

***Reading*** *Comprehension*

TEPS

# Listening Comprehension

## Directions

1. In the Listening Comprehension section, all content will be presented orally rather than in written form.
2. This section contains four parts, each with fifteen individual items. For each part, you will receive separate instructions. Listen to the instructions carefully, and choose the best answer from the options for each item.

Scripts P 308 / 정답 P 332

**Part I** **Questions 1–15**

You will now hear fifteen individual spoken questions or statements, each followed by four spoken responses. Choose the most appropriate response for each item.

**Part II** **Questions 16–30**

You will now hear fifteen short conversation fragments, followed by four spoken responses. Choose the most appropriate response to complete each conversation.

**Part III** **Questions 31—45**

You will now hear fifteen complete conversations. For each conversation, you will be asked to answer a question. Each conversation and its corresponding question will be read twice. Then you will hear four options which will be read only once. Based on the given information, choose the option that best answers the question.

**Part IV** **Questions 46—60**

You will now hear fifteen short talks. After each talk, you will be asked to answer a question. Each talk and its corresponding question will be read twice. Then you will hear four options which will be read only once. Based on the given information, choose the option that best answers the question.

TEPS

# GRAMMAR

**DIRECTIONS**

This section tests your grammar skills. You will have 25 minutes to complete the 50 questions. Be sure to follow the directions given by the proctor.

정답 P 332

## Part I Questions 1—20

Choose the option that best completes each gap.

**1.** A: Shall I get you a cup of coffee?
B: No, thanks. I already have ___________.

(a) any
(b) one
(c) none
(d) much

**2.** A: I wish I knew how to play chess.
B: I'll teach you. The rules of the game ___________ that hard.

(a) isn't
(b) aren't
(c) hasn't been
(d) haven't been

**3.** A: Jimmy daydreams when he should be doing his homework.
B: I know. He'd better ___________, or his grades will drop.

(a) stopping
(b) stopped
(c) to stop
(d) stop

**4.** A: How was the trip to France, Peggy?
B: Good, but it would have been better if you ___________ with me.

(a) had come
(b) have come
(c) were coming
(d) were to come

**5.** A: Did you get invited to Clara's house next Sunday?
B: Yes, but I heard the party she ___________ is potluck, and I don't know what to bring.

(a) has
(b) is having
(c) would have
(d) will have had

**6.** A: Is Ted studying math again?
B: Yes, he finds the subject ___________.

(a) interest
(b) interested
(c) to interest
(d) interesting

**7.** A: Did you say your mom did a 10 km run?
B: Yes, and in only 74 minutes, ___________ I think is very impressive for a woman her age.

(a) that
(b) who
(c) which
(d) whom

**8.** A: Are you happy you moved departments?
B: No. Actually I regret ___________ to sales.

(a) transfer
(b) to transfer
(c) to be transferred
(d) having transferred

9. A: Can we buy new office computers?
B: We don't usually spend large amounts like that without ___________.

(a) the boss giving us permission
(b) giving the permission from boss
(c) the boss has given us permission
(d) permission was given from the boss

10. A: Is Al still planning to be an architect?
B: Yes, but so far he ___________ a position with a firm.

(a) doesn't find
(b) hasn't found
(c) hadn't found
(d) wasn't finding

11. A: I like our new hiring strategy.
B: Me, too. I'm all ___________ it.

(a) at
(b) to
(c) for
(d) up

12. A: Did Andy set our work schedules according to our requests?
B: No. I wish he ___________.

(a) did set
(b) had so
(c) had
(d) set

13. A: The students can't be happy about the college's remote location.
B: ___________, the students actually prefer it.

(a) Most people believe contrarily
(b) To the contrary of most believing
(c) What people believe most contrary to
(d) Contrary to what most people believe

14. A: Did you recover any data after your computer crashed?
B: No, and among the files I lost ___________ one containing a week's worth of research!

(a) was
(b) were
(c) has been
(d) have been

15. A: I'm sorry your cat got sick while I was cat-sitting him.
B: In no way ___________. It wasn't your fault.

(a) do I blame you
(b) I do blame you
(c) do you I blame
(d) you I do blame

16. A: Should you quit your job in this tough economy?
B: That's something ___________ before I decide.

(a) I need to consider
(b) I need considering it
(c) that I need considering
(d) that I need to consider it

17. A: I have an extra ticket to the concert.
B: Sorry, I already have ___________.

(a) plan
(b) other plans
(c) another plans
(d) any other plan

**18.** A: Did the students understand the grammar rule?
B: They finally comprehended it ____________ I explained it with examples.

(a) whenever
(b) although
(c) whereas
(d) once

**19.** A: Tour Europe with me in July.
B: I can barely afford a short vacation at home, ____________ this summer.

(a) a trip less than
(b) much less a trip
(c) much less of a trip
(d) a trip much less than

**20.** A: Will there ever be a cure for heart disease?
B: ____________ new discoveries being made every day, I'm sure there will be.

(a) As
(b) With
(c) Since
(d) After

## Part II Questions 21—40

Choose the option that best completes each gap.

**21.** The spectators were shocked to see that Marcy ____________ break the track record so easily.

(a) may
(b) need
(c) could
(d) should

**22.** Harry accepted the offer on his house because it was ____________ one, far better than any other offer.

(a) profitable
(b) profitably
(c) more profitable
(d) the most profitable

**23.** Alternative energy use is on the rise in parts of the developing world, ____________ it is a necessity, not a choice.

(a) that
(b) what
(c) where
(d) of which

**24.** Larry knew he ____________ waste his money on lottery tickets, but he bought one anyway, hoping to get lucky and win.

(a) can't
(b) won't
(c) might not
(d) should not

**25.** The task of reexamining past test results ___________ assigned to the newest researcher.

(a) has
(b) have
(c) has been
(d) have been

**26.** The salary offered to Miss Turner was ___________ over the amount she expected.

(a) such
(b) very
(c) well
(d) too

**27.** ___________ the environmental hazards of aerosol cans, conservationists have recommended banning them.

(a) Given
(b) Giving
(c) To give
(d) Having given

**28.** Since it is a difficult hike to the bottom of the canyon, hardly ___________ people actually make it there.

(a) a little
(b) some
(c) few
(d) any

**29.** Petsco's Shiny Coat Vitamin keeps your dog's hair thick and lustrous when ___________ orally to your pet daily.

(a) administering
(b) to administer
(c) administered
(d) administer

**30.** Although scientists do not completely understand the "El Niño" weather effect, computer-generated models have allowed them ___________.

(a) better to predict the phenomenon
(b) to better predict the phenomenon
(c) predicting the phenomenon better
(d) to predicting the phenomenon better

**31.** Although TV violence may ___________ aggressive behavior in children, it is a contributing factor.

(a) not only be cause of
(b) be not the only cause
(c) be a cause of not only
(d) not be the only cause of

**32.** Upon the emperor's untimely death, his kingdom ___________ and fell under the control of one of his enemies.

(a) usurped
(b) has usurped
(c) was usurped
(d) has been usurped

**33.** As ever more complaints poured in, Roxanne felt there would be ___________ end to the list of dissatisfied customers.

(a) an
(b) no
(c) the
(d) few

**34.** Having come home soaked from the rain, Jamie did not want to do anything until he ___________ into dry clothes first.

(a) has changed
(b) had changed
(c) was changing
(d) would change

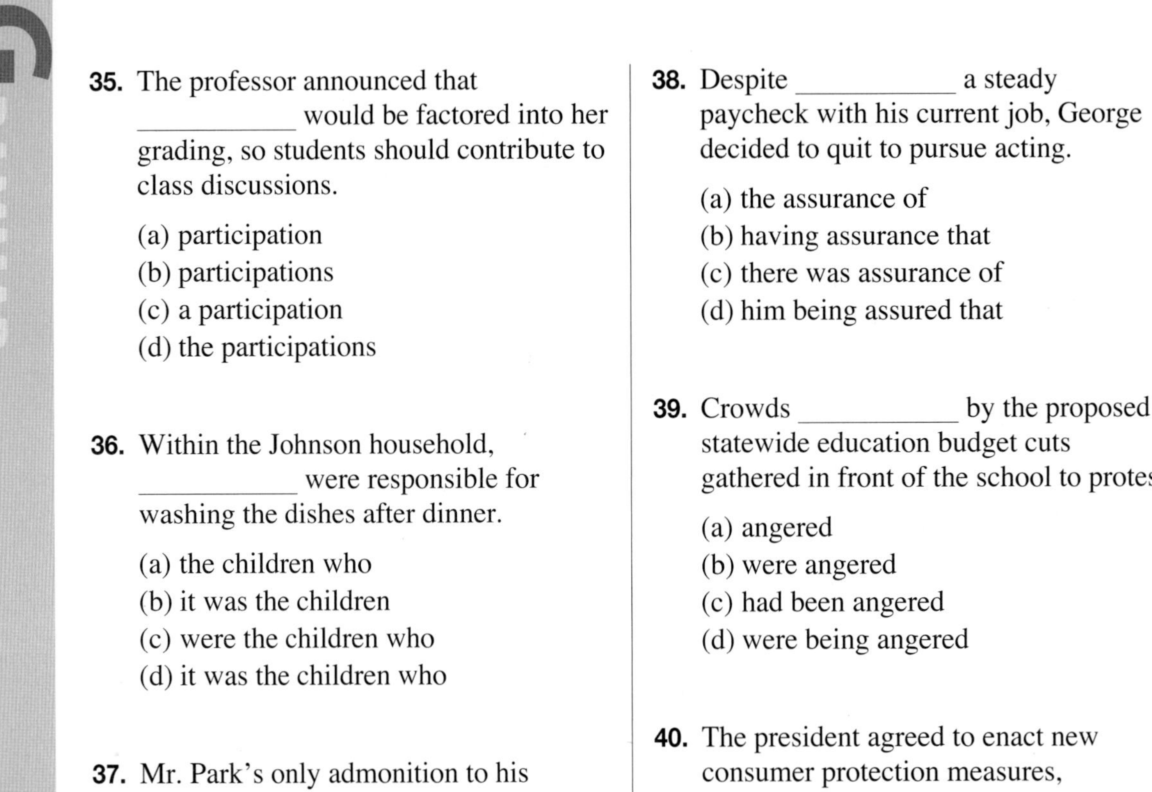

**35.** The professor announced that __________ would be factored into her grading, so students should contribute to class discussions.

(a) participation
(b) participations
(c) a participation
(d) the participations

**36.** Within the Johnson household, __________ were responsible for washing the dishes after dinner.

(a) the children who
(b) it was the children
(c) were the children who
(d) it was the children who

**37.** Mr. Park's only admonition to his daughter was that she __________ more judicious with her spending.

(a) will be
(b) were
(c) was
(d) be

**38.** Despite __________ a steady paycheck with his current job, George decided to quit to pursue acting.

(a) the assurance of
(b) having assurance that
(c) there was assurance of
(d) him being assured that

**39.** Crowds __________ by the proposed statewide education budget cuts gathered in front of the school to protest.

(a) angered
(b) were angered
(c) had been angered
(d) were being angered

**40.** The president agreed to enact new consumer protection measures, __________ certain economic concessions were first guaranteed.

(a) as well as
(b) as though
(c) rather than
(d) provided that

GRAMMAR

**Part III** **Questions 41–45**

Read each sentence carefully and identify the option that contains a grammatical error.

**41.** (a) A: Waiter, may I have some coffee, please?
(b) B: Certainly. I'll be back with it momentary.
(c) A: I'd also like some dessert. Is there a menu?
(d) B: Of course. I'll bring it with your coffee.

**42.** (a) A: I've read that there are a lot of benefits for babies if their mothers eat a healthy diet.
(b) B: Definitely. A mother's diet can even influence her baby's food preferences.
(c) A: Really? But how do babies get exposed to their mothers' diet choices?
(d) B: It happens when babies feed their mothers' breast milk.

**43.** (a) A: What do you think the basketball team's odds are of winning the division title?
(b) B: I'd say it's highly unlikely unless the team somehow manages to win the next two games.
(c) A: That seems totally possible to me. You don't think they'll be able to pull through?
(d) B: It's doubtful, especially they're playing against the defending champions.

**44.** (a) A: Did you hear that Mike has switched majors again?
(b) B: Yep, for the third time during just this semester alone.
(c) A: Any idea why he had changed his mind so frequently?
(d) B: I'm betting it's just that he has a lot of interests.

**45.** (a) A: Thank you for calling the Emergency Road Service. How may I be of assistance?
(b) B: Hi, I'm stuck out here on Sunset Road with a flat tire. Can you send some help?
(c) A: Sure. Allow about 15 minutes our getting there. In the meantime, try to pull over.
(d) B: Oh, I already have. I managed to get over onto the left shoulder before calling.

## Part IV Questions 46–50

Read each sentence carefully and identify the option that contains a grammatical error.

**46.** (a) Pratibha Patil, the former leader of India, became the country's first female president in 2007. (b) Her nomination in the election was unexpected as up until then she had kept a low political profile. (c) Nevertheless, she won the election by a landslide, securing nearly twice the votes of her opponent. (d) In a country which women face widespread discrimination, Patil's election was certainly a significant event.

**47.** (a) While proficient readers may be able to read material rapidly, they know they should not always do so. (b) Good reading depends not on the ability to read fast but on the ability to vary reading rates for different content. (c) For instance, efficient readers often decrease their speed when they will come across unfamiliar ideas. (d) However, they will move rapidly over unnecessary information and scan easy-to-understand material.

**48.** (a) Finland is one of the highest-achieving nations in annual international educational assessments. (b) Other countries, envied Finland's success, have tried to figure out what makes its system work so well. (c) Observers generally agree that Finland's extremely competent teachers are key to the high test scores. (d) Indeed, only top university students go on to major in education, so those who become teachers are eminently qualified.

**49.** (a) The Sarbanes-Oxley Act was introduced in the US after a string of major corporate scandals in the early 2000s. (b) The act imposed a number of strict government controls on corporate accounting practices. (c) It also created a semi-public entity to oversee and regulate accounting firms acting as auditors for companies. (d) Although debate continues today as to it is effective, several other nations have seen fit to adopt similar laws.

**50.** (a) Bats are one of the few mammal species that use echolocation to navigate and avoid collisions. (b) Their finely-tuned sensory systems enable them to avoid objects in the dark by using sound waves. (c) Nevertheless, there is something bats do run into it on a regular basis with deadly consequences: wind turbines. (d) Scientists have searched for the reason why bats fail to avoid these objects, but they have yet to figure out why.

This is the end of the Grammar section. Do NOT move on to the next section until instructed to do so. You are NOT allowed to turn to any other section of the test.

# VOCABULARY

## DIRECTIONS

This section tests your vocabulary skills. You will have 15 minutes to complete the 50 questions. Be sure to follow the directions given by the proctor.

정답 P 332

## Part I Questions 1–25

Choose the option that best completes each gap.

1. A: Should we loosen up before hitting some golf balls?
   B: Sure, let's ___________ first so we don't strain anything.

   (a) slide
   (b) grasp
   (c) utilize
   (d) stretch

2. A: Have you made plans for the summer?
   B: No, I'm still ___________ my options.

   (a) resuming
   (b) advancing
   (c) mentioning
   (d) contemplating

3. A: The medicine isn't helping my cold.
   B: Try a home ___________, such as honey tea or chicken soup.

   (a) mercy
   (b) remedy
   (c) ailment
   (d) support

4. A: Will we be able to get this couch into the den?
   B: No, the door is too ___________.

   (a) weary
   (b) scanty
   (c) narrow
   (d) clasped

5. A: Jen seemed genuinely sorry for forgetting your birthday.
   B: Yes, I could tell her apology was ___________.

   (a) accurate
   (b) ethical
   (c) sincere
   (d) engraved

6. A: Why are you so late?
   B: Sorry. Traffic was just ___________, and it delayed me.

   (a) hailing
   (b) slurring
   (c) crawling
   (d) blending

7. A: Ed? I can't hear you over all the noise.
   B: I'll call you back. There's too much ___________ on the line.

   (a) static
   (b) disorder
   (c) agitation
   (d) turbulence

8. A: How can I get Bruce to stop playing video games?
   B: ___________ his attention to something else, like sports.

   (a) Operate
   (b) Redeem
   (c) Divert
   (d) Warn

9. A: Do Muslims ___________ during Ramadan?
B: Yes, they don't eat anything from sunrise to sunset all month.

(a) fast
(b) cease
(c) strive
(d) evade

10. A: Have I returned all the books I checked out?
B: No, there's one that is still ___________. The title is *Fantastica*.

(a) indebted
(b) overtaken
(c) underrated
(d) outstanding

11. A: Let's go to the movies on Saturday.
B: I can't. I need to make a(n) ___________ at my cousin's wedding.

(a) turnout
(b) disposal
(c) emergence
(d) appearance

12. A: Ben has totally changed. He's a lot more outgoing than before.
B: Yes, he really has ___________.

(a) barked up the wrong tree
(b) turned over a new leaf
(c) gone through the roof
(d) gotten away scot-free

13. A: Joey says he was teased at school.
B: Yeah, a classmate ___________ him about his new haircut.

(a) invoked
(b) taunted
(c) clipped
(d) bustled

14. A: Does Main Street divide into two roads?
B: Yes, it ___________ into Ferry Street and Bay Avenue.

(a) forks
(b) veers
(c) slices
(d) shifts

15. A: It's nice to meet someone who isn't afraid to express his opinion.
B: Thanks. I guess I've always been ___________.

(a) tractable
(b) credulous
(c) outspoken
(d) resounding

16. A: Peter, congratulations on your promotion! You must feel great!
B: Totally. I'm ___________.

(a) walking on air
(b) laying it on thick
(c) passing the buck
(d) shooting the breeze

17. A: Life in the city is too busy and fast paced.
B: I agree. It is far too ___________.

(a) cryptic
(b) sturdy
(c) thrifty
(d) hectic

VOCABULARY

**18.** A: I don't want to spend too much money on our anniversary.

B: Come on. It's a special occasion, so it's OK to __________.

(a) fling
(b) hoard
(c) splurge
(d) rampage

**19.** A: Can I offer you a glass of wine?

B: No. I need to stay __________ tonight because I'm the designated driver.

(a) sparse
(b) sober
(c) lurid
(d) lofty

**20.** A: How could you have booked the wrong day for our flight?

B: It was a mistake made in __________. I was rushing and didn't check it.

(a) dash
(b) haste
(c) surge
(d) prompt

**21.** A: The hospitality industry has really grown over the years.

B: Indeed, it has __________ into a billion-dollar industry.

(a) curtailed
(b) peppered
(c) stockpiled
(d) burgeoned

**22.** A: The professor looks just like someone famous, but I can't think of his name.

B: I'd say he's a __________ for Winston Churchill.

(a) double whammy
(b) roll of the dice
(c) sitting duck
(d) dead ringer

**23.** A: The debate team lost again, but they're determined to win next time.

B: I admire their __________ spirit.

(a) tenacious
(b) pernicious
(c) immaculate
(d) intermittent

**24.** A: Your wife said you two met completely by chance.

B: Yes, it was a __________ meeting. I never would have expected it.

(a) capricious
(b) fortuitous
(c) languid
(d) truant

**25.** A: James sweet-talked his father into buying him a car.

B: That's James. He has __________ his father into giving him gifts before.

(a) excised
(b) dawdled
(c) wheedled
(d) lampooned

**Part II** **Questions 26–50**

Choose the option that best completes each gap.

**26.** A simple blood pressure test can help detect early __________ of high blood pressure.

(a) signs
(b) notices
(c) symbols
(d) methods

**27.** The police __________ the suspect from custody because they learned he was innocent of the crime.

(a) cleared
(b) arrested
(c) released
(d) witnessed

**28.** The school's emphasis on rote learning showed that it __________ memorization over creativity.

(a) recounted
(b) enrolled
(c) attained
(d) valued

**29.** Snoring __________ when blockages obstruct a person's airway during sleep.

(a) suffers
(b) ensues
(c) catches
(d) extends

**30.** Students can be __________ for mispronouncing Vladimir Nabokov's surname, as even reference books disagree on its pronunciation.

(a) beholden
(b) forgiven
(c) mended
(d) fixed

**31.** The PicMax digital camera is __________ with a meter that indicates when battery power is low.

(a) geared
(b) charged
(c) parceled
(d) equipped

**32.** Because illegal immigrants are not protected by workers' rights, they are often taken advantage of and __________ by dishonest employers.

(a) flattered
(b) enforced
(c) mistreated
(d) undertaken

**33.** Joyce preferred novels that kept her in a state of suspense, so that she was always __________ as to what would happen next.

(a) quaint
(b) curious
(c) meddling
(d) deviating

VOCABULARY

34. The cradle makes a gentle rocking ____________ that helps lull the baby to sleep.

(a) drift
(b) stroke
(c) motion
(d) gesture

35. Coffee and cigarettes can ____________ teeth, causing them to become brownish yellow.

(a) blot
(b) blur
(c) stain
(d) smear

36. Dmitri's goal was a(n) ____________ moment in the game, as it lifted the team's spirits and inspired an unexpected comeback.

(a) pivotal
(b) derisive
(c) desperate
(d) incremental

37. The earthquake opened holes on Hammond Street that ____________ so wide that they swallowed entire buses.

(a) gaped
(b) duped
(c) lunged
(d) severed

38. Japan has been ____________ to open its agricultural markets to foreign trade because of worries over the impact on local farmers.

(a) inadvertent
(b) redundant
(c) reluctant
(d) vigilant

39. When using a projector, ____________ the room so that bright lights do not interfere with the images.

(a) dim
(b) pale
(c) fade
(d) cloud

40. Needing a safe place, the refugees sought ____________ in a peaceful country.

(a) abyss
(b) asylum
(c) docility
(d) delirium

41. *American Road* is a novel that ____________ race, class conflict, and fate together into a complex tapestry.

(a) routes
(b) whines
(c) weaves
(d) surmises

42. The angry customer ____________ into the sales manager's office without permission, demanding to speak to her.

(a) sloughed
(b) barged
(c) binged
(d) griped

43. Freedom of speech should be upheld on the condition that it does not oppress or ____________ upon the rights of others.

(a) spoil
(b) malign
(c) infringe
(d) presuppose

**44.** People often look back on their college ___________ and feel shocked by their own reckless behavior.

(a) cascades
(b) crusades
(c) escapades
(d) promenades

**45.** The company's executives will convene to reach a(n) ___________ regarding salaries, which have been the subject of ongoing debate.

(a) accord
(b) affinity
(c) palaver
(d) partition

**46.** Recent bans on chimpanzee testing have ___________ scientists who relied on such animals as research subjects.

(a) imbued
(b) stymied
(c) reneged
(d) atrophied

**47.** Fierce opposition has caused the government to ___________ its plans to change the tax code, so the old system will remain in place.

(a) bolt
(b) scrap
(c) twitch
(d) conflate

**48.** Dehydrated from the triathlon, Victoria ___________ large quantities of water to replenish her body.

(a) purged
(b) infused
(c) gargled
(d) imbibed

**49.** The professor's book on the Korean economy is considered the best in the field, receiving universally ___________ reviews.

(a) archetypal
(b) laudatory
(c) equivocal
(d) nebulous

**50.** George Patton earned a reputation for being ___________ by abusing his power and treating those under his command poorly.

(a) despotic
(b) voracious
(c) scrupulous
(d) ingratiating

This is the end of the Vocabulary section. Do NOT move on to the Reading Comprehension section until instructed to do so. You are NOT allowed to turn to any other section of the test.

TEPS

# Reading Comprehension

## Directions

This section tests your ability to comprehend reading passages. You will have 45 minutes to complete the 40 questions. Be sure to follow the directions given by the proctor.

정답 P 332

## Part I Questions 1–16

Read the passage and choose the option that best completes the passage.

**1.** This October, Koala Language Institute is ____________________________. Take advantage of our celebratory mood by receiving discounts of 10% on our regular five-week courses. Also, on October 29, the school's foundation day, our staff will hold a reception with snacks and beverages. All of us at Koala wish to thank you for supporting us for the past two decades, helping us become Australia's leading language school, and we hope you join us in celebrating this landmark anniversary.

(a) being nationally recognized
(b) marking 20 years in business
(c) announcing its grand opening
(d) offering a series of free classes

**2.** Sir Arthur Conan Doyle, author of the Sherlock Holmes detective stories, felt serialized novels were problematic because ____________________________. To fully appreciate them, readers had to be familiar with the story and understand references to previous events and characters. The reader could not keep up without having read every installment. Therefore, Doyle constructed his tales as self-contained stories, which were still linked to previous and subsequent episodes through the use of some of the same characters.

(a) they often had inconsistencies between the installments
(b) they were published too frequently to remain exciting
(c) readers got bored of the same recurring characters
(d) readers became lost if they missed an installment

3. When designing Gothic cathedrals, French architects wanted to erect imposing buildings with enormous stained-glass windows to let in a lot of light. But walls with these delicate windows would not support the heavy weight of the stone roof, so engineers devised a way to relieve the pressure on the walls. The results were "flying buttresses," external fixtures built outside the main structure and connected to the roof, as a way to redirect part of the weight burden. This crucial innovation allowed architects to realize their goals by ______________________.

(a) angling sunlight strategically into the dark cathedrals
(b) making the use of lighter materials in church roofs possible
(c) drastically cutting down on the time and cost of building
(d) distributing weight away from walls that had stained-glass windows

4. PostExpress is a website that lets you ______________________. If you love getting mail, this site is for you! PostExpress is different from traditional pen pal exchange sites, where you are set up to exchange letters with one person with whom you stay connected. With PostExpress, you send a postcard to a random person, and in turn, receive one from another random person, so you can have several cards coming and going at once. It's a pleasant surprise every time you open your mailbox!

(a) stay in touch with your friends online
(b) exchange postcards with people worldwide
(c) track packages quickly and cheaply on the Internet
(d) find a pen pal you can build a lasting relationship with

5. St. George School would like to advise all parents of ______________________. In keeping with our tradition of teaching good nutritional habits, we ask that on your child's birthday, or for other classroom party events, you send healthy treats like fruit. Also, please ask your child's teacher if any of the students have food allergies. In the past, we have had problems with peanuts and strawberries. So please check before sending refreshments that may contain these allergens.

(a) certain severe food allergies among our student body
(b) a plan to teach children about health and nutrition
(c) the upcoming parties our school will be holding
(d) our food guidelines for your child's classroom

**6.** Charles Darwin's *The Expression of the Emotions in Man and Animals* argues that basic facial expressions ______________________________. Drawing on his evolutionary theory, which posits humankind's descent from apelike ancestors, Darwin was keen to show that modern human behavior has primeval roots. He did so by demonstrating that facial expressions occur as a kind of basic instinct in reaction to stimuli, and because of this, they are universal and can be observed in other primates such as monkeys. One example would be how the face contorts into the facial expression associated with anger when the individual is engaged in fighting.

(a) are tied to fundamental instinctual responses
(b) differ between species such as humans and apes
(c) have become more complex as humans have evolved
(d) are a function of cultural conditioning in each generation

**7.** Pure liberal arts programs in this country are becoming scarce. Small liberal arts colleges, originally devoted to educating students in the Western tradition, are downsizing humanities departments to make way for more career-oriented majors and co-op programs with direct professional applications. In defense of this move, administrators at these institutions claim that, like many other businesses, they must keep up with the times and such decisions are driven largely by financial pressures and enrollment trends. Nevertheless, many still lament the ______________________________.

(a) way market forces are hurting the humanities
(b) overall declining quality of college instruction
(c) emphasis on humanities to the exclusion of all else
(d) administration's refusal to adapt to changing times

**8.** After honeybees find suitable places to forage, they return to their hives and perform an elaborate dance. A popular theory explaining the dance, which was proposed by Karl von Frisch, ______________________________. Frisch asserted that the movements of the dance reflect the distance and direction of the foraging site. Detractors of this view, however, suggested that information about foraging sites is instead communicated by auditory or olfactory signals. Subsequent research confirmed Frisch's theory, and his is now accepted as the authoritative interpretation of the bee dance.

(a) has been successfully refuted by subsequent observations
(b) was initially debated but ultimately proven to be accurate
(c) claimed the dance was to show off how much a bee foraged
(d) stated that dancing bees produced a scent that guided other bees

9. Thomas Carlyle's 1843 work *Past and Present* addressed the "Condition of England" question, a term he coined to describe the social ills and declining morals brought about by the Industrial Revolution and capitalism. Carlyle observed that corrupt industrial magnates exploited the poor for the sake of profit and that English society as a whole had lost its spiritual and creative footing. Capitalist industrialism, driven by utilitarianism and laissez-faire economics, had effectively ______________________________.

(a) brought corrupt industrial magnates to justice
(b) deflected attention from other pressing problems
(c) reduced the country's problem of acute inequality
(d) caused the moral bankruptcy that was plaguing England

10.

Dear Ms. Kelly,

I am writing regarding ______________________________. As discussed in our last meeting, I will leave 50 necklaces and 30 bracelets on consignment with you. You agree to display and sell said items until the end of 2012, for which you will receive 30% of the revenue. While in your possession, all items will be covered by your store's insurance policy. If these terms are acceptable to you, I will arrange delivery of the merchandise.

Yours Truly,
Ramona Finley

(a) the sale of my jewelry in your shop
(b) our agreement on a new insurance policy
(c) the removal of your outdated merchandise
(d) the delivery of goods I purchased from you

**11.** The 1925 case *Pierce v. Society of Sisters* clarified the role of the state in a child's upbringing. The case came to trial when Oregon passed the Compulsory Education Act, requiring that all children between the ages of eight and sixteen attend public schools in their home districts. This enraged parents and private schools, who argued that children were not "creatures of the state" but should be raised based on their parents' will. The Supreme Court ruled in their favor, ______________________________.

(a) deeming that too much power was being given to parents
(b) backing the policy of placing education under state control
(c) requiring that Oregon's private schools be open to the public
(d) granting parents the ultimate say in their children's education

**12.** The cataclysmic eruption of the Indonesian volcano Krakatoa in August 1883 ______________________________. Heralded by years of heavy seismic activity, the eruption was the largest ever recorded, resulting in a massive discharge of superheated gas, molten rock, and volcanic ash. Following the eruption, worldwide temperatures dropped by an average of 2.2 degrees Fahrenheit, as sulfur dioxide collected in the atmosphere and produced cirrus clouds that blocked sunlight. Only after half a decade of acid rain had emptied the clouds of their toxic chemicals did these disruptive effects subside.

(a) disrupted weather so severely that its effects persist to this day
(b) unleashed materials that wreaked havoc on the global climate
(c) blanketed the sky with toxic ash that hindered precipitation
(d) heated up the globe with vast quantities of burning gases

**13.** Most democracies can be classified as presidential or parliamentary. In a presidential system, the nation's leader is selected by voters, whereas in a parliamentary system, the leader is chosen by the legislature. Certain countries, however, ______________________________. One example of such a country is France, where the president is elected by popular vote and then appoints a prime minister. Power is meted out between these two positions, which can give rise to efficient checks and balances within the system. Such political systems are often termed semi-presidential.

(a) flout these conventional notions of leadership altogether
(b) elect a president whose role is largely that of a figurehead
(c) have used a prime minister to check the legislature's power
(d) have adopted models incorporating elements of both systems

**14.** As an investment advisor, I have seen first-hand how even the savviest clients _______________________________. Consider the famous "endowment effect" proposed by behavioral economist Richard Thaler. The idea is that once we own something, we begin to perceive it as having greater value. In this twisted form of reasoning, investors notoriously hold on to stocks too long, even as their value dwindles. This happens not because of any objective assessment of value but simply because of the psychological effect of ownership.

(a) have allowed greed to overpower their principles
(b) liquidate their holdings rashly in the pursuit of profit
(c) let irrational tendencies distort their perception of value
(d) endow stocks they wish to purchase with illusory qualities

**15.** Code-switching is the practice of alternating between two or more languages within the same conversation. This phenomenon is common among bi- or multi-lingual speakers. It does not signify lack of fluency in a language, as some believed in the 1940s and 1950s. _______________________________, using two languages in a way that is consistent in terms of syntax and phonology demonstrates great linguistic proficiency. Code-switching also serves several sophisticated functions such as asserting authority and establishing familiarity.

(a) Even so
(b) To sum up
(c) As a result
(d) On the contrary

**16.** In 2008, hundreds of thousands of babies across China fell ill with kidney complications after being fed milk made from powder contaminated with melamine. This toxic substance was apparently added to make the protein content of diluted milk appear higher. The Chinese government promised to rectify the situation, and dairy companies have compensated the victims' families. _______________________________, many are still infuriated over the incident and skeptical about the overall safety of China's food supply.

(a) Hence
(b) In effect
(c) For all that
(d) In the same vein

**Part II** **Questions 17–37**

Read the passage, question, and options. Then, based on the given information, choose the option that best answers the question.

**17.** Millions are still without electricity after a snowstorm swept through the northeastern United States this past weekend. Coming two months before the official start of winter, the storm caught many people off guard. Power lines were damaged by tree branches that broke under the weight of the snow. Crews are still working to restore power to affected neighborhoods. The storm set a record for the largest snowfall for the month of October.

Q: What is the best title for the news article?
(a) No End to Winter in Sight
(b) Early Snowstorm Causes Trouble
(c) Preparing for Unpredictable Weather
(d) Cold Weather Drives Residents Indoors

**18.** When the red light on your Scanofax printer starts to flash, open the lid and remove the spent roll located next to the ink cartridges. Then gently place a new roll of Scanofax paper into the paper bay. Making sure that the glossy side faces out, thread the paper through the feeder. Press "Load" and the machine will do the rest. If the paper is not loaded correctly, nothing will be printed.

Q: What are the instructions mainly about?
(a) Fixing a jam in a printer's paper tray
(b) Refilling the paper in a Scanofax printer
(c) Sending multi-page scans on a fax machine
(d) Replacing a Scanofax printer's ink cartridge

**19.** As impressive as the trunk is, an elephant's ivory tusks are just as striking. Made of a material called dentin, tusks are long, hollow incisor teeth that are covered with hard, creamy-white enamel. Despite their intimidating appearance, tusks are used more as tools than as weapons. Tusks are the pickaxes an elephant uses to dig to find water. They are also used as crowbars to strip bark from a tree for food.

Q: What is the main topic of the passage?
(a) How elephants sharpen their tusks
(b) Features and functions of elephant tusks
(c) The physical structure of an elephant's trunk
(d) How an elephant's trunk and tusks work together

20. There are special films, stickers, and cases for wireless electronic devices on the market that purport to protect users from the electromagnetic fields created by such devices. But before buying these accessories, you should be aware of a few facts that bear on their supposed usefulness. First, electronic device manufacturers already follow international guidelines restricting the emissions of electromagnetic radiation. Furthermore, there are no proven health drawbacks linked to the regular use of wireless electronic devices. So the protective coverings are there if you wish to buy them, but it is likely just as safe to do without them.

Q: What is the main purpose of the announcement?
(a) To state the dangers of electromagnetic radiation
(b) To discourage the use of wireless electronic devices
(c) To explain how protective coverings filter radiation
(d) To point out that protective coverings are superfluous

21.

Dear Ms. Cho,

To begin with, we would like to thank you for being a loyal customer at Korea Cable TV and Internet for the past few years. I am contacting you today because the credit card you have registered with our automatic payment system is scheduled to expire next month. To avoid any service disruptions, we request that you inform us of your updated credit card number and expiration date either by phone or through your online account. Thank you for your cooperation.

Sincerely,
Jake Yoon
KCTV Customer Service

Q: What is the main purpose of the letter?
(a) To request payment for cable TV services
(b) To ask Ms. Cho for updated billing information
(c) To provide advice on setting up an online account
(d) To enroll Ms. Cho in a new automatic payment plan

**22.** Due to the rise of the so-called "BRIC" countries—Brazil, Russia, India, and China—traditional patterns of global economic activity have shifted. Once the undisputed powerhouse of the global economy, the United States has seen its share of the world's economy shrink for 25 years. American workers who once earned good salaries in manufacturing have seen their jobs shipped overseas to developing countries and newly advanced economies. American workers are now waking up to the realization that they face increasingly skilled international competitors who can do the same work at a lower cost.

Q: What is the main idea of the passage?
(a) Companies are facing a debilitating shortage of skilled labor in the US.
(b) The US is becoming the world's largest importer of foreign-made goods.
(c) BRIC countries are struggling to match the US's level of economic output.
(d) Developing countries have undermined the US's economic dominance.

**23.** The use of skin care products dates as far back as ancient Egypt. Ancient Egyptian men and women took great pride in how they looked. They used various cosmetics like oils, perfumes, and makeup to both enhance their beauty and protect their skin from the harsh desert weather. Indeed, skin products were so valued that workers often accepted them as payment for all or part of their wages.

Q: Which of the following is correct according to the passage?
(a) Ancient Egyptian men did not use any beauty products.
(b) Oils were used solely for healing purposes in ancient Egypt.
(c) Ancient Egypt's pleasant climate promoted naturally healthy skin.
(d) Skin products were used as payment for some jobs in ancient Egypt.

**24.** Before purchasing a pet frog, make sure it is the right pet for you. Domestic frogs live from 4 to 15 years, much longer than the average goldfish. Each species has specific habitat and dietary needs that you must meet, even if it means feeding your frog live mice or crickets. Owners should be aware that handling frogs is discouraged because they breathe through their skin. Raising amphibians is prohibited in some areas, so check your local laws.

Q: Which of the following is correct about pet frogs according to the passage?
(a) They live approximately as long as goldfish.
(b) They should never be given live mice or crickets.
(c) Regular handling of them is recommended.
(d) Some areas do not allow them as pets.

25. My great-grandmother's ninth pregnancy at age 46 was especially difficult. At the time, her eldest child, my grandfather, was away at college, putting an extra emotional and financial strain on the family. So she decided to move back to the farm where she was raised as an only child and where she had married my great-grandfather two decades earlier. She carried the baby to term and in 1905 gave birth to a healthy boy.

Q: Which of the following is correct about the writer according to the passage?
(a) His grandfather was the youngest of nine children.
(b) His great-grandmother grew up in the city.
(c) His great-grandmother did not have any siblings.
(d) His grandfather's parents married in 1905.

26. Beethoven revolutionized the structure of the symphony with an extended format, a wider range and density of sound, and inclusion of new instruments. Composers before him had created simpler symphonies and had been quite prolific—Haydn wrote 106 symphonies and Mozart 41. Those after Beethoven, however, found it difficult, if not impossible, to write more than the nine he composed. Brahms, for instance, was so overawed by Beethoven's example that he did not produce his First Symphony until he was 43, and his final total was four.

Q: Which of the following is correct according to the passage?
(a) Beethoven shortened the performance time of the symphony.
(b) Haydn's symphonies surpassed Beethoven's in terms of complexity.
(c) Later symphony composers found it hard to exceed Beethoven's output.
(d) Brahms wrote all four of his symphonies before he reached the age of 43.

27. Wine tastings involve certain conventions of drinking etiquette. A glass of red wine is held at the base of the bowl, while a glass of white wine is held by the stem so that its chill is unaffected by body temperature. Before drinking, swirl the wine in the glass to examine its body. Younger red wines are more vivid, whereas more aged red wines are browner in color. Sniff the wine and take a small sip first, exhaling as you swallow. Most wine tastings will provide bread or cheese to cleanse your palate between wines.

Q: Which of the following is correct according to the passage?
(a) White wine should be kept away from body heat.
(b) The color of red wine becomes more vibrant as it ages.
(c) Tasters should not exhale when swallowing the first sip of wine.
(d) Food is not served at wine tastings to avoid ruining the palate.

**28.** The Myers-Briggs Type Indicator (MBTI), a well-known personality test based on the psychological theories of Carl Jung, was developed by Katharine Cook Briggs and Isabel Briggs Myers during World War II to help women identify jobs that would suit them. Today, the MBTI is used by many companies for recruitment and training purposes. And while the test's use for career counseling has increased, the MBTI has been criticized as unreliable. Specifically, the test claims to reveal a person's innate personality type, but studies have shown that 76% of test subjects fall into different types when tested twice.

Q: Which of the following is correct about the MBTI according to the passage?
(a) It is based on the psychological theories of Briggs and Myers.
(b) It originated as a test for identifying suitable jobs for women.
(c) Criticisms of it have caused its use in career counseling to wane.
(d) Almost half of its test takers receive differing results when retested.

**29.** American playwright Tom Lanier Williams, who later adopted the name "Tennessee" after his father's home state, was born in 1911 in Columbus, Mississippi. He redefined American theater with his memorable characters and authentic depiction of the American South. *A Streetcar Named Desire*, set in New Orleans, netted him his first Pulitzer Prize in 1948. He was awarded the same honor for his 1955 play *Cat on a Hot Tin Roof*, the last of his truly great commercial triumphs. Williams's works inspired numerous adaptations for the ballet, opera, and screen.

Q: Which of the following is correct about Tennessee Williams according to the passage?
(a) His father named him Tennessee after his native state.
(b) *Cat on a Hot Tin Roof* was his first play to garner acclaim.
(c) Two of the plays he wrote were awarded Pulitzer Prizes.
(d) His plays were critical successes but commercial failures.

**30.** During the previous year, 80% of Veritelecom's customers had errors on their phone bills, most of which were in the phone company's favor and went overlooked by customers. In cases where the errors were detected, many claims were declared void because the 90-day window in which customers can receive a full refund on billing errors had expired. Some disgruntled customers have gotten their money back by hiring lawyers to help recover up to 12 months' worth of refunds, but such legal assistance typically costs 50% of whatever credit is earned.

Q: Which of the following is correct according to the article?
(a) The majority of billing errors that were found benefited Veritelecom.
(b) Veritelecom received complaints from 80% of its customers last year.
(c) Veritelecom's policy is to refund billing mistakes claimed within one year.
(d) Lawyers are powerless to secure refunds after the refund window closes.

**31.** Exercise programs need to incorporate recovery periods to maximize results for athletes because training without adequate rest depletes muscles of energy and causes muscle breakdown. A sophisticated training schedule will include both short- and long-term recovery periods. The former are rest days following strenuous workouts; they allow muscles to repair. Long-term recovery periods occur at regular intervals in seasonal training schedules to prevent the body from adapting to training. As such, long-term recovery periods typically involve cross-training, or alternating the type of exercise being performed.

Q: Which of the following is correct according to the article?
(a) Uninterrupted exercise increases the energy that is stored in muscles.
(b) Short-term recovery involves taking short breaks during a workout session.
(c) The ultimate goal of long-term recovery periods is adaptation to training.
(d) A different type of exercise from normal is used during long-term recovery.

**32.** Snowflakes embody the dual principles of symmetry and irregularity. Their symmetry owes to the shape of the water molecule, whose four triangular surfaces combine to form layers of hexagonal (six-sided) ice crystals. This is common to all snowflakes. What make snowflakes infinitely diverse, however, are the conditions under which they form, namely air currents, temperature, and humidity. The presence of dirt and dust also affect the formation of a snowflake: they make it heavier and easier to melt. All of these factors account for why, statistically, it is not impossible for two snowflakes to look exactly the same, but the chances of it happening are very slim.

Q: Which of the following is correct according to the passage?
(a) Snowflakes' irregularity comes from water's molecular structure.
(b) A water molecule's six triangular surfaces cause hexagonal ice crystals.
(c) The presence of dirt and dust facilitates the melting of snowflakes.
(d) It is statistically impossible for two snowflakes to be identical.

**33.** Do you find yourself arriving at work only to worry if you've left your coffeemaker or oven on? Put your mind at ease with a HomeSmart system. It lets you log in to your account and with a few simple mouse clicks control your home appliances. You can even turn them on before leaving work so that your home is warm and the lights are on when you arrive. Discover the convenience of HomeSmart today.

Q: What can be inferred about the HomeSmart system from the advertisement?
(a) It can grant its users peace of mind.
(b) It is activated by a portable remote control.
(c) It can only be accessed from outside the home.
(d) It tracks users' monthly home electricity usage.

**34.** As a life-long California resident, I know that our Central Valley is nothing short of an agricultural wonderland. After all, it produces 8% of our nation's farm output on less than 1% of the total farm area. So I can appreciate the public's concern that Central Valley is attracting developers seeking to build cheap housing. Preservationists claim that such urban sprawl at the expense of farmland will adversely affect the region. However, based on plain economics, development might prevail over agriculture, and perhaps it should. After all, urban growth could mean a more diverse job base and a solution to unemployment.

Q: Which statement about Central Valley would the writer most likely agree with?
(a) It needs to be preserved from urban development.
(b) Its economy is being hampered by high housing prices.
(c) Sacrificing some of its farmland could boost the economy.
(d) Developing its land is key to increasing its agricultural output.

**35.** The first adhesive postage stamp was known as the Penny Black. It featured an image of Queen Victoria on a black background. The stamp stopped being used after about one year over concerns about its design: the red cancellation mark that is applied to stamps to designate them as used virtually disappeared into the black background, and any red ink that was visible was easily wiped off, rendering the stamp as good as new. What followed was the Penny Red, which had the same image on a red background. At the same time, cancellation devices began being issued with black ink.

Q: What can be inferred about the Penny Black from the passage?
(a) Its design lent itself to being illegally reused.
(b) It gave rise to a need for cancellation stamps.
(c) It was discontinued out of respect for the monarch.
(d) Its ink rubbed off easily and made the stamp unusable.

**36.**

To the Editor:

Recently, state officials decided to use taxpayers' money on rehabilitation programs for gambling addicts. While I realize that addictions are diseases and must be dealt with accordingly, I believe it would be more effective to tackle the root of the problem and get rid of it once and for all. If gambling venues remain available and unregulated, people will continue to fall victim, creating a continuous burden on the state. If this threat can be eliminated, however, we can use our funds on more productive endeavors.

Lawrence Hall

Q: Which statement would the writer most likely agree with?
(a) State authorities should ban gambling establishments.
(b) State programs for gambling addiction deserve more funding.
(c) Addiction programs should take a more compassionate stance.
(d) Government-run casinos are effective at solving state budget shortfalls.

**37.** Before reading Rebecca Asher's *Shattered: Modern Motherhood and the Illusion of Equality*, the book's title gave me the impression it would follow the polemical conventions of most feminist parenting tomes. That it does not merely carp about women's traditional role as primary caregiver to newborn children came as a breath of fresh air. What Asher does is offer tangible solutions, scouring the developed world for social programs that support new mothers' participation in the workforce and new fathers' investment of personal time in their children's upbringing.

Q: What can be inferred from the review?
(a) *Shattered* defied the reviewer's initial expectations.
(b) Asher is an apologist for traditional roles in parenting.
(c) *Shattered* overlooks the government's role in family life.
(d) Asher's book criticizes feminism's polemical tendencies.

## Part III Questions 38–40

Read the passage and identify the option that does NOT belong.

**38.** Dietary supplements' classification as food means they are not subject to the same regulations as prescription drugs. (a) To reach the market, prescription drugs have to go through strict laboratory and clinical trials. (b) The tests performed must demonstrate that the products are safe for consumers. (c) On the other hand, deficiencies in certain vitamins and minerals can be extremely dangerous. (d) Dietary supplements, classified under the umbrella of food, are able to skirt these requirements.

**39.** Even after the Romans withdrew from Britain in the early fifth century AD, several distinctly Roman elements persisted in British culture. (a) Initially, Britons still spoke Latin and tried to keep up Roman forms of economic and political life. (b) Roman England became a prosperous colony with a population of three to four million people. (c) Many buildings, in terms of style and materials used, retained the influence of classical Roman architecture. (d) The survival of Christianity, the Romans' religion, was another example of the persistence of the old ways of life.

**40.** The Springfield Police Department used a local baseball game to conduct a controversial surveillance experiment on unsuspecting spectators. (a) Law enforcement was caught off guard by the spectators' reactions to the unorthodox security method. (b) About 20,000 random spectators unknowingly got their faces scanned and matched against mug shots from police files. (c) The experiment resulted in nine potential troublemakers being identified, but no arrests were actually made. (d) Despite the police's insistence that no harm was done, news of the experiment has raised questions about spectators' right to privacy.

This is the end of the Reading Comprehension section. Please remain seated until the proctor has instructed otherwise. You are NOT allowed to turn to any other section of the test.

# 서울대 최신기출 6

***Listening** Comprehension*

***Grammar***

***Vocabulary***

***Reading** Comprehension*

# LISTENING COMPREHENSION

## DIRECTIONS

1. In the Listening Comprehension section, all content will be presented orally rather than in written form.
2. This section contains four parts, each with fifteen individual items. For each part, you will receive separate instructions. Listen to the instructions carefully, and choose the best answer from the options for each item.

Scripts P 318 / 정답 P 333

**Part I** **Questions 1—15**

You will now hear fifteen individual spoken questions or statements, each followed by four spoken responses. Choose the most appropriate response for each item.

**Part II** **Questions 16—30**

You will now hear fifteen short conversation fragments, followed by four spoken responses. Choose the most appropriate response to complete each conversation.

**Part III** **Questions 31–45**

You will now hear fifteen complete conversations. For each conversation, you will be asked to answer a question. Each conversation and its corresponding question will be read twice. Then you will hear four options which will be read only once. Based on the given information, choose the option that best answers the question.

**Part IV** **Questions 46–60**

You will now hear fifteen short talks. After each talk, you will be asked to answer a question. Each talk and its corresponding question will be read twice. Then you will hear four options which will be read only once. Based on the given information, choose the option that best answers the question.

TEPS

# GRAMMAR

## DIRECTIONS

This section tests your grammar skills. You will have 25 minutes to complete the 50 questions. Be sure to follow the directions given by the proctor.

정답 P 333

## Part I Questions 1–20

Choose the option that best completes each gap.

**1.** A: Is it too late to call Joanne?
B: I'm afraid ___________. It's already 11 pm.

(a) ever
(b) well
(c) that
(d) so

**2.** A: Have they finished the building inspection?
B: Yes, it ___________ yesterday.

(a) completed
(b) is completed
(c) was completed
(d) had completed

**3.** A: Claudia seemed so cold and reserved at first, but she's not like that at all.
B: Yes, looks can be ___________. She's actually very friendly and warm.

(a) to deceive
(b) deceiving
(c) deceived
(d) deceive

**4.** A: How is living with Eric and Jim going?
B: Great! Living with friends definitely ___________ advantages.

(a) has
(b) have
(c) was having
(d) were having

**5.** A: How much would it cost to take a vacation to Hawaii?
B: That depends on the hotel ___________ you choose to stay at.

(a) that
(b) where
(c) in what
(d) in which

**6.** A: Are you joining that aerobics class again this month?
B: No, I'm too busy with work ___________.

(a) going
(b) to go
(c) gone
(d) goes

**7.** A: That dress looks great on you.
B: Really? I think it's ___________ too short.

(a) such
(b) very
(c) real
(d) far

**8.** A: Can you make it to Andrew's play tonight?
B: Unfortunately, I can't. If I had time, I definitely ___________.

(a) would have come
(b) will have come
(c) would come
(d) will come

9. A: Some students in my class have a very contagious flu.
B: I know. I wonder how many ___________.

(a) they have passed on it
(b) they have passed it on to
(c) of whom have passed on it
(d) of them have passed on it to

10. A: It's great having that exchange student from Africa here.
B: Yeah. ___________ people from so far away come to our town.

(a) Do we have rarely
(b) We do have rarely
(c) Rarely do we have
(d) Rarely we do have

11. A: Does James travel a lot for work?
B: Of course. Over a third of his work hours ___________ spent on the road.

(a) is
(b) are
(c) has
(d) have

12. A: What did Mr. Sedgwick want?
B: Just to thank me for ___________ his roof.

(a) such a good job doing to repair
(b) doing a such good job to repair
(c) a such good job to do repairing
(d) doing such a good job repairing

13. A: Do you have a refund policy?
B: Yes. If the item isn't ___________, you can return it within 15 days.

(a) liked to you
(b) to your liking
(c) liked it to you
(d) to your liking it

14. A: We need to call a handyman to fix our water heater.
B: No, let's just get a new one installed. It's ___________ repair.

(a) beneath
(b) beyond
(c) beside
(d) below

15. A: Do you know if Paul has moved to Paris yet?
B: Since I haven't seen him for a while, I think ___________.

(a) he may have done well so
(b) he may well have done so
(c) so he may well have done to
(d) so he well may have done to

16. A: Are you all set for the bake sale?
B: Yep! I ___________ so many treats over the last few days.

(a) make
(b) am making
(c) will have made
(d) have been making

17. A: Can we meet tomorrow at 2 pm?
B: Sorry, I can't. ___________ a class then.

(a) I'll teach
(b) I've taught
(c) I'm teaching
(d) I'll have taught

18. A: Ms. Roberts is pretty annoyed with Ted.
B: I have no idea ___________ to get on her nerves like that.

(a) what he said was it
(b) it was what he said
(c) he said what was it
(d) what it was he said

GRAMMAR

19. A: I'm glad you're joining tomorrow's protest.
B: Thanks. It's high time I ___________ a stand for something important.

(a) have taken
(b) am taking
(c) will take
(d) took

20. A: How many people can the conference room accommodate?
B: It has ___________ of 200 people.

(a) capacity
(b) a capacity
(c) all capacity
(d) each capacity

**Part II** **Questions 21–40**

Choose the option that best completes each gap.

21. Asafa Powell ran the 100-meter dash in 9.74 seconds at the Rieti Grand Prix, ___________ 0.03 seconds off the previous world record.

(a) shaved
(b) shaving
(c) had shaved
(d) being shaved

22. Professor Davis emphasized that final papers for his course ___________ be submitted on time, without exception.

(a) might
(b) could
(c) must
(d) may

23. At one point, Philadelphia ___________ the largest city in the US, surpassing even New York City.

(a) is
(b) was
(c) is being
(d) has been

24. Everyone in the office came to the outing ___________ Leonard, who had to stay home because of a cold.

(a) besides
(b) opposite
(c) in case of
(d) contrary to

25. For many years, paramount among the goals of the Homeless Advocacy Center ___________ improving public awareness of homelessness.

(a) is
(b) are
(c) has been
(d) have been

26. ___________ behavioral psychology, B. F. Skinner wrote many books on the subject.

(a) Pioneered in the field
(b) A pioneer in the field of
(c) A pioneer was in the field
(d) Pioneered was in the field of

**27.** Ron had told his roommates that he ___________ the following month, so they were surprised when he decided to stay.

(a) was moving out
(b) had moved out
(c) has moved out
(d) will move out

**28.** Over ___________ few decades, the shipbuilding and steel industries have contributed greatly to South Korea's economic growth.

(a) past
(b) the past
(c) any past
(d) each past

**29.** There ___________ so many layoffs in previous months that Sarah began to fear for her own job.

(a) are
(b) will be
(c) had been
(d) have been

**30.** ___________ the hotel room to be spacious and modern, the tourists were disappointed by the rustic decor of the cramped room.

(a) Expected
(b) To expect
(c) Had expected
(d) Having expected

**31.** ___________ the International Whaling Commission banned commercial whaling in 1986, it continues to allow whaling for scientific purposes.

(a) Until
(b) While
(c) Before
(d) Unless

**32.** Employees who had lunch while attending to other business ate twice as much food as ___________ who did not multitask during their meal.

(a) those
(b) them
(c) they
(d) that

**33.** After a disastrous investment, Jason tried his best to avoid bankruptcy, but he still ___________ not recoup his losses.

(a) should
(b) could
(c) must
(d) need

**34.** ___________ he had finished writing his annual report, Bruno submitted it to his supervisor for approval.

(a) So
(b) Once
(c) Though
(d) Whether

**35.** Children ___________ face an increased risk of respiratory infections, severe asthma, and other maladies.

(a) exposed to secondhand smoke
(b) with secondhand smoke exposed
(c) who expose to secondhand smoke
(d) to whom secondhand smoke exposes

**36.** Tim received extra vacation time when he renewed his contract at work, ___________ was a significant factor in his decision to stay.

(a) that
(b) what
(c) which
(d) where

**37.** All items on the agenda ___________ discussed, the meeting was finally brought to a close.

(a) been
(b) have been
(c) were being
(d) having been

**38.** A laboratory ___________ with computers and audio language tools is considered a necessity in many language schools.

(a) to equip
(b) equipped
(c) equipping
(d) is equipped

**39.** Mindy did not book a hotel in advance, but she realized that she ___________ when she could not find any vacancies.

(a) ought
(b) ought to
(c) ought to have
(d) ought to book

**40.** As World War II was ending, many German scientists sought ___________ by Russian forces, preferring to surrender to America instead.

(a) to evade capture
(b) to evade capturing
(c) evading to capture
(d) evading to have captured

GRAMMAR

**Part III** **Questions 41–45**

Read each sentence carefully and identify the option that contains a grammatical error.

**41.** (a) A: So how was your night out at the cinema after work on Friday?
(b) B: Great. My brother and I wound up catching a mystery together.
(c) A: Was it worthy of a recommendation? I might go out this weekend.
(d) B: I wouldn't say it was spectacular, but the movie was worth watching it.

**42.** (a) A: I heard you got a new place downtown. How do you like it?
(b) B: It's great! It's quite a change from staying in the country.
(c) A: I bet. So I guess you are getting used to live in Bangkok.
(d) B: I am. It's still a bit overwhelming, but I'm finding my niche.

**43.** (a) A: Does this subway line that goes to Ledderose Station?
(b) B: Yes, but I'm afraid you'll have to go to the other platform.
(c) A: Oh. Isn't this the main circle line around the city?
(d) B: Yes. But trains on this side go in the opposite direction.

**44.** (a) A: Excuse me, are you good with cameras? I'm having trouble.
(b) B: I do know a bit about them. What are you having difficulty?
(c) A: I'm trying to remove the lens, but it refuses to budge.
(d) B: It's a left-handed thread, so you have to turn the lens the other way.

**45.** (a) A: You're still on the lookout for those concert tickets, right?
(b) B: Yes, but I haven't been able to find anyone willing to sell.
(c) A: I've been keeping an eye out, too, but nothing's come up.
(d) B: Maybe it's time to give up and start making other plan.

Read each sentence carefully and identify the option that contains a grammatical error.

**46.** (a) When reading a good book, the reader feels that his or her emotions are stirred. (b) An expert author is one which books have the power to draw out the reader's feelings. (c) On the other hand, poor writers try to manipulate their readers. (d) Too often, their novels merely offer hollow phrases and empty feelings.

**47.** (a) In ancient times, it was customary to ascribe terrible acts of nature to divine forces. (b) These powerful beings often had erratic, malevolent, and mischievous temperaments. (c) Extreme acts of nature often attributed to deities that had been offended by people. (d) To prevent misfortune, people would make offerings intended to appease their gods.

**48.** (a) South America's Amazon River is the longest river on the continent. (b) The river's sources can be found throughout Peru, Ecuador, and Bolivia. (c) It flows thousands of miles across Brazil, emptying into the Atlantic Ocean. (d) The Amazon carries most water than any other river on Earth.

**49.** (a) Many technical terms used by volcanologists who are derived from the Hawaiian language. (b) They were adopted by researchers interested in Hawaii's numerous active volcanoes. (c) Such terms include *pahoehoe*, which denotes slow-moving lava under a smooth crust. (d) Another is *Pele's hair*, which is a term for lava that has formed thin strands in the wind.

**50.** (a) The Parthenon is an ancient Greek temple located in the city of Athens. (b) It was dedicated to Athena, the goddess of wisdom, courage, and justice. (c) Situated on top of the Acropolis, it has survived much wars and fires since 438 BC. (d) However, its bronze and stone decorations have mostly been destroyed.

This is the end of the Grammar section. Do NOT move on to the next section until instructed to do so. You are NOT allowed to turn to any other section of the test.

TEPS

# VOCABULARY

**DIRECTIONS**

This section tests your vocabulary skills. You will have 15 minutes to complete the 50 questions. Be sure to follow the directions given by the proctor.

정답 P 333

## Part I Questions 1—25

Choose the option that best completes each gap.

**1.** A: Northland Savings Bank, how can I help you?

B: I'd like to open a savings ___________.

(a) branch
(b) invoice
(c) account
(d) statement

**2.** A: Can I cut through these woods to get to the bus station?

B: Yes, there's a small hiking ___________ that leads there.

(a) leash
(b) trace
(c) aisle
(d) trail

**3.** A: Is the team still debating who to hire after Alan leaves?

B: Yeah, we still haven't ___________ a replacement.

(a) held
(b) meant
(c) chosen
(d) connected

**4.** A: I wonder when we'll get those new spring blouses to sell.

B: The ___________ will be delivered tomorrow, I think.

(a) quality
(b) entrance
(c) shipment
(d) substance

**5.** A: Do you throw out your old bills?

B: Yes, but I ___________ them into little pieces first for security.

(a) whip
(b) shred
(c) refrain
(d) decline

**6.** A: Why did Terry leave in such a huff?

B: I don't know. He just ___________ out of the room suddenly.

(a) wavered
(b) pressed
(c) startled
(d) bolted

**7.** A: Do you think Tom was acting strange today?

B: No, his behavior didn't seem especially ___________ to me.

(a) fertile
(b) prolific
(c) tedious
(d) peculiar

**8.** A: Did you ask Molly out for a date?

B: Yes, but she ___________. I was so disappointed.

(a) talked me up
(b) put me away
(c) bailed me out
(d) turned me down

**9.** A: Are you sure this tent can make it through a windstorm?

B: It has strong poles, so it can ___________ even strong gusts.

(a) withstand
(b) conserve
(c) condone
(d) remedy

**10.** A: Can I use air miles to get bumped up from economy to business class?

B: Sorry, we can't offer ___________ on this flight.

(a) relief
(b) disposal
(c) upgrades
(d) donations

**11.** A: I wish I didn't have to take that psychology course.

B: It's a(n) ___________ course, so you can't avoid it.

(a) compulsory
(b) inquisitive
(c) superficial
(d) explicit

**12.** A: Is this food enough for all our guests?

B: Don't worry, there's ___________ food to go around.

(a) avid
(b) voluble
(c) abundant
(d) competent

**13.** A: Did you take a nap?

B: Yeah, I ___________ while watching TV after lunch.

(a) shoved off
(b) nodded off
(c) headed out
(d) dropped out

**14.** A: Did I overreact in my fight with Jen?

B: No, you were ___________. You had every right to be mad.

(a) justified
(b) clinched
(c) apprised
(d) entrusted

**15.** A: Theresa and Liz need to learn to work together.

B: I know. They should ___________ their differences and cooperate.

(a) enclose
(b) reconcile
(c) correspond
(d) complement

**16.** A: Ann's so upset about losing her job.

B: I ___________ with her. I've been let go myself.

(a) sympathize
(b) apprehend
(c) contrive
(d) comply

**17.** A: Look at Maggie's origami! She's so good with her hands.

B: Wow! I knew she was ___________, but this is amazing.

(a) acute
(b) affluent
(c) diffident
(d) dexterous

**18.** A: Excuse me, I can't find my son. I think he's lost in the store.

B: I'll ___________ him over the loudspeaker.

(a) air
(b) page
(c) pitch
(d) voice

**19.** A: Do you think Zack will recover quickly from losing the writing contest?

B: He's a ___________ young man, so he'll likely return to normal soon.

(a) sedentary
(b) resilient
(c) dilatory
(d) cursory

**20.** A: Is there a big price difference between these two phones?

B: No, the difference is ___________.

(a) spare
(b) wanton
(c) negligible
(d) meritorious

**21.** A: Why is management renovating the office when we're so in debt?

B: It's probably a ___________ to hide the company's financial troubles from the clients.

(a) ploy
(b) hunch
(c) demise
(d) garnish

**22.** A: Mr. Jensen is so strict about his classroom discipline.

B: He thinks it's important to be ___________ with students.

(a) deft
(b) stern
(c) ample
(d) evasive

**23.** A: Do you think my new jeans would be appropriate for the party?

B: Well, it's a formal event, so you might ___________ there.

(a) feel out of place
(b) be dressed to kill
(c) have one too many
(d) be the worse for wear

**24.** A: Where should we place the logo on our t-shirt design?

B: Let's ___________ it across the front so it's really visible.

(a) inaugurate
(b) emblazon
(c) embezzle
(d) inundate

**25.** A: Aren't you annoyed that your husband goes golfing so often?

B: No, he works hard, so I don't ___________ him his golf trips.

(a) pester
(b) eschew
(c) reprieve
(d) begrudge

**Part II** **Questions 26–50**

Choose the option that best completes each gap.

**26.** Although they come with no financial rewards, ___________ positions are a good way to get work experience.

(a) sacrifice
(b) volunteer
(c) candidate
(d) retirement

**27.** Chuseok is a major Korean holiday which is ___________ every autumn.

(a) withheld
(b) celebrated
(c) responded
(d) acquainted

**28.** The postman approached the house ___________ because he did not want to provoke the fierce dog.

(a) slightly
(b) precisely
(c) cautiously
(d) nominally

**29.** James Joyce's novels contain so many details of Dublin that if the city were destroyed, it could be ___________ from his fiction.

(a) transferred
(b) persuaded
(c) sponsored
(d) recreated

**30.** Already a major supplier of fur, Russia initially explored Siberia intending to ___________ its trade using additional fur found there.

(a) abide
(b) convey
(c) expand
(d) unravel

**31.** To keep the park clean for our community, anyone caught ___________ will be fined.

(a) chattering
(b) muddling
(c) shuffling
(d) littering

**32.** The philanthropist devoted his life to ___________ causes such as distributing emergency food supplies and making health care available to the needy.

(a) haughty
(b) vulnerable
(c) pessimistic
(d) humanitarian

**33.** After the terrible tornado, hundreds of people were left living in tents and other temporary ___________.

(a) crusades
(b) shelters
(c) terrains
(d) cliques

**34.** Ryan's long, ___________ speech cost him points with the judges, who prefer debaters to keep their speeches concise.

(a) taciturn
(b) rambling
(c) abandoned
(d) impeccable

**35.** New evidence suggests that a certain type of protein may be the ___________ responsible for male pattern balding.

(a) culprit
(b) partisan
(c) opponent
(d) dependant

**36.** Sam negotiated for an increase in her weekly ___________, arguing that her value to the company merited higher compensation.

(a) stints
(b) assets
(c) wages
(d) gauges

**37.** Preston's Auto Center can ___________ your ordinary car with unique paint or special wheels and rims to suit your individual preferences.

(a) impersonate
(b) propagate
(c) customize
(d) indispose

**38.** Arthritis is among the most ___________ illnesses because it can severely restrict the sufferer's movements.

(a) irradiating
(b) debilitating
(c) conciliating
(d) expostulating

**39.** Francesca ___________ her tall figure from her mother, who comes from a long line of tall women.

(a) gleaned
(b) inherited
(c) resembled
(d) bequeathed

**40.** Sean was awakened by a ___________ crowd protesting in front of the government office next to his apartment.

(a) canonical
(b) credulous
(c) clamorous
(d) clandestine

**41.** Street food vendors continue to ___________ in America as more customers are turning to food trucks for their affordability and convenience.

(a) fumble
(b) swelter
(c) conceive
(d) proliferate

**42.** Musicians' personal romantic experiences often ___________ them to write songs about love.

(a) regale
(b) inspire
(c) promise
(d) commission

**43.** Made with soft lamb's wool, Toasty Feet baby shoes have a thick ___________ layer to keep your child's feet safe and warm.

(a) sultry
(b) sparse
(c) thermal
(d) parched

**44.** The speaker asserted that the world's high rate of oil consumption puts the natural resource in danger of total __________.

(a) recession
(b) depletion
(c) detention
(d) repression

**45.** The Lapindo mud volcano continues to exact a devastating __________ on East Java, displacing people and destroying villages.

(a) bait
(b) gall
(c) toll
(d) lag

**46.** In the American judicial system, defendants have the right not to __________ themselves, and so may refuse to answer compromising questions.

(a) adjourn
(b) abdicate
(c) proscribe
(d) incriminate

**47.** The principal announced that students found __________ idly in the hall during class hours would be issued a warning.

(a) pining
(b) longing
(c) loitering
(d) enduring

**48.** Kate thought that buying a separate blender would be __________, since her food processor already performed this function.

(a) insolent
(b) manifold
(c) redundant
(d) nonchalant

**49.** Some household products that seem harmless, such as toothpaste and mouthwash, can be toxic if __________ in large amounts.

(a) ingested
(b) incurred
(c) consoled
(d) convened

**50.** Thanks to the prompt call of a bystander, paramedics were able to __________ a swimmer who was found unconscious after almost drowning.

(a) obfuscate
(b) resuscitate
(c) incarcerate
(d) promulgate

This is the end of the Vocabulary section. Do NOT move on to the Reading Comprehension section until instructed to do so. You are NOT allowed to turn to any other section of the test.

# READING COMPREHENSION

## DIRECTIONS

This section tests your ability to comprehend reading passages. You will have 45 minutes to complete the 40 questions. Be sure to follow the directions given by the proctor.

정답 P 333

**Part I** **Questions 1–16**

Read the passage and choose the option that best completes the passage.

**1.** We at Dr. Gerson's dermatology clinic would like to notify patients of the following policy change affecting those with CHP Health insurance coverage. Starting January 1, treatments designated as nonemergency cosmetic procedures, such as laser hair removal, will no longer be covered by CHP Health. Therefore, patients with this insurance plan undergoing these procedures ______________________________. Please call Dr. Gerson's office if you have any questions.

(a) need to classify them as elective to be covered
(b) must be referred by their normal family doctor
(c) will have to pay for them out of their own pocket
(d) should apply directly to CHP Health for reimbursement

**2.** Now a major means of mass transit, the first bus was actually ______________________________. In 1826, French businessman Stanislas Baudry organized a regularly scheduled carriage route in Nantes to attract more customers to his establishment on the outskirts of the town. Noting that riders were using the service to get off at intermediate points along the way instead of continuing to the bathhouse, Baudry altered the shuttle service to focus purely on transportation. Thus, the world's first public transit service using buses was born.

(a) introduced to shuttle patrons to a public bath
(b) regarded as unsafe by many people at the time
(c) too slow to serve as a viable option for mass transit
(d) inefficient since it did not make stops along its route

**3.** One important part of giving an exam is ______________________________. On a typical exam, the majority of students should be able to score around 75%. However, if your students do not do as well as you had expected, you may need to scale their scores. One method you can use in such cases is simply to take the class average, excluding any outliers, and then multiply that number by four-thirds to get a new maximum possible score. Then, make each student's individual score a percentage of this maximum, rather than of the original maximum score.

(a) adhering to the content of the course
(b) deciding how to calculate final grades
(c) including questions of varying difficulty
(d) determining whether to award a partial score

**4.** In a recent book, political economists Daron Acemoglu and James Robinson make a powerful case that ______________________________. Factors such as natural resources and access to transportation corridors are of course taken into account in their argument. But Acemoglu and Robinson cite examples from a variety of countries over several millennia to show how policies which create positive incentives, reward innovation, and mitigate inequality are what ultimately lead to prosperity. When individuals' actions are guided by effective policy-making, they argue, everyone benefits.

(a) economic lessons from ancient countries are no longer pertinent
(b) governments should not try to manipulate economic growth
(c) good national policy is the result of a favorable economy
(d) economic success depends largely on good governance

**5.** *House of Ghosts*, like other horror movies in the so-called "found-footage" genre, employs shaky camerawork and haphazard editing to imitate spontaneous amateur video footage and convey the impression of capturing some supernatural being on tape. And while earlier horror movies in this genre came across as obviously fictional and unconvincing, *House of Ghosts* has managed to overcome that obstacle by taking the genre in a new direction. In this case, we get a film that ______________________________.

(a) shows events that come across as fake
(b) fails to live up to the standards of prior films
(c) has the feel of authentic impromptu videotaping
(d) emulates early found-footage movies successfully

**6.** The Treaty of Versailles, which officially ended World War I, ______________________. The agreement aroused resentment in Germany by stripping it of contested land, forcing it to pay large reparations, and saddling it with the sole responsibility for starting the war. At the same time, it failed to weaken Germany enough to prevent it from regaining power and retaliating through another global conflict. As a result, the treaty has gone down in history for precipitating a reiteration of the very events it purported to remedy.

(a) actually set the stage for the Second World War
(b) was circumspect about assigning blame for conflict
(c) effectively resolved long-standing territorial disputes
(d) succeeded in practical terms while failing ideologically

**7.** Flashing speed signs, which show drivers their speeds, might seem like an ineffective deterrent to speeding, as they do not issue speeding tickets. Yet they are an excellent example of how cognitive feedback loops can modify behavior. Such signs utilize the four stages of feedback loops: evidence, relevance, consequence, and action. They capture the driver's speed as evidence and show it on a visual display to make it relevant. The consequence is public exposure of speeding, which prompts action, in that the driver slows down. In this way, these four stages of cognitive feedback loops effectively ______________________.

(a) enforce the rules with automatic fines
(b) get people to regulate their own behavior
(c) counteract the effects of external pressures
(d) explain the motivations behind regulations

**8.** Youngmusan Temple would like to announce that for the first time ever, we are ______________________. Following recent renovations, guests can join us for overnight or week-long programs to experience the daily and nightly routines of traditional temple life, including meditation, monastic meals, and lantern-making. Previously, we offered only limited opening hours for educational tours and day programs, but now you can fully experience Buddhist life at our peaceful temple. Register today and take advantage of our introductory discount.

(a) going to improve our buildings and grounds
(b) allowing daily tours of monks' living quarters
(c) promoting educational courses on Buddhist traditions
(d) offering extended cultural programs with accommodations

9. Choosing a dissertation topic is no easy task. You should refrain from facile projects that yield immediate results, as the findings will be mundane and will not be beneficial to the expansion of scientific knowledge. In addition, conundrums that continue to baffle scholars should be avoided, as they are not likely to yield useful results within the time frame of a single degree. To prevent either of these missteps, you should ensure that your topic ______________________.

(a) matches your supervisor's area of expertise
(b) is accessible to both academics and laypeople
(c) focuses on empirical rather than theoretical issues
(d) is challenging but not beyond practical limitations

10. Before I talked to Carlisle Floyd, I assumed he'd be like other composers I'd interviewed. As a journalist, I've dealt with quite a few composers and, while I usually avoid stereotyping, they have uniformly been self-involved or preoccupied with their music at the expense of everything else. Mr. Floyd was a notable exception to this; he was polite and charismatic and took great interest in me and my job. Our meeting showed me how a single encounter can ______________________.

(a) lead to totally revised career aspirations
(b) establish professional boundaries quickly
(c) completely shatter one's prior expectations
(d) make people let go of their self-involvement

11. Condo hotels, which allow people to purchase hotel rooms for personal use or to rent out, ______________________. Hotels have been promoting the practice because they receive the majority of rental proceeds, as well as the purchase price of the room. But those who have purchased these condo hotels have also profited from their investments, as they have seen the value of these properties increase several times over in recent years. Their success has been a great incentive, resulting in a wave of new investors flocking to buy them.

(a) are a gain for hotels but a loss for investors
(b) have raised concerns among hotel owners
(c) have been becoming increasingly popular
(d) are a low-risk and low-profit investment

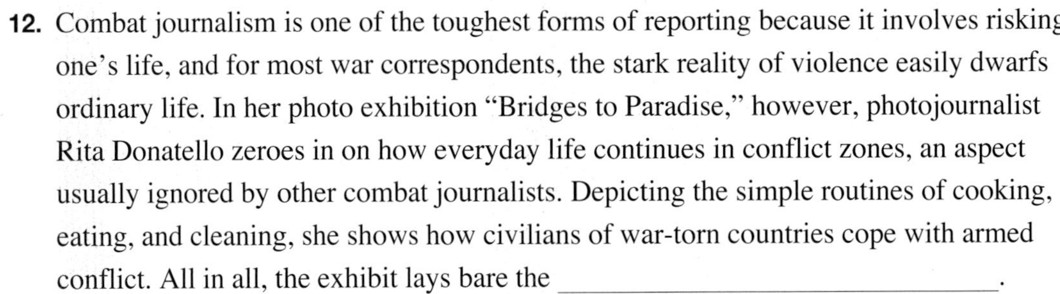

**12.** Combat journalism is one of the toughest forms of reporting because it involves risking one's life, and for most war correspondents, the stark reality of violence easily dwarfs ordinary life. In her photo exhibition "Bridges to Paradise," however, photojournalist Rita Donatello zeroes in on how everyday life continues in conflict zones, an aspect usually ignored by other combat journalists. Depicting the simple routines of cooking, eating, and cleaning, she shows how civilians of war-torn countries cope with armed conflict. All in all, the exhibit lays bare the ______________________.

(a) tremendous courage of fellow combat journalists
(b) types of violence that most war-torn countries share
(c) rituals soldiers use to bring a sense of normalcy to war
(d) overlooked quotidian aspects of life that persist despite war

**13.** The first emperor of China, Shihuangdi, is credited with unifying the country and undertaking large reform projects, including the standardization of writing. Yet in his attempts to consolidate the nation under his rule, Shihuangdi ______________________. His purported aim was the standardization of the writing system, but in fact he was more concerned about the seditious nature of the texts. He particularly feared that works on philosophy and history undermined his authority as emperor, and he had most of them destroyed, writing his own histories instead.

(a) underestimated the competence of his political enemies
(b) eventually had to prioritize unification over these reforms
(c) overlooked the disruptive potential of certain historical texts
(d) greatly restricted access to potentially subversive information

**14.**

> To the Editor:
>
> Being a doctor myself, and having major reservations about the state of modern medicine, I appreciated last week's article on the ethically questionable rewards that pharmaceutical companies are giving doctors. But I think you failed to elucidate the scope of the issue: not only do these companies influence doctors, but they also shape academic research agendas and lobby legislators aggressively. I commend the coverage you did provide, but I think the article should have
>
> ______________________________.
>
> Jonathan Arlen, MD

(a) given more credit to legislators' efforts to regulate the industry
(b) revealed that the issue extends far beyond perks offered to doctors
(c) mentioned that drug companies actually conduct high-level research
(d) exposed the unethical collusion between doctors and pharmaceutical firms

**15.** The term "long-term memory," which refers to the larger component of the memory system, carries an implication that it holds older memories but not recent ones. But in fact, long-term memory has no relationship to how long ago information was learned: it can hold information learned either a few minutes or many decades ago. ______________________________, the term "short-term memory" does mean what it implies: some neurological researchers believe that short-term memory holds elements for no longer than a minute.

(a) Indeed
(b) Similarly
(c) As an illustration
(d) On the other hand

**16.** Americorps, a popular nationwide public service program in the US, has undergone funding cuts during the last two years. ______________________________, the number of applicants has increased about 62% over the same period. With less money than ever, Americorps simply does not have the resources to accept so many applicants, and many are being turned away.

(a) Instead
(b) Meanwhile
(c) Particularly
(d) Subsequently

**Part II** **Questions 17—37**

Read the passage, question, and options. Then, based on the given information, choose the option that best answers the question.

**17.** I still remember the talk I attended last year entitled "Math in Daily Life." The speaker, a renowned professor, was one of the most skilled public speakers I've ever seen. He made sure the material was easily understandable, drawing pictures and using visual aids to demonstrate theoretical concepts. He also engaged with the audience by asking questions and making small jokes during the lecture. Thanks to his excellent speaking abilities, the whole experience was not only enjoyable but wholly memorable.

Q: What is the main topic of the passage?
(a) A university lecture on public speaking
(b) How to apply mathematics to everyday life
(c) An impressive lecture that used effective techniques
(d) How the writer was inspired to become a public speaker

**18.** Bella's Bistro would like to advise all of our customers that the empty lot next door has recently been sold to a new owner and is no longer available for restaurant parking. From now on, we are advising diners to park either in the municipal lot on State Street or to use the metered street parking in front of our establishment, both of which cost $1 per hour. We apologize for the inconvenience and thank you for your continued patronage.

Q: What is the announcement mainly about?
(a) A restaurant's purchase by new owners
(b) The cost of parking in city-owned spaces
(c) A change in a restaurant's parking options
(d) The opening of a new customer parking lot

**19.**

> Dear Ms. Yang,
>
> Congratulations again on your hard work and acceptance to Fairson College. At your request, we at the admissions office extended our offer of enrollment until July 1, and we would like to remind you that your intent to enroll must be confirmed by that date. Enrolling students are also required to send a copy of their final high school transcript. We are hoping to see you on campus this fall, and we congratulate you again on all you have accomplished.
>
> Best wishes,
> Nigel Wright
> Office of Admissions

Q: What is the main purpose of the letter?
(a) To present the recipient with a tentative scholarship offer
(b) To inform the recipient that her college transcript is ready
(c) To notify the recipient that her enrollment needs to be confirmed
(d) To grant the recipient an extension for a college application deadline

**20.** The good organization and easy readability of the Diagnostic and Statistical Manual of Mental Disorders (DSM) make it the preferred diagnostic guide of psychiatrists. However, despite its accessibility, laypeople and health care professionals who have not studied psychiatry should not use it to make assessments of mental health. Used indiscriminately by those without clinical training, it can lead to harmful misdiagnoses. The American Psychiatric Association, which publishes the DSM, cautions that it is not a substitute for a trained psychiatrist.

Q: What is the writer's main point about the DSM?
(a) It is the ultimate authority on physiological disorders.
(b) The American Psychiatric Association has endorsed it.
(c) Non-specialists should not use it to diagnose mental health.
(d) It benefits general practitioners by explaining mental disorders.

**21.** The United States Constitution gives the president the power to appoint the chief justice of the United States, who is the head judge of the Supreme Court, but it does not specify the qualifications of the nominee. In practice, there are certain conventions that have been established by precedent. Professional qualifications and ability obviously play a large role, and a candidate's ideological leanings and the amount of political support he or she receives are hugely important. The nominee must also be able to meet the approval of the Senate, which has the final say in whether to accept or reject the candidate.

Q: What is the passage mainly about?
(a) The practical considerations of nominating a chief justice
(b) The chief justice's responsibility to enforce the Constitution
(c) The power of the Senate to overturn the chief justice's decisions
(d) The distribution of power between the president and Supreme Court

**22.** Among archaeologists, it is well known that stone tools discovered in Asia are remarkably simple compared to the complex stone tools found in Europe and Africa from the same period. A number of explanations for this have been put forth: some archaeologists believe that Stone Age humans in Asia lacked the technological know-how to produce advanced stone tools. Others have posited that instead of stone, they made tools from the abundant bamboo in their environment. Still others have suggested that the region lacked appropriate raw materials for making stone tools.

Q: What is the passage mainly about?
(a) How complex tools evolved at different times in Europe and Asia
(b) How the geology of prehistoric Asia affected its tool development
(c) Hypotheses about why stone tools found in Asia lacked complexity
(d) Archaeological research about the usage of ancient stone tools in Asia

**23.** People typically lose anywhere from fifty to one hundred hairs a day. This is not a sign of a scalp abnormality or permanent hair loss but a natural process. Every strand undergoes a growth phase that lasts two to three years, growing about half an inch each month. Normally, approximately 90% of the hair on your head is in this phase. The remaining 10% is in the "resting phase," which lasts between three to four months, after which the resting hairs fall out and new ones are generated in their place.

Q: Which of the following is correct according to the passage?
(a) Losing more than fifty hairs a day is considered abnormal.
(b) Strands of hair grow about half an inch every two months.
(c) The resting phase of hair can last from two to three years.
(d) Strands of hair in the resting phase will subsequently fall out.

**24.** Since 1980, Clear-Flow's mission has been to improve bodies of water the natural way. Our equipment mimics nature's own processes in oxygenating and cleaning waterways. Without using chemicals, we can reduce algae and increase oxygen levels in aquatic environments ranging from ponds to rivers to huge reservoirs. Our proven approach also means you never need to worry about your water containing toxins. Let the experts at Clear-Flow clean up your water supply today.

Q: Which of the following is correct about Clear-Flow according to the advertisement?
(a) It uses technology to remove excess oxygen from water.
(b) It employs gentle and environmentally-friendly chemicals.
(c) It promotes algal growth to improve the health of bodies of water.
(d) Its processes can be used in a wide variety of water environments.

**25.** Throughout history, many parts of the world developed large, stable agricultural communities. But in mountainous areas with inadequate rainfall and poor soil, pastoral societies that depended on herding and small-scale agriculture formed. These communities were found in many parts of Asia, Africa, and Europe and were often small, averaging about 72 members in a community. Of such societies, 90% were nomadic, moving from place to place to find water, better weather, or more pasture for their livestock to feed on.

Q: Which is correct about pastoral societies according to the passage?
(a) They developed in areas with heavy rainfall.
(b) They subsisted solely on herding activity.
(c) They existed across several continents.
(d) They were primarily stationary groups.

**26.** On August 12, 2000, the Russian nuclear submarine *Kursk* exploded and sank off the coast of Norway. Fearing that the submarine's leaking nuclear reactors could destroy the pristine fishing grounds in the area, an international consortium called the Kursk Foundation was set up in Belgium three months after the disaster to collect funds to raise the sunken submarine. After months of delays due to financial shortcomings and several failed negotiations between Russia and the foundation, the *Kursk* was finally lifted from the seabed in October of the following year.

Q: Which of the following is correct according to the article?
(a) The Belgian submarine *Kursk* sank near Norway.
(b) The Kursk Foundation was established in Russia.
(c) The salvage mission initially had trouble raising money.
(d) The *Kursk* was raised three months after its sinking.

**27.**

Dear Mr. Hansen,

This is in reference to the scheduled replacement of the oxygen sensor in the emission system of your Minova ST50 minivan, which you left at our shop on Monday. Your warranty covers only the cost of replacement parts, so you will have to pay for the labor involved. Once the part arrives this Friday, it should take one day to install. Please call us if you have any questions.

Bob Hopkins
Minova Service Center

Q: Which of the following is correct according to the letter?
(a) Mr. Hansen is asked to drop off his vehicle at the service center next Monday.
(b) The minivan has a warranty that covers labor costs for all needed repairs.
(c) Mr. Hansen's warranty covers his vehicle's replacement part.
(d) The mechanics have already received the part for the minivan.

**28.** Neckwear worn primarily for decoration dates back to seventeenth-century France. King Louis XIII, a fashion aficionado, was influenced by the colorful silk handkerchiefs worn by a regiment of Croatian mercenary soldiers fighting on France's behalf in the Thirty Years' War. King Louis called the fabric a "cravat" based on "Croat," the French word for a native of Croatia, and the style quickly spread among French military and civilians and then to other European countries. Subsequently, under Louis XVI's reign, the cravat was replaced by the "steinkirk," a neckcloth more similar to the modern necktie.

Q: Which of the following is correct according to the passage?
(a) The Croatian soldiers fought on behalf of France's enemies in the Thirty Years' War.
(b) The word "cravat" reflects the ethnic group from which it originated.
(c) French soldiers picked up the trend of wearing cravats from civilians.
(d) Steinkirks were replaced by cravats under King Louis XVI.

**29.** For years, experts have predicted that declining fertility in Mexico would lead to a decrease in Mexican immigration to the US. And demographic statistics do indeed show that Mexico's fertility rate—that is, the average number of children per woman—is half of what it was fifty years ago. Yet data reveal that the Mexican immigrant population in the US actually grew more than ten-fold over the same fifty-year period. In fact, experts have yet to find strong proof for a correlation between fertility and immigration trends.

Q: Which of the following is correct according to the passage?
(a) Mexican immigration to the US was predicted to decrease.
(b) Mexico's total fertility rate doubled over the last half century.
(c) Immigration to the US from Mexico rose 10% over the last fifty years.
(d) Substantial evidence has conclusively linked fertility rates and immigration.

**30.** Drinking too much water can lead to a state called water intoxication. Because of the presence of excess water in the body, the fluid surrounding cells becomes less concentrated than the fluid inside the cells. In an effort to reach equilibrium and balance out this gradient, cells absorb water and swell. Although not as common as dehydration, water intoxication can cause dangerous effects such as swelling in the brain and lungs. The remedy for water intoxication, a solution containing high amounts of sodium, is injected into the bloodstream to draw water out of the cells.

Q: Which of the following is correct about water intoxication according to the passage?
(a) It occurs when the fluid outside cells becomes too diluted.
(b) It results in the shriveling of cells because of a lack of water.
(c) People are more likely to suffer from it than from dehydration.
(d) The treatment for it is an orally-administered sodium solution.

**31.** Sociologists used to believe that prior to industrialization, the majority of people in England lived in extended family arrangements. But this is now known to be incorrect: nuclear family households, which comprise a pair of adults and their children, were common long before the Industrial Revolution. Pre-industrial households did typically have more members than today's households, but the difference is not very large, especially considering that servants were included in household counts. For example, the average household size in England remained around 4.75 people throughout the seventeenth century, while the figure for 2010 was 2.4.

Q: Which of the following is correct according to the passage?
(a) Nuclear family households began in England with industrialization.
(b) Pre-industrial household size counts included domestic workers.
(c) Household size changed drastically during the seventeenth century.
(d) The average household size in England is currently 4.75 persons.

**32.** Although they are hardy enough birds to manage an annual autumn migration from Alaska to Argentina, Buff-breasted Sandpipers are being threatened by human activities at both ends of their journey. Their Arctic summer home, which also acts as their breeding grounds, is being ravaged by oil development. At the other end, the transformation of grasslands into soybean fields in South America is completely restructuring the landscape where the species spends the winter. They had a near-miraculous comeback after widespread hunting had taken them to the brink of extinction in the 1920s, but with both habitats steadily shrinking, Buff-breasted Sandpipers' numbers are again diminishing.

Q: Which of the following is correct about Buff-breasted Sandpipers according to the passage?
(a) They migrate to Argentina when spring starts.
(b) Their breeding grounds are in South America.
(c) Their winter habitat is being disrupted by oil development.
(d) They previously faced extinction because of widespread hunting.

**33.** The Cannery Seafood Restaurant invites you to come try our authentic, home-style specials like Broiled Atlantic Salmon or Ipswich Whole Belly Clams. Our mouthwatering set menu options and generous portions are guaranteed to have you coming back for more. Who needs seafood shipped across the country or imported from exotic lands when you can eat here and support area fishermen? We're located right next to the bay, so visit today to discover our exclusive culinary delights!

Q: What can be inferred about the Cannery Seafood Restaurant from the advertisement?
(a) It has several locations.
(b) It is a family-run business.
(c) Its seafood is caught locally.
(d) It is an all-you-can-eat buffet.

**34.** A number of food products on the market today include the term "natural" in their labels. And people often believe that the description indicates that the product's ingredients have not been changed from their original state or that the product promotes health in some way. But in fact, a company can label anything as natural because the interpretation of the word is flexible and government approval is not needed to use it.

Q: What can be inferred about products labeled as "natural" from the passage?
(a) They generally live up to their claimed health benefits.
(b) They have been carefully reviewed by the government.
(c) They are not necessarily unaltered from their natural state.
(d) They are more trustworthy than products without the label.

**35.** Looking for a good deal on golf? Join the Allenville Golf Club (AGC)! We're a group of dedicated golfers who collectively negotiate discounts at participating courses in Allenville and surrounding areas for the best deals possible, even getting up to 60% off regular green fees! As an AGC member, you'll have access to our convenient online reservation system, where you can book tee times as early as a week in advance. And once you sign up, you'll always have priority when it's time to re-register each year. Memberships are running out, so visit our website to join before it's too late!

Q: What can be inferred about the Allenville Golf Club?
(a) It offers a limited number of memberships.
(b) Its memberships are valid for multiple years.
(c) New members need a referral from current members.
(d) The discount rate is the same at all Allenville golf courses.

**36.** Home births are often regarded as being risky. Indeed, one recent study showed that home deliveries had a considerably higher infant mortality rate than hospital deliveries. However, a close examination revealed that home deliveries assisted by trained midwives were perfectly safe; the mortality rate was higher only when a midwife was not present during the delivery. Insurance companies that do not cover midwifery services should consider the implications of this and rethink their policies, particularly because the cost of home births can be much less than hospital care costs.

Q: Which statement would the writer most likely agree with?
(a) Covering midwifery services would not increase demand for home birth.
(b) Home birth is an outdated practice that should be discontinued.
(c) Midwives should start attending more hospital deliveries.
(d) Insurance companies should cover midwifery services.

**37.** Earlier this week, Brownsville Leopards point guard Max LeBraun announced that he would sit out Saturday's All-Star Game. LeBraun, who has struggled the last several seasons with a recurring shoulder injury, says he wants to avoid last year's mistake and be in his best condition for the playoffs. Leopards coach Tim Paterson says he supports LeBraun's decision, and with the team's record getting stronger each week, he is optimistic that this year his star player will get a chance to shine in the playoffs.

Q: What can be inferred from the report?
(a) LeBraun aggravated his injury before the playoffs last year.
(b) The All-Star Game is scheduled to be played after the playoffs.
(c) LeBraun resents Paterson's plan to bench him at the All-Star Game.
(d) Paterson is doubtful about the team's chances of reaching the playoffs.

**Part III** **Questions 38–40**

Read the passage and identify the option that does NOT belong.

**38.** Work-induced stress that employees are subjected to can inflict great financial damage on a company. (a) Productivity usually drops when employees are under too much pressure, reducing the company's profits. (b) Highly stressed workers are also more likely to call in sick or to quit, putting further financial strain on the company. (c) Organizational restructuring can be a major source of stress in many workplaces, for employees at all levels. (d) Therefore, managers often consider it worthwhile to help employees limit their stress levels before the bottom line is damaged.

**39.** Since the design of front-loading washers makes them prone to mold, users should take steps to prevent mold growth. (a) Manufacturers recommend running the cleaning cycle of your machine regularly to prevent mold from developing. (b) In humid weather especially, a moldy smell may develop on garments if they are not dried thoroughly. (c) Furthermore, using low-suds detergents designed for front-loading washers can help limit mold growth. (d) Removing clothes promptly and allowing the inside of the washer to dry out is another easy way to keep your washer mold-free.

**40.** Western classical music was introduced to Thailand in the nineteenth century following increased contact with the West. (a) Thai composer Phra Chen Duriyang greatly contributed to its development in Thailand by establishing orchestras and educational programs. (b) Through certain programs, Thai music students were sent abroad to be trained in the Western classical music tradition. (c) Western students benefited from studying Thai traditional music, which has simple linear progressions in contrast to the complex harmonies of Western music. (d) When these students returned to Thailand, a variety of public and private agencies helped them share what they had learned with their nation.

This is the end of the Reading Comprehension section. Please remain seated until the proctor has instructed otherwise. You are NOT allowed to turn to any other section of the test.

# ***Listening*** Comprehension Scripts

# 서울대 최신기출 1

## Listening Comprehension Scripts

**1**

W How was lunch?

M ______________________

(a) Let's go tomorrow.
(b) The food was great.
(c) I'll meet you.
(d) I've already eaten.

**2**

M Sorry I missed class yesterday, Professor.

W ______________________

(a) That's fine. Just get the notes from someone.
(b) Don't worry. I'll make up the work.
(c) I'll let you know beforehand.
(d) It's OK. You weren't that late.

**3**

W What's the cheapest way to the airport?

M ______________________

(a) Traffic is pretty bad.
(b) The shuttle doesn't go there.
(c) Maybe two hours ago.
(d) Probably the subway.

**4**

M What are you reading?

W ______________________

(a) A recently released sci-fi thriller.
(b) I need to build my vocabulary.
(c) A documentary I rented.
(d) My favorite classic film.

**5**

W The party's outside? What if it starts to rain?

M ______________________

(a) They all kept pretty dry.
(b) I'll just move everyone indoors.
(c) I'll invite more people, then.
(d) It wasn't raining that hard.

**6**

M The line is so long! Let's go somewhere else.

W ______________________

(a) Let's stay. I don't like waiting in line.
(b) Trust me. It'll be worth the wait.
(c) That's what the sign says.
(d) It really paid off in the end.

**7**

W What time should I pick you up?

M ______________________

(a) Until 10:30 in the morning.
(b) Whenever's convenient for you.
(c) I can be there by then.
(d) This isn't my first time.

**8**

M How come you weren't at the meeting?

W ______________________

(a) I forgot to bring it.
(b) It wasn't until this morning.
(c) I was told I could skip it.
(d) I couldn't make it, so I'm not sure.

**9**

W What qualifies you for this sales position?

M ______________________

(a) Your performance keeps improving.
(b) I've worked in retail for years.
(c) There are a lot of excellent candidates.
(d) It sounds nice, but I have a job.

**10**

M How do you manage to stay so slim?

W ______________________

(a) I got it right after my workout.
(b) I always overeat during the holidays.
(c) I try to do something active daily.
(d) I'm inclined to think so, too.

## 11

W Do you recognize this song? It sounds familiar.

M ______________________________

(a) It rings a bell, but I can't name it.
(b) It seems like a reasonable request.
(c) I wouldn't know what to listen to.
(d) That sounds like an effective strategy.

## 12

M Our team's new goalkeeper is impressive.

W ______________________________

(a) Well, I guess I could play goalie.
(b) Yeah, he used to play professionally.
(c) That game isn't until tomorrow.
(d) I wouldn't say he's that bad.

## 13

W Did you put this furniture on our credit card?

M ______________________________

(a) No, it belongs in the family room.
(b) I tried, but the store wouldn't accept cash.
(c) It wasn't necessary—my parents took care of it.
(d) Sure, since they offered to buy it.

## 14

M I finally got the accounting error sorted out.

W ______________________________

(a) Let me see if I can identify the problem.
(b) I should have it fixed tomorrow.
(c) I'm relieved there were no mistakes.
(d) I knew you'd find a solution in the end.

## 15

W How are you handling the night shift?

M ______________________________

(a) I have to get everyone's approval first.
(b) I think it's taking a toll on my health.
(c) My boss used to work nights.
(d) I don't think it's ready.

## 16

M Are you ordering the hamburger or burrito?

W I don't know; they both look good.

M How about we share?

W ______________________________

(a) Good thinking. We can split one of each.
(b) I don't know what they serve.
(c) No, the meal is on me.
(d) Sure, we can get something else.

## 17

W How's your job search going?

M I've submitted several applications.

W But no offers yet?

M ______________________________

(a) No, but I'm staying hopeful.
(b) I'll decide soon enough.
(c) Right. I don't know which to choose.
(d) I haven't applied there yet.

## 18

M What'd you think of the movie?

W It wasn't my kind of thing.

M But you love comedies.

W ______________________________

(a) I'd recommend it.
(b) This was especially hilarious.
(c) It wasn't the kind of humor I enjoy.
(d) It was funnier than I expected.

## 19

W There's a baseball game Sunday.

M Oh, did you get tickets?

W Yes, I bought several. Are you free?

M ______________________________

(a) No, they're not that expensive.
(b) But the season's over.
(c) I'll check and get back to you.
(d) I think they're sold out.

## 20

M Did you get everything on the grocery list?

W Almost—they were out of cherries.

M But I need those for the muffins.

W ______________________________

(a) OK, I'll take them out.
(b) Just don't include them.
(c) They didn't have those, either.
(d) No, that recipe needs cherries.

## 21

W Is this your first job in a law office?

M Yes, I just became a paralegal.

W Have you always wanted a legal career?

M ______________________________

(a) No, I decided on it fairly recently.
(b) Of course, as soon as I get the job.
(c) I need to talk to my lawyer first.
(d) I'm glad you took the offer.

## 22

M We should cut back on processed foods.

W But they're so convenient.

M Well, they're full of chemicals.

W ______________________________

(a) Yeah, I guess we need them.
(b) Fine, let's eat more fresh food.
(c) That's why we don't eat produce.
(d) I refuse to sacrifice taste for convenience.

## 23

W Have you tried those new e-readers?

M I got one for Christmas, but I never use it.

W Why not? I hear they're great.

M ______________________________

(a) Well, I use mine regularly.
(b) I'm not really into those high-tech gadgets.
(c) I can't afford to purchase one.
(d) Because I prefer my e-reader.

## 24

M Hi, I'm calling to speak with Mr. Pitkin.

W Sorry, he's gone for the day.

M When can I reach him?

W ______________________________

(a) Just ask him to call me back tomorrow.
(b) Early morning is your best bet.
(c) It'll take longer than that.
(d) I guess that will have to do.

## 25

W Have you ever been to New Zealand?

M Once, on a tour of the entire country.

W What was your favorite part?

M ______________________________

(a) It'd be tough to pick one country.
(b) I haven't decided on the dates yet.
(c) The capital was the most memorable.
(d) My first trip was probably the most fun.

## 26

M Have you memorized your lines for the play?

W Not yet. But I've still got a week.

M Oh—that's not much time.

W ______________________________

(a) Well, at least I memorized everything.
(b) I know, but I like to start early.
(c) Yeah, but I work better under pressure.
(d) Don't worry, we can see the play together.

## 27

W Did you finish your paper on time?

M Just barely. I only need to print it out.

W But I thought it was due yesterday.

M ______________________________

(a) Actually, I handed mine in already.
(b) Oh, I like to budget my time.
(c) Nope, the deadline's in an hour.
(d) Well, I was denied an extension.

**28**

M Joan, what's wrong? You look livid.
W I was just lambasted by my boss for her mistake.
M Why were you reprimanded, then?
W ______________________________

(a) Well, I really couldn't intervene.
(b) She said that I hadn't done my part.
(c) It's a good thing she excluded you.
(d) Oh, I couldn't have gotten away with it.

**29**

W Thanks to you, I got a good deal on insurance.
M From that broker I recommended?
W Yes. I hope you don't mind that I mentioned your name.
M ______________________________

(a) No, I can't take all the credit.
(b) Sure, I'd love a recommendation.
(c) Not at all. I'm glad he helped you out.
(d) OK, let's go tomorrow, then.

**30**

M Ray said that the company might start laying people off.
W How would he know?
M He overheard someone talking. Do you think it's true?
W ______________________________

(a) Well, he's not one to spread false rumors.
(b) He doesn't have the final say in hiring.
(c) Not if you heard he was there, too.
(d) No, I don't think he was laid off.

**31**

M I need to pick up some bread. Do you know a good bakery?
W Well, there's a bakery not too far from here.
M I've never noticed one before. Where, exactly?
W It's next to the gas station right on the corner.
M Isn't that where the coffee shop is?
W Yes, the bakery's right behind there.

Q: What are the man and woman mainly discussing?
(a) The woman's favorite bread shop
(b) An errand the man has to do
(c) Directions to a coffee shop
(d) The location of a bakery

**32**

W Excuse me. I'm looking to buy a desktop computer.
M Do you have a specific model in mind?
W No, I just need something for college.
M Then I'd recommend this model, which is on sale.
W Really? What about this one with all the upgrades?
M That'd work, but it's geared toward gaming or video editing.

Q: What is the man mainly trying to do?
(a) Convince the woman to upgrade her computer
(b) Help the woman find a suitable computer
(c) Advise the woman to get a laptop instead of a desktop
(d) Find out what word processor the woman uses

**33**

M Do you know anyone who speaks Spanish?
W My friend Jon does. Why?
M I have a document in Spanish that needs to be translated.
W Do you want me to ask him?
M That'd be great. I'm willing to pay him.
W I'll ask and get back to you.

Q: What is the man mainly trying to do?
(a) Find someone who can translate Spanish
(b) Translate a document into Spanish
(c) Find someone to teach him Spanish
(d) Befriend a Spanish translator

## 34

W I'm having trouble finding references for my paper.

M Have you tried searching on the library website?

W I know how to log in, but I don't know where to go from there.

M Just click "Resources," and you can search for books and journals.

W And then I can print them out?

M Yeah, many are in electronic format, but some you have to check out in person.

Q: What is the man mainly trying to do?

(a) Demonstrate how to take materials out of the library
(b) Teach the woman how to access print journals
(c) Explain how to use the library website to find research sources
(d) Recommend the woman put more references in her paper

## 35

M I heard that we're not getting a raise after all.

W But I was counting on that money!

M Yeah, I think the entire office was.

W This is the second time they've gone back on their word!

M Management said we'll get it next year.

W I'm not sure how many times I'll believe that.

Q: What is the woman mainly complaining about?

(a) Management's mistrust of employees
(b) Her company's unfulfilled promises
(c) An unexpectedly low pay raise
(d) A coworker's hypocrisy

## 36

W Shouldn't you have a mechanic check that weird car noise?

M Yeah, but the warranty has run out.

W How much could it cost to have it looked at?

M Lots! And I'm living paycheck to paycheck.

W The longer you let it go, the more it'll cost.

M I'll get it checked out once I have the money.

Q: What is the man mainly doing in the conversation?

(a) Dissuading the woman from going to a mechanic
(b) Explaining why he is not having his car inspected
(c) Grumbling about the sharp increase in car repair costs
(d) Refusing the woman's request to fix her car

## 37

M Our lawyer called. You won't believe this.

W Is there a problem with our law suit?

M The defendant lodged an appeal.

W But he was found responsible for the accident.

M He's appealing the severity of the payout.

W I wouldn't worry since we just got the cost of repairs.

Q: What are the man and woman mainly discussing?

(a) Whether they should appeal a court case
(b) Changes to the estimated cost of repairs
(c) The defendant's appeal over an accident's cause
(d) An unanticipated appeal against them in a court case

## 38

W Northeastern Airlines, may I help you?

M I'd like one ticket to Washington this Friday.

W Sure, roundtrip or one-way?

M Roundtrip, but can I leave the return date open?

W Certainly. That will cost an extra $250, though.

M OK. I'll be charging it on my company's credit card.

Q: Which is correct about the man according to the conversation?

(a) He is buying a one-way ticket to Washington.
(b) His flight departs Washington on Friday.
(c) His ticket has an additional fee.
(d) He is covering his own travel expenses.

## 39

M You're quite a talented flutist.
W Thanks, I've been playing for six years.
M Wow! Did you attend an academy?
W My father's a concert flutist, and he taught me at home.
M Have you thought about entering a competition?
W I used to, in my teens, and even won some small awards, but I just play for fun now.

Q: Which is correct about the woman according to the conversation?
(a) She started playing the flute when she was six.
(b) She learned to play the flute at an academy.
(c) She has entered music competitions before.
(d) She plays the flute professionally.

## 40

W My house has been on the market for two months, but still no sale.
M Have people been coming by to look at it?
W Yes, several people. But no offers.
M Maybe you're asking too much.
W Well, I just lowered the price to $200,000.
M Then I'm sure you'll get an offer soon.

Q: Which is correct about the woman according to the conversation?
(a) She put her house up for sale two weeks ago.
(b) Her house has received no visits from prospective buyers.
(c) She recently decreased the house's asking price.
(d) The original asking price for her house was $200,000.

## 41

M Have you seen the Impressionist exhibition at the museum?
W Not yet. It features mostly twentieth-century artists, right?
M It showcases masterpieces from the 1860s onward.
W Interesting. I'll have to check it out sometime next week.
M Actually, you only have until Friday.
W Oh, right. I forgot the collection is moving to Washington, DC.

Q: Which is correct according to the conversation?
(a) The woman has been to the Impressionist exhibition.
(b) The exhibition presents nineteenth- and twentieth-century art.
(c) The woman says she will see the exhibit Friday.
(d) The exhibit is simultaneously being shown in Washington, DC.

## 42

W I heard you're moving out of your parents' house.
M Yup, in a couple of weeks.
W That's great! But I thought you couldn't afford your own place.
M Luckily, I found a second part-time job to supplement my income.
W Wow, you must be busy. Let me know if you need help.
M Thanks! I'll take you up on that.

Q: Which is correct about the man according to the conversation?
(a) He currently lives by himself.
(b) He moved a couple of weeks ago.
(c) He works at more than one job.
(d) He declines the woman's offer of help.

## 43

M Thank you for calling Bayside Restaurant. Can I help you?
W I'd like to make a reservation for six tonight at 7 P.M.
M Unfortunately, only patio seating is left. Is that OK?
W Hmm. Is smoking allowed in that area?
M Actually, smoking is banned on our premises.
W Oh, then the outdoor table works.

Q: What can be inferred from the conversation?
(a) The woman would prefer to sit inside.
(b) The restaurant is an entirely outdoor venue.
(c) The woman prefers not to be around smokers.
(d) The restaurant does not take advance reservations.

## 44

W Hi, I'm Megan Williams. You must be Bob.
M Nice to meet you. You work in sales, right?
W No, that's Megan Adams. I work in accounting.
M Sorry! I'm still trying to learn everyone's name.
W No problem. It took some time before I knew everyone.
M With a company this size, it'll take me weeks.

Q: What can be inferred from the conversation?
(a) The man works in accounting.
(b) The man is relatively new to the company.
(c) The woman confuses names easily.
(d) The woman has not met Megan Adams.

## 45

M Can you stay late tomorrow since we're launching the new web browser?
W To work the help desk? Sure, no problem.
M Oh, good. You'll need to stay three hours after it goes into effect.
W Who else is staying? One extra person won't be enough.
M There'll be six of us, including you.
W OK, we should be able to handle the calls.

Q: What can be inferred from the conversation?
(a) The man is asking the woman to switch shifts with him.
(b) The woman is not used to working overtime.
(c) The man is expecting an increased number of customer calls.
(d) The help desk is usually covered by one person.

## 46

Have you been practicing your golf swing at indoor ranges, waiting for the snow to thaw? Why not treat yourself to a week of golf in beautiful, warm Florida? At fabulous PGA-quality golf courses surrounded by beautiful beaches and palm trees, you can play the round of your life. Florida's premier golf tour company, Florida Greens offers a selection of golf package tours throughout the state according to your specific requirements. Visit www.floridagreens.net for more information!

Q: What is mainly being advertised?
(a) A popular golf resort in Florida
(b) Golf tour packages to Florida
(c) A selection of golf schools in Florida
(d) Florida's most famous tourist attractions

## 47

Contrary to majority opinion, I believe that newspapers have every right to charge subscription fees for their online articles. With print revenues declining and more people relying on online sources for their news, newspapers need to make their livelihood somehow. If they cannot charge for online content, then they have no other option than to add more advertisements. I would much rather pay a nominal fee that would minimize advertising than deal with an increasing number of annoying and distracting advertisements splashed across news pages.

Q: What is the speaker's main point?
(a) Subscription fees are more profitable than advertising.
(b) Fees are acceptable if bothersome ads are decreased.
(c) Newspapers need to have more ads to make money.
(d) Charging subscription fees will alienate readers.

## 48

In this course, we'll look at the beginnings of psychology. First we will talk about Socrates and Plato and their influence on early psychological theory. These men, although considered philosophers, sowed the seeds that would one day become psychology. And so in this class we will examine their views on the mind and free will and consider how their views have shaped generations of psychologists.

Q: What is the main purpose of the lecture?
(a) To provide a brief history of philosophy
(b) To introduce psychology's general principles
(c) To give students an overview of the psychology course
(d) To introduce the concepts of free will and thought

## 49

Photographing a subject when it is in the center of your camera's frame is easy, but what if your subject is off to the side? Simply move your camera so that your object is in the center of your frame, then hold the shutter button down halfway. The camera will lock in the proper focus and lighting for that object. Then, without releasing the shutter button, move the camera back to the original position before snapping away.

Q: What is the talk mainly about?
(a) Framing portraits of people
(b) Capturing an off-center shot
(c) The importance of proper lighting
(d) How to arrange objects for a photograph

## 50

With winter approaching, it's crucial to take precautions. In addition to regular car maintenance, which should be done year-round, the most important thing to check is the tread on your tires. Snowy roads require good traction, so if your tread is worn, get your tires replaced. You may also want to consider getting snow tires, which are specifically designed to improve traction on snow and ice, before you brave winter's treacherous roads.

Q: What is the main purpose of the talk?
(a) To advise drivers to tune-up their cars regularly
(b) To suggest safe driving maneuvers for snowy roads
(c) To caution drivers about winter's effect on tire treads
(d) To urge drivers to take measures to have good tire traction in winter

## 51

In her book, *Raising Minnie*, Alice Jenkins writes about raising Minnie, her boisterous puppy. In this account of the tribulations of life with a new canine companion, Jenkins lovingly reminisces about the joys and frustrations she experienced while raising Minnie. The puppy proves to be a handful as she has no idea how to behave or what not to chew. Even with training, Minnie remains a tumbling 60 pounds of energy who is hard to control. Dog lovers everywhere will relate to this delightful memoir.

Q: What is the reviewer's main point about *Raising Minnie*?
(a) It focuses on how to train intractable puppies.
(b) It tells the story of Minnie and her litter of puppies.
(c) It is the story of raising an unruly puppy for dog lovers.
(d) It is a fun memoir from a puppy's point of view.

## 52

The concept of space-time, or a continuum in which time is not constant, shocked the scientific community when it was first proposed by Albert Einstein. In his most famous theory, the theory of relativity, Einstein supposed that the three dimensions of space—depth, width, and length—and the fourth dimension, time, are all affected by gravity. Until this theory was presented, time had been considered universal and constant. However, accounting for time's fluctuation has led to a better understanding of other theories about the universe.

Q: What is the main purpose of the lecture?
(a) To describe how Einstein came up with a theory
(b) To explain the theory of relativity and its scientific impact
(c) To define the multitude of forces that affect time
(d) To show how time influences other dimensions in space

## 53

Now for today's forecast. Expect today's foggy weather to continue through to the end of the weekend. The low-pressure system that has settled over the region shows no sign of moving on until Sunday, when a high-pressure system will bring cool air and clear skies. Even the daily highs are expected to remain constant, and the nightly lows should fall to about 50 degrees Fahrenheit by Sunday and then to 45 next week.

Q: Which is correct according to the weather report?
(a) The weather is expected to clear up later today.
(b) The region is currently under a low-pressure system.
(c) A low-pressure system is expected on Monday of next week.
(d) Nighttime temperatures should rise late next week.

## 54

Italy was not always the unified nation that we know today. In the 1400s, it consisted of many independent states, each under various forms of government. Southern Italy was ruled by a series of monarchies, while central Italy, known as the Papal States, was controlled by the Roman Catholic Church. Northern Italy was ruled by prominent families, and the three regions fought against each other in an effort to increase their respective influence.

Q: Which is correct according to the lecture?
(a) Italy was a unified country in the fifteenth century.
(b) Central Italy was controlled by monarchies.
(c) The Roman Catholic Church ruled Northern Italy.
(d) The three regions competed for power.

## 55

Mathematics has a long history. The earliest known mathematical texts are about 4,000 years old from ancient Egypt and Babylonia. These mathematical concepts spread to Greece, where they were refined over the following millennium. At the same time, mathematics was developing in India. Indian, as well as Greek, mathematical texts were translated into Latin, and mathematics was introduced to Western Europe through these texts. The mathematics of Western Europe eventually became the basis of modern mathematics.

Q: Which is correct according to the lecture?
(a) The oldest mathematics text was written around 4000 BC.
(b) Ancient Greece is credited with creating modern mathematics.
(c) Mathematical texts spread from Greece to Egypt and Babylonia.
(d) Indian mathematical texts were translated into Latin.

## 56

Regular ovens rely on the combination of heat radiation from the walls and air convection to heat food; however, a convection oven uses a fan to force circulation. Thus, the cooking temperature need not be as high as a conventional oven, yet food is cooked more quickly and evenly because there are no hot spots. While special cookware isn't required, convection ovens need adjustments in cooking times. They are not recommended for very delicate cakes or soufflés, as the air circulated by the fan can cause them to collapse.

Q: Which is correct about convection ovens according to the talk?
(a) They rely on natural air circulation to heat food.
(b) They operate at lower temperatures than conventional ovens.
(c) Their cooking times are the same as those of conventional ovens.
(d) They create hot spots that can collapse delicate foods.

## 57

And now for traffic. The ongoing Tacony Bridge expansion project resumed yesterday and will continue until Monday, which means all eastbound lanes of Interstate 70, shut down for the roadwork, will remain closed till then. Though construction is expected to continue for the next 12 weeks, Interstate 70 will only be affected this weekend. Motorists are encouraged to use alternate routes including Interstate 90 during this period, or use trains or the subway, which will be running according to the normal schedule.

Q: Which is correct according to the news report?
(a) The eastbound lanes of Interstate 70 are now closed.
(b) The Tacony Bridge expansion will be completed on Monday.
(c) Interstate 70 will be closed for the next 12 weeks.
(d) Motorists should use Interstate 70 instead of 90.

## 58

Mariton City's newest hotspot is the Mix 'n' Match, a restaurant with a twist. At Mix 'n' Match, you'll get good food and a blind date. No one eats alone, and everyone has a good time. Just fill out a brief survey, and our friendly wait staff will seat you with your perfect match. Come to Mix 'n' Match, where we make good food and you make new friends!

Q: What can be inferred about the restaurant from the advertisement?
(a) It is marketed toward singles.
(b) It requires a registration fee.
(c) It mainly serves fast food.
(d) It has several locations.

## 59

To end my presentation on the wisdom of mandating school uniforms for all New York City schools, I reference two examples—Brooklyn and Queens. Schools in both districts had suffered from discipline problems and low test scores. With the introduction of uniforms, these issues improved—a change that administrators attributed to instituting a dress code. It's time for us to follow suit. Let's make uniforms standard citywide.

Q: What can be inferred from the speech?
(a) Individual districts can elect to require uniforms.
(b) Uniforms are identical in most New York City schools.
(c) Test scores are improving throughout New York City.
(d) Inner-city schools typically mandate a dress code.

## 60

Today we're going to talk about the political system of ancient Carthage. Unlike other parts of the Phoenician Empire, Carthage became a constitutional monarchy. It preceded Greece, where democracy is often considered to have been founded, by hundreds of years. Indeed, Aristotle—the great Greek philosopher—commented favorably on the egalitarian society of the Carthaginians. Eventually, however, Carthage was destroyed completely by the Romans, and its once-thriving political system became little more than a historical memory.

Q: What can be inferred about Carthage from the lecture?
(a) Its influence on democracy is generally overlooked.
(b) Aristotle's teachings were the basis of its government.
(c) The Phoenician Empire expanded from its prosperity.
(d) Roman envy of its political system led to its downfall.

# 서울대 최신기출 2

## Listening Comprehension Scripts

**1**

M Where's the financial aid office?
W ______________________

(a) Give it later.
(b) Down this hallway.
(c) That's really helpful.
(d) They're very friendly.

**2**

W Try my homemade ice cream.
M ______________________

(a) You'll like it.
(b) Without ice, please.
(c) Just help yourself.
(d) I'd love to, thanks.

**3**

M Do you mind if I sit here?
W ______________________

(a) I'd rather stand here.
(b) I already have one.
(c) Of course not. Go ahead.
(d) Please take it home.

**4**

W Isn't your dentist appointment later today?
M ______________________

(a) Right, it wasn't bad.
(b) It's causing my tooth problem.
(c) I rescheduled it to tomorrow.
(d) Yes. You must be in pain.

**5**

M These scissors can barely cut anything!
W ______________________

(a) At least they're sharp.
(b) They've dulled over time.
(c) Slice them in half.
(d) Switch to cutting instead.

**6**

W You ought to eat less meat.
M ______________________

(a) I prefer not sharing food.
(b) But it's so hard to resist.
(c) True, I never order it rare.
(d) Then cook it longer.

**7**

M Hello, I'm calling for Ms. Andrews.
W ______________________

(a) No problem. I'll hold.
(b) She's called me, too.
(c) I'm afraid she's out today.
(d) Sorry, she'll get some later.

**8**

W Isn't your train commute boring?
M ______________________

(a) Just the opposite. I keep myself occupied.
(b) If we wait, it'll be less crowded.
(c) I don't mind driving occasionally.
(d) Absolutely! I never have time to finish it.

**9**

M Can we go back home for my phone charger?
W ______________________

(a) Just use mine—it should work.
(b) Sorry, my spare battery is drained.
(c) That's unnecessary. I can borrow yours.
(d) Oh, I must've left it on.

**10**

W I'm taking my doctor's advice to exercise regularly.
M ______________________

(a) That's something I should do, too.
(b) I'm glad we worked out our differences.
(c) It's nice to binge every now and then.
(d) He meant you should exercise regularly.

**11**

M Should we mention Sue and Pete's breakup during the party?

W ______________________________

(a) OK, let's keep the party private.
(b) That's likely a touchy subject.
(c) We'd better not. It's best if we tell everyone.
(d) It's time we set them up together.

**12**

W You were supposed to be home two hours ago!

M ______________________________

(a) I know. I wasn't late.
(b) Sorry, I lost track of time.
(c) There's plenty left for you.
(d) Don't worry. You can do it.

**13**

M I was disappointed by how disorganized the new science museum was.

W ______________________________

(a) Too bad, but we'll go when it opens.
(b) I'm disappointed you couldn't come with us, too.
(c) Yeah, and it's not really organized, either.
(d) That's a shame. You had high hopes for it.

**14**

W Is it wise to take out a loan for an apartment?

M ______________________________

(a) No, it's worth more than that.
(b) Well, it's fine if you can offer that.
(c) Only if there's no other option.
(d) Sure, my parents covered my housing.

**15**

M Why wasn't I asked to sign off on this projector before it was ordered?

W ______________________________

(a) Because we were waiting for your say-so.
(b) Don't trouble yourself. I'll make sure it gets ordered.
(c) I was under the impression you had approved it.
(d) Someone had to sign for the delivery, so I did.

**16**

W Sorry to hear you're sick.

M Thanks. This flu is terrible.

W Can I do anything for you?

M ______________________________

(a) OK, but I can't do anything.
(b) It should warm up soon.
(c) No, but thanks for offering.
(d) Tea might help you.

**17**

M How was dance class?

W Fun! We're preparing for the recital.

M When is that?

W ______________________________

(a) A month from now.
(b) Maybe I can perform then.
(c) We stretch first.
(d) It'll take two hours.

**18**

W I'll get the check.

M No, let me—I invited you!

W You paid last time. It's my turn.

M ______________________________

(a) Glad you ordered it.
(b) Then I'll use my card.
(c) I insist. You're my guest.
(d) Nonsense, they overcharged us.

**19**

M I couldn't reach you last week.

W I was in Paris.

M Paris? That must have been exciting!

W ______________________________

(a) Not really. I was there on business.
(b) I know. I'd love to go.
(c) Of course. Let's stay in touch.
(d) Call me when you're back.

## 20

W When should we head home?

M Oh, aren't you enjoying Beth's party?

W I'm just getting tired.

M ______________________________

(a) We can cancel the party.
(b) That's no reason to leave home.
(c) Then let's leave shortly.
(d) Beth warned us she'd be early.

## 21

M Have you seen Linda's new baby?

W Yes, and he's adorable!

M Doesn't he resemble his dad?

W ______________________________

(a) Linda swears it'll be a girl.
(b) I think he looks more like Linda.
(c) His dad looks after him.
(d) I'll decide once I see him.

## 22

W Can you come to Friday's basketball game?

M Hmm... Friday's not great for me.

W Don't tell me you've already got plans!

M ______________________________

(a) I do, but I'll try to change them.
(b) Even so, I hope you'll come.
(c) I can make it if you move it to Friday.
(d) Honestly, I won't forget.

## 23

M Ma'am, is this your carry-on bag?

W Yes, it's mine.

M Do you have any liquids in it?

W ______________________________

(a) Sure, I'll take some.
(b) It doesn't seem wet.
(c) No, I bring my own.
(d) Just a few toiletries.

## 24

W How was your appointment with my acupuncturist?

M Great! I'm seeing him again next week.

W Isn't he just the best?

M ______________________________

(a) Yeah, you won't regret it.
(b) Definitely—thanks for the referral.
(c) He should improve within a week.
(d) Well, I won't be going back.

## 25

M How can I repay you for picking up my daughter today?

W It was no problem. It was on the way.

M I'd still love to return the favor.

W ______________________________

(a) I'll return it right away.
(b) Sounds good. She was waiting.
(c) There's no need to give permission.
(d) Really, you don't have to reciprocate.

## 26

W Can you cater a party at my house this Saturday?

M How many people will there be?

W Fifteen. Can you manage?

M ______________________________

(a) A generous offer, but I've got to work.
(b) For a group that size, I'll need assistance.
(c) Actually, I'm not expecting company.
(d) Sure, but I'll keep the number down.

## 27

M Why did you cancel your vacation?

W Something came up at work, so I had to get a refund.

M Oh, too bad. Well, at least you didn't lose any money.

W ______________________________

(a) Actually, that's the reason I couldn't go.
(b) Hardly a consolation for missing the trip, though.
(c) No, I didn't have enough money.
(d) I thought of that, but I still can't make it.

**28**

W The new mall opens this weekend. Want to go?

M Not really. I do need some things, but it'll be a madhouse.

W Please? I need help picking out gifts.

M ______________________________

(a) OK. But let's go early to avoid the crowds.
(b) But we just went to that mall yesterday.
(c) Thanks for your offer, but I've done all my shopping.
(d) You're welcome to, but don't feel obligated.

**29**

M Would getting an advanced degree be a good idea?

W Personally, I'd argue it's not.

M Wouldn't it open more doors professionally?

W ______________________________

(a) Yes, but at the expense of your education.
(b) Honestly, I doubt it'd be worth the investment.
(c) That is true. It'd boost your grades.
(d) Professionalism isn't your concern, though.

**30**

W Jake, this study schedule you've made is unrealistic.

M How so? We'll cover all the major chemistry concepts.

W Yeah, if we study morning to night with no breaks!

M ______________________________

(a) It won't matter if the concepts aren't realistic.
(b) You're right. We should prioritize chemistry.
(c) Put that way, it does seem too ambitious.
(d) Let's continue studying right after the break.

**31**

M Tammy, I heard you finally got the teaching position.

W Yeah, I found out today!

M Good luck with your new job.

W Thanks. It's been my dream for a while.

M I hope you have a successful career. You definitely deserve it.

W You're sweet to say so.

Q: What is the man mainly doing in the conversation?

(a) Helping the woman choose a career
(b) Congratulating the woman on her educational achievements
(c) Wishing the woman well in her new job
(d) Complimenting the woman's working style

**32**

W Should we get a head start on driving? Looks like it might snow.

M Five inches, according to the forecast.

W Then let's start driving now.

M But we were going to have lunch first.

W Food can wait. We want to get home safely.

M OK, you're right.

Q: What are the man and woman mainly discussing?

(a) Why driving in snow is dangerous
(b) How much farther they have to travel
(c) Changing their driving plans because of the weather
(d) Taking a different route to avoid snow-clogged roads

**33**

M What other dishes do we need for the potluck?

W A salad and a dessert.

M I can bring a salad.

W Then I'll bring a crumb cake for dessert.

M Will you have enough time to make it?

W I'll just get one from a bakery.

Q: What are the man and woman mainly doing in the conversation?

(a) Deciding to have a potluck dinner
(b) Choosing how to spend their dinner budget
(c) Planning what to bring to a potluck meal
(d) Debating who will bring dessert

## 34

W I can't get this essay going.
M What are you having trouble with?
W I'm stuck on the introduction.
M Do that last. Focus on the body first.
W Hm... That actually makes perfect sense.
M Of course it does! You can't introduce your essay until you've written it!

Q: What is the man's main advice to the woman?
(a) To make an outline of her introduction
(b) To include a better introduction in her essay
(c) To proofread her introduction carefully
(d) To write her introduction after writing the essay

## 35

M Is this the right street? I don't see the hotel.
W According to the map, it's just off Miles Square.
M I don't see any signs. What's the name again?
W The Hotel Lexington. Let's keep walking.
M OK, I guess we'll stumble on it sooner or later.
W Right. It must be nearby.

Q: What are the man and woman mainly doing in the conversation?
(a) Arguing about an unfamiliar area of the city
(b) Talking about how to locate their hotel on foot
(c) Discussing how their hotel is poorly marked
(d) Deciding which hotel to stay at for the night

## 36

W I heard you rent an art studio in addition to your apartment.
M Yes. It's a necessary expenditure.
W Many would call it a luxury.
M Not me. I need my own space to produce my art.
W Even if it costs you an arm and a leg?
M Yes, I simply couldn't do what I do without it.

Q: What is the man mainly doing in the conversation?
(a) Arguing that expensive art studios are of better value
(b) Defending renting a studio as essential to his work
(c) Justifying the use of his apartment as a studio space
(d) Complaining that he cannot afford to rent an art studio

## 37

M My university doesn't deserve its reputation.
W But the senior faculty there are top-notch.
M They mostly do research, though. They only teach a handful of classes.
W So they don't bring their knowledge to the classroom?
M Not much. Most classes are conducted by junior faculty.
W Oh, that would be frustrating.

Q: What is the man mainly complaining about?
(a) The lack of senior faculty in the classroom
(b) The scant research required of professors
(c) The high student-to-faculty ratio
(d) The low reputation his university has

## 38

W Happy belated birthday, Ernie. I brought you a present.
M Wow, a new tie! Thanks!
W Sorry I missed the office celebration yesterday.
M You missed a great lunch.
W Did everyone else go?
M Yes, we went to a nearby sushi restaurant.

Q: Which is correct about the man according to the conversation?
(a) He receives a book as a gift from the woman.
(b) His office is celebrating his birthday today.
(c) He had lunch with his colleagues yesterday.
(d) He brought sushi to the office for his birthday.

## 39

M Have you been to Gilda's Coffee Shop on Main Street yet?

W I've seen it, but haven't gone in.

M It opened two weeks ago, and I've been there every morning since!

W Why? There are so many coffee shops already on that street.

M True, but it offers free extra shots until 9 A.M.

W Ah! That explains the line out the door every morning!

Q: Which is correct about Gilda's Coffee Shop according to the conversation?

(a) It had its grand opening last week.
(b) It is frequented by the man.
(c) It is the only coffee shop on Main Street.
(d) It offers free extra shots all day.

## 40

W You know the shoes I bought to wear to Carrie's wedding?

M Yes, the black heels.

W Well, I didn't wear them. I wore an old gold pair instead.

M Why? You spent a fortune on them!

W I decided they weren't formal enough for a wedding.

M So, will you take them back to the store?

W Yes. I'm glad I kept the receipt.

Q: Which is correct about the woman's black heels according to the conversation?

(a) She purchased them for no particular purpose.
(b) She did not spend much to get them.
(c) She deemed them inappropriate for a wedding.
(d) She decided against returning them to the store.

## 41

M I heard you've worked at Live FM radio station. So have I.

W Is that right? I interned for them as a community correspondent.

M I was there for two years starting in 2003 as the public affairs assistant.

W Really? I went there right out of college in 2004.

M I wonder why we never met at the office. I practically lived there.

W Well, I worked mostly off-site.

Q: Which is correct according to the conversation?

(a) The man left Live FM in 2003.
(b) The woman interned at Live FM as a college student.
(c) The man was a public affairs assistant for two years.
(d) The man and woman both worked mostly off-site.

## 42

W Hello, may I speak to Mr. Morris?

M I'm sorry. He's relocated to the Riverway branch for the time being.

W Oh, is he no longer the regional manager?

M He is. He's just at Riverway because his office here is being refurbished.

W Then could you give me his new number?

M I'll transfer you directly instead.

Q: Which is correct according to the conversation?

(a) Renovations have caused Mr. Morris to temporarily relocate.
(b) Mr. Morris no longer works at the Riverway branch.
(c) The man has taken over Mr. Morris's position as regional manager.
(d) The man gives Mr. Morris's number to the woman.

## 43

M We've narrowed our list of job candidates to three.

W Great. Should I set up their flights and interviews?

M Yes. And please prepare summaries for the hiring committee.

W Sure. And do you need anything else?

M Please attach their résumés and cover letters.

W I'll do that right away.

Q: What can be inferred from the conversation?

(a) The woman is the head of the hiring committee.
(b) The company plans to hire more than three new employees.
(c) The job applicants will be traveling to attend the interviews.
(d) The hiring committee has already interviewed some candidates.

**44**

M Good morning, are you Mrs. Banks?

W Yes, you must be here to check my furnace.

M Yes. You said on the phone that it's an old model?

W Right. It had been working on and off before finally breaking down yesterday.

M Sounds like it'll likely need to be replaced.

W Ah well. Good thing I put aside some savings for it.

Q: What can be inferred from the conversation?

(a) Replacing the furnace would be at the woman's expense.

(b) Misuse is what caused the furnace to break down.

(c) The man's initial attempt to fix the furnace had failed.

(d) The man noticed the broken furnace during routine maintenance.

**45**

M I'm dreading the next company-wide seminar.

W Why? It's a chance to be out of the office.

M But all we do is socialize.

W What's wrong with that?

M Well, if I were in charge, I would make the seminars relevant to our jobs.

W But building office camaraderie is important.

Q: What can be inferred from the conversation?

(a) The seminars are only mandatory for new employees.

(b) The man fails to see the merit in the seminars.

(c) The woman has yet to attend her first seminar.

(d) The seminars leave little time for socializing.

**46**

As a community, we must stop the city council's proposal to sell Sturges Park to developers. This public space provides a peaceful place for residents to relax and a safe place for children to play. It has been valued by our community for the past 25 years. Don't let it become yet another high-rise! Come to City Hall on Saturday to protest the proposal and make your voice heard.

Q: What is the main purpose of the talk?

(a) To rally citizens to save a local park

(b) To explain a recently passed proposal

(c) To protest park maintenance budget cuts

(d) To announce plans to build more parks

**47**

The next stop on our tour is Laos, so let's go over the basics about its currency. Laos is a bit different from the other Southeast Asian countries we've visited so far. In Laos, US dollars are preferred for many transactions. Thai money, known as Baht, is also widely accepted. However, that doesn't mean you shouldn't carry any local currency, which is the Lao Kip. It's good to have some on hand for making small purchases.

Q: What is the main topic of the announcement?

(a) How to spot fake currency in Laos.

(b) Why the Lao Kip is not widely used.

(c) Where to exchange currency in Laos.

(d) Which currencies to carry in Laos.

**48**

As doctors, our role is to help our patients. We diagnose illnesses and recommend treatments. These are important responsibilities, of course, but there's something just as powerful we could be doing: anticipating diseases before they strike and taking measures to prevent them. As the old saying goes, "An ounce of prevention is worth a pound of cure." Let's remember this and focus as much of our energy on promoting health as on curing sickness.

Q: What is the speaker's main point?
(a) Preventing disease is as important as curing it.
(b) Patients should have a choice of treatment options.
(c) Treating illnesses early prevents them from becoming serious.
(d) Regular visits to the doctor are essential to good health.

## 49

Brooking University is proud to announce the start of renovations to the sports complex. Thanks to alumni donations, we have collected enough funds for the job. The Student Activities Council also helped: they formed three new athletic teams this year, which justified the expense of updating the sports complex. The project also wouldn't have gone ahead without the support of the student body. Again, thanks to all who made the project possible.

Q: What is the talk mainly about?
(a) Planned fundraising efforts for the sports complex
(b) Circumstances that enabled a sports complex's renovations
(c) Reasons why the campus sports complex needs to be renovated
(d) A campaign to better utilize the newly renovated sports complex

## 50

I'd like to address the confusion regarding the newly created social media director position. Because this is an internal promotion opportunity, only current employees are eligible to apply. We are seeking those who have been at the company for at least three years in the information technology or data management departments. Interested applicants must be willing to be on-call during evenings and on weekends.

Q: What is the main purpose of the talk?
(a) To recruit new applicants to a computer company
(b) To announce the creation of a new department
(c) To clarify requisites for a new job opening
(d) To outline expectations of all new employees

## 51

These days, busy schedules often prevent families from having meals together, but a recent study shows that family meals are worth the effort. The study found that children who didn't eat family meals missed out on quality family time and were more likely to use alcohol and tobacco later in life. What's more, kids who ate meals with their parents felt deeper bonds with their family members, which boosted their confidence and helped them perform better in school.

Q: What is the speaker's main point about family meals?
(a) They are hard to plan because of busy schedules.
(b) They foster family interaction that benefits children.
(c) They lead children to have healthier and more balanced meals.
(d) They are becoming popular again among young families.

## 52

The Center for Forestry is trying to accelerate the walnut tree's evolution. To save the notoriously sensitive tree from being ravaged by increasingly extreme weather conditions expected in the future, scientists have started a breeding program, looking at seeds from mature trees to see if they have developed any defense mechanisms against varying weather. From this program, they hope to develop walnut trees that can adapt to a range of environmental conditions.

Q: What is the talk mainly about?
(a) Alarm over the walnut tree's dwindling populations.
(b) Breeding walnut trees that can withstand harsh weather.
(c) Transplanting walnut trees to more moderate climates.
(d) Research focused on why certain walnut trees are growing weaker.

## 53

Use the Electric Power Watchdog to safeguard your home! When someone steps into your backyard, the Watchdog simulates a barking dog within your home, deterring potential intruders. The Watchdog's sensors can be attached to doors or windows, and it can operate on AC power or batteries. It can be set to simulate between one and three dogs, and the barking time is adjustable from one to ten minutes. Find out about the Electric Power Watchdog today!

Q: Which is correct about the Electric Power Watchdog according to the advertisement?
(a) It operates without the use of sensors.
(b) It cannot run on battery power.
(c) It simulates up to ten barking dogs.
(d) It can bark for different lengths of time.

## 54

In November 2011, a planet named Kepler-21b was discovered about 352 light years from Earth—a relatively close distance, astronomically speaking. Interestingly, however, although Kepler-21b's radius is similar in size to Earth's, approximately 1.6 times bigger, its mass is ten times that of our planet. Kepler-21b also differs significantly in terms of its temperature, which comes close to 3,000 degrees Fahrenheit, ruling out the possibility of liquid water on its surface or any chance of life.

Q: Which is correct about Kepler-21b according to the talk?
(a) It is considered relatively close to Earth.
(b) Its radius is ten times bigger than Earth's.
(c) Its temperature far exceeds 3,000 degrees Fahrenheit.
(d) It is thought to contain water that could support life.

## 55

A recent study has UK residents concerned about sodium in bread. The study revealed that people are generally unaware that commercial breads contain large amounts of salt. In fact, one slice of the popular Coleman's brand loaf bread contained as much sodium as a single-serving bag of potato chips. But at least Coleman's products have labels. Not so for the typically unlabeled artisan bread from specialty bakeries. Though the study participants perceived artisan breads as being healthy to eat, they contained some of the highest amounts of sodium.

Q: Which is correct according to the news report?
(a) The public was unaware of commercial bread's sodium content.
(b) One loaf of Coleman's bread equals the sodium of a single-serving bag of chips.
(c) Coleman's drew criticism for not labeling its products.
(d) Artisan breads from specialty bakeries are typically low in sodium.

## 56

Helen Keller made history for overcoming deafness and blindness to become an advocate for the disabled. What is generally less known about her these days is her impassioned leftist politics. In her day, she earned the label of "radical" by joining the Socialist Party and speaking on behalf of the working class. For this, she endured a significant backlash. Even journalists who had previously lauded her for overcoming her physical limitations pointed to those same disabilities to discredit her and her viewpoints.

Q: Which is correct about Helen Keller according to the talk?
(a) Her leftist activism is better known than her advocacy for the disabled.
(b) She was labeled a radical despite never officially embracing Socialism.
(c) She was generally praised by the media for defending the working class.
(d) Her critics used her disabilities to publicly undermine her.

## 57

New concepts are more easily recalled when presented as pictures rather than words. This is known as the picture superiority effect. But some factors, such as overconfidence, can negatively affect the picture superiority effect. A 2011 study found that when learning Swahili words, participants had better recall when the words were paired with the English text translation rather than an illustration. Researchers linked this anomaly to study participants being overconfident about their ability to recall from pictures. When researchers mitigated the overconfidence effect by warning participants against it, pictures were actually more effective.

Q: Which is correct about the study according to the talk?
(a) It proved overconfidence can enhance the picture superiority effect.
(b) It included both English texts and pictures representing Swahili words.
(c) Pictures consistently prompted the best recall from its participants.
(d) Researchers failed to address overconfidence in its participants.

## 58

Betty Boop debuted during America's Depression years. She was a cute but eccentric cartoon character who got herself into and out of hilarious predicaments. She was popular because she offered a form of escapism when people needed their spirits lifted. Much Depression-era entertainment was silly like this. The underlying message to the audience was to be optimistic. Though times were tough, things would work out. Gumption and a good attitude would carry you through.

Q: What can be inferred from the talk?
(a) Comic entertainment can gain popularity in hard economic times.
(b) Betty Boop was a character exclusively intended for children.
(c) Depression-era viewers did not appreciate the silliness of cartoons.
(d) Betty Boop cartoons became more somber after the Depression years.

## 59

Nonfiction authors like Roger Harrow, author of the book *Jungle Law,* don't have it easy. Not only do they have to painstakingly research real-life events, but they must also relate these events in a way that grips the reader. This is why in stories based on real life, attempts at suspense often fall flat. In *Jungle Law*, though, Harrow avoids that misstep. Drawing on interviews and field research, his vivid story of plane crash survivors encountering disease and hunger in a New Guinea jungle is captivating.

Q: Which statement about Roger Harrow's *Jungle Law* would the speaker most likely agree with?
(a) Its sustained suspense makes it a standout among nonfiction works.
(b) Its popularity owes to its blending of historical fact with fiction.
(c) It demonstrates Harrow's courage in writing about his own experiences.
(d) Its success as a historical account is marred by its lackluster style.

## 60

An alarming trend is gaining popularity among my fellow scientists: blogging one's research. Getting published in a reputable journal can be a frustratingly long process, I know. But journals demand that your research be reviewed by your peers, and this lends credibility to your work. Posting directly to the Internet and evading this review process only weakens your standing in the scientific community and calls into question your motives for avoiding peer review.

Q: Which statement would the speaker most likely agree with?
(a) Reputable journals should consider moving online.
(b) Peer review is an outdated concept that should be abandoned.
(c) Unverified scientific research is proliferating on the Internet.
(d) Publishing research quickly should be a scientist's priority.

# 서울대 최신기출 3

## Listening Comprehension Scripts

**1**

M How long does the train to Allentown take?

W ______________________

(a) About four times.
(b) Just over thirty minutes.
(c) Fifty miles an hour.
(d) Two hours ago.

**2**

W Is this the way to the subway station?

M ______________________

(a) I need a ticket.
(b) This is your train.
(c) No, it just left.
(d) Yeah, it's straight ahead.

**3**

M Do you sell stamps here?

W ______________________

(a) Sorry, I don't want any.
(b) No, you should try the post office.
(c) Sure, here's your receipt.
(d) Yes, I posted it already.

**4**

W Should we ask Gina to join us for lunch?

M ______________________

(a) Sure, it'd be nice to see her.
(b) No, I haven't eaten yet.
(c) She really enjoyed lunch.
(d) Thanks for inviting me.

**5**

M How's your new house working out so far?

W ______________________

(a) I'm still looking for work, actually.
(b) It wasn't as much as I expected.
(c) I'm so thrilled to have a place of my own.
(d) No, it's actually pretty close to here.

**6**

W Did your driver's test go OK?

M ______________________

(a) Yes, but I've never tried to before.
(b) I was nervous but I managed to pass.
(c) Not unless I can practice some more.
(d) Actually, it's already over.

**7**

M I'm taking the dog for a walk—I'll be back.

W ______________________

(a) That's fine. He'll be back.
(b) Make sure you don't forget the leash.
(c) No, it won't take me that long.
(d) All right, just take the dog, too.

**8**

W Are you flying to Portland next week?

M ______________________

(a) No, I got a good deal on the ticket.
(b) It wasn't my first time there.
(c) I'm driving a rental car instead.
(d) Doubtful. I prefer to travel by plane.

**9**

M Are you OK? You look pale.

W ______________________

(a) I've got an upset stomach.
(b) OK, that's fine with me.
(c) Maybe you should see a doctor.
(d) I couldn't find anything when I looked.

**10**

W My car's being serviced. Can I get a lift?

M ______________________

(a) No problem. Let me know which one's yours.
(b) If you don't mind waiting a few minutes, sure.
(c) I don't know much about repairs, but I'll try.
(d) I'd rather drive, but thanks for offering.

**11**

M One of your suitcases is over the weight limit, ma'am.

W ____________________

(a) All right. I'll check in early.
(b) That's fine. I only have one anyhow.
(c) Then I'll remove a few things.
(d) I thought I remembered to pack it.

**12**

W I see you got a new cell phone.

M ____________________

(a) I know. I'd like a new one, myself.
(b) I found it on sale last week.
(c) This? It isn't as old as it looks.
(d) I just might take you up on that.

**13**

M Will you be staying here in Seoul for a while?

W ____________________

(a) I'd like to, as soon as possible.
(b) I'll go there for a short visit.
(c) I'm staying at my friend's place.
(d) I'm planning to leave next month.

**14**

W Has this recession hurt your company's sales?

M ____________________

(a) Definitely, since it's only for a limited time.
(b) I wouldn't make predictions like that.
(c) No, that doesn't fit with our image.
(d) It's hit our whole industry pretty hard.

**15**

M What's included in your party's health care proposal, senator?

W ____________________

(a) We've made provisions to lower costs.
(b) I think they can reach an agreement.
(c) It'll probably wrap up soon.
(d) We're not ruling that out yet.

**16**

W Let's order together and share.

M Sure. But no shellfish; you know I'm allergic.

W OK, how about our usual, cashew chicken?

M ____________________

(a) But most fish is healthy.
(b) I'd rather try something different, for a change.
(c) Great. I've always wanted to try it.
(d) I thought you hated cooking, though.

**17**

M Hi, I'm calling to confirm an appointment.

W What's your name, please?

M William Ross. It's for tomorrow.

W ____________________

(a) I see you're booked for 2:30.
(b) We're open until 7 tomorrow.
(c) I'm sorry. Mr. Ross won't be in tomorrow.
(d) It usually takes 45 minutes.

**18**

W How are we getting this sofa home?

M Ryan is lending us his truck.

W Great! We should show him our appreciation somehow.

M ____________________

(a) OK, I'll find out if he can.
(b) I know he's grateful, anyway.
(c) I'll take him out to lunch tomorrow.
(d) Right. He really should reciprocate.

**19**

M You're dressed up today. What's the occasion?

W It's my wedding anniversary.

M Congratulations! What do you have planned?

W ____________________

(a) The wedding hall was fully booked all week.
(b) My husband won't tell me; he says it's a surprise.
(c) We'll be back from vacation.
(d) I'd have to arrange them in advance.

## 20

W Have you ever met my colleague, Bill?

M No, I haven't.

W Why don't I introduce you?

M ____________________

(a) OK, I'd love to meet him.
(b) Probably because I'm new here.
(c) Sure, I met him only once.
(d) I don't mind introducing him.

## 21

M I hear you started taking guitar lessons last month.

W Yeah, I'm enjoying it a lot.

M I thought you had given up playing years ago.

W ____________________

(a) You promised you wouldn't, though.
(b) Right. It's been a month since I quit.
(c) My interest was rekindled recently.
(d) Yeah, I don't know why I ever started.

## 22

W So, you got into graduate school!

M Yeah, I got the letter yesterday.

W Have you accepted the offer?

M ____________________

(a) I'm waiting to hear from other schools.
(b) I'd be thrilled if I got in.
(c) Of course, I'm happy to help.
(d) Not yet. I'll see if it gets accepted first.

## 23

M Is everything set for tomorrow's summit meeting?

W I've confirmed everything with the organizing committee.

M And all the participants have arrived safely?

W ____________________

(a) Oh, I'm sure there's no danger of that.
(b) Yes, they're at a group dinner right now.
(c) Everything except one hotel reservation.
(d) I'll check whether the committee planned to.

## 24

W Sam seems unhappy these days.

M We should try to cheer him up.

W Let's take him out for drinks tonight.

M ____________________

(a) He's taken your advice to heart, then.
(b) Good idea. He needs a night on the town.
(c) He'll want to send his condolences, too.
(d) Perfect. I'm glad he's back to his old self.

## 25

M Do we have a lot more shopping to do?

W Why? Are the bags getting heavy?

M Kind of. Does this mall have lockers somewhere?

W ____________________

(a) I didn't know where you went.
(b) I'll ask someone if it does.
(c) Just put it in your bag.
(d) I forgot to bring one.

## 26

W Is that you, Joe? What are you doing in Paris?

M Lauren! I'm here on vacation.

W What are the chances of meeting like this?

M ____________________

(a) Really! How nice of you to remember our meeting!
(b) I'll be traveling all next month.
(c) I know—it's an amazing coincidence!
(d) Just give me another chance.

## 27

M Andrea! I didn't know you were a member at this gym.

W I'm not. I just came in for a free trial.

M And how are you liking it?

W ____________________

(a) No, I'm just doing it to lose weight.
(b) It's nice, but I wish it had a pool.
(c) I don't know, maybe after New Year's.
(d) It's better than working out at the gym.

## 28

W What do you think of this shirt?

M The design looks good, but I'd go down a size.

W It might shrink in the wash, though.

M ______________________

(a) You're right. That can cause some stretching.
(b) OK, just stick with that one then.
(c) Good idea. I'll grab a smaller size.
(d) No, I think it's the perfect fit.

## 29

M I'm considering hiring a cleaning service.

W Aren't they expensive?

M Yeah, but I'm too busy to keep my house tidy.

W ______________________

(a) That's much longer than I spend.
(b) Then maybe it's worth the price.
(c) I usually keep mine at home.
(d) Ask for your money back.

## 30

W My bank started charging a two dollar fee on ATM withdrawals!

M Really? That seems excessive.

W Should I call them and complain?

M ______________________

(a) Just take your business elsewhere.
(b) There are plenty of cash machines nearby.
(c) Even so, you can't make withdrawals by phone.
(d) Well, maybe you are charging too much.

## 31

W You know that ad blocker program you mentioned?

M Yeah, what about it?

W How did you get it, again?

M It's a browser extension. I just downloaded it online.

W Could you tell me where?

M Sure, I'll email you the site.

Q: What is the woman mainly trying to do?
(a) Get help finding ad-blocking software
(b) Learn how to download a new web browser
(c) Upgrade her current ad-blocking program
(d) Find out how to block unwanted email

## 32

M I'm tired of all this overtime.

W I know. The workload is too much.

M I barely spend any time at home anymore.

W Neither do I. And I'm always exhausted.

M Has anyone complained to management?

W We've all been hoping that it's only temporary.

Q: What are the man and woman mainly discussing?
(a) Their frustration with having their hours cut
(b) Management's refusal to give them a raise
(c) The company's reaction to workers' complaints
(d) Their annoyance with their extra workload

## 33

W I don't know how I should get to my job interview.

M There's a subway station nearby, isn't there?

W There is, but I either have to transfer twice or take a long detour.

M What about the bus?

W That takes so long, and it can be so crowded.

M Well, maybe your sister can drop you off on her way downtown.

Q: What is the man mainly doing in the conversation?
(a) Trying to persuade the woman to take the subway
(b) Suggesting ways the woman can reach her interview
(c) Offering to drive the woman downtown
(d) Giving the woman directions to the interview location

## 34

M Oh, this sandwich has cheese on it.
W You asked for no cheese, right?
M Yeah. Should I send it back?
W I would if I were you.
M I feel like I'm being fussy, though.
W Just politely point out the mistake to the waiter.

Q: What is the woman's main advice to the man?
(a) To be more polite to the waiter
(b) To complain about the taste of the food
(c) To take more time to enjoy his meal
(d) To have the restaurant fix his order

## 35

W Hello, I have a question about the job ad you posted.
M You mean the one for a visiting nurse?
W Yes. What are the hours?
M You would take care of my mother from 9 to 6, while I'm at work.
W And that includes Saturdays?
M No, just Monday to Friday.

Q: What are the man and woman mainly discussing?
(a) The care the man's mother needs
(b) The woman's availability on weekends
(c) The scheduling details of a caregiver position
(d) The woman's nursing qualifications

## 36

M Hey, look who made it! Welcome to the party.
W Hi, Paul. Thanks for inviting me.
M You said you couldn't come. What happened?
W One of my clients cancelled, so here I am.
M Everyone will be happy to see you.
W I'm glad I didn't have to miss it!

Q: What are the man and woman mainly discussing?
(a) Why the woman declined an invitation
(b) The guests they expect to see at the party
(c) Why the woman's client had to cancel an appointment
(d) The woman's unexpected attendance at a party

## 37

W Ugh. I'm feeling so overfed.
M Me, too. I shouldn't have eaten so much during the holidays.
W There were so many events with friends and family...
M And all the cookies people brought to the office...
W It's hard to say no to people's generosity. But I wish I had.
M We have to cut back next Christmas.

Q: What are the man and woman mainly doing in the conversation?
(a) Complaining about unpleasant holiday guests
(b) Regretting their holiday overindulgence
(c) Wishing that holiday foods were more diverse
(d) Describing the things they ate during Christmas

## 38

W I'm so far behind on my readings this term.
M Your part-time job is getting in the way?
W No, it's just that I have to read several whole books every week.
M Oh, right. You switched your major from psychology to literature.
W Yeah, but I'm seriously thinking about switching back!
M Maybe that's not a bad idea.

Q: Which is correct about the woman according to the conversation?
(a) She is keeping up with her reading assignments.
(b) She thinks her job is the main cause of her time shortage.
(c) She has recently become a psychology student.
(d) She is considering reverting back to her previous major.

## 39

M That plant on the windowsill is beautiful!

W Thanks. It's a jade plant from South Africa.

M Hm, I need a plant for my place, too. Where did you get it?

W It was a housewarming gift from my neighbors.

M Is it easy to care for? I don't want one that needs a lot of attention.

W Yes, it only needs water about once a month.

Q: Which is correct according to the conversation?

(a) The woman's plant comes from South America.

(b) The woman purchased the plant when she moved in.

(c) The man wants a plant that needs minimal care.

(d) The jade plant requires weekly watering.

## 40

W I'm thinking about visiting the Grand Canyon this spring.

M Oh, I went there a few years ago.

W Really? I can't decide if I should fly or drive.

M If it were me, I'd definitely go by car.

W But in that case, I'd want a travel companion.

M Well, I'd come if I weren't so busy with work.

Q: Which is correct according to the conversation?

(a) The woman is planning her summer vacation.

(b) The man went to the Grand Canyon last year.

(c) The man recommends taking a road trip.

(d) The woman prefers to drive to the Grand Canyon alone.

## 41

M You must have paid a lot for those new running shoes.

W I did, but I've started running more, so they're worth it.

M Your old sneakers couldn't take it, huh?

W I still go for strolls in them. But they were too worn out for running.

M Are those new ones comfortable?

W Yep, the extra cushioning is great, since I always run outdoors.

Q: Which is correct about the woman according to the conversation?

(a) She denies paying a lot for her shoes.

(b) She has stopped running so much lately.

(c) She has not thrown out her old shoes.

(d) She usually runs on a treadmill.

## 42

W Hi, do you take walk-ins? I'd like to have my teeth cleaned.

M Unfortunately, our dental hygienist is booked until 4:30.

W Hmm, that's about an hour wait.

M Yes. Or you can come back at 8:30 tomorrow.

W Since I'm here, I'll just wait.

M OK. Once you're in, it shouldn't take more than half an hour.

Q: Which is correct according to the conversation?

(a) The woman has arrived early for her scheduled appointment.

(b) The woman has come because of dental pain.

(c) There are no openings until tomorrow.

(d) The dental service is expected to take less than thirty minutes.

## 43

M You know that liquidation sale I was telling you about?

W Yeah, I'm going there tomorrow to buy a camera.

M Well, it actually ended yesterday.

W Oh, I was really looking forward to it.

M I'm sorry. I must have misread the ad.

W That's OK. Maybe I'll look for a camera online.

Q: What can be inferred from the conversation?

(a) The woman is buying a camera for the man.

(b) The sale will happen again at a future date.

(c) The man gave the woman incorrect dates for the sale.

(d) The woman has found a camera sale online.

## 44

W My bike is gone!

M Really? Maybe you left it somewhere else.

W No, I left it at this exact bike rack.

M Did you lock it up?

W I'm not sure. I was in a hurry.

M Uh-oh. You'd better report it to campus security.

Q: What can be inferred from the conversation?

(a) The woman has reported the bike missing.

(b) The man suspects the bike has been stolen.

(c) The woman usually locks her bike somewhere else.

(d) The man works for campus security.

## 45

M I might buy this car. The price seems reasonable.

W That's what you said about your last used car.

M But this only has 60,000 miles—that's pretty good!

W You've said that before, too.

M Well, what should I do? I'm on a budget.

W At least have a mechanic check it this time.

Q: What can be inferred about the man from the conversation?

(a) He is prepared to spend more for a new car.

(b) He worries that the car's mileage is suspiciously low.

(c) He mainly considers appearance when car shopping.

(d) He did not have his previous car inspected before purchase.

## 46

The traditional model of retirement—saving enough money to maintain your lifestyle in old age—is undergoing a transformation. As people live longer, they are finding it harder to put aside sufficient funding to ensure the kind of retirement they want. Their health care costs are rising, while their support from the government is diminishing. It is becoming necessary for people to save more, work longer, and live more modestly after retirement.

Q: What is the main idea of the talk?

(a) The government is responsible for supporting retirees.

(b) Retirees are living healthier lives than ever before.

(c) People with enjoyable jobs do not want to retire.

(d) It is becoming harder to afford a comfortable retirement.

## 47

The birth of democracy in ancient Greece was more than just a political development; it was also the starting point for a creative revolution. The notion that people could select their own leaders and voice their opinions led to a vigorous questioning of traditional dogma. This pursuit of truth and exchange of ideas produced an explosion of innovation in the arts, literature, and philosophy.

Q: What is the main topic of the lecture?

(a) The events that led to democracy in ancient Greece.

(b) How the ancient Greeks shaped Western thought.

(c) How democracy in ancient Greece affected culture.

(d) The limits of political freedom in ancient Greece.

## 48

Jonathan Swift's eighteenth-century narrative *A Tale of a Tub* appears at first to be a straightforward story of three brothers. However, each of the brothers actually represents one of the three branches of Western Christianity—the Catholic, Anglican, and Protestant churches. Swift uses this simple allegorical device to parody contemporary theology and creates a multifaceted critique of contemporary religious excesses.

Q: What is the speaker's main point about *A Tale of a Tub*?

(a) It disguises religious satire as a simple story.

(b) It was written to convey Christian values to readers.

(c) Its narrative supported prevailing religious views.

(d) Its purpose was to promote the author's own religion.

## 49

In public speaking, your voice and gestures are very important, so if you want to be more effective, try videotaping yourself giving a speech. Are you varying your intonation to prevent a monotonous delivery? Is your upper body relaxed? Are you pausing to allow the audience to reflect? Reviewing these recordings can help you evaluate your performance objectively and develop techniques to maximize your impact as a speaker.

Q: What is the main idea of the talk?
(a) Feedback from viewers is useful for public speakers.
(b) Speakers should learn techniques for impromptu speaking.
(c) Recording and reviewing speeches can enhance one's performance.
(d) A speech's delivery is more important than its content.

## 50

Academic tracking, or assigning students to different classes based on aptitude, is supposed to challenge stronger students and provide support for weaker ones. But I'd argue that tracking does most students far more harm than good. Being designated an underachiever, or even average, is a powerful social stigma. I believe that the damage that tracking systems can do to students' self-esteem ultimately hinders their intellectual growth.

Q: What is the speaker's main point about academic tracking?
(a) Its classification of students is often inaccurate.
(b) It only uses standardized tests to measure academic potential.
(c) It labels students in ways harmful to their development.
(d) It fails to support the growth of gifted students.

## 51

Are the days of the Internet café really over? These popular coffee shops were a booming business until the growth of home Internet access and smartphones caused their popularity to wane. Now people are predicting their demise. Although it is unlikely that Internet cafés will regain their former popularity, such predictions about their demise seem overly pessimistic. They fail to consider Internet café patrons like international travelers, who will ensure the Internet café's survival for years to come.

Q: What is the main idea of the talk?
(a) Internet cafés are regaining popularity after a period of decline.
(b) The future of Internet cafés is not as bleak as predicted.
(c) Internet technology is evolving in unexpected directions.
(d) Internet cafés will need new technology to survive.

## 52

Many investors are attracted by the rapid economic growth of developing countries, yet concerned about the risk of political turmoil, regulatory changes, and security incidents in these emerging markets. Noting that these dangers are highly unpredictable, investment strategists strongly recommend geographic diversification to reduce these dangers—as political and security risks tend to be highly localized, it is unlikely that any single event will wipe out a properly diversified portfolio.

Q: What is the speaker's main point about investing in emerging markets?
(a) Investors' worry over perceived risks make it unpopular.
(b) It must be based on accurate assessments of political threats.
(c) Distributing investments in multiple regions can mitigate its risks.
(d) It has an unpredictable effect on countries' political climates.

## 53

If you think crocodiles are fearsome, imagine one with jaws three times larger than the largest crocodile today. In fact, this so-called "supercroc" actually lived around 110 million years ago, meaning it was a contemporary of dinosaurs. Although parts of it were first discovered by French paleontologists in the Sahara Desert in the 1940s, it wasn't until American paleontologist Paul Sereno began excavating in 1997 that knowledge of the supercroc took shape: findings indicated that they could grow to 12 meters in length and weigh up to eight tons.

Q: Which is correct about the supercroc according to the speaker?
(a) Its jaws were equal in size to those of modern crocodiles.
(b) It lived more than 100 million years ago.
(c) It preceded the age of dinosaurs.
(d) It was first discovered by paleontologist Paul Sereno.

## 54

Citizens of northeastern Queensland are preparing for what will be the biggest storm in the state's history. Cyclone Mira is expected to make landfall around sunrise tomorrow, with winds up to 270 kilometers per hour. Thirty thousand coastal residents have been urged to evacuate their homes, and patients at hospitals in the coastal city of Cairns have already been flown to Brisbane. The cyclone is expected to start letting up by midday tomorrow as it moves toward the interior of the country.

Q: Which is correct about Cyclone Mira according to the news report?
(a) It will surpass Queensland's previous storms in size.
(b) It is forecasted to arrive in the early evening.
(c) It has prompted hospital patients to be evacuated to Cairns.
(d) It will begin slowing around midnight tomorrow.

## 55

I'd like to begin this town hall meeting by addressing Danville's garage sale ordinances. Please remember that residents must obtain a free permit prior to holding garage sales. Requests for permits must be submitted no later than two weeks in advance. Sales may operate between 8 A.M. and 7 P.M. One sale of no more than three consecutive days is allowed per month. The posting of signs on trees, utility poles, or any public property is strictly prohibited. The city council thanks you for your cooperation.

Q: Which is correct according to the announcement?
(a) Garage sale permits must be purchased prior to the sale.
(b) Danville restricts the hours when sales may take place.
(c) Residents may hold up to three garage sales per month.
(d) Posting signs on public property requires approval.

## 56

Born to Irish immigrants in Boston, Massachusetts in 1738, John Singleton Copley was one of the most talented and financially successful artists of colonial America. After a productive career in America that spanned more than two decades, during which he created oil portraits, pastels, and miniatures, he moved to London at the age of 36. It was in London, where his interest shifted from portraiture to historical painting, that he became internationally famous.

Q: Which is correct about John Singleton Copley according to the lecture?
(a) He was born in Ireland and immigrated to colonial America.
(b) His renown as an artist did not bring him financial success.
(c) He had a prolific career in America that lasted for over twenty years.
(d) His interest shifted to portraiture after he relocated to London.

## 57

A study on acupuncture for chronic headaches found that the popular alternative treatment worked better than conventional treatment alone. The study consisted of two groups, a control group receiving conventional treatments and an experimental group receiving both conventional treatments and acupuncture. Initially the difference between the groups was not significant, but after a year researchers observed substantial variance. The experimental group experienced 22 fewer days of headaches and made 25% fewer doctor's visits. And while they still missed work because of severe headaches, they took fewer sick days than the control group.

Q: Which is correct according to the talk?
(a) The experimental group was treated solely with acupuncture.
(b) Significant differences between the study groups appeared immediately.
(c) The control group suffered more headaches than the experimental group.
(d) The group receiving acupuncture stopped taking sick days.

## 58

Hello. This is your captain. We apologize once more for the delay this afternoon and request that all passengers remain seated until we get off the ground. The runway has been cleared of snow, and planes have begun to take off. We'll be departing in about ten minutes, and we expect to make up the lost time during the flight. Thank you for your patience.

Q: What can be inferred from the announcement?
(a) The plane has experienced some mechanical difficulties.
(b) The captain is making his first announcement to passengers.
(c) The flight is expected to arrive at its destination on time.
(d) The airline has not had to delay any of its other flights.

## 59

People have recognized the antimicrobial properties of wine for centuries. For instance, ancient Greeks and Romans recommended wine as a disinfectant for wounds. Today's microbiologists have experimentally confirmed that wine's combination of acids and alcohol is indeed inhospitable to microbes. Scientists have proven that as a marinade for meat, wine can kill the Campylobacter and Salmonella bacteria, both of which cause food poisoning.

Q: What can be inferred about wine from the talk?
(a) Its use as a marinade spreads food contamination.
(b) Its health benefits mainly pertain to psychological well-being.
(c) Its traditional uses have stood up to modern scientific scrutiny.
(d) Its potency is increased when its acids and alcohol are separated.

## 60

In US-Japan trade relations, rice has long been a sticking point. Eager to protect its domestic farmers, Japan refused to import American-grown rice until 1995, when the World Trade Organization forced the country to allow rice imports. Today, American rice in Japan is mostly used for processed foods or animal feed, and much of it lies stockpiled in warehouses. American farmers have protested these uses, saying they flout the spirit of international trade regulations. But Japanese policymakers respond that their nation's consumers simply prefer the taste of domestic rice and would not buy imported rice.

Q: What can be inferred from the talk?
(a) Japanese policymakers are eager to please the World Trade Organization.
(b) American rice is unpopular in Japan because of its high price.
(c) Japanese consumers have limited direct access to American rice.
(d) Japanese farmers refuse to sell their rice for processed foods.

# 서울대 최신기출 4

## Listening Comprehension Scripts

**1**

W Welcome to the company!
M ______________________

(a) I can manage, thanks.
(b) It's no problem at all.
(c) I wouldn't mind some company.
(d) I'm honored to be here.

**2**

M May I borrow a pen?
W ______________________

(a) Sure, I'll jot it down.
(b) There wasn't enough ink.
(c) Sorry, I only have one.
(d) Thanks for lending it to me.

**3**

W Want to go to the noodle restaurant for lunch?
M ______________________

(a) I would if I'd had dinner.
(b) No, I'll have noodles instead.
(c) You bet. I'll meet you there.
(d) I'd rather eat out.

**4**

M This prescription I got isn't making me feel any better.
W ______________________

(a) It's time to see a doctor again, then.
(b) Maybe you need a prescription.
(c) We never expected such a strong effect.
(d) Try reducing your dosage.

**5**

W The selection at in-flight duty-free shops is so limited.
M ______________________

(a) Yeah, there's not much to choose from.
(b) Right. I wasn't expecting such a wide variety.
(c) I'm afraid the complimentary meal isn't, either.
(d) I was pleasantly surprised, too.

**6**

M Avoid Fifth Street going home. The traffic's terrible.
W ______________________

(a) Thanks, but I'll take my chances.
(b) It was closed on my way home.
(c) I'm glad the traffic is light.
(d) OK, I'll detour down Fifth Street.

**7**

W Your dog's adorable—what breed is he?
M ______________________

(a) I've never had a pet before.
(b) Oh, he's big for his breed.
(c) He's a mix, nothing special.
(d) I'm not allergic to dogs.

**8**

M Peter just fell asleep, so please try to be quiet.
W ______________________

(a) OK, I'll tell him right away.
(b) I'll be careful not to wake him.
(c) Here—let me try to get him to sleep.
(d) No wonder he's being so fussy.

**9**

W Is the printer still out of order?
M ______________________

(a) It was jammed, but I fixed it.
(b) I'm not sure if one's been ordered.
(c) Actually, I don't have a printer.
(d) No, it's still being repaired.

**10**

M Are you teaching much this semester?

W ______________________

(a) No, my classes are all full.
(b) I'll say—I have a full load.
(c) Yes, I'm still on the waiting list.
(d) Those classes are in session.

**11**

W You must be upset about not getting the account.

M ______________________

(a) I've decided to move past it.
(b) Yeah, it hasn't turned up anywhere.
(c) It still might fall through.
(d) It's fine. I have a backup copy.

**12**

M Do we need reservations for the restaurant tonight?

W ______________________

(a) I doubt it, since it's a weeknight.
(b) Yes, I think I left them at the restaurant.
(c) No, we should make them in advance.
(d) Sleep on it. We'll discuss it in the morning.

**13**

W I'm debating pulling out of the stock market.

M ______________________

(a) Well, it'll work on any occasion.
(b) Me, too. That would've been a gamble.
(c) I would. The instability is too much to handle right now.
(d) You should. This is the best time to invest in stocks.

**14**

M When's the conference starting?

W ______________________

(a) Until 11 A.M.
(b) Ten on the dot
(c) Not usually this much
(d) An hour longer this time

**15**

W It's virtually impossible to shop for Ann.

M ______________________

(a) That's because she's so particular.
(b) No, I didn't go shopping with her, either.
(c) Actually, she didn't buy anything this time.
(d) It'd be easier if she knew your birthday.

**16**

M Hi, it's Rick calling. Is Lisa home?

W Sorry, she's stepped out.

M Would you have her call me back?

W ______________________

(a) OK, I'll put you through.
(b) She's expecting your return.
(c) Sure, I'll relay the message.
(d) I haven't asked her yet.

**17**

W Did you show my blueprint to your boss?

M He's interested but wants more details.

W Great! What should I do?

M ______________________

(a) The next step is a formal presentation.
(b) No need to despair. He'll come around eventually.
(c) Come up with a blueprint.
(d) Maybe you can ask for a second chance.

**18**

M Have you decided what to order?

W Well, I'm not very hungry.

M Same here. It'd be a waste to get two entrées.

W ______________________

(a) Then I'll try the full course.
(b) Let's split something, then.
(c) At least it'd be easy to cook.
(d) Right, let's get two entrées.

## 19

W There's a coffee stain on my shirt!
M Try buttoning your jacket.
W There. Is it still noticeable?
M ______________________________

(a) I'll watch it for you.
(b) Sure, it'll dry in no time.
(c) It's completely hidden.
(d) Not once it's stained like that.

## 20

M I can't access the online English homework.
W Did you enter the password we got in class today?
M It doesn't work. Could I have written it down wrong?
W ______________________________

(a) Here, check it against what I wrote down.
(b) Try resending the homework.
(c) No, you're supposed to do it online.
(d) You should've written it down.

## 21

W Hi, I placed an online order but accidentally gave the wrong address.
M OK, do you know if it's been shipped yet?
W I doubt it. I placed it a minute ago.
M ______________________________

(a) You can just order it online.
(b) We apologize for the mistake.
(c) Then I can help you change it online.
(d) Sorry, the order hasn't been shipped.

## 22

M Your new apartment is so spacious!
W It costs more, but my last place was too cramped.
M So it's worth paying more rent?
W ______________________________

(a) Only if I can find a good discount.
(b) Definitely. I love the extra room.
(c) Exactly. That's why I chose not to.
(d) My last apartment cost a lot more.

## 23

W How was Ken's dinner party?
M I completely stuffed myself.
W I take it he knows his way around a kitchen.
M ______________________________

(a) Without a doubt, he's quite the chef.
(b) No kidding, since we were ordering in.
(c) No, he cooked everything himself.
(d) I'll let you know after the party.

## 24

M Have you mapped out our route to the ski resort?
W Yeah, let's take Highway 5.
M Isn't that a roundabout way?
W ______________________________

(a) It's the straightest road home.
(b) I didn't know it would take that long.
(c) Factoring in traffic, it's the quickest way.
(d) That's why we're flying there.

## 25

W I missed class on Monday because I was sick.
M That day was mostly review, so you didn't miss much.
W May I borrow your notes? I don't want to fall behind.
M ______________________________

(a) You may be able to submit them later.
(b) We didn't learn anything new, so I didn't take any.
(c) I found out when I went to class.
(d) Don't worry. I'll be sure to give them back.

## 26

M Front desk? Can I talk to hotel maintenance?
W I can help. Is there a problem?
M The air conditioner isn't working, and the room is too warm.
W ______________________________

(a) I'll have someone come up.
(b) There isn't a thermometer.
(c) A new manual was recently ordered.
(d) I'll have it heated up right away.

## 27

W Mr. Sanders is coming back to work tomorrow.

M Isn't he supposed to be in Hawaii till the end of next week?

W He had to cut his vacation short because something important came up.

M ______________________

(a) Wow, he must be really disappointed.
(b) I know. He told me once he got back.
(c) I wasn't aware he was leaving.
(d) The exact date hasn't been set yet.

## 28

M Want to come to happy hour with me on Friday?

W I'll probably be too drained after work.

M It'll be a good way to unwind.

W ______________________

(a) In that case, either place will do.
(b) I suppose I can swing by for a bit.
(c) Fine, if you cancel your plans.
(d) I would go, but I'll be at work tonight.

## 29

W I was disappointed by the restaurant you recommended.

M I'm surprised—the food was wonderful when I went.

W But the service was abysmal.

M ______________________

(a) That can really ruin a dining experience.
(b) The same goes for the food.
(c) Reviews call the food overrated, too.
(d) You should try it before deciding.

## 30

M My leg muscles are killing me after my run.

W Didn't you go hiking yesterday, too? You're really pushing yourself.

M Well, I'm trying to build my endurance these days.

W ______________________

(a) That's not done by dieting, though.
(b) Still, you should try to get some exercise.
(c) You seem to be overdoing it.
(d) Seriously, I'm not exaggerating.

## 31

W Hi, I'd like to apply for a new passport.

M Sure, do you have identification?

W Yes. I brought my birth certificate with me.

M Good, but we need something with your photo on it, too.

W OK, then here's my driver's license.

M Great, those'll do.

Q: What is the main topic of the conversation?

(a) Identification required for a passport
(b) Documentation needed for a travel visa
(c) Types of pictures needed for a new passport
(d) Reasons why the woman must show identification

## 32

M Shouldn't you be studying? Why are you watching TV?

W I'm not—it's on for the background noise.

M But don't you find it distracting?

W Actually, it helps. I can't study in silence.

M Still, won't you retain more without it on?

W I've gotten all A's this semester studying like this.

Q: What is the woman mainly doing in the conversation?

(a) Justifying her study habit
(b) Complaining about being distracted by the TV
(c) Advising the man to watch less TV
(d) Describing how to get straight A's

## 33

W Sorry, Kevin, I lost your drill. I'll get you a new one.

M There's no need. It was old, anyway.

W No, I should. Where'd you get it?

M It was so long ago that I don't remember.

W I'll get a similar model, then. It would make me feel better.

M If you want to, thanks.

Q: What is the woman mainly doing in the conversation?

(a) Determining how long ago the man bought a drill
(b) Offering the man money for a drill she used
(c) Insisting on replacing the man's drill
(d) Apologizing to the man for breaking a drill

## 34

M Is it true that John's in the hospital?
W Yes. He fell off a ladder.
M Oh, no! What was he doing?
W Putting up Christmas lights.
M Was he badly hurt?
W A few broken ribs and a concussion.
M That's awful. I hope he recovers soon.

Q: What are the man and woman mainly discussing?
(a) Injuries that can be caused by falling from a ladder
(b) The steps John is taking in order to recover
(c) Precautions to take when using a ladder
(d) The circumstances surrounding John's hospitalization

## 35

W I heard you're looking for an executive assistant.
M Yes, and I'm starting to get desperate.
W Well, Rachel, my cousin, is more than qualified.
M Does she have any experience?
W Of course, and references to back it up.
M Forward me her résumé, and I'll take a look.

Q: What is the woman mainly trying to do?
(a) Suggest the man widen his job search
(b) Recommend her cousin for a job opening
(c) Boast about her cousin's accomplishments
(d) Persuade the man to make her his assistant

## 36

M Our cable bill went up again.
W Maybe we should go with a different provider.
M But I enjoy all the premium channels we get.
W Other companies have them, too.
M But their rates are probably just as high.
W Well, at least we could get an introductory deal.

Q: What is the woman mainly doing in the conversation?
(a) Convincing the man to downgrade their cable plan
(b) Suggesting the man stop watching cable television
(c) Proposing to switch cable companies
(d) Recommending cutting utility costs

## 37

W Everyone has a smartphone but me. Maybe I should get one, too.
M Well, you barely use the phone you have.
W Still, I feel out of date for not having a smartphone.
M That's a silly excuse to buy something you won't use.
W Yeah, I guess. And it would triple my phone bill.
M All the more reason not to cave in.

Q: What is the man mainly doing in the conversation?
(a) Complaining about a smartphone he never uses
(b) Defending his rationale for purchasing a smartphone
(c) Dissuading the woman from getting a smartphone
(d) Chastising the woman for upgrading to a smartphone

## 38

M Hi, I'm Jim. Are you a freshman, too?
W No, I'm a sophomore. I'm Bella. Where are you from?
M A small town in Canada. You?
W I grew up in Boston, but I was born in India.
M Oh, when did you move to Boston?
W A long time ago, when I was a small kid.

Q: Which is correct about the woman according to the conversation?
(a) She is a college freshman.
(b) She was born in Canada.
(c) She recently moved from India.
(d) She relocated to Boston in her childhood.

## 39

W All your practice really paid off! The presentation went great.
M Yeah, the slide show seemed quite effective. Thanks to your help!
W Oh, please. You did all the research.
M Still, you helped tie it together with the visuals.
W I just hope my presentation goes as well next week.
M It will! Let me know if I can help.

Q: Which is correct according to the conversation?
(a) The man did not rehearse his presentation.
(b) The man's presentation involved a slide show.
(c) The woman helped the man with his research.
(d) The woman has already given her presentation.

## 40

M I heard you had an interview with a radio station for a hosting job.
W Yes, I have another one with them tomorrow.
M Great! You're making me nostalgic for when I used to host a show.
W I didn't know you did that! When?
M Every morning as an undergrad at my college's station.
W Wow, I'll be sure to ask for advice if I get this job.

Q: Which is correct according to the conversation?
(a) The woman has applied for an off-air position.
(b) The woman's first interview is tomorrow.
(c) The man currently hosts his own radio show.
(d) The man was a radio host during his college days.

## 41

W That website you suggested sent me the wrong thing.
M The sporting goods store? What did you order?
W I bought golf balls, but they sent the wrong brand.
M You can exchange them for free. I've done it.
W They've messed up your order, too?
M Yes, they sent me a wrong-sized shirt, and I exchanged it for free.

Q: Which is correct according to the conversation?
(a) The woman ordered from an online sports shop.
(b) The woman received golf clubs instead of balls.
(c) The man suggests the woman ask for a refund.
(d) The man had to pay shipping costs for an exchange.

## 42

M I don't think I can finish painting my living room in time.
W You mean before your wife gets back?
M Yeah. Her flight's tomorrow at noon.
W Haven't you been working on it all weekend?
M Yeah, but I still have an entire wall and the trim to do.
W Then I'll stop by after work to give you a hand.

Q: Which is correct about the man according to the conversation?
(a) He is confident that he can finish the painting by tomorrow.
(b) His wife's flight arrives today at noon.
(c) He spent the weekend painting the living room.
(d) His living room walls are done but not the trim.

## 43

W Would you recommend laser eye surgery?
M Absolutely. Are you thinking about doing it?
W Maybe. My contact lenses have been irritating my eyes.
M I had the same problem, and I didn't want to wear glasses.
W I hate glasses, too. It'd be great to not need anything in order to see.
M Well, everyone has different results, but I've never looked back.

Q: What can be inferred about the man from the conversation?
(a) He performs laser eye surgeries.
(b) He has had laser eye surgery.
(c) His contact lenses were too expensive to maintain.
(d) His eyesight is worse than the woman's.

## 44

M Are you entering the *Daily News* photo contest?
W I'm just an amateur. I don't do those big professional contests.
M The contest is open to amateurs, too. They have a "new talent" category.
W Still, I don't think I'm experienced enough.
M Just try. Your nature photos are spectacular.
W I don't know. Maybe next year.

Q: What can be inferred from the conversation?
(a) The woman entered last year's *Daily News* photo contest.
(b) The man is a judge in the photo contest.
(c) The photo contest has strict eligibility restrictions.
(d) The photo contest has multiple categories.

## 45

W I found out I'm in charge of the new cereal ad contract.
M So we snagged that contract? That's great!
W Not really. The company's taking on more work than it can handle.
M It'll be all the more impressive when it's completed.
W Not if it's rushed and turns out badly, though.
M It'll be a lot of work, but you'll manage.

Q: What can be inferred from the conversation?
(a) The woman is eager to oversee the new project.
(b) The woman was responsible for negotiating the contract.
(c) The man believes that the new project is feasible.
(d) The man put the woman in charge of the project.

## 46

Come to Nova Gallery this weekend to help us celebrate! Ten years ago, Nova opened and began promoting new and established artists. To mark this milestone, all of the artists from our three currently running shows will be on hand to answer questions about their art. So come by this Saturday, enjoy some light refreshments, talk to the artists, and maybe even pick up a one-of-a-kind artwork!

Q: What is mainly being advertised?
(a) Nova Gallery's grand opening
(b) Art being discounted at Nova Gallery
(c) A gallery's newest exhibition
(d) An art gallery's anniversary event

## 47

The Department of State is dedicated to providing citizens traveling abroad with updates about their destination countries. Simply log onto our website before your journey to learn about the current political situation of the country you are bound for. Or if you're already abroad and concerned about a deteriorating political climate or social unrest, please check the department website for up-to-date news on your location regarding potential threats and recommended courses of action.

Q: What is mainly being announced?
(a) Travel tips from foreign websites
(b) A website with information about international destinations
(c) Areas that are experiencing social unrest
(d) Evacuation procedures during emergencies abroad

## 48

The cheetah is one of the fastest land animals, achieving speeds of up to 75 miles per hour. A number of evolutionary features support its incredible velocity. Unlike most cats, a cheetah has semi-retractable claws, which offer better gripping ability. Additionally, its nostrils, heart, and lungs are enlarged, allowing better oxygen intake and circulation. Finally, its tail serves as a kind of rudder, increasing agility.

Q: What is the main purpose of the lecture?
(a) To illustrate how oxygen affects a cheetah's speed
(b) To show how running ability is an advantage for cheetahs
(c) To explain the different stages in the cheetah's evolution
(d) To detail physical characteristics that enhance a cheetah's speed

## 49

Flamenco music is associated with the region of Andalusia, Spain, but it was originally the signature musical style of the Romani people. Centuries ago, flamenco songs were simple chants that lamented the persecution and loss suffered by the Romani, with the only accompaniment being a cane hit upon the floor for rhythm. The music that was added later had a heavy Moorish influence, using minor scales and elaborate melodies. The melding of these characteristics with influences from the people of Andalusia made flamenco what it is today, a music quite different from its original form.

Q: What is the speaker's main point about flamenco music?
(a) Its original form has been preserved by the Romani.
(b) It was influenced by several cultures as it developed.
(c) Its popularity waned after being introduced to Spain.
(d) It was a form of protest against persecution.

## 50

Sending aid money to other countries is admirable and builds international goodwill. Yet the pros of foreign aid do not outweigh the cons, and continuing our current course will only cause further harm to our country. Aiding other countries has been done at the expense of our own citizens, millions of whom are still jobless or living in poverty. The situation at home calls for allocating the funds here rather than elsewhere.

Q: What is the speaker's main point about foreign aid?
(a) It cannot be used to improve the domestic economy.
(b) It is irrelevant in building international goodwill.
(c) It should be distributed abroad more evenly.
(d) It has detrimental effects domestically.

## 51

There is much that first-generation immigrants can do to encourage their children to achieve proficiency in their family's native language. Children will learn and use English at school, so parents should make sure they expose their children to their native language daily. They should make sure to spend a lot of time talking in their native tongue. Additionally, introducing children to other children who speak their native language is beneficial. Exposing them to books, movies, and music in their language is also useful.

Q: What is the talk mainly about?
(a) The advantages of having children retain their native language
(b) Ways to help children learn their parents' native language
(c) Reasons children have forgotten their native language
(d) Methods parents can use to become bilingual

## 52

New Harmony was a socialist community in Indiana created by Robert Owen in 1825. Although it was deemed a failure, dissolving after only four years, it was based on a plan that had been successful. During a time when working conditions were deplorable, Owen had managed a profitable and humane industrial community at his cotton mill in Scotland. When he attempted to apply these precepts on a larger scale at New Harmony, though, they proved to be unsustainable.

Q: What is the speaker's main point about New Harmony?
(a) It failed despite being based on a successful model.
(b) Its socialist leaders ignored harsh working conditions.
(c) It became a prototype of future socialist communities.
(d) Its failure resulted from Owen changing his stance on socialism.

## 53

As director of Fairview Soccer Camp, I'd like to welcome you to our summer program! We'll be meeting every weekday from 9:00 A.M. to 3:30 P.M. this week. The camp will be split into two teams: red and blue. There'll be a series of practice matches, culminating in a final match between the two teams this Friday, which is the last day of camp. I'll be the coach for the red team, and Martin, my co-director, will take the blue team. Let's have some fun!

Q: Which is correct according to the announcement?
(a) The camp will be held on the weekend.
(b) The duration of the program is one month.
(c) The blue team will be coached by the speaker.
(d) The red and blue teams will play against each other.

## 54

Mining for utilitarian and precious metals was prevalent throughout the Roman Empire. In fact, Caesar's desire for new sources of tin, a metal necessary in the production of bronze, was a driving factor in his decision to invade the British Isles. By the time the empire reached its zenith, mining was taking place in every part of the realm, from the Iberian Peninsula, the leading supplier of lead, to Noricum, where gold and iron ore were mined.

Q: Which is correct about the Roman Empire according to the lecture?
(a) It limited its mining to precious metals.
(b) It sought bronze in order to create tin.
(c) It invaded Britain for its tin deposits.
(d) It mined most of its lead in Noricum.

## 55

A former mayor's proposition to rebuild parts of the Berlin Wall, which was torn down over twenty years ago, is causing controversy. Eberhard Diepgen, Berlin's mayor in the decade after Germany's reunification, wants to restore the Wall's original graffiti, barbed wire, and watch towers. Residents supporting the proposal say that it would serve as a memorial, but others have dismissed the idea, seeing it as merely a tourist attraction that fails to reflect the harsh history behind the Wall.

Q: Which is correct according to the report?
(a) The proposition entails rebuilding the entire Berlin Wall.
(b) The memorial was proposed by the current mayor of Berlin.
(c) Diepgen proposed including the Berlin Wall's original graffiti in the memorial.
(d) Diepgen's proposal has failed to draw any support from residents.

## 56

The US government needs to enact stricter online privacy protection measures. Currently, websites only have an obligation to obtain parental consent for collecting personal information from children under the age of 13. For other minors and adults, there is no comprehensive federal law that restricts the collection, retention, or sharing of personal information. Websites that collect payment, medical, or financial information are subject to certain security standards regarding that information, but they can share other information with third parties.

Q: Which is correct according to the talk?
(a) Websites need parental permission to collect the personal information of all minors.
(b) Retention of personal information is subject to federal privacy laws.
(c) Sites that gather medical information must abide by relevant security standards.
(d) Sites collecting financial information cannot share any user information with third parties.

## 57

The British period drama *The Gentleman's Wife* was the big winner at the Film Critics' Awards last night, surprising many in the industry. Most critics had picked *Break Free*, a story about the American Civil War, as the most likely winner. Yet despite its 15 nominations, the slavery drama only won awards for Best Screenplay and Best Musical Score. The British film, by contrast, took home six awards, including the two biggest, Best Picture and Best Director.

Q: Which is correct about *The Gentleman's Wife* according to the news report?
(a) It had been favored as a winner by critics.
(b) It won a Film Critics' Award for Best Screenplay.
(c) It garnered more awards than *Break Free*.
(d) It failed to win the two biggest awards of last night.

## 58

"Easy English News" is a dynamic radio program for learners of English. Our daily program reports current news and events with easily comprehensible vocabulary and syntax. Our news stories are also available on our website, along with vocabulary study aids and listening exercises. Learn the basics of English while catching up on the latest news from around the world. Catch our show live on 101FM every day at 9 P.M.!

Q: What can be inferred about the program?
(a) It was designed for use in public schools.
(b) It is targeted at English learners who are not yet proficient.
(c) Its content was created by English learners.
(d) Its policy is to avoid news about politics.

## 59

The ongoing global effort to eradicate polio met with some disheartening news earlier today. The Global Polio Eradication Initiative, or GPEI, found a resurgence of the disease in countries where it had previously disappeared. The GPEI is looking for methods to better maintain vaccine efficacy in the warm climates of the resurgent countries, as the vaccine currently used is heat-sensitive. Doctors suggest that a proposed oral vaccine could be the answer to the problem. The oral vaccine should help keep the disease at bay in locations where refrigeration is not readily available.

Q: What can be inferred from the speech?
(a) The current polio vaccine must be stored at a certain temperature.
(b) The resurgence of polio is attributed to the new oral vaccine.
(c) The GPEI believed polio had been defeated globally.
(d) The polio virus requires a warm climate to survive.

## 60

In the 1920s, painter Georgia O'Keeffe changed her artistic style. She had been doing abstract painting, but during this time she started creating more representational images. This was an attempt to try to steer critics away from their tendency to impose gendered interpretations onto her work. What she wanted to express were the parallels between nature and humanity, and she was bothered that critics pigeonholed her work as only feminist.

Q: What can be inferred about Georgia O'Keeffe from the speech?
(a) She deliberately made her paintings hard to interpret.
(b) She tried to evoke parallels between nature and feminism.
(c) Critical interpretations of her work influenced her painting style.
(d) Gender issues were her main source of inspiration.

# 서울대 최신기출 5

## Listening Comprehension Scripts

**1**

M Would you like a drink?

W ______________________

(a) Glad you like it.
(b) Juice would be great.
(c) You're very welcome.
(d) All I can offer is water.

**2**

W I'm annoyed with my unstable Internet connection.

M ______________________

(a) You mistyped it.
(b) Contact your service provider.
(c) Bookmark that site.
(d) Internet information is unreliable.

**3**

M Congratulations on your engagement! Eric's a lucky guy!

W ______________________

(a) But he planned it.
(b) Thanks for the advice.
(c) That's sweet of you to say.
(d) What a nice idea!

**4**

W It's weird that Sue missed tonight's meeting.

M ______________________

(a) There's no reason to cancel it.
(b) I hope she gets here before it starts.
(c) It's definitely unlike her.
(d) Well, I'll be there instead.

**5**

M Why haven't you left for work?

W ______________________

(a) I'm not going. I called in sick.
(b) Once I finish up, I'll go home.
(c) Of course! I knew I left it behind.
(d) I was caught in traffic.

**6**

W I appreciated the thank-you flowers you sent.

M ______________________

(a) They're just a token of my gratitude.
(b) Nonsense! I love receiving gifts.
(c) I'll accept them for you.
(d) Oh, you shouldn't have sent them.

**7**

M Paul's reason for skipping the party sounded made-up.

W ______________________

(a) You're right. We should trust him.
(b) I suspected that as well.
(c) No one knew it was his party.
(d) I'm positive he was there, too.

**8**

W When can I receive the shirt I ordered?

M ______________________

(a) Take your time with it.
(b) Exchange it as soon as possible.
(c) Delivery will take a few days.
(d) Order through the website.

**9**

M I hope rain won't cancel the kids' soccer game.

W ______________________

(a) Too bad it was called off.
(b) I doubt we can move it outdoors.
(c) Good thing we can both attend.
(d) They'd be inconsolable if it did.

**10**

W Hello, front desk? My room hasn't been cleaned.

M ______________________

(a) Sorry, that room is unavailable.
(b) I'll send someone up right away.
(c) Our rooms only accommodate two.
(d) I apologize for the commotion.

## 11

M Our tickets don't have seat numbers.

W ______________________________

(a) Because it's first-come, first-served seating.
(b) Check the number on the seat.
(c) Tickets must have been sold out.
(d) Go ahead. I'll watch your seat.

## 12

W Was that the train to Berlin that just left?

M ______________________________

(a) Yes, I'm about to board it now.
(b) No, the one that left was to Berlin.
(c) Right, but leave as quickly as you can.
(d) It was. Another will be along shortly, though.

## 13

M Courtesy is disappearing these days, wouldn't you say?

W ______________________________

(a) Etiquette isn't as prevalent as you claim.
(b) The world could do with more manners.
(c) It's better, since we have to get along.
(d) I'd say being courteous makes up for it.

## 14

W I worry my friends are more successful than I am.

M ______________________________

(a) Sounds like you've reached your goal.
(b) No need to worry them yet.
(c) Don't. You have plenty of achievements to be proud of.
(d) Unlikely. Your success won't intimidate others.

## 15

M With so many people involved, how can we reach a consensus about the project?

W ______________________________

(a) No wonder it was much easier than I thought.
(b) Compromise. Not everyone can have their way.
(c) Duly noted. I'll get more people involved.
(d) Good idea. Things could possibly work out that way.

## 16

M How'd your exam go?

W Not very well.

M Oh, you're being modest.

W ______________________________

(a) It won't take long.
(b) You answered incorrectly.
(c) No, I should study for it.
(d) Really, it was a disaster.

## 17

W Is there a deli nearby?

M No, but there's a diner.

W I just need lunch to-go.

M ______________________________

(a) I've never eaten there, either.
(b) It does takeout orders.
(c) Tables fill up quickly.
(d) I'll grab the check, then.

## 18

M I heard you were in a car accident.

W Yes, a minor one.

M Were there any injuries?

W ______________________________

(a) No, I'm still healing.
(b) I'm glad I wasn't there.
(c) Fortunately, no one was hurt.
(d) It was my fault, actually.

## 19

W Did you hear about the fire?

M At the factory? Yeah.

W The news must be spreading quickly.

M ______________________________

(a) Well, every news channel is covering it.
(b) It's the first I've heard of it.
(c) I can't believe you haven't heard yet.
(d) Because I don't follow the news.

## 20

M Excuse me, didn't we meet at Jon's party?
W Oh, right! We had an interesting talk.
M Yeah, about politics, right?
W ______________________________

(a) Yes, and it got pretty lively.
(b) OK, but I'd prefer another subject.
(c) There're several opinions about that.
(d) That's an interesting point you make.

## 21

W What do you do for a living?
M I'm a stockbroker.
W That's a pretty demanding job.
M ______________________________

(a) I'm not demanding at all.
(b) True, but I enjoy it.
(c) Sounds like a risky investment.
(d) Good guess, but I'm a stockbroker.

## 22

M Have you made a New Year's resolution?
W I decided not to this year.
M Why not?
W ______________________________

(a) I always keep my resolutions to myself.
(b) I decided to learn Spanish this year.
(c) It feels pointless since I never keep them.
(d) New Year's Eve isn't much fun, after all.

## 23

W Do you have any bags to check?
M That depends. Would it cost extra?
W Yes. It's $20 per bag.
M ______________________________

(a) No, mine aren't hand luggage.
(b) I have enough bags, thanks.
(c) In that case, I'll just carry mine.
(d) Then I'll claim both.

## 24

M Luke's work is full of mistakes.
W Maybe we should offer constructive criticism.
M What if he takes it personally?
W ______________________________

(a) That's why we shouldn't mention it.
(b) If he does, it mustn't be his work.
(c) He doesn't criticize anyone.
(d) I'm sure he'll be receptive to feedback.

## 25

W What was your meeting with Mr. Vicks about?
M I'm not supposed to discuss it.
W Come on. Was it about the rumored merger?
M ______________________________

(a) I promised I'd keep it confidential.
(b) Honestly, I'd like to know, too.
(c) If you don't want to say, that's fine.
(d) Everyone says so, but I wasn't there.

## 26

M Isn't your art show next month?
W A scheduling conflict pushed it back.
M You must be disappointed.
W ______________________________

(a) There's a chance I won't.
(b) Hardly. I welcome extra prep time.
(c) I'll always wish I did better.
(d) Once it's over, I'll know for sure.

## 27

W I'm thinking of adopting a third dog.
M Can you care for that many?
W Not really, but I can't say no to a helpless animal.
M ______________________________

(a) You shouldn't have given it away that easily.
(b) That's how you teach them to behave.
(c) Don't feel helpless. Try adopting one.
(d) You shouldn't take on more than you can manage.

## 28

M Hello, I'm surveying public opinion about the upcoming election.

W I'm not the best person to ask. I'm not into politics.

M That's no problem. Will you answer a few questions?

W ______________________________

(a) I'm not good at conducting them.
(b) If you think I can be of use, sure.
(c) I'm afraid I haven't voted yet.
(d) Essentially, the issue is local politics.

## 29

W I'm sorry about the typo that got published.

M It was a real embarrassment to our newspaper.

W I won't let it happen again.

M ______________________________

(a) I'll have to take you at your word on that.
(b) It wasn't even misspelled, though.
(c) Just please correct it before it goes to press.
(d) Nobody overlooked it, anyway.

## 30

M You're late getting home. We missed our dinner reservation.

W There were no cabs because of the rain, so I had to walk.

M Should we go and see if they'll still seat us?

W ______________________________

(a) I'm too disheveled—let me freshen up first.
(b) I don't see any free tables.
(c) Better that than trudging back out again.
(d) Don't worry. We'll still be on time for our reservation.

## 31

M I miss my high school days.

W Me, too. It was a special time.

M Remember chemistry with Mrs. Smith?

W Of course. It was fun being lab partners.

M That made the class more enjoyable.

W Yeah, I'm glad we signed up for it together.

Q: What are the man and woman mainly doing?

(a) Recalling a time in high school
(b) Planning a high school reunion
(c) Remembering how they met as teenagers
(d) Discussing an old teacher

## 32

W I'd like to apply for a passport.

M OK, fill out this form.

W It asks for my occupation, but I'm out of work.

M Just put down "unemployed."

W And who can be my emergency contact?

M A close family member is usually best.

Q: What is the man mainly doing in the conversation?

(a) Reviewing the woman's completed form
(b) Assisting the woman with an application form
(c) Asking for a passport application form
(d) Renewing an expired passport

## 33

M Welcome to my new apartment.

W It's smaller than your old place but looks cozy.

M It's all I could afford since rents are skyrocketing.

W Yeah, a lot of people are downsizing.

M Even this was barely in my price range.

W And your old place was twice the size!

Q: What are the man and woman mainly discussing?

(a) Whether a bigger apartment is worth the price
(b) How much it would cost for the man to move
(c) Whether the man will have to move again
(d) How rent prices forced the man to rent a smaller apartment

## 34

W There's a new folk art exhibit at the museum.
M What makes folk art different or special, anyway?
W It's usually made by indigenous peoples.
M Nothing else sets it apart?
W Well, folk art is also utilitarian, rather than purely aesthetic.
M Huh, I never knew that.

Q: What is the woman mainly doing in the conversation?
(a) Explaining what makes folk art distinct from other art
(b) Describing the different exhibits at the museum
(c) Differentiating between various kinds of folk art
(d) Defining folk art as a purely aesthetic artistic genre

## 35

M What's with the news reporting so much on celebrities?
W Perhaps people find it entertaining?
M But it's unbefitting of a formal news program.
W I agree. It's frivolous.
M And it distracts from important issues.
W Yeah, gossip is better suited for talk shows.

Q: What is the main topic of the conversation?
(a) How TV programs distort celebrity life
(b) Why the public prefers entertainment over news
(c) The news as an inappropriate medium for celebrity gossip
(d) Criticism of celebrities hosting news programs

## 36

W The job applicants we interviewed were quite something.
M I know. Deciding who to hire won't be easy!
W Yeah, they all seem very competent.
M That was my feeling, too.
W And I was pleased to see each has a unique skill set.
M Yes. We've got plenty of choice!

Q: What are the man and woman mainly doing in the conversation?
(a) Debating employee hiring criteria
(b) Deciding which applicants to interview
(c) Discussing their impression of the interviewees
(d) Comparing the interviewees' strengths and weaknesses

## 37

M I feel awful. My daughter seems to feel that I don't trust her.
W Oh, because you had your neighbor check up on her?
M Yeah. I was worried she might misbehave when I left her home alone.
W And did she misbehave?
M Not at all. I should've trusted her.
W Just talk with her to smooth things over.

Q: What is the man mainly doing in the conversation?
(a) Complaining about his daughter's misbehavior
(b) Regretting that he showed too little faith in his daughter
(c) Showing remorse for leaving his daughter home alone
(d) Explaining his reasons for mistrusting his daughter

## 38

W Nick, is that new red sedan yours?
M It's just a temporary rental.
W What happened to your old minivan?
M It's at the mechanic's for a brake problem.
W Ah, so they provided you with a replacement car?
M Yeah, I'll be driving it until tomorrow.

Q: Which is correct about the man according to the conversation?
(a) He recently purchased a new car.
(b) He traded in his sedan for a minivan.
(c) He is getting his minivan repaired.
(d) He must return the rental car today.

## 39

M Ms. Jones, your husband's here to see you.

W Oh, he's 30 minutes early. We weren't supposed to have lunch until one.

M He says he'll wait if you can't leave right away.

W Well, just tell him I can be out in five minutes.

M Sure. I'll make a reservation, if you need me to.

W Thanks, but we already have one.

Q: Which is correct about the woman according to the conversation?

(a) Her husband surprised her with an unplanned lunch date.

(b) She worked past her usual 1 P.M. lunch time.

(c) Her husband will have to wait 30 minutes.

(d) She declines the man's offer to make a reservation.

## 40

W Where's Gate 5? My flight begins boarding in ten minutes.

M I can have a cart take you there.

W Isn't there a shortcut?

M The cart's your best option. It'll take two minutes.

W OK, then I'll take it. Sorry for the trouble.

M No problem. I'll get one right now.

Q: Which is correct according to the conversation?

(a) The woman's flight began boarding ten minutes ago.

(b) The man suggests taking a shortcut instead of a cart.

(c) The woman agrees to take a cart to her gate.

(d) The man apologizes for the lack of available carts.

## 41

M I'm dying to see Australia since my buddy, Rick, just raves about it.

W Hasn't he only been there once on business?

M Yeah, but he went sightseeing, too.

W I'm sure Australia's great, but what about the flight?

M You and I have plenty of savings. We can afford it.

W That's not it. I couldn't endure 12 hours on a plane.

Q: Which is correct according to the conversation?

(a) Rick's enthusiasm spurred the man's interest in Australia.

(b) Rick has made several business trips to Australia.

(c) The man can only pay for the trip if he saves more money.

(d) The woman cannot afford the flight to Australia.

## 42

W What did the dermatologist say about your rash?

M It's another rosacea flare-up. Annoying but harmless.

W Did he say what triggered it?

M He wasn't sure what caused it, but I think it was all that sun I got.

W I see. It's easily treatable, right? With a topical cream?

M There's no cure, but he said I should avoid sun exposure, just in case.

Q: Which is correct about the man according to the conversation?

(a) He is experiencing a recurring skin condition.

(b) His skin condition could adversely affect his health.

(c) His doctor pinpointed sun exposure as the cause of his skin problem.

(d) He can cure his skin problem with a topical sunblock cream.

## 43

W Man, I can't send the ball where I want to.

M Please, you're the ace of our tennis team.

W My backhand slice was off at practice, too.

M You're probably stressed from all the pressure.

W Well, I can't afford to look bad in front of these college recruiters.

M Relax, you have nothing to worry about.

Q: What can be inferred about the woman from the conversation?

(a) Her current tennis scholarship is in jeopardy.

(b) She hopes to pursue tennis at the collegiate level.

(c) She is forgoing college to be a professional athlete.

(d) Her grades may disqualify her from school athletics.

## 44

M That couple sitting across from us is so loud.
W Yeah, I can hear their entire conversation.
M Should I say something?
W Best not to. They might get angry.
M But they should know better than to talk so loudly in public.
W I know, but let's not cause any trouble.

Q: What can be inferred about the woman from the conversation?
(a) She finds the content of the couple's conversation offensive.
(b) She has already asked the couple to lower their voices.
(c) She fears confronting the couple could worsen the situation.
(d) She is curious about the couple's argument.

## 45

M The estimate for my basement water damage is $2,000.
W You have homeowners' insurance, though, right?
M Yes, but it doesn't cover flood damage.
W Yikes. The flooding could've been worse, though.
M You're right, like Mr. Sampson next door.
W Yeah, his was really bad. It's a good thing his insurance covered it.

Q: What can be inferred about the man from the conversation?
(a) He has a separate flood insurance policy.
(b) His insurance covered more than he expected.
(c) He was with Mr. Sampson when the flood occurred.
(d) His neighbor, Mr. Sampson, had flood damage insurance.

## 46

The leader that Genghis Khan ultimately became was perhaps influenced by events from his childhood. Following his father's death, the nine-year-old Genghis Khan tried to claim his father's position as clan chieftain. The clan refused to follow such a young boy, and his family was ostracized. Having to subsist without protection and in poverty toughened the young Genghis Khan. This toughness, and his knowledge of Mongolia's unstable politics, helped him rise to power.

Q: What is the main purpose of the lecture about Genghis Khan?
(a) To explain his impact on history
(b) To analyze his effectiveness as a leader
(c) To describe how key events from his early life affected him
(d) To emphasize his father's influence on him

## 47

In reconstructing the history of the earth's climate, geologists look to glaciers. Changes in temperature and weather patterns affect how a glacier evolves and, as such, a glacier's history reflects climate history. For instance, glaciers grow and shrink over time according to environmental factors. When they shrink, they leave behind rock and soil debris known as moraines that provide information about changes in climate.

Q: What is the talk mainly about?
(a) Glaciers as sources of information about climate change
(b) Typical weather patterns in glacial areas
(c) The way global warming is melting glaciers
(d) The impact glaciers have on the environment

## 48

Good morning, staff. I know you have concerns about the company's tightened security. I assure you these new rules are necessary and were created in response to a breach that happened recently. An employee used his cell phone to take pictures of classified documents and sold them to our competitors. In my role as manager, I must ensure that such a violation is never repeated, and that is why we have no choice but to ban cell phone use in security-sensitive areas.

Q: What is the main purpose of the announcement?
(a) To justify a new security measure
(b) To identify a problem with employee morale
(c) To state how cell phone use is limiting productivity
(d) To dispel rumors about a cell phone ban

## 49

In a few minutes we'll be interviewing Joe Banks, who came out of nowhere to win the comedy festival's best-newcomer award. Banks had planned to perform at one of the festival's minor venues, simply to hone his skills. But his one hour stand-up performance earned him a five-star review that propelled him into the spotlight. Banks expressed surprise at the attention he's been getting but couldn't be happier about his new-found success.

Q: What is the speaker's main point about Joe Banks?
(a) He refuses to give up his dream of becoming a comedian.
(b) He advanced from obscurity to fame with one show.
(c) His award has revitalized public interest in comedy.
(d) His debut was the festival's most anticipated event.

## 50

Though deemed by some to be the greatest biography written in English, James Boswell's *The Life of Samuel Johnson* has received its share of negative criticism. Most of it has been leveled at the book's undue emphasis on the later part of Johnson's life. Boswell had only met Johnson when the latter was in his fifties, so his biography for the most part leaves out Johnson's early years. For this reason, several critics assert that Boswell's biography does not constitute a comprehensive telling of Johnson's life.

Q: What is the speaker's main point about James Boswell's *The Life of Samuel Johnson*?
(a) It is critical of Johnson's behavior in his later years.
(b) It is well-written but lacks historical accuracy.
(c) It has drawn criticism due to scant coverage of Johnson's youth.
(d) It was crafted to omit information that could discredit Boswell.

## 51

Want to change your look but not sure if the style will suit you? Salonstyle.com has a solution. Our website lets you preview several options before heading to the hairstylist. Here's how our virtual hair-imaging program works: you simply upload your photo at salonstyle.com and choose different style, length, and color options to apply to your image. There are thousands of possible combinations, so you're sure to find the right look for you!

Q: What is mainly being advertised?
(a) A website that recommends hairstyles suited to your face
(b) Software that guides users through at-home hair styling
(c) Technology that is used to train new hairstylists
(d) An online program that simulates hairstyles

## 52

Most couples informally discuss plans regarding their future together. Not Richard and Estelle Parson of Ontario, Canada, though. Before marrying, they drew up a 15-page agreement that stipulated every part of their married life, and have happily adhered to it ever since. Under this contract, each spouse has different responsibilities. It even includes the number of times Estelle must cook breakfast per week and how often Richard must give his wife a back massage. Unconventional as this arrangement may be, it works for the Parsons.

Q: What is mainly being reported about the Parsons?
(a) Why they chose to divide housework equitably
(b) Why they try to chronicle their daily married life
(c) How a detailed marriage contract facilitated their marital harmony
(d) How they overcame adversity in their marriage

## 53

The American Legacy Foundation, or ALF, was established in 1998 to reduce tobacco use among the youth. In 2000, ALF launched the nationwide "truth" campaign. It targeted youths aged 12 to 17 and aimed to expose the facts about tobacco without explicitly saying that youngsters should not smoke. It was the first national antismoking campaign that was successful at preventing and stopping teens from smoking.

Q: Which is correct about ALF's "truth" campaign according to the talk?
(a) It targeted smokers of all ages.
(b) It used emotions rather than facts as a persuasive tool.
(c) It avoided directly telling youths not to smoke.
(d) It fell short of preventing youths from smoking.

## 54

When traveling with your pet internationally, you must know the rabies classification for both your origin and destination countries. Countries are classified either as rabies-free countries, as countries with a high incidence of rabies, or as "third countries." Third countries are those with a low incidence of rabies and include the US and Canada. Veterinary certificates are required for all, even when traveling to and from countries with the same classification.

Q: Which is correct according to the talk?
(a) Rabies classifications are only relevant for destination countries.
(b) Countries are categorized into one of three rabies classifications.
(c) Third countries are those with no information about rabies rates.
(d) Traveling between rabies-free countries requires no paperwork.

## 55

Attention, students, for an announcement about Saber University's parking policy. Students parking on campus must purchase a permit at the Student Union Building. Note that permits are now good for one three-month semester at a time. This differs from the old permits, which were valid for the entire academic year. The permits are non-refundable and not transferable, and they must be displayed at all times. As a reminder, students must not park in areas that are exclusively designated for university staff and faculty.

Q: Which is correct according to the announcement?
(a) Parking permits are now valid for one month at a time.
(b) This year's permits have a longer period of validity than last year's.
(c) Ownership of the parking permit cannot be passed to another person.
(d) Students are allowed to park in any campus parking area.

## 56

According to the World Bank's definition of poverty, which is living on less than US$1.25 a day, the world's poorest region in 1981 was East Asia, with nearly 80% of its population living below the poverty line. However, the poverty rate of this region was reduced to under 20% by 2005. Why hasn't the same happened in Africa? Donor countries send $50 billion annually to the continent—a trillion dollars over the past 60 years—and yet the situation remains appalling. The poverty rate has remained pretty much the same for 25 years.

Q: Which is correct according to the speech?
(a) The World Bank defines poverty as living on less than US $1.25 a day.
(b) 80% of East Asians were living above the poverty line in 1981.
(c) Africa has received a total of $50 billion in aid.
(d) Africa's poverty rate has been declining slowly for twenty years.

## 57

When it comes to North American mapping and exploration, Lewis and Clark often spring to mind. Lesser known but prolific in his contributions is David Thompson. Thompson mapped an astonishing one-fifth of North America. Despite this remarkable achievement, Thompson died destitute and in obscurity in 1857. It was not until geologist J.B. Tyrell published Thompson's unfinished book nearly 60 years after Thompson's death that the explorer finally got his due.

Q: Which is correct about David Thompson according to the talk?
(a) His prominence in history overshadows that of Lewis and Clark.
(b) He is credited with mapping the entire North American continent.
(c) His unfinished book was published by J.B. Tyrell in 1857.
(d) He received much deserved recognition posthumously.

## 58

Our next stop is the North Shore, where you'll experience the Shark Adventure. We'll start by taking a boat ride three miles out from Haleiwa Harbor. Once there, you'll have a chance to swim with sharks and see them in their natural habitat, all from the safety of an enclosed underwater cage. You'll encounter gray reef, Galapagos, and sandbar sharks. If you're really lucky, you may even see hammerhead sharks. Those who would prefer to stay out of the water can shark-watch from the comfort of the boat.

Q: What can be inferred from the announcement?
(a) The sharks are caged for the tourists' safety.
(b) Those who opt to shark-watch on the boat will get a partial refund.
(c) All tourists on the boat ride must know how to swim.
(d) Hammerhead sharks are rare sights on the boat tour.

## 59

One issue raised by ocean warming is the dire consequences it has on temperature-sensitive coral reefs. Coral has algae called zooxanthellae living within it, from which the coral draws 80% of its energy. When coral becomes overheated, it releases this zooxanthellae. The algae are also what give coral its color, so without them, the coral becomes white or "bleached." Bleached coral, weakened from the lack of algae, typically dies.

Q: What can be inferred from the talk?
(a) Zooxanthellae kills coral by encroaching on its habitats.
(b) Color is an indicator of health in coral.
(c) Uncontrollable algae growth is suffocating coral.
(d) White coral thrives in cooler ocean environments.

## 60

Early cancer detection is critical to survival, but for certain cancers, the benefits of regular testing are debated within the medical community. For instance, in the case of prostate cancer, the accuracy of early detection tests is mediocre. Patients who receive ambiguous results go on to have more invasive screenings, but only about a quarter of these patients will actually turn out to have cancer. This means that the majority of men who are referred to these screenings unnecessarily expose themselves to the possibility of infections or worse.

Q: What can be inferred from the talk?
(a) Repeating cancer screenings regularly reduces their accuracy.
(b) Doctors unanimously recommend regular screenings for all cancers.
(c) Prostate cancer is easy to diagnose but difficult to treat.
(d) Cancer screenings carry risks of their own.

# 서울대 최신기출 6

## Listing Comprehension Scripts

**1**

W Hi. I'm calling to reserve a table for four tonight.
M ____________________

(a) Our tables only seat up to eight people.
(b) Sorry, we're all booked.
(c) Right this way, please.
(d) Thanks for the invitation.

**2**

M Max and Tracy are splitting up.
W ____________________

(a) Sorry, I didn't mean to.
(b) Yeah? They'll make a great couple.
(c) I guess they're happy together.
(d) They are? I never expected that.

**3**

W Hello. May I speak with the head of the household?
M ____________________

(a) That would be me.
(b) Sure, I'll try again.
(c) I'm calling about your Internet service.
(d) Sorry, this is the Jones residence.

**4**

M What should we do with the dog while we're away?
W ____________________

(a) I'll leave you everything he needs.
(b) I'd rather take a trip instead.
(c) Don't worry. He'll be back soon.
(d) My brother can look after him.

**5**

W I heard you ran into Brian today.
M ____________________

(a) I doubt I'll have time.
(b) He told me that, too.
(c) Well, we needed the exercise.
(d) Yep, at the department store.

**6**

M Is this the gate for flight 221?
W ____________________

(a) Yes, let me look in my bag.
(b) There aren't that many gates.
(c) Actually, it's one gate over.
(d) That sounds like the right time.

**7**

W Can I give you a ride to the bus station?
M ____________________

(a) I'll drop you off outside.
(b) You need to buy a ticket first.
(c) Yes, I got one from my friend.
(d) If it's no trouble, sure.

**8**

M Shouldn't you lock your door at night?
W ____________________

(a) I rarely get home early enough.
(b) That's why I'm staying in.
(c) I usually do. I just forgot.
(d) Don't worry—I'll open it later.

**9**

W That store's salespeople are too aggressive!
M ____________________

(a) Yeah, but don't be afraid to help the customers.
(b) I know. It's really intimidating.
(c) I don't want to chase customers away.
(d) Me, too. They barely noticed us.

**10**

M What brings you to this history conference?
W ____________________

(a) I took the subway this morning.
(b) I'm presenting a paper with a colleague.
(c) I'm sure I'll see you there.
(d) I haven't decided where yet.

**11**

W Have you read Robert Green's latest novel? I loved it!

M ______________________________

(a) I prefer his more recent novel.
(b) Sure, I'll lend it to you.
(c) I haven't gotten around to it.
(d) Then you really should read it.

**12**

M There's a rumor that Sarah's quitting.

W ______________________________

(a) Not unless they renew her contract.
(b) Really? That's news to me.
(c) Yes, she says retirement's been great.
(d) She wouldn't let anyone go like that.

**13**

W You think the wrestling team will maintain its winning streak?

M ______________________________

(a) Only if they lose another match.
(b) They'll recover from it eventually.
(c) They've got to win at some point.
(d) I'd say the chances are good.

**14**

M Weren't you going to fix that broken step?

W ______________________________

(a) I keep meaning to do it.
(b) I agree. We should let it go.
(c) I know. I must've misplaced it.
(d) I didn't want to skip any steps.

**15**

W How about that CEO giving half his wealth to charity!

M ______________________________

(a) Amazing. To think a charity can make so many donations.
(b) I thought he was planning to give it away, though.
(c) I can't believe he's donating everything he has to them.
(d) I know. Hopefully others will follow his lead.

**16**

W Is your wife coming to Jackie's baby shower?

M She can't make it.

W Oh, Jackie will be disappointed.

M ______________________________

(a) Well, she told me it was a great party.
(b) No, she isn't going, either.
(c) I'm sure Jackie will make it up to her.
(d) Yeah, but she has a prior engagement.

**17**

M What are you doing Friday night?

W Nothing. Let's plan something.

M How about ice skating?

W ______________________________

(a) I hope you can.
(b) Maybe on Friday instead.
(c) I'm busy then.
(d) Sounds like a plan.

**18**

W You must be the new tenant in Apartment 401.

M Yes, I just finished unpacking.

W I saw the moving van outside. I'm Milly.

M ______________________________

(a) Great, thanks for offering.
(b) I'm Timothy Duffy—call me Tim.
(c) Actually, the van's coming soon.
(d) You'll like living here. It's great.

**19**

M Let's review the sales figures this afternoon.

W Actually, I've got a conference call at 3.

M Can we meet when it's over?

W ______________________________

(a) I'd rather talk in person, actually.
(b) That's what I was going to suggest.
(c) Good idea. Three o'clock it is, then.
(d) The sale is starting soon.

**20**

W Is the cake ready?

M No, it needs more time in the oven.

W When will it be done?

M ______________________________

(a) Until ten minutes ago.
(b) Probably in five more minutes.
(c) Whenever you feel you're ready.
(d) That's a reasonable length of time.

**21**

M How much farther is it to the concert hall?

W We've still got a ways to go.

M Won't we miss the start of the show?

W ______________________________

(a) No, I'm sure it'll start on time.
(b) Not if heavy traffic slows us down.
(c) I'm hoping to get there just in time.
(d) It's been a long time since I've seen one.

**22**

W How's your economics presentation going?

M Great. I finished preparing it in just two hours!

W You must be good with presentation software.

M ______________________________

(a) Well, I've had a lot of practice.
(b) That's why it took me so long.
(c) Actually I used software, since it's faster.
(d) No, it still needs some preparation.

**23**

M Can I give you a hand with your groceries, ma'am?

W Oh, that would be great.

M Where should I take them to?

W ______________________________

(a) In a plastic bag is fine.
(b) Just let me return them first.
(c) They're at the checkout.
(d) My car is right over there.

**24**

W I feel great today, and you'll never guess why.

M You and your husband booked a vacation to Hawaii?

W How did you know?

M ______________________________

(a) I prefer to plan my vacations ahead.
(b) I thought about it before deciding.
(c) I don't need any excuse to go there again.
(d) I ran into him an hour ago.

**25**

M Welcome to Smooth Rentals. Have you reserved a car?

W Yes, it's under Wendy Lee.

M OK. You wanted a minivan with a child seat?

W ______________________________

(a) Sorry, we forgot to make the reservation.
(b) Oh, we don't offer free child seats.
(c) That's right, I'm travelling with my toddler.
(d) No, we're not going that far, actually.

**26**

W Did you finish the library book you were reading yesterday?

M You mean *Beloved*? I still have a few chapters left.

W Well, it's due tomorrow, in case you forgot.

M ______________________________

(a) Ask them to hold it for you.
(b) Maybe it was already checked out.
(c) OK. I'd better finish it tonight, then.
(d) The library was closed last night, though.

**27**

M Nice jersey! I didn't know you followed sports.

W Yep. I'm a fan of the Springville Tigers.

M Who's your favorite player?

W ______________________________

(a) Probably soccer, I'd say.
(b) It's hard to pick just one team.
(c) They're having a great season.
(d) The one whose name I'm wearing, of course.

## 28

W Interested in going to tonight's campus talent show?
M I'm already going with some friends.
W Oh, I thought just the two of us could go together.
M ___________________

(a) I wish I'd gone, too.
(b) My friends will be happy to.
(c) Let's get dinner tomorrow instead.
(d) I can't go to both shows at once.

## 29

M They announced Sophia's promotion yesterday.
W Sophia? But she's only been here a year.
M I know. Doesn't that seem unfair to you?
W ___________________

(a) It should've gone to someone with more seniority.
(b) Yes, but her long tenure here qualifies her.
(c) Put that way, it seems reasonable.
(d) No, I'm sure you deserved it.

## 30

W What was that movie you recommended, again?
M The one with Jeremy Kelly in it?
W I mean the documentary about organic farming.
M ___________________

(a) I don't think he's in that one, either.
(b) I forget what it was called. I'll check.
(c) Yes, that's the one you recommended.
(d) No, that wasn't any better.

## 31

M You're working at your family's restaurant?
W Just for the summer.
M Could I possibly work there as well?
W I'll ask, but I think all the positions are filled.
M Well, let me know. I'll take anything I can get.
W OK, I'll get back to you after I talk to my dad.

Q: What is the man mainly trying to do?
(a) Complain about his summer job
(b) Get a job through the woman
(c) Find out about the woman's family
(d) Learn about the restaurant business

## 32

W Is that jacket leather?
M Nah, it's fake. I don't wear leather.
W Oh, since it's expensive?
M No, I avoid it for moral reasons.
W Really? But it's so fashionable.
M Well, I think it supports animal cruelty.

Q: What is the conversation mainly about?
(a) Why leather jackets are fashionable
(b) The high price of leather jackets
(c) Why real leather is better than fake leather
(d) The man's choice not to wear real leather

## 33

M Have you checked out the new sports complex?
W Yes. There's a pool, a basketball court, and an indoor track.
M What about the gym?
W It's great. It has lots of machines.
M Wow. Sounds like it's worth joining.
W Yeah, they have a sauna, too. It's really nice.

Q: What is the main topic of the conversation?
(a) How the woman has joined a new gym
(b) The amenities of a new athletics facility
(c) The anticipated launch of a recreational facility
(d) Why the local sports complex needs to be remodeled

## 34

M Estelle seems unhappy at college.
W That's common for freshmen.
M She says the workload is overwhelming.
W Does she have some friends to support her?
M She hasn't met many people yet. She's not adapting well.
W She will. It just takes time.

Q: What is the conversation mainly about?
(a) How Estelle is struggling to adjust to college life
(b) How Estelle's social life is hindering her studies
(c) Estelle's desire for a more challenging workload
(d) Estelle's anxiety about leaving for college

## 35

W You know that stack of papers that was on the desk?

M Yeah, I cleared it off.

W What did you do with it?

M Some of it I recycled. I kept anything that looked important.

W Did you see that bill I was saving from Dr. Grimsby's office?

M Yeah, I pinned it on the cork board near the door.

Q: What is the woman mainly trying to do?

(a) Get the man to help her clean off the desk

(b) Locate a document she had been saving

(c) Find out which papers the man wants to keep

(d) Determine whether a doctor's bill has arrived

## 36

M What should we do when our lease expires next month?

W I don't know. We could sign on for another year.

M You think? Our rent is so expensive here.

W But don't you like this area?

M I guess. I'm ready for a change of scenery, though.

W Well, let's just think it over.

Q: What are the man and woman mainly discussing?

(a) Whether they can afford to buy a house

(b) Whether they should renew their lease

(c) How to negotiate for lower rent

(d) What area to move to next

## 37

W I'm appalled by these staff restructuring decisions.

M I know. Our workload has really increased.

W Not only that, but people are being shifted to other departments.

M I've already started getting some different tasks.

W I have to help with accounting, despite having no experience.

M This shake-up doesn't seem well planned.

Q: What is the conversation mainly about?

(a) Rumors of staff changes to be implemented

(b) Increased work for the employees in accounting

(c) Workplace upheaval due to abrupt staffing changes

(d) Confusion caused by the renaming of departments

## 38

M I wish I hadn't taken the bus to work today.

W Why? Was traffic held up on the freeway?

M Yeah, the icy roads really slowed everyone down.

W That's why I took the subway today.

M You must've gotten here on time, then.

W Yep, only a couple of people were here earlier than me.

Q: Which is correct according to the conversation?

(a) The man drove to work this morning.

(b) Traffic was held up because of an accident on the freeway.

(c) The woman got to work by subway.

(d) The office was empty when the woman arrived.

## 39

M Honey, take a look at these purses online.

W You know I don't like anything too flashy.

M Actually, it's for my sister's birthday this weekend.

W Oh, they'd be perfect for her. She loves bright colors.

M Do you think she'd prefer a larger tote or smaller purse?

W The small ones are cuter.

Q: Which is correct about the man according to the conversation?

(a) He is shopping online for the woman.

(b) His sister has a birthday next week.

(c) His sister does not like bright colors.

(d) He asks the woman what size bag to buy.

## 40

W You sang really well at the party on Friday.

M Thanks. I had no idea I'd be singing that night.

W Even the boss said you sounded professional.

M Well, I sang in an amateur rock group years ago.

W Really? So why did you stop?

M The band broke up after we graduated from college.

Q: Which is correct about the man according to the conversation?

(a) He had prepared a song for the party.
(b) His boss praised his vocal performance.
(c) He used to be a professional rock singer.
(d) His band broke up when they started college.

## 41

W You've really lost weight!

M Thanks, I'm halfway to my goal of shedding 30 pounds.

W What's your strategy?

M I've been substituting veggies for grains and starchy stuff.

W Don't you feel weaker?

M Just the opposite. I've been doing it for three weeks and I feel more energetic.

Q: Which is correct about the man according to the conversation?

(a) His diet has helped him lose 30 pounds.
(b) He has been eating more grains in place of vegetables.
(c) He has spent over three months on his diet.
(d) His energy levels are up since changing his diet.

## 42

M Can you pick Jill up from school today?

W You can't get her on your way home?

M I've got that client dinner I mentioned.

W I have to work until 4:30.

M She's got soccer practice after school until 5 anyway.

W OK, then I'll swing by right after work and get her.

Q: Which is correct according to the conversation?

(a) The man asks the woman to give Jill a ride to school.
(b) The man forgot to tell the woman about a work dinner.
(c) The woman is scheduled to work until 4:30 pm.
(d) The woman agrees to leave work early to pick up Jill.

## 43

W Want to go watch a play tonight?

M It depends. What's on?

W Well, *Transformations* got good reviews when it premiered.

M Oh, is that still running? Will they have seats for tonight's show?

W I checked, and they do.

M Great! I'll make the reservations.

Q: What can be inferred from the conversation?

(a) *Transformations* has been running for some time already.
(b) The man is open to seeing any play the woman chooses.
(c) *Transformations* has received mostly negative reviews recently.
(d) The man is unfamiliar with the play the woman suggests.

## 44

M You're already back to work? How's your back?

W It's still stiff, but the doctor gave me the all-clear.

M You should file a complaint about the company's negligence and seek reimbursement.

W I like working here, so I don't want to cause any trouble.

M Well, the management should require warning signs when floors are wet.

W That's true. I'll think it over.

Q: What can be inferred from the conversation?

(a) The woman's request for medical leave was denied.
(b) The woman's injury resulted from a slip at work.
(c) The company has covered the woman's medical costs.
(d) The man blames the woman's negligence for her injury.

## 45

W How were the football tryouts?

M The pickings were slim. It ended a lot earlier than I expected.

W Not much athletic talent among the students?

M I wouldn't know. They're not trying out.

W Maybe they're discouraged by last year's state championship.

M That was a fluke! They should be begging to join a team with a record as good as ours.

Q: What can be inferred from the conversation?

(a) The man is trying to recruit coaches for the football team.

(b) The team made a good showing at last year's state championship.

(c) The woman assisted the man with the football tryouts.

(d) Fewer people tried out for the team than the man expected.

## 46

Teachers and professors are increasingly seeing the problematic effect of the Internet on students' writing. Specifically, the abbreviations that make online communication efficient are appearing in students' essays and exams. For many students, the majority of writing done outside the classroom is through blogging and social networking services, so it is understandable that shortening has permeated their style. However, it is not appropriate in an academic context.

Q: What is the speaker's main point?

(a) Online communication has negatively affected academic writing.

(b) Students communicate less effectively through online media.

(c) Professors are assessing students' writing using the Internet.

(d) Standard language is becoming too outdated for academic writing.

## 47

The Zenith Instant Noodle Company has announced a labeling error on their new extra spicy flavor noodle snack. The product was made in a factory that processes peanuts, a fact which was not included on the new packaging. As this could have health risks for peanut allergy sufferers, they are advised to discard the product and send proof of purchase to the company for a refund. Stores have been asked to remove the product from their shelves.

Q: What is the announcement mainly about?

(a) A new instant noodle offering from Zenith

(b) Stores that are offering Zenith products

(c) A potentially dangerous mislabeled product

(d) The health risks of eating processed foods

## 48

Nutritionists have long encouraged people to eat broccoli, and they can now point to new evidence that proves why the vegetable is so important. A paper published in a leading medical journal shows that chemical compounds in broccoli block proteins produced by mutated genes. These proteins have been implicated in about 50% of all human cancers. These findings support the idea that broccoli may prevent serious illness.

Q: What is the main topic of the talk?

(a) The nutritional benefits of protein-rich foods

(b) An experiment using broccoli to cure cancer

(c) The failure of conventional wisdom in dietary health

(d) Scientific confirmation of broccoli's health benefits

**49**

The State High School Athletic Association regrets to announce the passing of one of our greatest founding members. Bob Petrillo acted as the director of our organization from its inception in 1962 until 1975. He served as a consultant to the state department of education until 1995 and worked to extend athletic scholarship opportunities to disadvantaged students. We invite everyone to join us in commemorating his outstanding achievements, as we carry his legacy of athletic excellence forward.

Q: What is the announcement mainly about?
(a) The history of the state's athletic association
(b) The death of a prominent figure in state athletics
(c) The expansion of athletic scholarship opportunities
(d) The commemoration of one of the state's most talented athletes

**50**

Is sugar addictive? On one hand, research shows that sugar shares many neurological and behavioral effects with addictive chemicals like nicotine: consuming it leads to the activation of pleasure centers in the brain, and people can experience intense cravings for it. On the other hand, sugar in its simplest form—glucose—is the basis of human metabolism and is necessary for survival. The inability to agree about whether a fundamental nutrient can be considered addictive has made it impossible for medical professionals to reach a consensus on sugar.

Q: What is the main purpose of the talk?
(a) To describe how foods containing sugar affect the brain
(b) To outline the chemical similarities between sugar and nicotine
(c) To present the debate over whether sugar is addictive
(d) To explain recent research about sugar's addictive properties

**51**

As the United States seeks new clean energy sources, offshore wind farms have been proposed for the Gulf of Mexico. This solution is attractive but ultimately impractical in light of the area's hurricanes. One study predicted that half the turbines in a Gulf wind farm could be destroyed by the area's frequent hurricanes over a 20-year period. Some have suggested that the probability of damage could be reduced with modifications that allow the turbines to rotate in high winds. But these modifications could take years to engineer and may be expensive, rendering them unfeasible.

Q: What is the speaker's main point about offshore wind farms?
(a) They can provide the US with cleaner energy.
(b) They can be modified to resist hurricane damage.
(c) They are not a viable solution for America's energy needs.
(d) They should be implemented more quickly in the Gulf of Mexico.

**52**

The First Punic War, fought between Rome and Carthage, ended in 241 BC in a Carthaginian defeat. Following the war, Rome demanded large sums of gold as reparations. This was a problem for Carthage: its defense relied on an army of 20,000 mercenaries, and after paying reparations to Rome, it could not afford to pay its hired military. Thus, the mercenaries turned on their former employer, and started another war that lasted from 240-238 BC.

Q: What is the main topic of the talk?
(a) The war that resulted from Rome's inability to pay reparations
(b) How the terms of the First Punic War's settlement led to further conflict
(c) The treaty ending the Second Punic War between Rome and Carthage
(d) How Carthaginian mercenaries waged another war on Rome

## 53

Mexico City, originally called Tenochtitlan, was founded by the Aztecs in 1325. Built on a small island, Tenochtitlan is considered remarkable for its time: the city had running water, drainage systems, and paved roads. When the Spanish colonizer Cortés arrived in 1519 and conquered the city, he found Tenochtitlan difficult to pronounce, so the Spaniards adopted the city's secondary name, Mixico. Over time, this became Mexico City.

Q: Which is correct about Tenochtitlan according to the lecture?
(a) It was founded by Spanish explorers in the year 1325.
(b) It is noted for its advanced infrastructure.
(c) It was conquered by an alliance of Aztecs and Spaniards.
(d) It was renamed so the Aztecs could pronounce it more easily.

## 54

Since today is the first day of class, let's review the syllabus. This class meets twice a week, on Monday and Wednesday, from 9 to 10:20 A.M. We will often start class with a quiz, and there are no make-ups, so I expect everyone to arrive on time. There will be a total of ten quizzes this semester, but the two lowest scores will be dropped from your final grade.

Q: Which is correct according to the talk?
(a) The class meets on Monday, Wednesday, and Friday.
(b) Late students cannot take a missed quiz later.
(c) Quizzes are scheduled for the final ten minutes of class.
(d) Final grades incorporate only the students' top two quiz scores.

## 55

A program called Parent View, offered by the UK government, now allows parents to rate their children's schools in online surveys. Through the surveys, parents can give anonymous feedback about their satisfaction with their child's educational and social experiences in school. The public will also be able to view the results online. Teachers have voiced their discontent over the surveys, claiming that such feedback should be more private and direct, but parents' groups strongly support the plan.

Q: Which is correct according to the news report?
(a) The new survey includes parents' names with the feedback.
(b) The survey results will not be available for the general public.
(c) Teachers have expressed enthusiasm about the survey.
(d) Parents' groups are backing the government's new survey program.

## 56

For children who stutter, therapists recommend seeking treatment from an early age. They also remind parents that stuttering is unrelated to general intelligence or social skills. Therapy for stuttering focuses on stopping the most common problems, which include prolonging vowels and repeating consonant sounds. To overcome this, therapists counsel children to maintain eye contact with listeners and to speak slowly with a melodic voice. As no drug therapy has ever proven effective in stopping stuttering, such behavioral strategies are the best treatment currently available.

Q: Which is correct according to the talk?
(a) Doctors warn against treating stuttering at an early age.
(b) Stuttering is not linked to general intelligence.
(c) Doctors stress that eye contact can worsen stuttering.
(d) There are currently several effective pharmaceutical remedies for stuttering.

## 57

Throughout its long history, the American telecommunications corporation AT&T has had a changing relationship with anti-trust regulation. In 1907, company president Theodore Vail successfully argued that AT&T's functions were of sufficient national importance that it should be allowed to operate as a monopoly, albeit with government regulation. In 1913, facing legal challenges over its size, the company divested its telegraph business in exchange for sole control over local calling networks nationwide. Challenges to the company's monopoly again surfaced in the 1950s, but the biggest blow came in 1974, when the Department of Justice ordered AT&T to break up.

Q: Which is correct according to the talk?
(a) Vail suggested that AT&T be exempt from government regulation.
(b) AT&T enlarged its telegraph services in 1913.
(c) AT&T once had a national monopoly on local calling networks.
(d) The Department of Justice ordered AT&T to break up in 1950.

## 58

The best example of Robert Browning's dramatic monologue is "My Last Duchess." In the poem, the Duke of Ferrara acts as narrator and explains the fate of his late wife, whose demise was brought about by his possessiveness and unwarranted jealousy. Browning skillfully handles the duke as a narrator. The duke speaks casually as if what he did was the most natural thing to do, and unsuspecting readers follow him as he tells his story. But they are horrified when they realize that he had his innocent wife killed.

Q: What can be inferred from the lecture?
(a) Browning suggests that the duchess deserved her fate.
(b) Browning views the duke's plight with sympathy.
(c) The duke's narrative voice is not remorseful.
(d) The duke is portrayed as being aware that others will be appalled at him.

## 59

The *Kumbh Mela* is a Hindu festival that is held on a rotating basis at one of four places in India, each location hosting it every 12 years. It attracts tens of millions of people, who participate in ritual river bathing to purify themselves. But during various celebrations over the years, the event has precipitated tragedy: large crowds have led to stampedes, sometimes resulting in dozens of participant casualties. Fortunately, in 2010, the Indian Space Research Organization began taking satellite photos of pilgrims, with the aim of improving the organization and safety of the event in the future.

Q: What can be inferred from the talk?
(a) The Indian government is planning to cancel the *Kumbh Mela*.
(b) Only the clergy are allowed to participate in the *Kumbh Mela*.
(c) The *Kumbh Mela's* casualties have not resulted from deliberate violence.
(d) Pilgrims from many different faiths participate in the *Kumbh Mela*.

## 60

Over 100 pilots have called in sick this month, forcing World Airways to cancel 20 more flights amid a salary dispute with employees. Two or three pilots scheduled on a single flight have been reporting sick on the same day after the airline announced a 7% pay cut over two years. In response to the threat of further sick leave requests, World Airways is preparing contingency plans for additional flight disruptions but has no intention of backing down.

Q: What can be inferred from the news report?
(a) The pilots called in sick as a form of protest.
(b) The flights were cancelled to prevent passengers from getting sick.
(c) The dispute centers on pilots' demands for paid sick leave.
(d) The pay cuts are a repercussion of the abuse of sick leave.

# Answer Keys

## 서울대 최신기출 · 1

### Listening Comprehension

| | | | | | | | | | |
|---|---|---|---|---|---|---|---|---|---|
| **1** (b) | **2** (a) | **3** (d) | **4** (a) | **5** (b) | **6** (b) | **7** (b) | **8** (c) | **9** (b) | **10** (c) |
| **11** (a) | **12** (b) | **13** (c) | **14** (d) | **15** (b) | **16** (a) | **17** (a) | **18** (c) | **19** (c) | **20** (b) |
| **21** (a) | **22** (b) | **23** (b) | **24** (b) | **25** (c) | **26** (c) | **27** (c) | **28** (b) | **29** (c) | **30** (a) |
| **31** (d) | **32** (b) | **33** (a) | **34** (c) | **35** (b) | **36** (b) | **37** (d) | **38** (c) | **39** (c) | **40** (c) |
| **41** (b) | **42** (c) | **43** (c) | **44** (b) | **45** (c) | **46** (b) | **47** (b) | **48** (c) | **49** (b) | **50** (d) |
| **51** (c) | **52** (b) | **53** (b) | **54** (d) | **55** (d) | **56** (b) | **57** (a) | **58** (a) | **59** (a) | **60** (a) |

### Grammar

| | | | | | | | | | |
|---|---|---|---|---|---|---|---|---|---|
| **1** (d) | **2** (c) | **3** (b) | **4** (a) | **5** (a) | **6** (d) | **7** (b) | **8** (b) | **9** (d) | **10** (b) |
| **11** (a) | **12** (c) | **13** (b) | **14** (a) | **15** (b) | **16** (a) | **17** (d) | **18** (b) | **19** (a) | **20** (d) |
| **21** (b) | **22** (a) | **23** (a) | **24** (c) | **25** (b) | **26** (d) | **27** (c) | **28** (a) | **29** (d) | **30** (b) |
| **31** (b) | **32** (d) | **33** (c) | **34** (b) | **35** (c) | **36** (a) | **37** (b) | **38** (c) | **39** (c) | **40** (b) |
| **41** (a) | **42** (b) | **43** (c) | **44** (d) | **45** (b) | **46** (a) | **47** (c) | **48** (c) | **49** (c) | **50** (d) |

### Vocabulary

| | | | | | | | | | |
|---|---|---|---|---|---|---|---|---|---|
| **1** (c) | **2** (b) | **3** (d) | **4** (b) | **5** (d) | **6** (a) | **7** (a) | **8** (d) | **9** (d) | **10** (b) |
| **11** (a) | **12** (a) | **13** (c) | **14** (a) | **15** (b) | **16** (b) | **17** (d) | **18** (a) | **19** (d) | **20** (a) |
| **21** (b) | **22** (b) | **23** (a) | **24** (a) | **25** (d) | **26** (b) | **27** (a) | **28** (b) | **29** (b) | **30** (c) |
| **31** (c) | **32** (a) | **33** (c) | **34** (d) | **35** (a) | **36** (c) | **37** (c) | **38** (a) | **39** (c) | **40** (b) |
| **41** (a) | **42** (b) | **43** (b) | **44** (c) | **45** (a) | **46** (a) | **47** (a) | **48** (d) | **49** (d) | **50** (a) |

### Reading Comprehension

| | | | | | | | | | |
|---|---|---|---|---|---|---|---|---|---|
| **1** (c) | **2** (c) | **3** (a) | **4** (d) | **5** (d) | **6** (c) | **7** (a) | **8** (b) | **9** (d) | **10** (a) |
| **11** (d) | **12** (b) | **13** (d) | **14** (d) | **15** (b) | **16** (d) | **17** (c) | **18** (a) | **19** (c) | **20** (c) |
| **21** (b) | **22** (c) | **23** (c) | **24** (b) | **25** (c) | **26** (d) | **27** (d) | **28** (c) | **29** (b) | **30** (c) |
| **31** (d) | **32** (d) | **33** (d) | **34** (d) | **35** (c) | **36** (b) | **37** (b) | **38** (c) | **39** (a) | **40** (b) |

# 서울대 최신기출 · 2

## ***Listening*** *Comprehension*

| | | | | | | | | | |
|---|---|---|---|---|---|---|---|---|---|
| **1** (b) | **2** (d) | **3** (c) | **4** (c) | **5** (b) | **6** (b) | **7** (c) | **8** (a) | **9** (a) | **10** (a) |
| **11** (b) | **12** (b) | **13** (d) | **14** (c) | **15** (c) | **16** (c) | **17** (a) | **18** (c) | **19** (a) | **20** (c) |
| **21** (b) | **22** (a) | **23** (d) | **24** (b) | **25** (d) | **26** (b) | **27** (b) | **28** (a) | **29** (b) | **30** (c) |
| **31** (c) | **32** (c) | **33** (c) | **34** (d) | **35** (b) | **36** (b) | **37** (a) | **38** (c) | **39** (b) | **40** (c) |
| **41** (c) | **42** (a) | **43** (c) | **44** (a) | **45** (b) | **46** (a) | **47** (d) | **48** (a) | **49** (b) | **50** (c) |
| **51** (b) | **52** (b) | **53** (d) | **54** (a) | **55** (a) | **56** (d) | **57** (b) | **58** (a) | **59** (a) | **60** (c) |

## ***Grammar***

| | | | | | | | | | |
|---|---|---|---|---|---|---|---|---|---|
| **1** (d) | **2** (b) | **3** (b) | **4** (d) | **5** (a) | **6** (b) | **7** (b) | **8** (c) | **9** (c) | **10** (b) |
| **11** (d) | **12** (c) | **13** (b) | **14** (d) | **15** (d) | **16** (d) | **17** (c) | **18** (a) | **19** (a) | **20** (d) |
| **21** (b) | **22** (c) | **23** (b) | **24** (c) | **25** (a) | **26** (a) | **27** (d) | **28** (d) | **29** (b) | **30** (c) |
| **31** (a) | **32** (c) | **33** (c) | **34** (b) | **35** (b) | **36** (b) | **37** (a) | **38** (a) | **39** (c) | **40** (b) |
| **41** (d) | **42** (d) | **43** (c) | **44** (d) | **45** (b) | **46** (c) | **47** (d) | **48** (a) | **49** (d) | **50** (d) |

## ***Vocabulary***

| | | | | | | | | | |
|---|---|---|---|---|---|---|---|---|---|
| **1** (b) | **2** (c) | **3** (d) | **4** (a) | **5** (a) | **6** (d) | **7** (b) | **8** (b) | **9** (a) | **10** (c) |
| **11** (c) | **12** (c) | **13** (a) | **14** (b) | **15** (c) | **16** (d) | **17** (c) | **18** (a) | **19** (d) | **20** (c) |
| **21** (c) | **22** (a) | **23** (b) | **24** (c) | **25** (b) | **26** (a) | **27** (c) | **28** (c) | **29** (d) | **30** (b) |
| **31** (a) | **32** (c) | **33** (b) | **34** (b) | **35** (b) | **36** (b) | **37** (c) | **38** (c) | **39** (b) | **40** (c) |
| **41** (b) | **42** (d) | **43** (b) | **44** (c) | **45** (b) | **46** (d) | **47** (c) | **48** (b) | **49** (c) | **50** (c) |

## ***Reading*** *Comprehension*

| | | | | | | | | | |
|---|---|---|---|---|---|---|---|---|---|
| **1** (d) | **2** (a) | **3** (a) | **4** (c) | **5** (c) | **6** (c) | **7** (a) | **8** (b) | **9** (d) | **10** (b) |
| **11** (d) | **12** (b) | **13** (c) | **14** (b) | **15** (a) | **16** (a) | **17** (a) | **18** (c) | **19** (b) | **20** (c) |
| **21** (d) | **22** (b) | **23** (b) | **24** (d) | **25** (c) | **26** (a) | **27** (d) | **28** (d) | **29** (b) | **30** (b) |
| **31** (d) | **32** (d) | **33** (a) | **34** (a) | **35** (d) | **36** (a) | **37** (b) | **38** (c) | **39** (b) | **40** (c) |

# Answer Keys

## 서울대 최신기출 · 3

### Listening Comprehension

| | | | | | | | | | |
|---|---|---|---|---|---|---|---|---|---|
| **1** (b) | **2** (d) | **3** (b) | **4** (a) | **5** (c) | **6** (b) | **7** (b) | **8** (c) | **9** (a) | **10** (b) |
| **11** (c) | **12** (b) | **13** (d) | **14** (d) | **15** (a) | **16** (b) | **17** (a) | **18** (c) | **19** (b) | **20** (a) |
| **21** (c) | **22** (a) | **23** (b) | **24** (b) | **25** (b) | **26** (c) | **27** (b) | **28** (b) | **29** (b) | **30** (a) |
| **31** (a) | **32** (d) | **33** (b) | **34** (d) | **35** (c) | **36** (d) | **37** (b) | **38** (d) | **39** (c) | **40** (c) |
| **41** (c) | **42** (d) | **43** (c) | **44** (b) | **45** (d) | **46** (d) | **47** (c) | **48** (a) | **49** (c) | **50** (c) |
| **51** (b) | **52** (c) | **53** (b) | **54** (a) | **55** (b) | **56** (c) | **57** (c) | **58** (c) | **59** (c) | **60** (c) |

### Grammar

| | | | | | | | | | |
|---|---|---|---|---|---|---|---|---|---|
| **1** (d) | **2** (b) | **3** (d) | **4** (a) | **5** (a) | **6** (a) | **7** (a) | **8** (c) | **9** (c) | **10** (c) |
| **11** (b) | **12** (a) | **13** (c) | **14** (a) | **15** (a) | **16** (d) | **17** (b) | **18** (d) | **19** (b) | **20** (b) |
| **21** (d) | **22** (b) | **23** (a) | **24** (a) | **25** (a) | **26** (c) | **27** (d) | **28** (c) | **29** (b) | **30** (d) |
| **31** (a) | **32** (a) | **33** (c) | **34** (b) | **35** (d) | **36** (b) | **37** (d) | **38** (a) | **39** (d) | **40** (a) |
| **41** (d) | **42** (b) | **43** (c) | **44** (b) | **45** (d) | **46** (d) | **47** (c) | **48** (d) | **49** (b) | **50** (a) |

### Vocabulary

| | | | | | | | | | |
|---|---|---|---|---|---|---|---|---|---|
| **1** (a) | **2** (c) | **3** (b) | **4** (b) | **5** (c) | **6** (a) | **7** (a) | **8** (c) | **9** (c) | **10** (b) |
| **11** (d) | **12** (c) | **13** (c) | **14** (a) | **15** (a) | **16** (d) | **17** (d) | **18** (b) | **19** (c) | **20** (b) |
| **21** (a) | **22** (b) | **23** (b) | **24** (d) | **25** (a) | **26** (d) | **27** (a) | **28** (b) | **29** (c) | **30** (b) |
| **31** (a) | **32** (c) | **33** (d) | **34** (a) | **35** (c) | **36** (b) | **37** (a) | **38** (c) | **39** (b) | **40** (b) |
| **41** (c) | **42** (b) | **43** (d) | **44** (b) | **45** (b) | **46** (d) | **47** (c) | **48** (c) | **49** (a) | **50** (d) |

### Reading Comprehension

| | | | | | | | | | |
|---|---|---|---|---|---|---|---|---|---|
| **1** (b) | **2** (d) | **3** (c) | **4** (c) | **5** (c) | **6** (b) | **7** (d) | **8** (a) | **9** (d) | **10** (b) |
| **11** (d) | **12** (d) | **13** (c) | **14** (c) | **15** (c) | **16** (a) | **17** (d) | **18** (a) | **19** (b) | **20** (c) |
| **21** (c) | **22** (c) | **23** (d) | **24** (b) | **25** (c) | **26** (b) | **27** (c) | **28** (b) | **29** (b) | **30** (d) |
| **31** (b) | **32** (b) | **33** (d) | **34** (b) | **35** (c) | **36** (d) | **37** (a) | **38** (c) | **39** (c) | **40** (c) |

## 서울대 최신기출 · 4

### *Listening Comprehension*

| | | | | | | | | | |
|---|---|---|---|---|---|---|---|---|---|
| **1** (d) | **2** (c) | **3** (c) | **4** (a) | **5** (a) | **6** (a) | **7** (c) | **8** (b) | **9** (a) | **10** (b) |
| **11** (a) | **12** (a) | **13** (c) | **14** (b) | **15** (a) | **16** (c) | **17** (a) | **18** (b) | **19** (c) | **20** (a) |
| **21** (c) | **22** (b) | **23** (a) | **24** (c) | **25** (b) | **26** (a) | **27** (a) | **28** (b) | **29** (a) | **30** (c) |
| **31** (a) | **32** (a) | **33** (c) | **34** (d) | **35** (b) | **36** (c) | **37** (c) | **38** (d) | **39** (b) | **40** (d) |
| **41** (a) | **42** (c) | **43** (b) | **44** (d) | **45** (c) | **46** (d) | **47** (b) | **48** (d) | **49** (b) | **50** (d) |
| **51** (b) | **52** (a) | **53** (d) | **54** (c) | **55** (c) | **56** (c) | **57** (c) | **58** (b) | **59** (a) | **60** (c) |

### *Grammar*

| | | | | | | | | | |
|---|---|---|---|---|---|---|---|---|---|
| **1** (d) | **2** (b) | **3** (d) | **4** (d) | **5** (c) | **6** (a) | **7** (a) | **8** (b) | **9** (c) | **10** (b) |
| **11** (c) | **12** (b) | **13** (b) | **14** (a) | **15** (a) | **16** (d) | **17** (b) | **18** (c) | **19** (b) | **20** (a) |
| **21** (c) | **22** (b) | **23** (d) | **24** (d) | **25** (b) | **26** (a) | **27** (d) | **28** (b) | **29** (a) | **30** (d) |
| **31** (d) | **32** (b) | **33** (b) | **34** (d) | **35** (a) | **36** (d) | **37** (b) | **38** (b) | **39** (d) | **40** (c) |
| **41** (c) | **42** (d) | **43** (c) | **44** (b) | **45** (d) | **46** (b) | **47** (d) | **48** (c) | **49** (c) | **50** (c) |

### *Vocabulary*

| | | | | | | | | | |
|---|---|---|---|---|---|---|---|---|---|
| **1** (c) | **2** (c) | **3** (d) | **4** (b) | **5** (c) | **6** (b) | **7** (b) | **8** (a) | **9** (a) | **10** (b) |
| **11** (d) | **12** (d) | **13** (c) | **14** (c) | **15** (c) | **16** (b) | **17** (b) | **18** (b) | **19** (c) | **20** (b) |
| **21** (c) | **22** (d) | **23** (c) | **24** (a) | **25** (c) | **26** (b) | **27** (a) | **28** (c) | **29** (a) | **30** (a) |
| **31** (a) | **32** (b) | **33** (a) | **34** (c) | **35** (b) | **36** (c) | **37** (b) | **38** (a) | **39** (c) | **40** (a) |
| **41** (b) | **42** (b) | **43** (a) | **44** (a) | **45** (c) | **46** (c) | **47** (a) | **48** (b) | **49** (d) | **50** (d) |

### *Reading Comprehension*

| | | | | | | | | | |
|---|---|---|---|---|---|---|---|---|---|
| **1** (d) | **2** (a) | **3** (d) | **4** (a) | **5** (a) | **6** (d) | **7** (d) | **8** (c) | **9** (a) | **10** (c) |
| **11** (a) | **12** (c) | **13** (a) | **14** (d) | **15** (a) | **16** (c) | **17** (b) | **18** (b) | **19** (d) | **20** (a) |
| **21** (c) | **22** (b) | **23** (d) | **24** (a) | **25** (c) | **26** (b) | **27** (d) | **28** (a) | **29** (b) | **30** (b) |
| **31** (a) | **32** (c) | **33** (c) | **34** (a) | **35** (d) | **36** (d) | **37** (b) | **38** (a) | **39** (d) | **40** (b) |

# Answer Keys

## 서울대 최신기출 · 5

### Listening Comprehension

| | | | | | | | | | |
|---|---|---|---|---|---|---|---|---|---|
| **1** (b) | **2** (b) | **3** (c) | **4** (c) | **5** (a) | **6** (a) | **7** (b) | **8** (c) | **9** (d) | **10** (b) |
| **11** (a) | **12** (d) | **13** (b) | **14** (c) | **15** (b) | **16** (d) | **17** (b) | **18** (c) | **19** (a) | **20** (a) |
| **21** (b) | **22** (c) | **23** (c) | **24** (d) | **25** (a) | **26** (b) | **27** (d) | **28** (b) | **29** (a) | **30** (a) |
| **31** (a) | **32** (b) | **33** (d) | **34** (a) | **35** (c) | **36** (c) | **37** (b) | **38** (c) | **39** (d) | **40** (c) |
| **41** (a) | **42** (a) | **43** (b) | **44** (c) | **45** (d) | **46** (c) | **47** (a) | **48** (a) | **49** (b) | **50** (c) |
| **51** (d) | **52** (c) | **53** (c) | **54** (b) | **55** (c) | **56** (a) | **57** (d) | **58** (d) | **59** (b) | **60** (d) |

### Grammar

| | | | | | | | | | |
|---|---|---|---|---|---|---|---|---|---|
| **1** (b) | **2** (b) | **3** (d) | **4** (a) | **5** (b) | **6** (d) | **7** (c) | **8** (d) | **9** (a) | **10** (b) |
| **11** (c) | **12** (c) | **13** (d) | **14** (a) | **15** (a) | **16** (a) | **17** (b) | **18** (d) | **19** (b) | **20** (b) |
| **21** (c) | **22** (d) | **23** (c) | **24** (d) | **25** (c) | **26** (c) | **27** (a) | **28** (d) | **29** (c) | **30** (b) |
| **31** (d) | **32** (c) | **33** (b) | **34** (b) | **35** (a) | **36** (d) | **37** (d) | **38** (a) | **39** (a) | **40** (d) |
| **41** (b) | **42** (d) | **43** (d) | **44** (c) | **45** (c) | **46** (d) | **47** (c) | **48** (b) | **49** (d) | **50** (c) |

### Vocabulary

| | | | | | | | | | |
|---|---|---|---|---|---|---|---|---|---|
| **1** (d) | **2** (d) | **3** (b) | **4** (c) | **5** (c) | **6** (c) | **7** (a) | **8** (c) | **9** (a) | **10** (d) |
| **11** (d) | **12** (b) | **13** (b) | **14** (a) | **15** (c) | **16** (a) | **17** (d) | **18** (c) | **19** (b) | **20** (b) |
| **21** (d) | **22** (d) | **23** (a) | **24** (b) | **25** (c) | **26** (a) | **27** (c) | **28** (d) | **29** (b) | **30** (b) |
| **31** (d) | **32** (c) | **33** (b) | **34** (c) | **35** (c) | **36** (a) | **37** (a) | **38** (c) | **39** (a) | **40** (b) |
| **41** (c) | **42** (b) | **43** (c) | **44** (c) | **45** (a) | **46** (b) | **47** (b) | **48** (d) | **49** (b) | **50** (a) |

### Reading Comprehension

| | | | | | | | | | |
|---|---|---|---|---|---|---|---|---|---|
| **1** (b) | **2** (d) | **3** (d) | **4** (b) | **5** (d) | **6** (a) | **7** (a) | **8** (b) | **9** (d) | **10** (a) |
| **11** (d) | **12** (b) | **13** (d) | **14** (c) | **15** (d) | **16** (c) | **17** (b) | **18** (b) | **19** (b) | **20** (d) |
| **21** (b) | **22** (d) | **23** (d) | **24** (d) | **25** (c) | **26** (c) | **27** (a) | **28** (b) | **29** (c) | **30** (a) |
| **31** (d) | **32** (c) | **33** (a) | **34** (c) | **35** (a) | **36** (a) | **37** (a) | **38** (c) | **39** (b) | **40** (a) |

## ***Listening*** *Comprehension*

| | | | | | | | | | |
|---|---|---|---|---|---|---|---|---|---|
| **1** (b) | **2** (d) | **3** (a) | **4** (d) | **5** (d) | **6** (c) | **7** (d) | **8** (c) | **9** (b) | **10** (b) |
| **11** (c) | **12** (b) | **13** (d) | **14** (a) | **15** (d) | **16** (d) | **17** (d) | **18** (b) | **19** (b) | **20** (b) |
| **21** (c) | **22** (a) | **23** (d) | **24** (d) | **25** (c) | **26** (c) | **27** (d) | **28** (c) | **29** (a) | **30** (b) |
| **31** (b) | **32** (d) | **33** (b) | **34** (a) | **35** (b) | **36** (b) | **37** (c) | **38** (c) | **39** (d) | **40** (b) |
| **41** (d) | **42** (c) | **43** (a) | **44** (b) | **45** (d) | **46** (a) | **47** (c) | **48** (d) | **49** (b) | **50** (c) |
| **51** (c) | **52** (b) | **53** (b) | **54** (b) | **55** (d) | **56** (b) | **57** (c) | **58** (c) | **59** (c) | **60** (a) |

## ***Grammar***

| | | | | | | | | | |
|---|---|---|---|---|---|---|---|---|---|
| **1** (d) | **2** (c) | **3** (b) | **4** (a) | **5** (a) | **6** (b) | **7** (d) | **8** (c) | **9** (b) | **10** (c) |
| **11** (b) | **12** (d) | **13** (b) | **14** (b) | **15** (b) | **16** (d) | **17** (c) | **18** (d) | **19** (d) | **20** (b) |
| **21** (b) | **22** (c) | **23** (b) | **24** (a) | **25** (c) | **26** (b) | **27** (a) | **28** (b) | **29** (c) | **30** (d) |
| **31** (b) | **32** (a) | **33** (b) | **34** (b) | **35** (a) | **36** (c) | **37** (d) | **38** (b) | **39** (c) | **40** (a) |
| **41** (d) | **42** (c) | **43** (a) | **44** (b) | **45** (d) | **46** (b) | **47** (c) | **48** (d) | **49** (a) | **50** (c) |

## ***Vocabulary***

| | | | | | | | | | |
|---|---|---|---|---|---|---|---|---|---|
| **1** (c) | **2** (d) | **3** (c) | **4** (c) | **5** (b) | **6** (d) | **7** (d) | **8** (d) | **9** (a) | **10** (c) |
| **11** (a) | **12** (c) | **13** (b) | **14** (a) | **15** (b) | **16** (a) | **17** (d) | **18** (b) | **19** (b) | **20** (c) |
| **21** (a) | **22** (b) | **23** (a) | **24** (b) | **25** (d) | **26** (b) | **27** (b) | **28** (c) | **29** (d) | **30** (c) |
| **31** (d) | **32** (d) | **33** (b) | **34** (b) | **35** (a) | **36** (c) | **37** (c) | **38** (b) | **39** (b) | **40** (c) |
| **41** (d) | **42** (b) | **43** (c) | **44** (b) | **45** (c) | **46** (d) | **47** (c) | **48** (c) | **49** (a) | **50** (b) |

## ***Reading*** *Comprehension*

| | | | | | | | | | |
|---|---|---|---|---|---|---|---|---|---|
| **1** (c) | **2** (a) | **3** (b) | **4** (d) | **5** (c) | **6** (a) | **7** (b) | **8** (d) | **9** (d) | **10** (c) |
| **11** (c) | **12** (d) | **13** (d) | **14** (b) | **15** (d) | **16** (b) | **17** (c) | **18** (c) | **19** (c) | **20** (c) |
| **21** (a) | **22** (c) | **23** (d) | **24** (d) | **25** (c) | **26** (c) | **27** (c) | **28** (b) | **29** (a) | **30** (a) |
| **31** (b) | **32** (d) | **33** (c) | **34** (c) | **35** (a) | **36** (d) | **37** (a) | **38** (c) | **39** (b) | **40** (c) |

# TEPS 등급표

| 등급 | 점수 | 영역 | 능력검정기준(Description) |
|---|---|---|---|
| 1+급<br>Level 1+ | 901~990 | 전반 | 외국인으로서 최상급 수준의 의사소통 능력<br>교양 있는 원어민에 버금가는 정도로 의사소통이 가능하고 전문분야 업무에 대처할 수 있음<br>(Native Level of Communicative Competence) |
| 1급<br>Level 1 | 801~900 | 전반 | 외국인으로서 거의 최상급 수준의 의사소통 능력<br>단기간 집중 교육을 받으면 대부분의 의사소통이 가능하고 전문분야 업무에 별 무리 없이 대처할 수 있음<br>(Near-Native Level of Communicative Competence) |
| 2+급<br>Level 2+ | 701~800 | 전반 | 외국인으로서 상급 수준의 의사소통 능력<br>단기간 집중 교육을 받으면 일반분야 업무를 큰 어려움 없이 수행할 수 있음<br>(Advanced Level of Communicative Competence) |
| 2급<br>Level 2 | 601~700 | 전반 | 외국인으로서 중상급 수준의 의사소통 능력<br>중장기간 집중 교육을 받으면 일반분야 업무를 큰 어려움 없이 수행할 수 있음<br>(High Intermediate Level of Communicative Competence) |
| 3+급<br>Level 3+ | 501~600 | 전반 | 외국인으로서 중급 수준의 의사소통 능력<br>중장기간 집중 교육을 받으면 한정된 분야의 업무를 큰 어려움 없이 수행할 수 있음<br>(Mid Intermediate Level of Communicative Competence) |
| 3급<br>Level 3 | 401~500 | 전반 | 외국인으로서 중하급 수준의 의사소통 능력<br>중장기간 집중 교육을 받으면 한정된 분야의 업무를 다소 미흡하지만 큰 지장 없이 수행할 수 있음<br>(Low Intermediate Level of Communicative Competence) |
| 4+급<br>Level 4+ | 301~400 | 전반 | 외국인으로서 하급 수준의 의사소통 능력<br>장기간의 집중 교육을 받으면 한정된 분야의 업무를 대체로 어렵게 수행할 수 있음<br>(Novice Level of Communicative Competence) |
| 4급<br>Level 4 | 201~300 | | |
| 5+급<br>Level 5+ | 101~200 | 전반 | 외국인으로서 최하급 수준의 의사소통 능력<br>단편적인 지식만을 갖추고 있어 의사소통이 거의 불가능함<br>(Near-Zero Level of Communicative Competence) |
| 5급<br>Level 5 | 10~100 | | |

앞면(Side1)

# TEPS

Test of English Proficiency
developed by
Seoul National University

| 수험번호 Registration No. | |
| --- | --- |
| 성명 Name 한글 | |
| 한자 | |

| 문 제 지 번 호 Test Booklet No. |
| --- |
| |

| 감독관확인란 |
| --- |
| |

## 청 해 Listening Comprehension

| | | | | | | | | | | | | | |
| --- | --- | --- | --- | --- | --- | --- | --- | --- | --- | --- | --- | --- | --- |
| 1 | a | b | c | d | 26 | a | b | c | d | 51 | a | b | c | d |
| 2 | a | b | c | d | 27 | a | b | c | d | 52 | a | b | c | d |
| 3 | a | b | c | d | 28 | a | b | c | d | 53 | a | b | c | d |
| 4 | a | b | c | d | 29 | a | b | c | d | 54 | a | b | c | d |
| 5 | a | b | c | d | 30 | a | b | c | d | 55 | a | b | c | d |
| 6 | a | b | c | d | 31 | a | b | c | d | 56 | a | b | c | d |
| 7 | a | b | c | d | 32 | a | b | c | d | 57 | a | b | c | d |
| 8 | a | b | c | d | 33 | a | b | c | d | 58 | a | b | c | d |
| 9 | a | b | c | d | 34 | a | b | c | d | 59 | a | b | c | d |
| 10 | a | b | c | d | 35 | a | b | c | d | 60 | a | b | c | d |
| 11 | a | b | c | d | 36 | a | b | c | d | | | | | |
| 12 | a | b | c | d | 37 | a | b | c | d | | | | | |
| 13 | a | b | c | d | 38 | a | b | c | d | | | | | |
| 14 | a | b | c | d | 39 | a | b | c | d | | | | | |
| 15 | a | b | c | d | 40 | a | b | c | d | | | | | |
| 16 | a | b | c | d | 41 | a | b | c | d | | | | | |
| 17 | a | b | c | d | 42 | a | b | c | d | | | | | |
| 18 | a | b | c | d | 43 | a | b | c | d | | | | | |
| 19 | a | b | c | d | 44 | a | b | c | d | | | | | |
| 20 | a | b | c | d | 45 | a | b | c | d | | | | | |
| 21 | a | b | c | d | 46 | a | b | c | d | | | | | |
| 22 | a | b | c | d | 47 | a | b | c | d | | | | | |
| 23 | a | b | c | d | 48 | a | b | c | d | | | | | |
| 24 | a | b | c | d | 49 | a | b | c | d | | | | | |
| 25 | a | b | c | d | 50 | a | b | c | d | | | | | |

## 문 법 Grammar

| | | | | | | | | | |
| --- | --- | --- | --- | --- | --- | --- | --- | --- | --- |
| 1 | a | b | c | d | 26 | a | b | c | d |
| 2 | a | b | c | d | 27 | a | b | c | d |
| 3 | a | b | c | d | 28 | a | b | c | d |
| 4 | a | b | c | d | 29 | a | b | c | d |
| 5 | a | b | c | d | 30 | a | b | c | d |
| 6 | a | b | c | d | 31 | a | b | c | d |
| 7 | a | b | c | d | 32 | a | b | c | d |
| 8 | a | b | c | d | 33 | a | b | c | d |
| 9 | a | b | c | d | 34 | a | b | c | d |
| 10 | a | b | c | d | 35 | a | b | c | d |
| 11 | a | b | c | d | 36 | a | b | c | d |
| 12 | a | b | c | d | 37 | a | b | c | d |
| 13 | a | b | c | d | 38 | a | b | c | d |
| 14 | a | b | c | d | 39 | a | b | c | d |
| 15 | a | b | c | d | 40 | a | b | c | d |
| 16 | a | b | c | d | 41 | a | b | c | d |
| 17 | a | b | c | d | 42 | a | b | c | d |
| 18 | a | b | c | d | 43 | a | b | c | d |
| 19 | a | b | c | d | 44 | a | b | c | d |
| 20 | a | b | c | d | 45 | a | b | c | d |
| 21 | a | b | c | d | 46 | a | b | c | d |
| 22 | a | b | c | d | 47 | a | b | c | d |
| 23 | a | b | c | d | 48 | a | b | c | d |
| 24 | a | b | c | d | 49 | a | b | c | d |
| 25 | a | b | c | d | 50 | a | b | c | d |

## 어 휘 Vocabulary

| | | | | | | | | | |
| --- | --- | --- | --- | --- | --- | --- | --- | --- | --- |
| 1 | a | b | c | d | 26 | a | b | c | d |
| 2 | a | b | c | d | 27 | a | b | c | d |
| 3 | a | b | c | d | 28 | a | b | c | d |
| 4 | a | b | c | d | 29 | a | b | c | d |
| 5 | a | b | c | d | 30 | a | b | c | d |
| 6 | a | b | c | d | 31 | a | b | c | d |
| 7 | a | b | c | d | 32 | a | b | c | d |
| 8 | a | b | c | d | 33 | a | b | c | d |
| 9 | a | b | c | d | 34 | a | b | c | d |
| 10 | a | b | c | d | 35 | a | b | c | d |
| 11 | a | b | c | d | 36 | a | b | c | d |
| 12 | a | b | c | d | 37 | a | b | c | d |
| 13 | a | b | c | d | 38 | a | b | c | d |
| 14 | a | b | c | d | 39 | a | b | c | d |
| 15 | a | b | c | d | 40 | a | b | c | d |
| 16 | a | b | c | d | 41 | a | b | c | d |
| 17 | a | b | c | d | 42 | a | b | c | d |
| 18 | a | b | c | d | 43 | a | b | c | d |
| 19 | a | b | c | d | 44 | a | b | c | d |
| 20 | a | b | c | d | 45 | a | b | c | d |
| 21 | a | b | c | d | 46 | a | b | c | d |
| 22 | a | b | c | d | 47 | a | b | c | d |
| 23 | a | b | c | d | 48 | a | b | c | d |
| 24 | a | b | c | d | 49 | a | b | c | d |
| 25 | a | b | c | d | 50 | a | b | c | d |

## 독 해 Reading Comprehension

| | | | | | | | | | |
| --- | --- | --- | --- | --- | --- | --- | --- | --- | --- |
| 1 | a | b | c | d | 26 | a | b | c | d |
| 2 | a | b | c | d | 27 | a | b | c | d |
| 3 | a | b | c | d | 28 | a | b | c | d |
| 4 | a | b | c | d | 29 | a | b | c | d |
| 5 | a | b | c | d | 30 | a | b | c | d |
| 6 | a | b | c | d | 31 | a | b | c | d |
| 7 | a | b | c | d | 32 | a | b | c | d |
| 8 | a | b | c | d | 33 | a | b | c | d |
| 9 | a | b | c | d | 34 | a | b | c | d |
| 10 | a | b | c | d | 35 | a | b | c | d |
| 11 | a | b | c | d | 36 | a | b | c | d |
| 12 | a | b | c | d | 37 | a | b | c | d |
| 13 | a | b | c | d | 38 | a | b | c | d |
| 14 | a | b | c | d | 39 | a | b | c | d |
| 15 | a | b | c | d | 40 | a | b | c | d |
| 16 | a | b | c | d | | | | | |
| 17 | a | b | c | d | | | | | |
| 18 | a | b | c | d | | | | | |
| 19 | a | b | c | d | | | | | |
| 20 | a | b | c | d | | | | | |
| 21 | a | b | c | d | | | | | |
| 22 | a | b | c | d | | | | | |
| 23 | a | b | c | d | | | | | |
| 24 | a | b | c | d | | | | | |
| 25 | a | b | c | d | | | | | |

## 주 민 등 록 번 호 National ID No.

| | | | | | | | | | | | | | |
| --- | --- | --- | --- | --- | --- | --- | --- | --- | --- | --- | --- | --- | --- |
| 0 | 0 | 0 | 0 | 0 | 0 | | | 0 | 0 | 0 | 0 | 0 | 0 |
| 1 | 1 | 1 | 1 | 1 | 1 | | 1 | 1 | 1 | 1 | 1 | 1 | 1 |
| 2 | 2 | | 2 | 2 | 2 | | 2 | 2 | 2 | 2 | 2 | 2 | 2 |
| 3 | 3 | | 3 | 3 | 3 | | 3 | 3 | 3 | 3 | 3 | 3 | 3 |
| 4 | 4 | | 4 | | 4 | – | 4 | 4 | 4 | 4 | 4 | 4 | 4 |
| 5 | 5 | | 5 | | 5 | | 5 | 5 | 5 | 5 | 5 | 5 | 5 |
| 6 | 6 | | 6 | | 6 | | 6 | 6 | 6 | 6 | 6 | 6 | 6 |
| 7 | 7 | | 7 | | 7 | | 7 | 7 | 7 | 7 | 7 | 7 | 7 |
| 8 | 8 | | 8 | | 8 | | 8 | 8 | 8 | 8 | 8 | 8 | 8 |
| 9 | 9 | | 9 | | 9 | | 9 | 9 | 9 | 9 | 9 | 9 | 9 |

## 고사실란 Room No.

| | |
| --- | --- |
| 0 | 0 |
| 1 | 1 |
| 2 | 2 |
| 3 | 3 |
| 4 | 4 |
| 5 | 5 |
| | 6 |
| | 7 |
| | 8 |
| | 9 |

## 수 험 번 호 Registration No.

| | | | | | | |
| --- | --- | --- | --- | --- | --- | --- |
| 0 | 0 | 0 | 0 | 0 | 0 | 0 |
| 1 | 1 | 1 | 1 | 1 | 1 | 1 |
| 2 | 2 | 2 | 2 | 2 | 2 | 2 |
| 3 | 3 | 3 | 3 | 3 | 3 | 3 |
| 4 | 4 | 4 | 4 | 4 | 4 | 4 |
| 5 | 5 | 5 | 5 | 5 | 5 | 5 |
| 6 | 6 | 6 | 6 | 6 | 6 | 6 |
| 7 | 7 | 7 | 7 | 7 | 7 | 7 |
| 8 | 8 | 8 | 8 | 8 | 8 | 8 |
| 9 | 9 | 9 | 9 | 9 | 9 | 9 |

## 비밀번호 Password

| | | | |
| --- | --- | --- | --- |
| 0 | 0 | 0 | 0 |
| 1 | 1 | 1 | 1 |
| 2 | 2 | 2 | 2 |
| 3 | 3 | 3 | 3 |
| 4 | 4 | 4 | 4 |
| 5 | 5 | 5 | 5 |
| 6 | 6 | 6 | 6 |
| 7 | 7 | 7 | 7 |
| 8 | 8 | 8 | 8 |
| 9 | 9 | 9 | 9 |

## 좌석번호 Seat No.

| | |
| --- | --- |
| A | 1 |
| B | 2 |
| C | 3 |
| D | 4 |
| E | 5 |
| | 6 |
| | 7 |

| 서 약 | 본인은 필기구 및 기재오류와 답안지 훼손으로 인한 책임을 지고, 부정행위 처리규정을 준수할 것을 서약합니다. | |
| --- | --- | --- |

## 답안작성시 유의사항

1. 답안 작성은 반드시 **컴퓨터용 싸인펜**을 사용해야 합니다.
2. 답안을 정정할 경우 수정테이프(수정액 불가)를 사용해야 합니다.
3. 본 답안지는 컴퓨터로 처리되므로 훼손해서는 안되며, 답안지 하단의 타이밍마크(▌▌▌)를 찢거나, 낙서 등으로 인한 훼손시 불이익이 발생할 수 있습니다.
4. 답안은 문항당 정답을 1개만 골라 ▌와 같이 정확히 기재해야 하며, 필기구 오류나 본인의 부주의로 잘못 표기한 경우에는 당 관리위원회의 OMR판독기의 판독결과에 따르며, 그 결과는 본인이 책임집니다.

   Good ▌ Bad

5. 감독관의 확인이 없는 답안지는 무효처리됩니다.

뒷면(Side2)

# TEPS

Test of English Proficiency
developed by
Seoul National University

| 성명 | 영문 | |
|---|---|---|
| | 서명 | |

응시일자 : 20 년 월 일

## <부정행위 및 규정위반 처리규정>

1. 모든 부정행위 및 규정위반 적발 및 이에 대한 조치는 TEPS관리위원회의 처리규정에 따라 이루어집니다.

2. 부정행위 및 규정위반 행위는 현장 적발 뿐만 아니라 사후에도 적발될 수 있으며 모두 동일한 조치가 취해집니다.

3. 부정행위 적발 시 당해 성적은 무효화되며 사안에 따라 최대 5년까지 TEPS관리위원회에서 주관하는 모든 시험의 응시자격이 제한됩니다.

4. 문제지 이외에 메모를 하는 행위와 시험 문제의 일부 또는 전부를 유출하거나 공개하는 경우 부정행위로 처리됩니다.

5. 각 파트별 시간을 준수하지 않거나, 시험 종료 후 답안 작성을 계속할 경우 규정위반으로 처리됩니다.

성 명 (성 · 이름순으로 기재)

| EX | H | O | N | G | | G | I | L | | D | O | N | G | | | | | | | |
|---|---|---|---|---|---|---|---|---|---|---|---|---|---|---|---|---|---|---|---|---|
| A | A | A | A | A | A | A | A | A | A | A | A | A | A | A | A | A | A | A | A | A |
| B | B | B | B | B | B | B | B | B | B | B | B | B | B | B | B | B | B | B | B | B |
| C | C | C | C | C | C | C | C | C | C | C | C | C | C | C | C | C | C | C | C | C |
| D | D | D | D | D | D | D | D | D | D | D | D | D | D | D | D | D | D | D | D | D |
| E | E | E | E | E | E | E | E | E | E | E | E | E | E | E | E | E | E | E | E | E |
| F | F | F | F | F | F | F | F | F | F | F | F | F | F | F | F | F | F | F | F | F |
| G | G | G | G | G | G | G | G | G | G | G | G | G | G | G | G | G | G | G | G | G |
| H | H | H | H | H | H | H | H | H | H | H | H | H | H | H | H | H | H | H | H | H |
| I | I | I | I | I | I | I | I | I | I | I | I | I | I | I | I | I | I | I | I | I |
| J | J | J | J | J | J | J | J | J | J | J | J | J | J | J | J | J | J | J | J | J |
| K | K | K | K | K | K | K | K | K | K | K | K | K | K | K | K | K | K | K | K | K |
| L | L | L | L | L | L | L | L | L | L | L | L | L | L | L | L | L | L | L | L | L |
| M | M | M | M | M | M | M | M | M | M | M | M | M | M | M | M | M | M | M | M | M |
| N | N | N | N | N | N | N | N | N | N | N | N | N | N | N | N | N | N | N | N | N |
| O | O | O | O | O | O | O | O | O | O | O | O | O | O | O | O | O | O | O | O | O |
| P | P | P | P | P | P | P | P | P | P | P | P | P | P | P | P | P | P | P | P | P |
| Q | Q | Q | Q | Q | Q | Q | Q | Q | Q | Q | Q | Q | Q | Q | Q | Q | Q | Q | Q | Q |
| R | R | R | R | R | R | R | R | R | R | R | R | R | R | R | R | R | R | R | R | R |
| S | S | S | S | S | S | S | S | S | S | S | S | S | S | S | S | S | S | S | S | S |
| T | T | T | T | T | T | T | T | T | T | T | T | T | T | T | T | T | T | T | T | T |
| U | U | U | U | U | U | U | U | U | U | U | U | U | U | U | U | U | U | U | U | U |
| V | V | V | V | V | V | V | V | V | V | V | V | V | V | V | V | V | V | V | V | V |
| W | W | W | W | W | W | W | W | W | W | W | W | W | W | W | W | W | W | W | W | W |
| X | X | X | X | X | X | X | X | X | X | X | X | X | X | X | X | X | X | X | X | X |
| Y | Y | Y | Y | Y | Y | Y | Y | Y | Y | Y | Y | Y | Y | Y | Y | Y | Y | Y | Y | Y |
| Z | Z | Z | Z | Z | Z | Z | Z | Z | Z | Z | Z | Z | Z | Z | Z | Z | Z | Z | Z | Z |

| 단체구분 | |
|---|---|
| 학생 | 일반 |

## 질 문 란

1. 귀하의 TEPS 응시목적은?
   ⓐ 입사지원 ⓑ 인사정책
   ⓒ 개인실력측정 ⓓ 입시
   ⓔ 국가고시 지원 ⓕ 기타

2. 귀하의 영어권 체류 경험은?
   ⓐ 없다 ⓑ 6개월 미만
   ⓒ 6개월 이상 1년 미만 ⓓ 1년 이상 3년 미만
   ⓔ 3년 이상 5년 미만 ⓕ 5년 이상

3. 귀하께서 응시하고 계신 고사장에 대한 만족도는?
   ⓐ 0점 ⓑ 1점
   ⓒ 2점 ⓓ 3점
   ⓔ 4점 ⓕ 5점

4. 최근 2년내 TEPS 응시횟수는?
   ⓐ 없다 ⓑ 1회
   ⓒ 2회 ⓓ 3회
   ⓔ 4회 ⓕ 5회 이상

| 학력 | 재학 | 졸업 | 전공 | 직업 |
|---|---|---|---|---|
| 초등학교 | | | 인문학 | 공무원 |
| 중학교 | | | 사회과학 · 법학 | 고시준비 |
| 고등학교 | | | 경제학 · 경영학 | 교사 |
| 전문대학 | | | 자연과학 | 군인 |
| 대학교 | | | 의학 · 약학 · 간호학 | 의료인 |
| 대학원 | | | 공학 | 자영업 |
| | | | 교육학 | 학생 |
| | | | 음악 · 미술 · 체육 | 회사원 |
| | | | 기타 | 무직 |
| | | | | 기타 |

| 직종 | | 직책 |
|---|---|---|
| 고위임직원 | 무역 | 임원 |
| 전문직(과학.공학) | 외환 | 부장 |
| 전문직(교육) | 자금 | 차장 |
| 전문직(법률.회계.금융) | 공무 | 과장 |
| 기술직 | 업무 | 대리 |
| 영업 | 품질관리 | 계장 |
| 홍보 | 전산 | 사원 |
| 총무 | 행정직 | 인턴 |
| 인사 | 생산관리 | 기타 |
| 경리 | 서비스 | |
| 기획 | 기타 | |
| 구매 | | |

앞면(Side1)

# TEPS

Test of English Proficiency
developed by
Seoul National University

| 수험번호 Registration No. | | |
|---|---|---|
| 성명 Name | 한글 | |
| | 한자 | |

| 문제지번호 Test Booklet No. | 감독관확인란 |
|---|---|
| | |

## 청해 Listening Comprehension

| No. | | | | | No. | | | | | No. | | | | |
|---|---|---|---|---|---|---|---|---|---|---|---|---|---|---|
| 1 | a | b | c | d | 26 | a | b | c | d | 51 | a | b | c | d |
| 2 | a | b | c | d | 27 | a | b | c | d | 52 | a | b | c | d |
| 3 | a | b | c | d | 28 | a | b | c | d | 53 | a | b | c | d |
| 4 | a | b | c | d | 29 | a | b | c | d | 54 | a | b | c | d |
| 5 | a | b | c | d | 30 | a | b | c | d | 55 | a | b | c | d |
| 6 | a | b | c | d | 31 | a | b | c | d | 56 | a | b | c | d |
| 7 | a | b | c | d | 32 | a | b | c | d | 57 | a | b | c | d |
| 8 | a | b | c | d | 33 | a | b | c | d | 58 | a | b | c | d |
| 9 | a | b | c | d | 34 | a | b | c | d | 59 | a | b | c | d |
| 10 | a | b | c | d | 35 | a | b | c | d | 60 | a | b | c | d |
| 11 | a | b | c | d | 36 | a | b | c | d | | | | | |
| 12 | a | b | c | d | 37 | a | b | c | d | | | | | |
| 13 | a | b | c | d | 38 | a | b | c | d | | | | | |
| 14 | a | b | c | d | 39 | a | b | c | d | | | | | |
| 15 | a | b | c | d | 40 | a | b | c | d | | | | | |
| 16 | a | b | c | d | 41 | a | b | c | d | | | | | |
| 17 | a | b | c | d | 42 | a | b | c | d | | | | | |
| 18 | a | b | c | d | 43 | a | b | c | d | | | | | |
| 19 | a | b | c | d | 44 | a | b | c | d | | | | | |
| 20 | a | b | c | d | 45 | a | b | c | d | | | | | |
| 21 | a | b | c | d | 46 | a | b | c | d | | | | | |
| 22 | a | b | c | d | 47 | a | b | c | d | | | | | |
| 23 | a | b | c | d | 48 | a | b | c | d | | | | | |
| 24 | a | b | c | d | 49 | a | b | c | d | | | | | |
| 25 | a | b | c | d | 50 | a | b | c | d | | | | | |

## 문법 Grammar

| No. | | | | | No. | | | | |
|---|---|---|---|---|---|---|---|---|---|
| 1 | a | b | c | d | 26 | a | b | c | d |
| 2 | a | b | c | d | 27 | a | b | c | d |
| 3 | a | b | c | d | 28 | a | b | c | d |
| 4 | a | b | c | d | 29 | a | b | c | d |
| 5 | a | b | c | d | 30 | a | b | c | d |
| 6 | a | b | c | d | 31 | a | b | c | d |
| 7 | a | b | c | d | 32 | a | b | c | d |
| 8 | a | b | c | d | 33 | a | b | c | d |
| 9 | a | b | c | d | 34 | a | b | c | d |
| 10 | a | b | c | d | 35 | a | b | c | d |
| 11 | a | b | c | d | 36 | a | b | c | d |
| 12 | a | b | c | d | 37 | a | b | c | d |
| 13 | a | b | c | d | 38 | a | b | c | d |
| 14 | a | b | c | d | 39 | a | b | c | d |
| 15 | a | b | c | d | 40 | a | b | c | d |
| 16 | a | b | c | d | 41 | a | b | c | d |
| 17 | a | b | c | d | 42 | a | b | c | d |
| 18 | a | b | c | d | 43 | a | b | c | d |
| 19 | a | b | c | d | 44 | a | b | c | d |
| 20 | a | b | c | d | 45 | a | b | c | d |
| 21 | a | b | c | d | 46 | a | b | c | d |
| 22 | a | b | c | d | 47 | a | b | c | d |
| 23 | a | b | c | d | 48 | a | b | c | d |
| 24 | a | b | c | d | 49 | a | b | c | d |
| 25 | a | b | c | d | 50 | a | b | c | d |

## 어휘 Vocabulary

| No. | | | | | No. | | | | |
|---|---|---|---|---|---|---|---|---|---|
| 1 | a | b | c | d | 26 | a | b | c | d |
| 2 | a | b | c | d | 27 | a | b | c | d |
| 3 | a | b | c | d | 28 | a | b | c | d |
| 4 | a | b | c | d | 29 | a | b | c | d |
| 5 | a | b | c | d | 30 | a | b | c | d |
| 6 | a | b | c | d | 31 | a | b | c | d |
| 7 | a | b | c | d | 32 | a | b | c | d |
| 8 | a | b | c | d | 33 | a | b | c | d |
| 9 | a | b | c | d | 34 | a | b | c | d |
| 10 | a | b | c | d | 35 | a | b | c | d |
| 11 | a | b | c | d | 36 | a | b | c | d |
| 12 | a | b | c | d | 37 | a | b | c | d |
| 13 | a | b | c | d | 38 | a | b | c | d |
| 14 | a | b | c | d | 39 | a | b | c | d |
| 15 | a | b | c | d | 40 | a | b | c | d |
| 16 | a | b | c | d | 41 | a | b | c | d |
| 17 | a | b | c | d | 42 | a | b | c | d |
| 18 | a | b | c | d | 43 | a | b | c | d |
| 19 | a | b | c | d | 44 | a | b | c | d |
| 20 | a | b | c | d | 45 | a | b | c | d |
| 21 | a | b | c | d | 46 | a | b | c | d |
| 22 | a | b | c | d | 47 | a | b | c | d |
| 23 | a | b | c | d | 48 | a | b | c | d |
| 24 | a | b | c | d | 49 | a | b | c | d |
| 25 | a | b | c | d | 50 | a | b | c | d |

## 독해 Reading Comprehension

| No. | | | | | No. | | | | |
|---|---|---|---|---|---|---|---|---|---|
| 1 | a | b | c | d | 26 | a | b | c | d |
| 2 | a | b | c | d | 27 | a | b | c | d |
| 3 | a | b | c | d | 28 | a | b | c | d |
| 4 | a | b | c | d | 29 | a | b | c | d |
| 5 | a | b | c | d | 30 | a | b | c | d |
| 6 | a | b | c | d | 31 | a | b | c | d |
| 7 | a | b | c | d | 32 | a | b | c | d |
| 8 | a | b | c | d | 33 | a | b | c | d |
| 9 | a | b | c | d | 34 | a | b | c | d |
| 10 | a | b | c | d | 35 | a | b | c | d |
| 11 | a | b | c | d | 36 | a | b | c | d |
| 12 | a | b | c | d | 37 | a | b | c | d |
| 13 | a | b | c | d | 38 | a | b | c | d |
| 14 | a | b | c | d | 39 | a | b | c | d |
| 15 | a | b | c | d | 40 | a | b | c | d |
| 16 | a | b | c | d | | | | | |
| 17 | a | b | c | d | | | | | |
| 18 | a | b | c | d | | | | | |
| 19 | a | b | c | d | | | | | |
| 20 | a | b | c | d | | | | | |
| 21 | a | b | c | d | | | | | |
| 22 | a | b | c | d | | | | | |
| 23 | a | b | c | d | | | | | |
| 24 | a | b | c | d | | | | | |
| 25 | a | b | c | d | | | | | |

## 주민등록번호 National ID No.

| | | | | | | – | | | | | | | |
|---|---|---|---|---|---|---|---|---|---|---|---|---|---|
| 0 | 0 | 0 | 0 | 0 | 0 | | | 0 | 0 | 0 | 0 | 0 | 0 |
| 1 | 1 | 1 | 1 | 1 | 1 | | 1 | 1 | 1 | 1 | 1 | 1 | 1 |
| 2 | 2 | | 2 | 2 | 2 | | 2 | 2 | 2 | 2 | 2 | 2 | 2 |
| 3 | 3 | | 3 | 3 | 3 | | 3 | 3 | 3 | 3 | 3 | 3 | 3 |
| 4 | 4 | | 4 | | 4 | – | 4 | 4 | 4 | 4 | 4 | 4 | 4 |
| 5 | 5 | | 5 | | 5 | | 5 | 5 | 5 | 5 | 5 | 5 | 5 |
| 6 | 6 | | 6 | | 6 | | 6 | 6 | 6 | 6 | 6 | 6 | 6 |
| 7 | 7 | | 7 | | 7 | | 7 | 7 | 7 | 7 | 7 | 7 | 7 |
| 8 | 8 | | 8 | | 8 | | 8 | 8 | 8 | 8 | 8 | 8 | 8 |
| 9 | 9 | | 9 | | 9 | | 9 | 9 | 9 | 9 | 9 | 9 | 9 |

## 고사실란 Room No.

| | |
|---|---|
| 0 | 0 |
| 1 | 1 |
| 2 | 2 |
| 3 | 3 |
| 4 | 4 |
| 5 | 5 |
| | 6 |
| | 7 |
| | 8 |
| | 9 |

## 수험번호 Registration No.

| | | | | | | |
|---|---|---|---|---|---|---|
| 0 | 0 | 0 | 0 | 0 | 0 | 0 |
| 1 | 1 | 1 | 1 | 1 | 1 | 1 |
| 2 | 2 | 2 | 2 | 2 | 2 | 2 |
| 3 | 3 | 3 | 3 | 3 | 3 | 3 |
| 4 | 4 | 4 | 4 | 4 | 4 | 4 |
| 5 | 5 | 5 | 5 | 5 | 5 | 5 |
| 6 | 6 | 6 | 6 | 6 | 6 | 6 |
| 7 | 7 | 7 | 7 | 7 | 7 | 7 |
| 8 | 8 | 8 | 8 | 8 | 8 | 8 |
| 9 | 9 | 9 | 9 | 9 | 9 | 9 |

## 비밀번호 Password

| | | | |
|---|---|---|---|
| 0 | 0 | 0 | 0 |
| 1 | 1 | 1 | 1 |
| 2 | 2 | 2 | 2 |
| 3 | 3 | 3 | 3 |
| 4 | 4 | 4 | 4 |
| 5 | 5 | 5 | 5 |
| 6 | 6 | 6 | 6 |
| 7 | 7 | 7 | 7 |
| 8 | 8 | 8 | 8 |
| 9 | 9 | 9 | 9 |

## 좌석번호 Seat No.

| | |
|---|---|
| A | 1 |
| B | 2 |
| C | 3 |
| D | 4 |
| E | 5 |
| | 6 |
| | 7 |

**서 약** | **본인은 필기구 및 기재오류와 답안지 훼손으로 인한 책임을 지고, 부정행위 처리규정을 준수할 것을 서약합니다.**

**답안작성시 유의사항**

1. 답안 작성은 반드시 **컴퓨터용 싸인펜**을 사용해야 합니다.
2. 답안을 정정할 경우 수정테이프(수정액 불가)를 사용해야 합니다.
3. 본 답안지는 컴퓨터로 처리되므로 훼손해서는 안되며, 답안지 하단의 타이밍마크(▎▎▎)를 찢거나, 낙서 등으로 인한 훼손시 불이익이 발생할 수 있습니다.
4. 답안은 문항당 정답을 1개만 골라 ▮와 같이 정확히 기재해야 하며, 필기구 오류나 본인의 부주의로 잘못 표기한 경우에는 당 관리위원회의 OMR판독기의 판독결과에 따르며, 그 결과는 본인이 책임집니다.

   Good ▮　Bad

5. 감독관의 확인이 없는 답안지는 무효처리됩니다.

뒷면(Side2)

**TEPS** Test of English Proficiency developed by Seoul National University

| 성명 | |
|---|---|
| 영문 | |
| 서명 | |

응시일자 : 20 년 월 일

**<부정행위 및 규정위반 처리규정>**

1. 모든 부정행위 및 규정위반 적발 및 이에 대한 조치는 TEPS관리위원회의 처리규정에 따라 이루어집니다.
2. 부정행위 및 규정위반 행위는 현장 적발 뿐만 아니라 사후에도 적발될 수 있으며 모두 동일한 조치가 취해집니다.
3. 부정행위 적발 시 당해 성적은 무효화되며 사안에 따라 최대 5년까지 TEPS관리위원회에서 주관하는 모든 시험의 응시자격이 제한됩니다.
4. 문제지 이외에 메모를 하는 행위와 시험 문제의 일부 또는 전부를 유출하거나 공개하는 경우 부정행위로 처리됩니다.
5. 각 파트별 시간을 준수하지 않거나, 시험 종료 후 답안 작성을 계속할 경우 규정위반으로 처리됩니다.

**성 명 (성 · 이름순으로 기재)**

| EX | H | O | N | G | | G | I | L | | D | O | N | G | | | | | | | |
|---|---|---|---|---|---|---|---|---|---|---|---|---|---|---|---|---|---|---|---|---|
| A | A | A | A | A | A | A | A | A | A | A | A | A | A | A | A | A | A | A | A | A |
| B | B | B | B | B | B | B | B | B | B | B | B | B | B | B | B | B | B | B | B | B |
| C | C | C | C | C | C | C | C | C | C | C | C | C | C | C | C | C | C | C | C | C |
| D | D | D | D | D | D | D | D | D | D | D | D | D | D | D | D | D | D | D | D | D |
| E | E | E | E | E | E | E | E | E | E | E | E | E | E | E | E | E | E | E | E | E |
| F | F | F | F | F | F | F | F | F | F | F | F | F | F | F | F | F | F | F | F | F |
| G | G | G | G | G | G | G | G | G | G | G | G | G | G | G | G | G | G | G | G | G |
| H | H | H | H | H | H | H | H | H | H | H | H | H | H | H | H | H | H | H | H | H |
| I | I | I | I | I | I | I | I | I | I | I | I | I | I | I | I | I | I | I | I | I |
| J | J | J | J | J | J | J | J | J | J | J | J | J | J | J | J | J | J | J | J | J |
| K | K | K | K | K | K | K | K | K | K | K | K | K | K | K | K | K | K | K | K | K |
| L | L | L | L | L | L | L | L | L | L | L | L | L | L | L | L | L | L | L | L | L |
| M | M | M | M | M | M | M | M | M | M | M | M | M | M | M | M | M | M | M | M | M |
| N | N | N | N | N | N | N | N | N | N | N | N | N | N | N | N | N | N | N | N | N |
| O | O | O | O | O | O | O | O | O | O | O | O | O | O | O | O | O | O | O | O | O |
| P | P | P | P | P | P | P | P | P | P | P | P | P | P | P | P | P | P | P | P | P |
| Q | Q | Q | Q | Q | Q | Q | Q | Q | Q | Q | Q | Q | Q | Q | Q | Q | Q | Q | Q | Q |
| R | R | R | R | R | R | R | R | R | R | R | R | R | R | R | R | R | R | R | R | R |
| S | S | S | S | S | S | S | S | S | S | S | S | S | S | S | S | S | S | S | S | S |
| T | T | T | T | T | T | T | T | T | T | T | T | T | T | T | T | T | T | T | T | T |
| U | U | U | U | U | U | U | U | U | U | U | U | U | U | U | U | U | U | U | U | U |
| V | V | V | V | V | V | V | V | V | V | V | V | V | V | V | V | V | V | V | V | V |
| W | W | W | W | W | W | W | W | W | W | W | W | W | W | W | W | W | W | W | W | W |
| X | X | X | X | X | X | X | X | X | X | X | X | X | X | X | X | X | X | X | X | X |
| Y | Y | Y | Y | Y | Y | Y | Y | Y | Y | Y | Y | Y | Y | Y | Y | Y | Y | Y | Y | Y |
| Z | Z | Z | Z | Z | Z | Z | Z | Z | Z | Z | Z | Z | Z | Z | Z | Z | Z | Z | Z | Z |

**단 체 구 분**

| 학생 | 일반 |
|---|---|
| ( ) | ( ) |

**질 문 란**

1. 귀하의 TEPS 응시목적은?
   - a 입사지원
   - b 인사정책
   - c 개인실력측정
   - d 입시
   - e 국가고시 지원
   - f 기타
2. 귀하의 영어권 체류 경험은?
   - a 없다
   - b 6개월 미만
   - c 6개월 이상 1년 미만
   - d 1년 이상 3년 미만
   - e 3년 이상 5년 미만
   - f 5년 이상
3. 귀하께서 응시하고 계신 고사장에 대한 만족도는?
   - a 0점
   - b 1점
   - c 2점
   - d 3점
   - e 4점
   - f 5점
4. 최근 2년내 TEPS 응시횟수는?
   - a 없다
   - b 1회
   - c 2회
   - d 3회
   - e 4회
   - f 5회 이상

| 학력 | 재학 | 졸업 | 전공 | 직업 |
|---|---|---|---|---|
| 초등학교 | ( ) | ( ) | 인문학 ( ) | 공무원 ( ) |
| 중학교 | ( ) | ( ) | 사회과학 · 법학 ( ) | 고시준비 ( ) |
| 고등학교 | ( ) | ( ) | 경제학 · 경영학 ( ) | 교사 ( ) |
| 전문대학 | ( ) | ( ) | 자연과학 ( ) | 군인 ( ) |
| 대학교 | ( ) | ( ) | 의학 · 약학 · 간호학 ( ) | 의료인 ( ) |
| 대학원 | ( ) | ( ) | 공학 ( ) | 자영업 ( ) |
| | | | 교육학 ( ) | 학생 ( ) |
| | | | 음악 · 미술 · 체육 ( ) | 회사원 ( ) |
| | | | 기타 ( ) | 무직 ( ) |
| | | | | 기타 ( ) |

| 직종 | | 직책 |
|---|---|---|
| 고위임직원 ( ) | 무역 ( ) | 임원 ( ) |
| 전문직(과학.공학) ( ) | 외환 ( ) | 부장 ( ) |
| 전문직(교육) ( ) | 자금 ( ) | 차장 ( ) |
| 전문직(법률.회계.금융) ( ) | 공무 ( ) | 과장 ( ) |
| 기술직 ( ) | 업무 ( ) | 대리 ( ) |
| 영업 ( ) | 품질관리 ( ) | 계장 ( ) |
| 홍보 ( ) | 전산 ( ) | 사원 ( ) |
| 총무 ( ) | 행정직 ( ) | 인턴 ( ) |
| 인사 ( ) | 생산관리 ( ) | 기타 ( ) |
| 경리 ( ) | 서비스 ( ) | |
| 기획 ( ) | 기타 ( ) | |
| 구매 ( ) | | |

앞면(Side1)

# TEPS

Test of English Proficiency
developed by
Seoul National University

| 수험번호 Registration No. | |
|---|---|
| 성명 Name 한글 | |
| 한자 | |

문 제 지 번 호 Test Booklet No.

감독관확인란

## 청 해 Listening Comprehension

## 문 법 Grammar

## 어 휘 Vocabulary

## 독 해 Reading Comprehension

주 민 등 록 번 호 National ID No.

고사실란 Room No.

수 험 번 호 Registration No.

비밀번호 Password

좌석번호 Seat No.

| 서 약 | 본인은 필기구 및 기재오류와 답안지 훼손으로 인한 책임을 지고, 부정행위 처리규정을 준수할 것을 서약합니다. |
|---|---|

**답안작성시 유 의 사 항**

1. 답안 작성은 반드시 **컴퓨터용 싸인펜**을 사용해야 합니다.
2. 답안을 정정할 경우 수정테이프(수정액 불가)를 사용해야 합니다.
3. 본 답안지는 컴퓨터로 처리되므로 훼손해서는 안되며, 답안지 하단의 타이밍마크(**|||**)를 찢거나, 낙서 등으로 인한 훼손시 불이익이 발생할 수 있습니다.
4. 답안은 문항당 정답을 1개만 골라 ▮와 같이 정확히 기재해야 하며, 필기구 오류나 본인의 부주의로 잘못 표기한 경우에는 당 관리위원회의 OMR판독기의 판독결과에 따르며, 그 결과는 본인이 책임집니다.

Good ▮ Bad

5. 감독관의 확인이 없는 답안지는 무효처리됩니다.

**뒷면(Side2)**

# TEPS

Test of English Proficiency
developed by
Seoul National University

| 성명 | 영문 | |
|---|---|---|
| | 서명 | |

응시일자 : 20    년    월    일

## <부정행위 및 규정위반 처리규정>

1. 모든 부정행위 및 규정위반 적발 및 이에 대한 조치는 TEPS관리위원회의 처리규정에 따라 이루어집니다.

2. 부정행위 및 규정위반 행위는 현장 적발 뿐만 아니라 사후에도 적발될 수 있으며 모두 동일한 조치가 취해집니다.

3. 부정행위 적발 시 당해 성적은 무효화되며 사안에 따라 최대 5년까지 TEPS관리위원회에서 주관하는 모든 시험의 응시자격이 제한됩니다.

4. 문제지 이외에 메모를 하는 행위와 시험 문제의 일부 또는 전부를 유출하거나 공개하는 경우 부정행위로 처리됩니다.

5. 각 파트별 시간을 준수하지 않거나, 시험 종료 후 답안 작성을 계속할 경우 규정위반으로 처리됩니다.

**성 명 (성 · 이름순으로 기재)**

EX H O N G  G I L  D O N G

A B C D E F G H I J K L M N O P Q R S T U V W X Y Z

**단체구분**

| 학생 | 일반 |
|---|---|
| ( ) | ( ) |

**질 문 란**

1. 귀하의 TEPS 응시목적은?
ⓐ 입사지원 ⓑ 인사정책
ⓒ 개인실력측정 ⓓ 입시
ⓔ 국가고시 지원 ⓕ 기타

2. 귀하의 영어권 체류 경험은?
ⓐ 없다 ⓑ 6개월 미만
ⓒ 6개월 이상 1년 미만 ⓓ 1년 이상 3년 미만
ⓔ 3년 이상 5년 미만 ⓕ 5년 이상

3. 귀하께서 응시하고 계신 고사장에 대한 만족도는?
ⓐ 0점 ⓑ 1점
ⓒ 2점 ⓓ 3점
ⓔ 4점 ⓕ 5점

4. 최근 2년내 TEPS 응시횟수는?
ⓐ 없다 ⓑ 1회
ⓒ 2회 ⓓ 3회
ⓔ 4회 ⓕ 5회 이상

| 학력 | 재학 | 졸업 | 전공 | 직업 |
|---|---|---|---|---|
| 초등학교 | ( ) | ( ) | 인문학 ( ) | 공무원 ( ) |
| 중학교 | ( ) | ( ) | 사회과학 · 법학 ( ) | 고시준비 ( ) |
| 고등학교 | ( ) | ( ) | 경제학 · 경영학 ( ) | 교사 ( ) |
| 전문대학 | ( ) | ( ) | 자연과학 ( ) | 군인 ( ) |
| 대학교 | ( ) | ( ) | 의학 · 약학 · 간호학 ( ) | 의료인 ( ) |
| 대학원 | ( ) | ( ) | 공학 ( ) | 자영업 ( ) |
| | | | 교육학 ( ) | 학생 ( ) |
| | | | 음악 · 미술 · 체육 ( ) | 회사원 ( ) |
| | | | 기타 ( ) | 무직 ( ) |
| | | | | 기타 ( ) |

| 직종 | | 직책 |
|---|---|---|
| 고위임직원 ( ) | 무역 ( ) | 임원 ( ) |
| 전문직(과학.공학) ( ) | 외환 ( ) | 부장 ( ) |
| 전문직(교육) ( ) | 자금 ( ) | 차장 ( ) |
| 전문직(법률.회계.금융) ( ) | 공무 ( ) | 과장 ( ) |
| 기술직 ( ) | 업무 ( ) | 대리 ( ) |
| 영업 ( ) | 품질관리 ( ) | 계장 ( ) |
| 홍보 ( ) | 전산 ( ) | 사원 ( ) |
| 총무 ( ) | 행정직 ( ) | 인턴 ( ) |
| 인사 ( ) | 생산관리 ( ) | 기타 ( ) |
| 경리 ( ) | 서비스 ( ) | |
| 기획 ( ) | 기타 ( ) | |
| 구매 ( ) | | |

앞면(Side1)

# TEPS

Test of English Proficiency
developed by
Seoul National University

| 수험번호 Registration No. | |
|---|---|
| 성명 Name | 한글 |
| | 한자 |

| 문제지번호 Test Booklet No. |
|---|
| |

| 감독관확인란 |
|---|
| |

## 청해 Listening Comprehension

1–60 ⓐ ⓑ ⓒ ⓓ

## 문법 Grammar

1–50 ⓐ ⓑ ⓒ ⓓ

## 어휘 Vocabulary

1–50 ⓐ ⓑ ⓒ ⓓ

## 독해 Reading Comprehension

1–40 ⓐ ⓑ ⓒ ⓓ

## 주민등록번호 National ID No.

## 고사실란 Room No.

## 수험번호 Registration No.

## 비밀번호 Password

## 좌석번호 Seat No.

A B C D E / 1 2 3 4 5 6 7

**서약** 본인은 필기구 및 기재오류와 답안지 훼손으로 인한 책임을 지고, 부정행위 처리규정을 준수할 것을 서약합니다.

**답안작성시 유의사항**

1. 답안 작성은 반드시 **컴퓨터용 싸인펜**을 사용해야 합니다.
2. 답안을 정정할 경우 수정테이프(수정액 불가)를 사용해야 합니다.
3. 본 답안지는 컴퓨터로 처리되므로 훼손해서는 안되며, 답안지 하단의 타이밍마크(▎▎▎)를 찢거나, 낙서 등으로 인한 훼손시 불이익이 발생할 수 있습니다.
4. 답안은 문항당 정답을 1개만 골라 ▮와 같이 정확히 기재해야 하며, 필기구 오류나 본인의 부주의로 잘못 표기한 경우에는 당 관리위원회의 OMR판독기의 판독결과에 따르며, 그 결과는 본인이 책임집니다.
   Good ▮ Bad
5. 감독관의 확인이 없는 답안지는 무효처리됩니다.

뒷면(Side2)

# TEPS

Test of English Proficiency
developed by
Seoul National University

| 성명 | 영문 | |
|---|---|---|
| | 서명 | |

응시일자 : 20 년 월 일

## <부정행위 및 규정위반 처리규정>

1. 모든 부정행위 및 규정위반 적발 및 이에 대한 조치는 TEPS관리위원회의 처리규정에 따라 이루어집니다.

2. 부정행위 및 규정위반 행위는 현장 적발 뿐만 아니라 사후에도 적발될 수 있으며 모두 동일한 조치가 취해집니다.

3. 부정행위 적발 시 당해 성적은 무효화되며 사안에 따라 최대 5년까지 TEPS관리위원회에서 주관하는 모든 시험의 응시자격이 제한됩니다.

4. 문제지 이외에 메모를 하는 행위와 시험 문제의 일부 또는 전부를 유출하거나 공개하는 경우 부정행위로 처리됩니다.

5. 각 파트별 시간을 준수하지 않거나, 시험 종료 후 답안 작성을 계속할 경우 규정위반으로 처리됩니다.

### 성 명 (성 · 이름순으로 기재)

EX H O N G G I L D O N G

A B C D E F G H I J K L M N O P Q R S T U V W X Y Z

### 단체구분

| 학생 | 일반 |
|---|---|
| ( ) | ( ) |

### 질 문 란

1. 귀하의 TEPS 응시목적은?
ⓐ 입사지원 ⓑ 인사정책
ⓒ 개인실력측정 ⓓ 입시
ⓔ 국가고시 지원 ⓕ 기타

2. 귀하의 영어권 체류 경험은?
ⓐ 없다 ⓑ 6개월 미만
ⓒ 6개월 이상 1년 미만 ⓓ 1년 이상 3년 미만
ⓔ 3년 이상 5년 미만 ⓕ 5년 이상

3. 귀하께서 응시하고 계신 고사장에 대한 만족도는?
ⓐ 0점 ⓑ 1점
ⓒ 2점 ⓓ 3점
ⓔ 4점 ⓕ 5점

4. 최근 2년내 TEPS 응시횟수는?
ⓐ 없다 ⓑ 1회
ⓒ 2회 ⓓ 3회
ⓔ 4회 ⓕ 5회 이상

| 학력 | 재학 | 졸업 | 전공 | 직업 |
|---|---|---|---|---|
| 초등학교 | ( ) | ( ) | 인문학 ( ) | 공무원 ( ) |
| 중학교 | ( ) | ( ) | 사회과학 · 법학 ( ) | 고시준비 ( ) |
| 고등학교 | ( ) | ( ) | 경제학 · 경영학 ( ) | 교사 ( ) |
| 전문대학 | ( ) | ( ) | 자연과학 ( ) | 군인 ( ) |
| 대학교 | ( ) | ( ) | 의학 · 약학 · 간호학 ( ) | 의료인 ( ) |
| 대학원 | ( ) | ( ) | 공학 ( ) | 자영업 ( ) |
| | | | 교육학 ( ) | 학생 ( ) |
| | | | 음악 · 미술 · 체육 ( ) | 회사원 ( ) |
| | | | 기타 ( ) | 무직 ( ) |
| | | | | 기타 ( ) |

| 직종 | | 직책 |
|---|---|---|
| 고위임직원 ( ) | 무역 ( ) | 임원 ( ) |
| 전문직(과학 공학) ( ) | 외환 ( ) | 부장 ( ) |
| 전문직(교육) ( ) | 자금 ( ) | 차장 ( ) |
| 전문직(법률,회계,금융) ( ) | 공무 ( ) | 과장 ( ) |
| 기술직 ( ) | 업무 ( ) | 대리 ( ) |
| 영업 ( ) | 품질관리 ( ) | 계장 ( ) |
| 홍보 ( ) | 전산 ( ) | 사원 ( ) |
| 총무 ( ) | 행정직 ( ) | 인턴 ( ) |
| 인사 ( ) | 생산관리 ( ) | 기타 ( ) |
| 경리 ( ) | 서비스 ( ) | |
| 기획 ( ) | 기타 ( ) | |
| 구매 ( ) | | |

앞면(Side1)

# TEPS

Test of English Proficiency
developed by
Seoul National University

| 수험번호 Registration No. | |
|---|---|
| 성 명 Name 한글 | |
| 한자 | |

| 문 제 지 번 호 Test Booklet No. | 감독관확인란 |
|---|---|
| | |

## 청 해 Listening Comprehension

| | | | | | | | | | | | | | | |
|---|---|---|---|---|---|---|---|---|---|---|---|---|---|---|
| 1 | a | b | c | d | 26 | a | b | c | d | 51 | a | b | c | d |
| 2 | a | b | c | d | 27 | a | b | c | d | 52 | a | b | c | d |
| 3 | a | b | c | d | 28 | a | b | c | d | 53 | a | b | c | d |
| 4 | a | b | c | d | 29 | a | b | c | d | 54 | a | b | c | d |
| 5 | a | b | c | d | 30 | a | b | c | d | 55 | a | b | c | d |
| 6 | a | b | c | d | 31 | a | b | c | d | 56 | a | b | c | d |
| 7 | a | b | c | d | 32 | a | b | c | d | 57 | a | b | c | d |
| 8 | a | b | c | d | 33 | a | b | c | d | 58 | a | b | c | d |
| 9 | a | b | c | d | 34 | a | b | c | d | 59 | a | b | c | d |
| 10 | a | b | c | d | 35 | a | b | c | d | 60 | a | b | c | d |
| 11 | a | b | c | d | 36 | a | b | c | d | | | | | |
| 12 | a | b | c | d | 37 | a | b | c | d | | | | | |
| 13 | a | b | c | d | 38 | a | b | c | d | | | | | |
| 14 | a | b | c | d | 39 | a | b | c | d | | | | | |
| 15 | a | b | c | d | 40 | a | b | c | d | | | | | |
| 16 | a | b | c | d | 41 | a | b | c | d | | | | | |
| 17 | a | b | c | d | 42 | a | b | c | d | | | | | |
| 18 | a | b | c | d | 43 | a | b | c | d | | | | | |
| 19 | a | b | c | d | 44 | a | b | c | d | | | | | |
| 20 | a | b | c | d | 45 | a | b | c | d | | | | | |
| 21 | a | b | c | d | 46 | a | b | c | d | | | | | |
| 22 | a | b | c | d | 47 | a | b | c | d | | | | | |
| 23 | a | b | c | d | 48 | a | b | c | d | | | | | |
| 24 | a | b | c | d | 49 | a | b | c | d | | | | | |
| 25 | a | b | c | d | 50 | a | b | c | d | | | | | |

## 문 법 Grammar

| | | | | | | | | | |
|---|---|---|---|---|---|---|---|---|---|
| 1 | a | b | c | d | 26 | a | b | c | d |
| 2 | a | b | c | d | 27 | a | b | c | d |
| 3 | a | b | c | d | 28 | a | b | c | d |
| 4 | a | b | c | d | 29 | a | b | c | d |
| 5 | a | b | c | d | 30 | a | b | c | d |
| 6 | a | b | c | d | 31 | a | b | c | d |
| 7 | a | b | c | d | 32 | a | b | c | d |
| 8 | a | b | c | d | 33 | a | b | c | d |
| 9 | a | b | c | d | 34 | a | b | c | d |
| 10 | a | b | c | d | 35 | a | b | c | d |
| 11 | a | b | c | d | 36 | a | b | c | d |
| 12 | a | b | c | d | 37 | a | b | c | d |
| 13 | a | b | c | d | 38 | a | b | c | d |
| 14 | a | b | c | d | 39 | a | b | c | d |
| 15 | a | b | c | d | 40 | a | b | c | d |
| 16 | a | b | c | d | 41 | a | b | c | d |
| 17 | a | b | c | d | 42 | a | b | c | d |
| 18 | a | b | c | d | 43 | a | b | c | d |
| 19 | a | b | c | d | 44 | a | b | c | d |
| 20 | a | b | c | d | 45 | a | b | c | d |
| 21 | a | b | c | d | 46 | a | b | c | d |
| 22 | a | b | c | d | 47 | a | b | c | d |
| 23 | a | b | c | d | 48 | a | b | c | d |
| 24 | a | b | c | d | 49 | a | b | c | d |
| 25 | a | b | c | d | 50 | a | b | c | d |

## 어 휘 Vocabulary

| | | | | | | | | | |
|---|---|---|---|---|---|---|---|---|---|
| 1 | a | b | c | d | 26 | a | b | c | d |
| 2 | a | b | c | d | 27 | a | b | c | d |
| 3 | a | b | c | d | 28 | a | b | c | d |
| 4 | a | b | c | d | 29 | a | b | c | d |
| 5 | a | b | c | d | 30 | a | b | c | d |
| 6 | a | b | c | d | 31 | a | b | c | d |
| 7 | a | b | c | d | 32 | a | b | c | d |
| 8 | a | b | c | d | 33 | a | b | c | d |
| 9 | a | b | c | d | 34 | a | b | c | d |
| 10 | a | b | c | d | 35 | a | b | c | d |
| 11 | a | b | c | d | 36 | a | b | c | d |
| 12 | a | b | c | d | 37 | a | b | c | d |
| 13 | a | b | c | d | 38 | a | b | c | d |
| 14 | a | b | c | d | 39 | a | b | c | d |
| 15 | a | b | c | d | 40 | a | b | c | d |
| 16 | a | b | c | d | 41 | a | b | c | d |
| 17 | a | b | c | d | 42 | a | b | c | d |
| 18 | a | b | c | d | 43 | a | b | c | d |
| 19 | a | b | c | d | 44 | a | b | c | d |
| 20 | a | b | c | d | 45 | a | b | c | d |
| 21 | a | b | c | d | 46 | a | b | c | d |
| 22 | a | b | c | d | 47 | a | b | c | d |
| 23 | a | b | c | d | 48 | a | b | c | d |
| 24 | a | b | c | d | 49 | a | b | c | d |
| 25 | a | b | c | d | 50 | a | b | c | d |

## 독 해 Reading Comprehension

| | | | | | | | | | |
|---|---|---|---|---|---|---|---|---|---|
| 1 | a | b | c | d | 26 | a | b | c | d |
| 2 | a | b | c | d | 27 | a | b | c | d |
| 3 | a | b | c | d | 28 | a | b | c | d |
| 4 | a | b | c | d | 29 | a | b | c | d |
| 5 | a | b | c | d | 30 | a | b | c | d |
| 6 | a | b | c | d | 31 | a | b | c | d |
| 7 | a | b | c | d | 32 | a | b | c | d |
| 8 | a | b | c | d | 33 | a | b | c | d |
| 9 | a | b | c | d | 34 | a | b | c | d |
| 10 | a | b | c | d | 35 | a | b | c | d |
| 11 | a | b | c | d | 36 | a | b | c | d |
| 12 | a | b | c | d | 37 | a | b | c | d |
| 13 | a | b | c | d | 38 | a | b | c | d |
| 14 | a | b | c | d | 39 | a | b | c | d |
| 15 | a | b | c | d | 40 | a | b | c | d |
| 16 | a | b | c | d | | | | | |
| 17 | a | b | c | d | | | | | |
| 18 | a | b | c | d | | | | | |
| 19 | a | b | c | d | | | | | |
| 20 | a | b | c | d | | | | | |
| 21 | a | b | c | d | | | | | |
| 22 | a | b | c | d | | | | | |
| 23 | a | b | c | d | | | | | |
| 24 | a | b | c | d | | | | | |
| 25 | a | b | c | d | | | | | |

## 주 민 등 록 번 호 National ID No.

| | | | | | | | | | | | | | |
|---|---|---|---|---|---|---|---|---|---|---|---|---|---|
| | | | | | | – | | | | | | | |
| 0 | 0 | 0 | 0 | 0 | 0 | | | 0 | 0 | 0 | 0 | 0 | 0 |
| 1 | 1 | 1 | 1 | 1 | 1 | | 1 | 1 | 1 | 1 | 1 | 1 | 1 |
| 2 | 2 | | 2 | 2 | 2 | | 2 | 2 | 2 | 2 | 2 | 2 | 2 |
| 3 | 3 | | 3 | 3 | 3 | | 3 | 3 | 3 | 3 | 3 | 3 | 3 |
| 4 | 4 | | 4 | | 4 | – | 4 | 4 | 4 | 4 | 4 | 4 | 4 |
| 5 | 5 | | 5 | | 5 | | 5 | 5 | 5 | 5 | 5 | 5 | 5 |
| 6 | 6 | | 6 | | 6 | | 6 | 6 | 6 | 6 | 6 | 6 | 6 |
| 7 | 7 | | 7 | | 7 | | 7 | 7 | 7 | 7 | 7 | 7 | 7 |
| 8 | 8 | | 8 | | 8 | | 8 | 8 | 8 | 8 | 8 | 8 | 8 |
| 9 | 9 | | 9 | | 9 | | 9 | 9 | 9 | 9 | 9 | 9 | 9 |

## 고사실란 Room No.

| | |
|---|---|
| 0 | 0 |
| 1 | 1 |
| 2 | 2 |
| 3 | 3 |
| 4 | 4 |
| 5 | 5 |
| | 6 |
| | 7 |
| | 8 |
| | 9 |

## 수 험 번 호 Registration No.

| | | | | | | |
|---|---|---|---|---|---|---|
| 0 | 0 | 0 | 0 | 0 | 0 | 0 |
| 1 | 1 | 1 | 1 | 1 | 1 | 1 |
| 2 | 2 | 2 | 2 | 2 | 2 | 2 |
| 3 | 3 | 3 | 3 | 3 | 3 | 3 |
| 4 | 4 | 4 | 4 | 4 | 4 | 4 |
| 5 | 5 | 5 | 5 | 5 | 5 | 5 |
| 6 | 6 | 6 | 6 | 6 | 6 | 6 |
| 7 | 7 | 7 | 7 | 7 | 7 | 7 |
| 8 | 8 | 8 | 8 | 8 | 8 | 8 |
| 9 | 9 | 9 | 9 | 9 | 9 | 9 |

## 비밀번호 Password

| | | | |
|---|---|---|---|
| 0 | 0 | 0 | 0 |
| 1 | 1 | 1 | 1 |
| 2 | 2 | 2 | 2 |
| 3 | 3 | 3 | 3 |
| 4 | 4 | 4 | 4 |
| 5 | 5 | 5 | 5 |
| 6 | 6 | 6 | 6 |
| 7 | 7 | 7 | 7 |
| 8 | 8 | 8 | 8 |
| 9 | 9 | 9 | 9 |

## 좌석번호 Seat No.

| | |
|---|---|
| A | 1 |
| B | 2 |
| C | 3 |
| D | 4 |
| E | 5 |
| | 6 |
| | 7 |

**서 약** 본인은 필기구 및 기재오류와 답안지 훼손으로 인한 책임을 지고, 부정행위 처리규정을 준수할 것을 서약합니다.

**답안작성시 유의사항**

1. 답안 작성은 반드시 **컴퓨터용 싸인펜**을 사용해야 합니다.
2. 답안을 정정할 경우 수정테이프(수정액 불가)를 사용해야 합니다.
3. 본 답안지는 컴퓨터로 처리되므로 훼손해서는 안되며, 답안지 하단의 타이밍마크(|||)를 찢거나, 낙서 등으로 인한 훼손시 불이익이 발생할 수 있습니다.
4. 답안은 문항당 정답을 1개만 골라 ▮와 같이 정확히 기재해야 하며, 필기구 오류나 본인의 부주의로 잘못 표기한 경우에는 당 관리위원회의 OMR판독기의 판독결과에 따르며, 그 결과는 본인이 책임집니다.
   Good ▮ Bad
5. 감독관의 확인이 없는 답안지는 무효처리됩니다.

Test of English Proficiency
developed by
Seoul National University

| 성명 | 영문 | |
|---|---|---|
| | 서명 | |

응시일자 : 20　　년　　월　　일

**<부정행위 및 규정위반 처리규정>**

1. 모든 부정행위 및 규정위반 적발 및 이에 대한 조치는 TEPS관리위원회의 처리규정에 따라 이루어집니다.
2. 부정행위 및 규정위반 행위는 현장 적발 뿐만 아니라 사후에도 적발될 수 있으며 모두 동일한 조치가 취해집니다.
3. 부정행위 적발 시 당해 성적은 무효화되며 사안에 따라 최대 5년까지 TEPS관리위원회에서 주관하는 모든 시험의 응시자격이 제한됩니다.
4. 문제지 이외에 메모를 하는 행위와 시험 문제의 일부 또는 전부를 유출하거나 공개하는 경우 부정행위로 처리됩니다.
5. 각 파트별 시간을 준수하지 않거나, 시험 종료 후 답안 작성을 계속할 경우 규정위반으로 처리됩니다.

**성 명 (성 · 이름순으로 기재)**

| EX | H | O | N | G | | G | I | L | | D | O | N | G | | | | | | | |
|---|---|---|---|---|---|---|---|---|---|---|---|---|---|---|---|---|---|---|---|---|
| A | A | A | A | A | A | A | A | A | A | A | A | A | A | A | A | A | A | A | A | A |
| B | B | B | B | B | B | B | B | B | B | B | B | B | B | B | B | B | B | B | B | B |
| C | C | C | C | C | C | C | C | C | C | C | C | C | C | C | C | C | C | C | C | C |
| D | D | D | D | D | D | D | D | D | D | D | D | D | D | D | D | D | D | D | D | D |
| E | E | E | E | E | E | E | E | E | E | E | E | E | E | E | E | E | E | E | E | E |
| F | F | F | F | F | F | F | F | F | F | F | F | F | F | F | F | F | F | F | F | F |
| G | G | G | G | G | G | G | G | G | G | G | G | G | G | G | G | G | G | G | G | G |
| H | H | H | H | H | H | H | H | H | H | H | H | H | H | H | H | H | H | H | H | H |
| I | I | I | I | I | I | I | I | I | I | I | I | I | I | I | I | I | I | I | I | I |
| J | J | J | J | J | J | J | J | J | J | J | J | J | J | J | J | J | J | J | J | J |
| K | K | K | K | K | K | K | K | K | K | K | K | K | K | K | K | K | K | K | K | K |
| L | L | L | L | L | L | L | L | L | L | L | L | L | L | L | L | L | L | L | L | L |
| M | M | M | M | M | M | M | M | M | M | M | M | M | M | M | M | M | M | M | M | M |
| N | N | N | N | N | N | N | N | N | N | N | N | N | N | N | N | N | N | N | N | N |
| O | O | O | O | O | O | O | O | O | O | O | O | O | O | O | O | O | O | O | O | O |
| P | P | P | P | P | P | P | P | P | P | P | P | P | P | P | P | P | P | P | P | P |
| Q | Q | Q | Q | Q | Q | Q | Q | Q | Q | Q | Q | Q | Q | Q | Q | Q | Q | Q | Q | Q |
| R | R | R | R | R | R | R | R | R | R | R | R | R | R | R | R | R | R | R | R | R |
| S | S | S | S | S | S | S | S | S | S | S | S | S | S | S | S | S | S | S | S | S |
| T | T | T | T | T | T | T | T | T | T | T | T | T | T | T | T | T | T | T | T | T |
| U | U | U | U | U | U | U | U | U | U | U | U | U | U | U | U | U | U | U | U | U |
| V | V | V | V | V | V | V | V | V | V | V | V | V | V | V | V | V | V | V | V | V |
| W | W | W | W | W | W | W | W | W | W | W | W | W | W | W | W | W | W | W | W | W |
| X | X | X | X | X | X | X | X | X | X | X | X | X | X | X | X | X | X | X | X | X |
| Y | Y | Y | Y | Y | Y | Y | Y | Y | Y | Y | Y | Y | Y | Y | Y | Y | Y | Y | Y | Y |
| Z | Z | Z | Z | Z | Z | Z | Z | Z | Z | Z | Z | Z | Z | Z | Z | Z | Z | Z | Z | Z |

**단체구분**

| 학생 | 일반 |
|---|---|
| ▯ | ▯ |

**질 문 란**

1. 귀하의 TEPS 응시목적은?
   - ⓐ 입사지원　ⓑ 인사정책
   - ⓒ 개인실력측정　ⓓ 입시
   - ⓔ 국가고시 지원　ⓕ 기타
2. 귀하의 영어권 체류 경험은?
   - ⓐ 없다　ⓑ 6개월 미만
   - ⓒ 6개월 이상 1년 미만　ⓓ 1년 이상 3년 미만
   - ⓔ 3년 이상 5년 미만　ⓕ 5년 이상
3. 귀하께서 응시하고 계신 고사장에 대한 만족도는?
   - ⓐ 0점　ⓑ 1점
   - ⓒ 2점　ⓓ 3점
   - ⓔ 4점　ⓕ 5점
4. 최근 2년내 TEPS 응시횟수는?
   - ⓐ 없다　ⓑ 1회
   - ⓒ 2회　ⓓ 3회
   - ⓔ 4회　ⓕ 5회 이상

| 학력 | 재학 | 졸업 | 전공 | 직업 |
|---|---|---|---|---|
| 초등학교 | ▯ | ▯ | 인문학 ▯ | 공무원 ▯ |
| 중학교 | ▯ | ▯ | 사회과학 · 법학 ▯ | 고시준비 ▯ |
| 고등학교 | ▯ | ▯ | 경제학 · 경영학 ▯ | 교사 ▯ |
| 전문대학 | ▯ | ▯ | 자연과학 ▯ | 군인 ▯ |
| 대학교 | ▯ | ▯ | 의학 · 약학 · 간호학 ▯ | 의료인 ▯ |
| 대학원 | ▯ | ▯ | 공학 ▯ | 자영업 ▯ |
| | | | 교육학 ▯ | 학생 ▯ |
| | | | 음악 · 미술 · 체육 ▯ | 회사원 ▯ |
| | | | 기타 ▯ | 무직 ▯ |
| | | | | 기타 ▯ |

| 직종 | | 직책 |
|---|---|---|
| 고위임직원 ▯ | 무역 ▯ | 임원 ▯ |
| 전문직(과학,공학) ▯ | 외환 ▯ | 부장 ▯ |
| 전문직(교육) ▯ | 자금 ▯ | 차장 ▯ |
| 전문직(법률,회계,금융) ▯ | 공무 ▯ | 과장 ▯ |
| 기술직 ▯ | 업무 ▯ | 대리 ▯ |
| 영업 ▯ | 품질관리 ▯ | 계장 ▯ |
| 홍보 ▯ | 전산 ▯ | 사원 ▯ |
| 총무 ▯ | 행정직 ▯ | 인턴 ▯ |
| 인사 ▯ | 생산관리 ▯ | 기타 ▯ |
| 경리 ▯ | 서비스 ▯ | |
| 기획 ▯ | 기타 ▯ | |
| 구매 ▯ | | |

앞면(Side1)

# TEPS

Test of English Proficiency
developed by
Seoul National University

| 수험번호 Registration No. | |
|---|---|
| 성명 Name 한글 | |
| 한자 | |

문 제 지 번 호 Test Booklet No.

감독관확인란

## 청 해 Listening Comprehension

1–60

## 문 법 Grammar

1–50

## 어 휘 Vocabulary

1–50

## 독 해 Reading Comprehension

1–40

## 주 민 등 록 번 호 National ID No.

## 고사실란 Room No.

## 수 험 번 호 Registration No.

## 비밀번호 Password

## 좌석번호 Seat No.

A B C D E

| 서 약 | 본인은 필기구 및 기재오류와 답안지 훼손으로 인한 책임을 지고, 부정행위 처리규정을 준수할 것을 서약합니다. | |
|---|---|---|

## 답안작성시 유의사항

1. 답안 작성은 반드시 **컴퓨터용 싸인펜**을 사용해야 합니다.
2. 답안을 정정할 경우 수정테이프(수정액 불가)를 사용해야 합니다.
3. 본 답안지는 컴퓨터로 처리되므로 훼손해서는 안되며, 답안지 하단의 타이밍마크(|||)를 찢거나, 낙서 등으로 인한 훼손시 불이익이 발생할 수 있습니다.
4. 답안은 문항당 정답을 1개만 골라 ▮와 같이 정확히 기재해야 하며, 필기구 오류나 본인의 부주의로 잘못 표기한 경우에는 당 관리위원회의 OMR판독기의 판독결과에 따르며, 그 결과는 본인이 책임집니다.

Good ▮ Bad

5. 감독관의 확인이 없는 답안지는 무효처리됩니다.

뒷면(Side2)

# TEPS

Test of English Proficiency
developed by
Seoul National University

| 성명 | 영문 | |
|---|---|---|
| | 서명 | |

응시일자 : 20　　년　　월　　일

**<부정행위 및 규정위반 처리규정>**

1. 모든 부정행위 및 규정위반 적발 및 이에 대한 조치는 TEPS관리위원회의 처리규정에 따라 이루어집니다.

2. 부정행위 및 규정위반 행위는 현장 적발 뿐만 아니라 사후에도 적발될 수 있으며 모두 동일한 조치가 취해집니다.

3. 부정행위 적발 시 당해 성적은 무효화되며 사안에 따라 최대 5년까지 TEPS관리위원회에서 주관하는 모든 시험의 응시자격이 제한됩니다.

4. 문제지 이외에 메모를 하는 행위와 시험 문제의 일부 또는 전부를 유출하거나 공개하는 경우 부정행위로 처리됩니다.

5. 각 파트별 시간을 준수하지 않거나, 시험 종료 후 답안 작성을 계속할 경우 규정위반으로 처리됩니다.

**성　명 (성 · 이름순으로 기재)**

EX H O N G　G I L　D O N G

A B C D E F G H I J K L M N O P Q R S T U V W X Y Z

**단체구분**

학생 ( )　일반 ( )

**질문란**

1. 귀하의 TEPS 응시목적은?
ⓐ 입사지원　ⓑ 인사정책
ⓒ 개인실력측정　ⓓ 입시
ⓔ 국가고시 지원　ⓕ 기타

2. 귀하의 영어권 체류 경험은?
ⓐ 없다　ⓑ 6개월 미만
ⓒ 6개월 이상 1년 미만　ⓓ 1년 이상 3년 미만
ⓔ 3년 이상 5년 미만　ⓕ 5년 이상

3. 귀하께서 응시하고 계신 고사장에 대한 만족도는?
ⓐ 0점　ⓑ 1점
ⓒ 2점　ⓓ 3점
ⓔ 4점　ⓕ 5점

4. 최근 2년내 TEPS 응시횟수는?
ⓐ 없다　ⓑ 1회
ⓒ 2회　ⓓ 3회
ⓔ 4회　ⓕ 5회 이상

| 학력 | 재학 | 졸업 | 전공 | 직업 |
|---|---|---|---|---|
| 초등학교 | ( ) | ( ) | 인문학 ( ) | 공무원 ( ) |
| 중학교 | ( ) | ( ) | 사회과학 · 법학 ( ) | 고시준비 ( ) |
| 고등학교 | ( ) | ( ) | 경제학 · 경영학 ( ) | 교사 ( ) |
| 전문대학 | ( ) | ( ) | 자연과학 ( ) | 군인 ( ) |
| 대학교 | ( ) | ( ) | 의학 · 약학 · 간호학 ( ) | 의료인 ( ) |
| 대학원 | ( ) | ( ) | 공학 ( ) | 자영업 ( ) |
| | | | 교육학 ( ) | 학생 ( ) |
| | | | 음악 · 미술 · 체육 ( ) | 회사원 ( ) |
| | | | 기타 ( ) | 무직 ( ) |
| | | | | 기타 ( ) |

| 직종 | | 직책 |
|---|---|---|
| 고위임직원 ( ) | 무역 ( ) | 임원 ( ) |
| 전문직(과학.공학) ( ) | 외환 ( ) | 부장 ( ) |
| 전문직(교육) ( ) | 자금 ( ) | 차장 ( ) |
| 전문직(법률.회계.금융) ( ) | 공무 ( ) | 과장 ( ) |
| 기술직 ( ) | 업무 ( ) | 대리 ( ) |
| 영업 ( ) | 품질관리 ( ) | 계장 ( ) |
| 홍보 ( ) | 전산 ( ) | 사원 ( ) |
| 총무 ( ) | 행정직 ( ) | 인턴 ( ) |
| 인사 ( ) | 생산관리 ( ) | 기타 ( ) |
| 경리 ( ) | 서비스 ( ) | |
| 기획 ( ) | 기타 ( ) | |
| 구매 ( ) | | |

앞면(Side1)

# TEPS

Test of English Proficiency
developed by
Seoul National University

| 수험번호 Registration No. | |
|---|---|
| 성명 Name 한글 | |
| 한자 | |

| 문 제 지 번 호 Test Booklet No. | 감독관확인란 |
|---|---|
| | |

## 청 해 Listening Comprehension

1–60: ⓐ ⓑ ⓒ ⓓ

## 문 법 Grammar

1–50: ⓐ ⓑ ⓒ ⓓ

## 어 휘 Vocabulary

1–50: ⓐ ⓑ ⓒ ⓓ

## 독 해 Reading Comprehension

1–40: ⓐ ⓑ ⓒ ⓓ

## 주 민 등 록 번 호 National ID No.

## 고사실란 Room No.

## 수 험 번 호 Registration No.

## 비밀번호 Password

## 좌석번호 Seat No.

A B C D E / 1 2 3 4 5 6 7

| 서 약 | 본인은 필기구 및 기재오류와 답안지 훼손으로 인한 책임을 지고, 부정행위 처리규정을 준수할 것을 서약합니다. | |
|---|---|---|

## 답안작성시 유 의 사 항

1. 답안 작성은 반드시 **컴퓨터용 싸인펜**을 사용해야 합니다.
2. 답안을 정정할 경우 수정테이프(수정액 불가)를 사용해야 합니다.
3. 본 답안지는 컴퓨터로 처리되므로 훼손해서는 안되며, 답안지 하단의 타이밍마크(|||)를 찢거나, 낙서 등으로 인한 훼손시 불이익이 발생할 수 있습니다.
4. 답안은 문항당 정답을 1개만 골라 ▮와 같이 정확히 기재해야 하며, 필기구 오류나 본인의 부주의로 잘못 표기한 경우에는 당 관리위원회의 OMR판독기의 판독결과에 따르며, 그 결과는 본인이 책임집니다.

   Good ▮ Bad

5. 감독관의 확인이 없는 답안지는 무효처리됩니다.

뒷면(Side2)

# TEPS

Test of English Proficiency
developed by
Seoul National University

| 성명 | 영문 | |
|---|---|---|
| | 서명 | |

응시일자 : 20　　년　　월　　일

**<부정행위 및 규정위반 처리규정>**

1. 모든 부정행위 및 규정위반 적발 및 이에 대한 조치는 TEPS관리위원회의 처리규정에 따라 이루어집니다.

2. 부정행위 및 규정위반 행위는 현장 적발 뿐만 아니라 사후에도 적발될 수 있으며 모두 동일한 조치가 취해집니다.

3. 부정행위 적발 시 당해 성적은 무효화되며 사안에 따라 최대 5년까지 TEPS관리위원회에서 주관하는 모든 시험의 응시자격이 제한됩니다.

4. 문제지 이외에 메모를 하는 행위와 시험 문제의 일부 또는 전부를 유출하거나 공개하는 경우 부정행위로 처리됩니다.

5. 각 파트별 시간을 준수하지 않거나, 시험 종료 후 답안 작성을 계속할 경우 규정위반으로 처리됩니다.

**성　명 (성 · 이름순으로 기재)**

| EX | H | O | N | G | | G | I | L | | D | O | N | G | | | | | | | |
|---|---|---|---|---|---|---|---|---|---|---|---|---|---|---|---|---|---|---|---|---|
| A | A | A | A | A | A | A | A | A | A | A | A | A | A | A | A | A | A | A | A | A |
| B | B | B | B | B | B | B | B | B | B | B | B | B | B | B | B | B | B | B | B | B |
| C | C | C | C | C | C | C | C | C | C | C | C | C | C | C | C | C | C | C | C | C |
| D | D | D | D | D | D | D | D | D | D | D | D | D | D | D | D | D | D | D | D | D |
| E | E | E | E | E | E | E | E | E | E | E | E | E | E | E | E | E | E | E | E | E |
| F | F | F | F | F | F | F | F | F | F | F | F | F | F | F | F | F | F | F | F | F |
| G | G | G | G | G | G | G | G | G | G | G | G | G | G | G | G | G | G | G | G | G |
| H | H | H | H | H | H | H | H | H | H | H | H | H | H | H | H | H | H | H | H | H |
| I | I | I | I | I | I | I | I | I | I | I | I | I | I | I | I | I | I | I | I | I |
| J | J | J | J | J | J | J | J | J | J | J | J | J | J | J | J | J | J | J | J | J |
| K | K | K | K | K | K | K | K | K | K | K | K | K | K | K | K | K | K | K | K | K |
| L | L | L | L | L | L | L | L | L | L | L | L | L | L | L | L | L | L | L | L | L |
| M | M | M | M | M | M | M | M | M | M | M | M | M | M | M | M | M | M | M | M | M |
| N | N | N | N | N | N | N | N | N | N | N | N | N | N | N | N | N | N | N | N | N |
| O | O | O | O | O | O | O | O | O | O | O | O | O | O | O | O | O | O | O | O | O |
| P | P | P | P | P | P | P | P | P | P | P | P | P | P | P | P | P | P | P | P | P |
| Q | Q | Q | Q | Q | Q | Q | Q | Q | Q | Q | Q | Q | Q | Q | Q | Q | Q | Q | Q | Q |
| R | R | R | R | R | R | R | R | R | R | R | R | R | R | R | R | R | R | R | R | R |
| S | S | S | S | S | S | S | S | S | S | S | S | S | S | S | S | S | S | S | S | S |
| T | T | T | T | T | T | T | T | T | T | T | T | T | T | T | T | T | T | T | T | T |
| U | U | U | U | U | U | U | U | U | U | U | U | U | U | U | U | U | U | U | U | U |
| V | V | V | V | V | V | V | V | V | V | V | V | V | V | V | V | V | V | V | V | V |
| W | W | W | W | W | W | W | W | W | W | W | W | W | W | W | W | W | W | W | W | W |
| X | X | X | X | X | X | X | X | X | X | X | X | X | X | X | X | X | X | X | X | X |
| Y | Y | Y | Y | Y | Y | Y | Y | Y | Y | Y | Y | Y | Y | Y | Y | Y | Y | Y | Y | Y |
| Z | Z | Z | Z | Z | Z | Z | Z | Z | Z | Z | Z | Z | Z | Z | Z | Z | Z | Z | Z | Z |

**단 체 구 분**

| 학생 | 일반 |
|---|---|
| ⬯ | ⬯ |

**질 문 란**

1. 귀하의 TEPS 응시목적은?
   - ⓐ 입사지원　ⓑ 인사정책
   - ⓒ 개인실력측정　ⓓ 입시
   - ⓔ 국가고시 지원　ⓕ 기타

2. 귀하의 영어권 체류 경험은?
   - ⓐ 없다　ⓑ 6개월 미만
   - ⓒ 6개월 이상 1년 미만　ⓓ 1년 이상 3년 미만
   - ⓔ 3년 이상 5년 미만　ⓕ 5년 이상

3. 귀하께서 응시하고 계신 고사장에 대한 만족도는?
   - ⓐ 0점　ⓑ 1점
   - ⓒ 2점　ⓓ 3점
   - ⓔ 4점　ⓕ 5점

4. 최근 2년내 TEPS 응시횟수는?
   - ⓐ 없다　ⓑ 1회
   - ⓒ 2회　ⓓ 3회
   - ⓔ 4회　ⓕ 5회 이상

| 학력 | 재학 | 졸업 | 전공 | 직업 |
|---|---|---|---|---|
| 초등학교 | ⬯ | ⬯ | 인문학 ⬯ | 공무원 ⬯ |
| 중학교 | ⬯ | ⬯ | 사회과학 · 법학 ⬯ | 고시준비 ⬯ |
| 고등학교 | ⬯ | ⬯ | 경제학 · 경영학 ⬯ | 교사 ⬯ |
| 전문대학 | ⬯ | ⬯ | 자연과학 ⬯ | 군인 ⬯ |
| 대학교 | ⬯ | ⬯ | 의학 · 약학 · 간호학 ⬯ | 의료인 ⬯ |
| 대학원 | ⬯ | ⬯ | 공학 ⬯ | 자영업 ⬯ |
| | | | 교육학 ⬯ | 학생 ⬯ |
| | | | 음악 · 미술 · 체육 ⬯ | 회사원 ⬯ |
| | | | 기타 ⬯ | 무직 ⬯ |
| | | | | 기타 ⬯ |

| 직종 | | 직책 |
|---|---|---|
| 고위임직원 ⬯ | 무역 ⬯ | 임원 ⬯ |
| 전문직(과학.공학) ⬯ | 외환 ⬯ | 부장 ⬯ |
| 전문직(교육) ⬯ | 자금 ⬯ | 차장 ⬯ |
| 전문직(법률.회계.금융) ⬯ | 공무 ⬯ | 과장 ⬯ |
| 기술직 ⬯ | 업무 ⬯ | 대리 ⬯ |
| 영업 ⬯ | 품질관리 ⬯ | 계장 ⬯ |
| 홍보 ⬯ | 전산 ⬯ | 사원 ⬯ |
| 총무 ⬯ | 행정직 ⬯ | 인턴 ⬯ |
| 인사 ⬯ | 생산관리 ⬯ | 기타 ⬯ |
| 경리 ⬯ | 서비스 ⬯ | |
| 기획 ⬯ | 기타 ⬯ | |
| 구매 ⬯ | | |

앞면(Side1)

# TEPS

Test of English Proficiency
developed by
Seoul National University

| 수험번호 Registration No. | |
|---|---|
| 성명 Name 한글 | |
| 한자 | |

| 문제지번호 Test Booklet No. | 감독관확인란 |
|---|---|
| | |

청해 Listening Comprehension (1–60)

문법 Grammar (1–50)

어휘 Vocabulary (1–50)

독해 Reading Comprehension (1–40)

주민등록번호 National ID No.

고사실란 Room No.

수험번호 Registration No.

비밀번호 Password

좌석번호 Seat No.

| 서 약 | 본인은 필기구 및 기재오류와 답안지 훼손으로 인한 책임을 지고, 부정행위 처리규정을 준수할 것을 서약합니다. | |
|---|---|---|

**답안작성시 유의사항**

1. 답안 작성은 반드시 **컴퓨터용 싸인펜**을 사용해야 합니다.
2. 답안을 정정할 경우 수정테이프(수정액 불가)를 사용해야 합니다.
3. 본 답안지는 컴퓨터로 처리되므로 훼손해서는 안되며, 답안지 하단의 타이밍마크(|||)를 찢거나, 낙서 등으로 인한 훼손시 불이익이 발생할 수 있습니다.
4. 답안은 문항당 정답을 1개만 골라 ▮와 같이 정확히 기재해야 하며, 필기구 오류나 본인의 부주의로 잘못 표기한 경우에는 당 관리위원회의 OMR판독기의 판독결과에 따르며, 그 결과는 본인이 책임집니다.
   Good ▮ Bad
5. 감독관의 확인이 없는 답안지는 무효처리됩니다.

뒷면(Side2)

# TEPS

Test of English Proficiency
developed by
Seoul National University

| 성명 | 영문 | |
|---|---|---|
| | 서명 | |

응시일자 : 20 년 월 일

**<부정행위 및 규정위반 처리규정>**

1. 모든 부정행위 및 규정위반 적발 및 이에 대한 조치는 TEPS관리위원회의 처리규정에 따라 이루어집니다.

2. 부정행위 및 규정위반 행위는 현장 적발 뿐만 아니라 사후에도 적발될 수 있으며 모두 동일한 조치가 취해집니다.

3. 부정행위 적발 시 당해 성적은 무효화되며 사안에 따라 최대 5년까지 TEPS관리위원회에서 주관하는 모든 시험의 응시자격이 제한됩니다.

4. 문제지 이외에 메모를 하는 행위와 시험 문제의 일부 또는 전부를 유출하거나 공개하는 경우 부정행위로 처리됩니다.

5. 각 파트별 시간을 준수하지 않거나, 시험 종료 후 답안 작성을 계속할 경우 규정위반으로 처리됩니다.

**성 명 (성 · 이름순으로 기재)**

EX H O N G G I L D O N G

A B C D E F G H I J K L M N O P Q R S T U V W X Y Z

**단체구분**

학생 ( ) 일반 ( )

**질 문 란**

1. 귀하의 TEPS 응시목적은?
ⓐ 입사지원 ⓑ 인사정책
ⓒ 개인실력측정 ⓓ 입시
ⓔ 국가고시 지원 ⓕ 기타

2. 귀하의 영어권 체류 경험은?
ⓐ 없다 ⓑ 6개월 미만
ⓒ 6개월 이상 1년 미만 ⓓ 1년 이상 3년 미만
ⓔ 3년 이상 5년 미만 ⓕ 5년 이상

3. 귀하께서 응시하고 계신 고사장에 대한 만족도는?
ⓐ 0점 ⓑ 1점
ⓒ 2점 ⓓ 3점
ⓔ 4점 ⓕ 5점

4. 최근 2년내 TEPS 응시횟수는?
ⓐ 없다 ⓑ 1회
ⓒ 2회 ⓓ 3회
ⓔ 4회 ⓕ 5회 이상

| 학력 | 재학 | 졸업 | 전공 | 직업 |
|---|---|---|---|---|
| 초등학교 | ( ) | ( ) | 인문학 ( ) | 공무원 ( ) |
| 중학교 | ( ) | ( ) | 사회과학 · 법학 ( ) | 고시준비 ( ) |
| 고등학교 | ( ) | ( ) | 경제학 · 경영학 ( ) | 교사 ( ) |
| 전문대학 | ( ) | ( ) | 자연과학 ( ) | 군인 ( ) |
| 대학교 | ( ) | ( ) | 의학 · 약학 · 간호학 ( ) | 의료인 ( ) |
| 대학원 | ( ) | ( ) | 공학 ( ) | 자영업 ( ) |
| | | | 교육학 ( ) | 학생 ( ) |
| | | | 음악 · 미술 · 체육 ( ) | 회사원 ( ) |
| | | | 기타 ( ) | 무직 ( ) |
| | | | | 기타 ( ) |

| 직종 | | 직책 |
|---|---|---|
| 고위임직원 ( ) | 무역 ( ) | 임원 ( ) |
| 전문직(과학.공학) ( ) | 외환 ( ) | 부장 ( ) |
| 전문직(교육) ( ) | 자금 ( ) | 차장 ( ) |
| 전문직(법률.회계.금융) ( ) | 공무 ( ) | 과장 ( ) |
| 기술직 ( ) | 업무 ( ) | 대리 ( ) |
| 영업 ( ) | 품질관리 ( ) | 계장 ( ) |
| 홍보 ( ) | 전산 ( ) | 사원 ( ) |
| 총무 ( ) | 행정직 ( ) | 인턴 ( ) |
| 인사 ( ) | 생산관리 ( ) | 기타 ( ) |
| 경리 ( ) | 서비스 ( ) | |
| 기획 ( ) | 기타 ( ) | |
| 구매 ( ) | | |

Memo

# TEPS

Test of English Proficiency
developed by
Seoul National University

실제 기출 어휘와 예문을 그대로 수록한
서울대 최신기출
NEW TEPS VOCA
최신 기출 예문 수록
서울대 최신기출
NEW TEPS VOCA
뉴텝스 보카
NEW TEPS 완벽 대비
최신판
www.nexusbook.com
MP3 듣기
미니 테스트
보너스 어휘
기출 예문 MP3 듣기
미니 테스트 풀기
수준별 보너스 어휘
어휘 테스트지
www.nexusbook.com